High Performance in-memory computing with Apache Ignite

Building low latency, near real time application

Shamim Ahmed Bhuiyan, Michael Zheludkov and Timur Isachenko

This book is for sale at http://leanpub.com/ignite

This version was published on 2017-04-04

Leanpub

This is a Leanpub book. Leanpub empowers authors and publishers with the Lean Publishing process. Lean Publishing is the act of publishing an in-progress ebook using lightweight tools and many iterations to get reader feedback, pivot until you have the right book and build traction once you do.

© 2016 - 2017 Shamim Ahmed Bhuiyan

Tweet This Book!

Please help Shamim Ahmed Bhuiyan, Michael Zheludkov and Timur Isachenko by spreading the word about this book on Twitter!

The suggested hashtag for this book is #shamim_ru.

Find out what other people are saying about the book by clicking on this link to search for this hashtag on Twitter:

https://twitter.com/search?q=#shamim_ru

In memory of my Father. - Shamim Ahmed Bhuiyan

Contents

Preface 1
    What this book covers 1
    Code Samples 2

About the authors 3

Acknowledgments 4

Introduction 5
    What is Apache Ignite? 6
    Modern application architecture with Apache Ignite 7
    Who uses Apache Ignite? 12
    Why Ignite instead of others? 12
    Our Hope 13

Chapter one: Installation and the first Ignite application 14
    Pre-requisites 14
    Installation 14
    Run multiple instances of Apache Ignite in a single host 17
    Configure a multi-node cluster in different host 18
    Rest client to manipulate with the Apache Ignite 19
    Java client 22
    SQL client 26
    Conclusion 31
    What's Next 32

Chapter two: Architecture overview 33
    Functional overview 33
    Cluster Topology 34
        Client and Server 35
        Embedded with the application 37
        Server in separate JVM (real cluster topology) 37
        Client and Server in separate JVM on single host 38
    Caching Topology 39

CONTENTS

  Partitioned caching topology 39
  Replicated caching topology 40
  Local mode 40
 Caching strategy 41
  Cache-aside 41
  Read-through and Write-through 42
  Write behind 43
 Data model 43
 CAP theorem and where does Ignite stand in? 47
 Clustering 49
  Cluster group 49
  Data collocation 51
  Compute collocation with Data 53
  Zero SPOF 54
 How SQL queries works in Ignite 55
 Multi-datacenter replication 56
 Asynchronous support 58
 Resilience 59
 Security 59
 Key API 59
 Conclusion 60
 What's next 60

Chapter three: In-memory caching 61
 Apache Ignite as a 2nd level cache 62
  MyBatis 2nd level cache 63
  Hibernate 2nd level cache 73
 Java method caching 87
 Web session clustering with Apache Ignite 95
 Apache Ignite as a big memory, off-heap memory 108
 Conclusion 115
 What's next 115

Chapter four: Persistence 116
 Persistence Ignite's cache 117
  Persistence in RDBMS (PostgreSQL) 120
  Persistence in MongoDB 127
 Cache queries 134
  Scan queries 136
  Text queries 141
 SQL queries 144
  Projection and indexing with annotations 146
  Query API 149

CONTENTS

    Collocated distributed Joins 149
    Non-collocated distributed joins 153
    Performance tuning SQL queries 155
Apache Ignite with JPA 155
Expiration & Eviction of cache entries in Ignite 165
    Expiration 165
    Eviction 169
Transaction 173
    Ignite transactions 175
    Transaction commit protocols 177
    Optimistic Transactions 179
    Pessimistic Transactions 180
    Performance impact on transaction 180
Conclusion 181
What's next 181

Chapter five: Accelerating Big Data computing 182
Hadoop accelerator 182
    In-memory Map/Reduce 184
    Using Apache Pig for data analysis 196
    Near real-time data analysis with Hive 203
    Replace HDFS by Ignite In-memory File System (IGFS) 209
    Hadoop file system cache 224
Ignite for Apache Spark 227
    Apache Spark – an introduction 228
    IgniteContext 230
    IgniteRDD 230
    Preparing the sandbox 231
    Spark-shell to run Spark jobs 234
    Spark application example in Scala to share states 237
Conclusion 239
What's next 240

Chapter six: Streaming and complex event processing 241
Introducing data streamer 242
IgniteDataStreamer 243
    StreamReceiver 249
    StreamVisitor 249
Camel data streamer 252
    Direct Ingestion 254
    Mediated Ingestion 259
Flume streamer 263
Storm data streamer 273

CONTENTS

    Conclusion 284
    What's next 284

Chapter seven: Distributed computing **285**
    Compute grid 287
        Distributed Closures 289
        MapReduce and Fork-join 294
        Per-Node share state 302
        Distributed task session 309
        Fault tolerance and checkpointing 312
        Collocation of computation and data 322
        Job scheduling 328
    Service Grid 330
        Developing services 332
        Cluster singleton 337
        Service management and configuration 339
    Developing microservices in Ignite 342
    Conclusion 351

Preface

My first acquaintance with High load systems was at the beginning of 2007, and I started working on a real-world project since 2009. From that moment, I spent most of my office time with Cassandra, Hadoop, and numerous CEP tools. Our first Hadoop project (the year 2011-2012) with a cluster of 54 nodes often disappointed me with its long startup time. I have never been satisfied with the performance of our applications and was always looking for something new to boost the performance of our information systems. During this time, I have tried HazelCast, Ehcache, Oracle Coherence as in-memory caches to gain the performance of the applications. I was usually disappointed from the complexity of using these libraries or from their functional limitations.

When I first encountered Apache Ignite, I was amazed! It was the platform that I'd been waiting on for a long time: a simple spring based framework with a lot of awesome features such as DataBase caching, Big data acceleration, Streaming and compute/service grids.

In 2015, I had participated in Russian HighLoad++ conference[1] with my presentation and started blogging in Dzone/JavaCodeGeeks and in my personal blog[2] about developing High-load systems. They became popular shortly, and I received a lot of feedback from the readers. Through them, I clarified the idea behind the book. The goal of the book was to provide a guide for those who really need to implement an in-memory platform in their projects. At the same time, the idea behind the book is not writing a manual. Although the Apache Ignite platform is very big and growing day by day, we concentrate only on the features of the platform (from our point of view) that can really help to improve the performance of the applications.

We hope that *High-performance in-memory computing with Apache Ignite* will be the go-to guide for architects and developers: both new and at an intermediate level, to get up and to develop with as little friction as possible.

Shamim Ahmed

What this book covers

Introduction gives an overview of the trends that have made in-memory computing such important technology today. By the end of this chapter, you will have a clear idea of what Apache Ignite are and how can you design application with Apache Ignite for getting maximum performance from your application.

Chapter one - Installation and the first Ignite application walks you through the initial setup of an Ignite grid and running of some sample application. At the end of the chapter, you will implement

---

[1] http://www.highload.ru/2015/abstracts/1875.html
[2] http://frommyworkshop.blogspot.ru

your first simple Ignite application to read and write entries from the Cache. You will also learn how to install and configure an SQL IDE to run SQL queries against Ignite caches.

Chapter two - Architecture overview covers the functional and architecture overview of the Apache Ignite data fabrics. Here you will learn the concepts and the terminology of the Apache Ignite. This chapter introduces the main features of Apache Ignite such as cluster topology, caching topology, caching strategies, transactions, Ignite data model, data collocation and how SQL queries works in Apache Ignite. You will become familiar with some other concepts like multi-datacenter replication, Ignite asynchronous support and resilience abilities.

Chapter three - In-memory caching presents some of the popular Ignite data grid features, such as 2nd level cache, java method caching, web session clustering and off-heap memory. This chapter covers developments and technics to improve the performance of your existing web applications without changing any code.

Chapter four - Persistence guides you through the implementation of transactions and persistence of the Apache Ignite cache. This chapter explores in depth: SQL feature and transaction of the Apache Ignite.

Chapter five - Accelerating Big Data computing, we focus on more advanced features and extensions to the Ignite platform. In this chapter, we will discuss the main problems of the Hadoop ecosystems and how Ignite can help to improve the performance of the exists Hadoop jobs. We detail the three main features of the Ignite *Hadoop accelerator*: in-memory Map/Reduce, IGFS, and Hadoop file system cache. We also provide examples of using Apache Pig and Hive to run Map/Reduce jobs on top of the Ignite in-memory Map/Reduce. At the end of the chapter, we show how to share states in-memory across different Spark applications easily.

Chapter six - Streaming and complex event processing takes the next step and goes beyond using Apache Ignite to solve complex real-time event processing problem. This chapter covers how Ignite can be used easily with other BigData technologies such as flume, storm, and camel to solve various business problems. We will guide you through with a few complete examples for developing real-time data processing on Apache Ignite.

Chapter seven - Distributive computing covers, how Ignite can help you to easily develop Microservice like application, which will be performed in parallel fashion to gain high performance, low latency, and linear scalability. You will learn about Ignite MapReduce & ForkJoin, Distributed closure execution, continuous mapping, etc. for data processing across multiple nodes in the cluster.

Code Samples

All code samples, scripts, and more in-depth examples can be found on GitHub at GitHub repo[3]

---

[3] https://github.com/srecon/ignite-book-code-samples

About the authors

Shamim Ahmed Bhuiyan

He received his Ph.D. in Computer Science from the University of Vladimir, Russia in 2007. He is currently working as an Enterprise architect, where he is responsible for designing and building out highhighly scalable, and high load middleware solutions. He has been in the IT field for over 16 years and is specialized in Java and Data science. Also, he is a former SOA solution designer, speaker, and Big data evangelist. Actively participates in the development and designing of high-performance software for IT, telecommunication and the banking industry. In spare times, he usually writes the blog frommyworkshop[4] and shares ideas with others.

Michael Zheludkov

Is a senior programmer at AT Consulting. Graduated from the *Bauman Moscow State Technical University* in 2002.

Lecturer at BMSTU since 2013, delivering course *Parallel programming and distributed systems*.

Timur Isachenko

Is a Full Stack Developer working for AT-Consulting, passionate about web development and solving biga wide variety of related challenges.

Timur spends his time learning cutting-edge technologies every day to make a best developer out of himself.

---

[4] http://frommyworkshop.blogspot.ru/

Acknowledgments

In the journey to writing this book, I have been encouraged and inspired by a lot of amazing peoples. My wife and my little son sacrificed a lot of weekends and holidays so that I could write. Thanks' a lot Katia for your tremendous help.

I would like to give a special thanks to the co-authors of this book, who helped me through the process. They spent countless nights and weekends to discuss and endure my caprice during the whole process.

There are many Apache Ignite users and committers who helped us to clear a lot of materials and made our life easier. Thanks' a lot you guys for your wonderful contributions.

A special thank you goes out to those, who read our book at the early stage and provides useful commentaries and reviews. Thanks' to Eduard Manas for providing reviews of the book. I appreciate Evgeni Pishunuk help for providing some early comments and encouragements.

I would also like to thank my colleagues and friends at AT Consulting, Sberbank and Fors Development center, who provided moral support, encouragements, and technical suggestions.

Introduction

The term *high-performance computing* has recently become very popular in the IT world. *High-performance computing* refers to the practice of aggregating computing power in such a way that it delivers much higher performance than a typical desktop computer or workstation in order to solve large problems in science, engineering, or business.

High-performance computing is not only used to model complex physical phenomena such as weather or astronomical calculations. Very common use cases are to improve applications, reduce production costs and decrease development times. Also, as our ability to collect Big Data increases, the need to analyze the data also increases. High-performance computing allows processing this data as quickly as possible.

We can achieve 2-3x times the performance of a workstation by aggregating a few computers together in one grid. If someone wants a 4-5x performance, flash storage (SSD, Flash on PCI-E) can do the job easily. They are cheap and can provide a modest performance boost. However, if we have to achieve more than 10-20x performance, then we need to find another paradigm or solution: in-memory computing.

> In plain English, `in-memory computing` primarily relies on keeping data in a server's RAM as a means of processing at faster speeds.

Why is it so popular? Because memory prices have come down a lot in recent times. In-memory computing can now be used to speed data-intensive processing. Imagine if you want to provide 16000 RPS for your customer internet banking portal or millions of transactions per second for online transaction processing system such as OW4. This is a common use case for in-memory computing that would be very hard to achieve with traditional disk-based computing. Best use cases for in-memory computing are as follows:

- High volume of ACID transactions processing.
- Cache as a Service (CaaS).
- Database caching.
- Complex event processing for IoT projects.
- Real-time analytics.
- HTAP business applications.

What is Apache Ignite?

Apache Ignite provides a convenient and easy-to-use interface for developers to work with large-scale data sets in real time and other aspects of in-memory computing. Apache Ignite has the following features:

1. Data grid.
2. Compute grid.
3. Service grid.
4. Bigdata accelerator;
5. and Streaming grid.

The following figure illustrates the basic features of Apache Ignite.

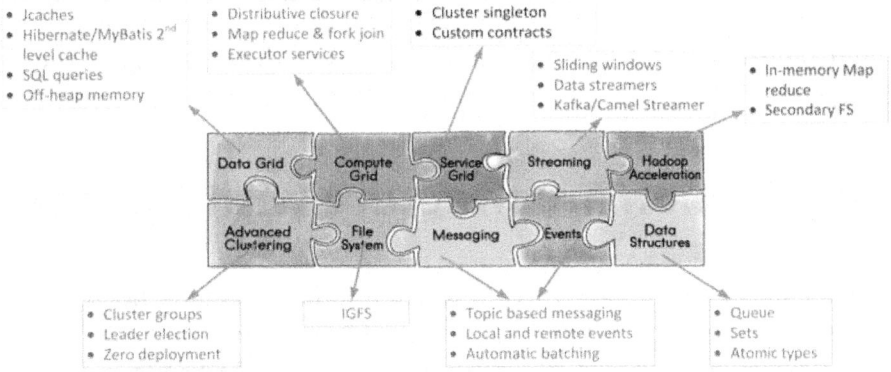

Ignite features

These are the core Apache Ignite technologies:

1. Open source.
2. Written in pure Java.
3. Supports java 7 and 8.
4. Based on Spring.
5. Supports .Net, C++ and PHP.

The primary capabilities that Apache Ignite provides are as follows

- Elasticity: An Apache Ignite cluster can grow horizontally by adding new nodes.
- Persistence: Apache Ignite data grid can persist cache entries in RDBMS, even in NoSQL like MongoDB or Cassandra.

- Cache as a Service (CaaS): Apache Ignite supports Cache-as-a-Service across the organization which allows multiple applications from different departments to access managed in-memory cache instead of slow disk base databases.
- 2nd Level Cache: Apache Ignite is the perfect caching tier to use as a 2nd level cache in Hibernate and MyBatis.
- High-performance Hadoop accelerator: Apache Ignite can replace Hadoop task tracker and job tracker and HDFS to increase the performance of big data analysis.
- Share state in-memory across Spark applications: Ignite RDD allows easily sharing of state in-memory between different Spark jobs or applications. With Ignite in-memory shared RDD's, any Spark application can put data into Ignite cache which will be accessible by another Spark application later.
- Distributed computing: Apache Ignite provides a set of simple APIs that allows a user to distribute computation and data processing across multiple nodes in the cluster to gain high performance. Apache Ignite distributed services is very useful to develop and execute **microservice** like architecture.
- Streaming: Apache Ignite allows processing continuous never-ending streams of data in scalable and fault-tolerant fashion in-memory, rather than analyzing the data after it has been stored in the database.

Modern application architecture with Apache Ignite

Let's take a quick look at an architecture of a traditional system. The traditional application architecture uses data stores which have synchronous read-write operations. This is useful for data consistency and data durability, but it is very easy to have a bottleneck if there are a lot of transactions waiting in the queue. Consider the following traditional architecture as shown below.

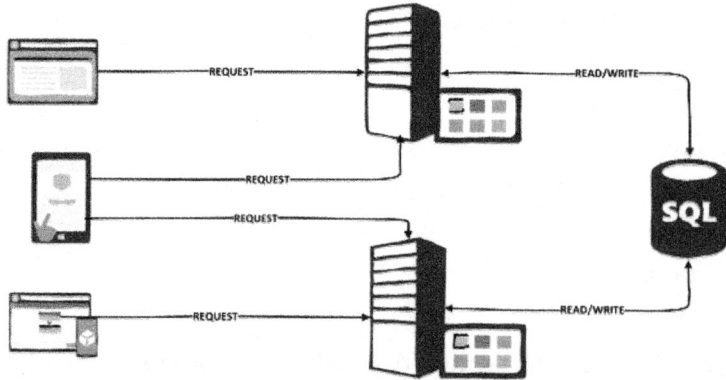

The traditional application architecture

High-volume transaction processing.

In-memory data grid adds an additional layer within an environment, which uses the Random-Access Memory (RAM) of the server to store most of all data required by the applications. In-memory data grid sits between the application servers and the data store. In-memory data grid uses a cache of frequently accessed data by the client in the active memory and then can access the persistence store whenever needed and even asynchronously send and receive updates from the persistence store. An application architecture with in-memory data grid is shown below.

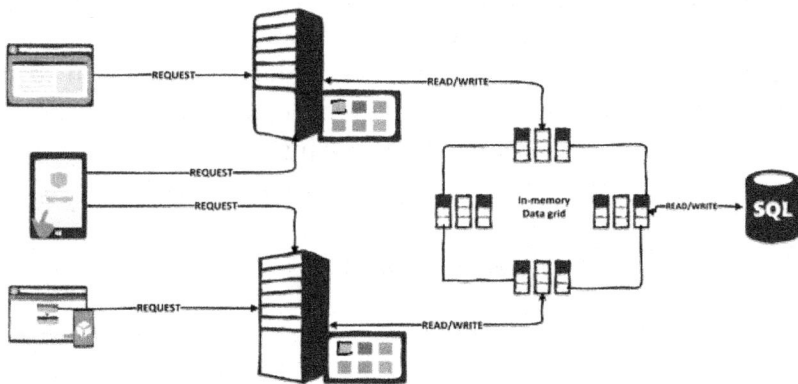

Application architecture with in-memory data grid

By using in-memory data grid, data moves closer to the application endpoints. This approach reduces the response times and can lower transactions times from a few seconds to fractions of a second. This way, the application can support extremely large numbers of concurrent transactions involving terabytes of operational data, providing a faster, more reliable transactional experience for customers. It is also a more modern scalable data management system than traditional RDBMS, able to elastically scale as demand increases.

Resilient web acceleration.

With in-memory data grid like Apache Ignite, you can provide fault tolerance to your web application and accelerate your web application's performance. Without changing any code, you can share session states between web applications through caches.

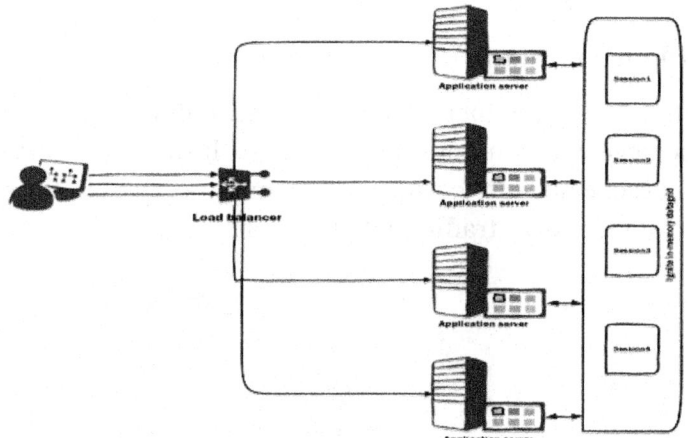

Fault tolerance web application

This above approach provides the highest level of high availability of a system and a customer experience. Since Ignite is an in-memory solution, the performance of the web session clustering and replication mechanism of user web sessions are very high.

Event processing & real-time analysis.

Data tells the story of what's happing with your business on the background right now. With the IoT as a continuous data source, the opportunities to take advantage of the hot data is greater than ever. Traditional data management system cannot process big data fast enough to notify the business of important events as they occur: such as online credit card fraud detection or risk calculation. Apache Ignite allows processing continuous never-ending streams of data in scalable and fault-tolerant fashion in-memory, rather than analyzing data after it's reached the database.

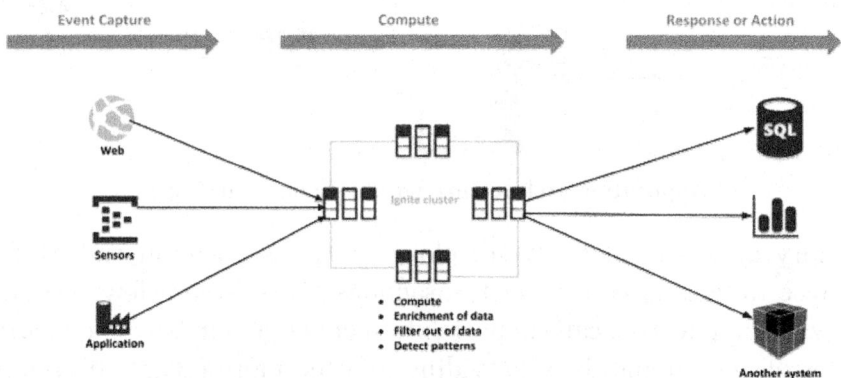

Complex event notification and processing

Not only does this enable you to correlate relationships and detect meaningful patterns from significantly more data but you can process it faster and much more efficiently. Apache Ignite in-memory data grid can manage a tremendous amount of incoming data and push notifications to the business application when changes occur with the server. The Apache Ignite continuous queries capability allows systems to quickly access a large amount of incoming never ending data and take action.

Microservices in distributed fashion.

Microservice architecture has a number of benefits and enforces a level of modularity that is extremely difficult to achieve with a monolithic code base. In-memory data grid like Apache Ignite can provide independent cache nodes to corresponding microservices in the same distributed cluster and gives you a few advantages over traditional approaches.

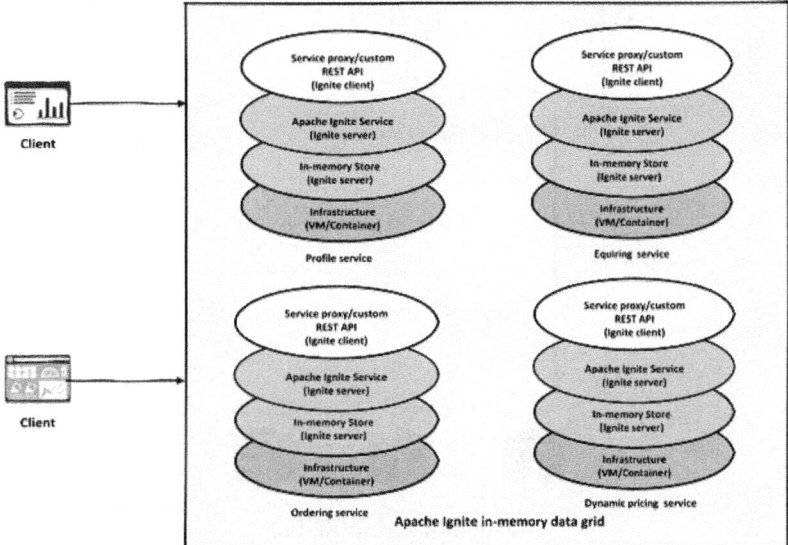

Apache Ignite microservice architecture

It allows you to make use to its maximum the data fabrics/grid resources. Services running on the in-memory cluster is much faster than the disk-based application server. Apache Ignite microservice based service grid provides a platform to automatically deploy any number of distributed service instance in the cluster.

BigData accelerator.

Hadoop has been widely used for its ability to store and analyze large data sets economically and has long passed the point of being nascent technology. However, it's batch scheduling overhead, and disk-based data storage have made it unsuitable for use in analyzing live, real-time data in the production environment. One of the main factors that limit performance scaling of Hadoop and Map/Reduce is the fact that Hadoop relies on a file system that generates a lot of input/output (I/O) files. An alternative is to store the needed distributed data within the memory. Placing Map/Reduce in- memory with the data it needs eliminates file I/O latency.

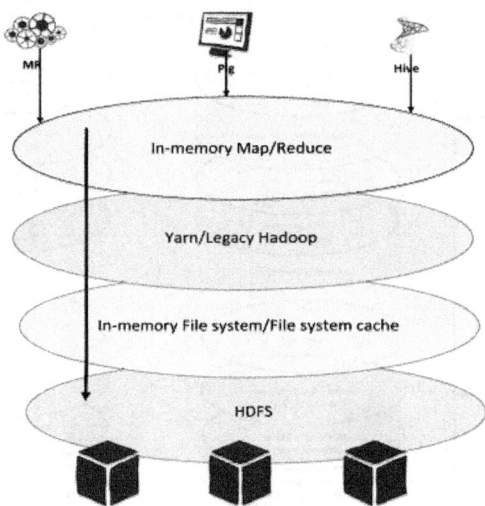

In-memory Map/Reduce

Apache Ignite has offered a set of useful components allowing in-memory Hadoop job executing and file system operations. Apache Ignite Hadoop accelerator can automatically deploy all necessary executable programs and libraries for the execution of Map/Reduce across the JVMs, which greatly reducing startup time down to milliseconds. This speeds up by avoiding delays in accessing secondary storage. Also, because the execution engine is integrated with the in-memory data grid, key/value pairs hosted within the data grid can be efficiently read into the execution engine to minimize access time.

Cache as a Service.

Data-driven applications that take too long to load are boring and frustrating to use. Four out of five online users will click away if a page stalls while loading. In-memory data grid can provide a common caching layer across the organization, which can allow multiple applications to access managed in-memory cache.

Introduction

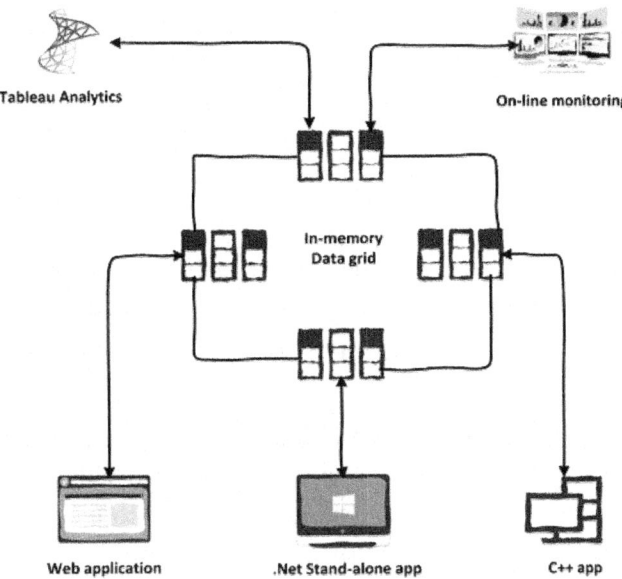

Cache as a Service

You can isolate the caching layer from the applications by separating the caching layer from the applications. Any applications (Java, .Net, C++) across the organization can store and read data from the cache. By using in-memory data grid as a service, it's not necessary to build and deploy local caching infrastructure for each application. Applications can use Apache Ignite as cache-aside or write behind to their database or load data from the database into the cache. It eliminates the complexity in the management of the hundred or more separate caching infrastructures.

These are some of the ways in-memory grids like Apache Ignite have served as an essential, architectural component for **transforming** the way businesses use their data to do business. But that's not all folks! We will cover a lot of in-memory data grid use cases and application architecture in more details through this book.

Who uses Apache Ignite?

Apache Ignite is widely used around the world and is growing all the time. Companies like Barclays, Misys, Sberbank (3rd largest bank in the Europe) all use Ignite to power pieces of their architecture that are critical to the day-to-day operations of those organizations.

Why Ignite instead of others?

There are a few others alternatives of Apache Ignite from other vendors such as HazelCast, Oracle, Ehcache, GemFire, etc. The main difference of Apache Ignite from the others is the quantity of functionality and simplicity of use. Apache Ignite provides a variety of functionalities, which you can use for different use cases. Unlike other competitors, Ignite provides a set of components called

Hadoop accelerator and Spark shared RDD that can deliver real-time performance to Hadoop & Spark users.

Our Hope

There is a lot to learn when diving into Apache Ignite. Just like any other distributed system, it can be complex. But by the end of this book, we hope to have simplified it enough for you to not only build an application based on in-memory computing but also to administer the cluster supporting your application.

The book is a *project-based* guide, where each chapter focuses on the complete implementation of a real-world scenario. The frequent challenges in each scenario will be discussed, along with tips, tricks and best practices on how to overcome them. For every topic, we will introduce a complete sample running application, which will help you to hit the ground running.

Chapter one: Installation and the first Ignite application

Ignite is a Java-Based application. Because of this, a few considerations need to be taken into account when installing it. This chapter will highlight the different installation type and configurations. First of all, we will install Ignite on a single machine and then we will dive into setting up a multi-node cluster to run a HelloWorld example.

Pre-requisites

Apache Ignite team officially supports Oracle JDK 7 version and above. However, we installed Apache Ignite with IBM J9 and OpenJDK 7 in a few projects.

N	Name	Value
1	JDK	Oracle JDK 7 and above
2	OS	Linux, MacOS (10.6 and above), Windows XP and above, Windows Server (2008 and above)
3	Network	10G
4	RAM	Default value 1 GB ram for development environment

Installation

This section covers the installation for binary distribution and the source code of Apache Ignite.

> **Note:**
> I am going to use macOS operating system for install and running Apache Ignite through the book. Most of the commands I am using also runs on Linux operating system.

Download the binaries.zip archive:

```
curl http://apache-mirror.rbc.ru/pub/apache/ignite/1.6.0/apache-ignite-fabric-1.6.0-bin.zip
```

Unpack the zip archive anywhere in your file system, such as /opt/ignite-1.6.0:

Chapter one: Installation and the first Ignite application

```
unzip apache-ignite-fabric-1.6.0-bin.zip
```

Set an environment variable *IGNITE_HOME* to the home directory (directory, where the Apache Ignite is installed) of the Apache Ignite:

```
export IGNITE_HOME=YOUR_IGNITE_HOME_PATH
export PATH=$PATH:$JAVA_HOME/bin:$IGNITE_HOME/bin:$HOME/bin
```

Copy the folder `$IGNITE_HOME/libs/optional/ignite-rest-http` to `IGNITE_HOME/libs`, this will enable the Ignite *rest interface*. Run `ignite.sh` in your any favorite terminal, which will run the Apache Ignite with default configuration. If you want to run Ignite with pre-configured cache called `example`, run the following command:

```
ignite.sh $IGNITE_HOME/examples/config/example-cache.xml
```

After executing the above command, you should get some responses as follows:

```
Ignite node started OK (id=ceb614ca)
Topology snapshot [ver=1, servers=1, clients=0, CPUs=3, heap=2.0GB]
```

```
[22:19:26] Ignite node started OK (id=27cb79fb)
[22:19:26] Topology snapshot [ver=1, servers=1, clients=0, CPUs=8, heap=1.0GB]
```

Figure 1.1

Sanity

Open the following URL in your favorite web browser.

```
http://IP_ADDRESS:8080/ignite?cmd=version
```

You should get the following response from the Ignite node:

```
{"error":"","response":"1.6.0","sessionToken":"","successStatus":0}
```

Compiling from the source code

You need to have apache Maven to be able to compile and build Ignite source code. If you already have a Maven installed on your computer, please skip this stage. Download and install maven.

Download and install maven.

```
curl http://apache-mirror.rbc.ru/pub/apache/maven/maven-3/3.3.9/binaries/apache-maven-3.3.\
9-bin.tar.gz
```

> **Note:**
> Your editor or IDE may have specific functionality for working with Maven, which is not addressed in this document. For information about the capabilities of your IDE (Eclipse/IntelliJ Idea), see the documentation for the product you are using.

Unzip the distribution archive in any directory.

```
tar xvf apache-maven-3.3.9-bin.tar.gz
```

Add the bin directory of the created directory apache-maven-3.3.9 to the PATH environment variable.

```
export PATH=$PATH:$JAVA_HOME/bin:$IGNITE_HOME/bin:$MAVEN_HOME/bin
```

Run, *mvn -v* in terminal, the result should look similar to the following:

```
Apache Maven 3.2.3 (33f8c3e1027c3ddde99d3cdebad2656a31e8fdf4; 2014-08-12T00:58:10+03:00)
Maven home: /Users/shamim/Development/java/maven/apache-maven-3.2.3
Java version: 1.8.0_45, vendor: Oracle Corporation
Java home: /Library/Java/JavaVirtualMachines/jdk1.8.0_45.jdk/Contents/Home/jre
Default locale: en_US, platform encoding: UTF-8
OS name: "mac os x", version: "10.11.5", arch: "x86_64", family: "mac"
```

Download the Ignite source code.

```
curl http://apache-mirror.rbc.ru/pub/apache/ignite/1.6.0/apache-ignite-1.6.0-src.zip
```

Unzip the archive file in any directory.

```
unzip apache-ignite-1.6.0-src.zip
```

Then change directory to the already extracted file with the command below,

Chapter one: Installation and the first Ignite application   17

```
cd apache-ignite-1.6.0-src
```

and run the following command

```
mvn clean install -DskipTests
```

If you want to build in-memory Hadoop accelerator release, run the following command.

```
mvn clean install -DskipTests -Dignite.edition=hadoop [-Dhadoop.version=X.X.X]
```

For the first time, it will take a few minutes to download all the dependencies from the maven repositories and build the release.

Run multiple instances of Apache Ignite in a single host

With multicast auto-discovery mechanism, Ignite allows cluster member to discover each other using multicast communication. It also allows you to run a few Ignite instances on a single host machine. You have to run the following commands in the different shell to run a few Ignite instances on a single host.

```
ignite.sh $IGNITE_HOME/examples/config/example-cache.xml
```

```
[22:19:26] Topology snapshot [ver=1, servers=1, clients=0, CPUs=8, heap=1.0GB]
[22:33:02] Topology snapshot [ver=2, servers=2, clients=0, CPUs=8, heap=2.0GB]
```

Figure 1.2

> **Note:**
> Before running the above command, please make sure that you have sufficient memory on your host machine. By default, Ignite consumes 1 GB memory per Ignite instance.

You can change the default configuration in **ignite.sh** file located in $IGNITE_HOME/bin directory. Find the following fragment of bash script in **ignite.sh** file

```
if [ -z "$JVM_OPTS" ] ; then
    if [[ `"$JAVA" -version 2>&1 | egrep "1\.[7]\."` ]]; then
        JVM_OPTS="-Xms1g -Xmx1g -server -XX:+AggressiveOpts -XX:MaxPermSize=256m"
    else
        JVM_OPTS="-Xms1g -Xmx1g -server -XX:+AggressiveOpts -XX:MaxMetaspaceSize=256m"
    fi
fi
```

Replace the *-Xms1g -Xmx1g* parameters with *-Xms512m -Xmx512m* for example. Next time when you restart the Ignite instance, your JVM will be started with Xms amount of memory and will be able to use a maximum of Xmx amount of memory. For example, starting a JVM with *-Xms512m -Xmx512m* parameter will start the JVM with 512MB of memory, and will allow the process to use up to 512MB of memory.

Configure a multi-node cluster in different host

This approach is very similar to a single-host cluster. First of all, on every host machine, we have to open a few ports in the iptables file. By adding the following commands to the **iptables** file, it will open all the necessary port on the host machine.

```
-A INPUT -m state --state NEW -m tcp -p tcp --dport 47500:47509 -j ACCEPT
-A INPUT -m state --state NEW -m tcp -p tcp --dport 47400 -j ACCEPT
-A INPUT -m state --state NEW -m tcp -p tcp --dport 47100 -j ACCEPT
-A INPUT -m state --state NEW -m tcp -p tcp --dport 47101 -j ACCEPT
-A INPUT -m state --state NEW -m tcp -p tcp --dport 48100 -j ACCEPT
-A INPUT -m state --state NEW -m tcp -p tcp --dport 48101 -j ACCEPT
-A INPUT -m state --state NEW -m tcp -p tcp --dport 31100 -j ACCEPT
-A INPUT -m state --state NEW -m tcp -p tcp --dport 31101 -j ACCEPT
```

And restart the *iptable service* as follows:

```
/etc/init.d/iptables restart
```

Next, we will make only one change in *example-cache.xml* file. We are going to replace the IP address **127.0.0.1** with the *actual host IP address* as follows:

Chapter one: Installation and the first Ignite application

```
<bean class="org.apache.ignite.spi.discovery.tcp.ipfinder.multicast.TcpDiscoveryMulticastI\
pFinder">
        <property name="addresses">
            <list>
                    <value>HOST_IP_ADDRESS:47500..47509</value>
            </list>
        </property>
</bean>
```

Now, we can start every instance of the Apache Ignite on the separate host machines, and every instance should locate each other.

> **Note:**
> If something went wrong, double check the *iptable* file settings and the actual IP address of the host machine.

Rest client to manipulate with the Apache Ignite

Now, we can use the Ignite rest API for manipulating Apache Ignite caches. Ignite out-of-the-box provides an HTTP REST client that gives you the ability to communicate with the Ignite grid over HTTP and HTTPS protocols using REST API.

Open your favorite browser and type the following URL:

```
http://IP_ADDR:8080/ignite?cmd=getorcreate&cacheName=testCache
```

where,

> cmd = Ignite rest command, for instance *getorcreate*. This creates a new cache if doesn't exist.
> cacheName = the name of the cache, in our case this is **testCache**.

The above URL on browser should return you the following JSON response.

```
{"error":"","response":null,"sessionToken":"","successStatus":0}
```

Once the Ignite node or cluster is up and running, you can use the command-line tool *ignitevisor* to show various statistics about the nodes in the cluster. Open a shell or terminal and run the following command.

Chapter one: Installation and the first Ignite application 20

```
$ignitevisorcmd.sh
```

The next figure shows what you should see now:

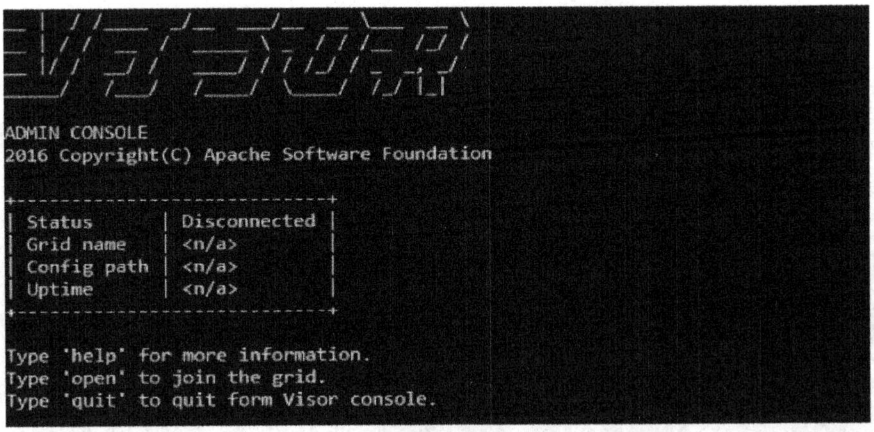

Figure 1.3

Ignite Visor is a CLI (command-line) tools for managing and monitoring the Ignite cluster. In *ignitevisor* console, you can look for your cache, which you have just created through rest API.

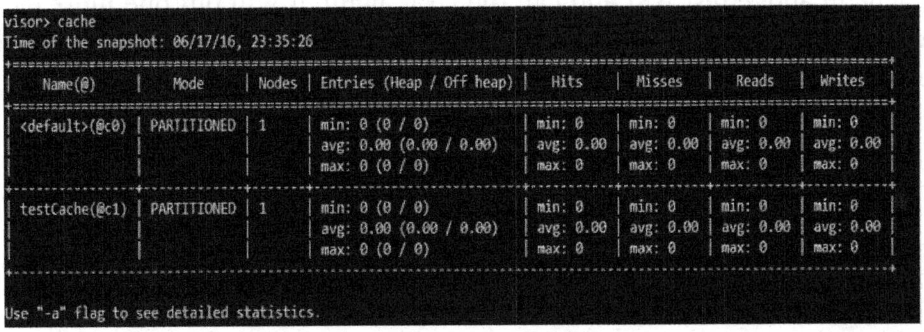

Figure 1.4

Let's put a few cache elements (entries) by using the rest API. Type the following URL in your browser.

```
http://IP_ADDRt:8080/ignite?cmd=put&key=moscow&val=777&cacheName=testCache
```

Where,

> cmd = command put, put an element to the cache.
>
> key = key of the cache, it must be unique. In our case it is Moscow.
>
> value = value of the cache. In our case, it is the region code of the Moscow, code 777.

Chapter one: Installation and the first Ignite application

> cacheName = the name of the cache. For example, *testCache*.

After calling the above RestFull API, we can check our cache on *ignitevisor*.

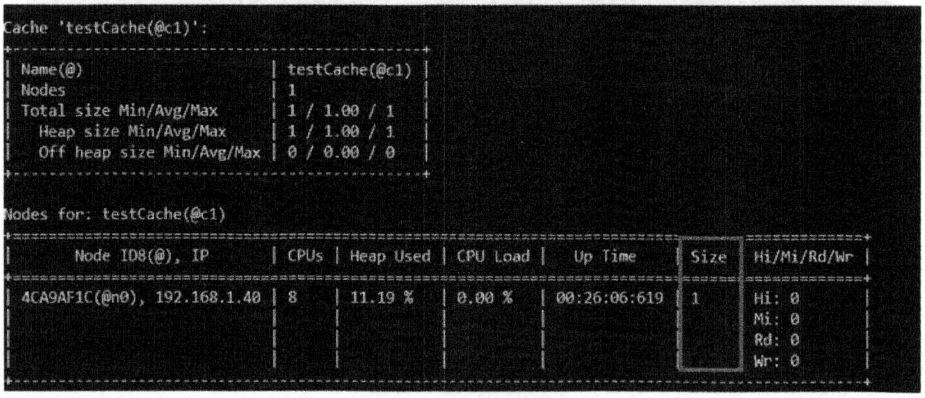

Figure 1.5

Now, cache size is 1, because we have just put one element in it. If you will change the key and the value of the cache in above rest API and call the URL again, it will put one more element into the cache and the cache size should be increased. For retrieving the element from the Ignite cache, type the following URL in the browser.

`http://localhost:8080/ignite?cmd=get&key=moscow&cacheName=testCache`

Where,

> cmd = command get, get the cache value.
>
> key = cache unique key, for example **Moscow**.
>
> cacheName = the name of the cache, in our case it should be **testCache**.

`{"affinityNodeId":"4ca9af1c-7404-4f30-a92d-2c2ae08b8b85","error":"","response":"777","sess\`
`ionToken":"","successStatus":0}`

It's also possible to get a few values from the cache with one rest API call. Here is an example as shown below.

```
http://localhost:8080/ignite?cmd=getall&k1=moscow&k2=vladimir&k3=tver&cacheName=testCache
```

The above URL will return the following result:

```
{"affinityNodeId":"","error":"","response":{"moscow":"777","tver":"39","vladimir":"33"},"s\
essionToken":"","successStatus":0}
```

Java client

In this section, we will take you through the creation of your first Ignite application to write and read (put/get) from the distributive cache. The complete source code can be downloaded from GitHub[5] (chapter-installation).

Start your Ignite single node cluster or multi-node cluster, if it's not started yet. Create an mvn project with the following command, or you can clone the *chapter-installation* from the GitHub.

```
mvn archetype:create -DartifactId=chapter-one -DgroupId=com.blu.imdg
```

Add the following Ignite maven dependency to the **pom.xml** file.

```xml
<dependency>
    <groupId>org.apache.ignite</groupId>
    <artifactId>ignite-core</artifactId>
    <version>${ignite.version}</version>
</dependency>
```

Also add the project properties section in the pom.xml file.

```xml
<properties>
    <project.build.sourceEncoding>UTF-8</project.build.sourceEncoding>
    <ignite.version>1.6.0</ignite.version>
</properties>
```

You can run the application from the command line with Maven. Or you can build a single executable JAR file that contains all the necessary dependencies, classes, and resources, and run that. This makes it easy to ship, version, and deploy the service as an application throughout the development lifecycle, across different environments, and so on. Add two more plugins to create a **fat executable jar** to run the application easily.

---

[5] https://github.com/srecon/ignite-book-code-samples

Chapter one: Installation and the first Ignite application

```xml
<build>
    <plugins>
        <plugin>
            <groupId>com.jolira</groupId>
            <artifactId>onejar-maven-plugin</artifactId>
            <version>1.4.4</version>
            <executions>
                <execution>
                    <id>build-query</id>
                    <configuration>
                        <mainClass>com.blu.imdg.HelloIgnite</mainClass>
                        <attachToBuild>true</attachToBuild>
                        <classifier>onejar</classifier>
                        <filename>HelloIgnite-runnable.jar</filename>
                    </configuration>
                    <goals>
                        <goal>one-jar</goal>
                    </goals>
                </execution>
            </executions>
        </plugin>
    </plugins>
</build>
```

Create a Java class with name *HelloIgnite* and import all the following libraries.

```java
import org.apache.ignite.Ignite;
import org.apache.ignite.IgniteCache;
import org.apache.ignite.Ignition;
import org.apache.ignite.configuration.IgniteConfiguration;
import org.apache.ignite.spi.discovery.tcp.TcpDiscoverySpi;
import org.apache.ignite.spi.discovery.tcp.ipfinder.multicast.TcpDiscoveryMulticastIpFinder;
```

Add the following fragments of code to your class *HelloIgnite*

```java
public static void main(String[] args) {
    System.out.println("Hello Ignite");
    // create a new instance of TCP Discovery SPI
    TcpDiscoverySpi spi = new TcpDiscoverySpi();
    // create a new instance of tcp discovery multicast ip finder
    TcpDiscoveryMulticastIpFinder tcMp = new TcpDiscoveryMulticastIpFinder();
    tcMp.setAddresses(Arrays.asList("localhost")); // change your IP address here
    // set the multi cast ip finder for spi
    spi.setIpFinder(tcMp);
    // create new ignite configuration
    IgniteConfiguration cfg = new IgniteConfiguration();
    cfg.setClientMode(false);
    // set the discovery spi to ignite configuration
    cfg.setDiscoverySpi(spi);
    // Start ignite
    Ignite ignite = Ignition.start(cfg);
    // get or create cache
    IgniteCache<Integer, String> cache = ignite.getOrCreateCache("myCacheName");
    // put some cache elements
    for(int i = 1; i <= 100; i++){
        cache.put(i, Integer.toString(i));
    }
    // get them from the cache and write to the console
    for(int i =1; i<= 100;i++){
        System.out.println("Cache get:"+ cache.get(i));
    }
    // close ignite instance
    ignite.close();
}
```

Although the above fragment code is straight forward, let me explain a little bit. First, we created the instance of a TCP Discovery SPI and set multicast IP finder instance on it. Later, we set the address of our Ignite cluster and create an Ignite configuration. After starting the Ignite instance, it joins with existing Ignite cluster as a new server. We putted 100 entries in the Ignite distributed cache and read those 100 entries from the cache and stop the Ignite instance.

Now you are ready to compile the source file. At the prompt of the terminal, type the following command and press enter.

```
mvn clean install
```

After successful compilation, an *executable jar* will be created in the *target* directory. Run the application by typing the following command:

Chapter one: Installation and the first Ignite application 25

```
java -jar .\target\HelloIgnite-runnable.jar
```

You should see a lot of logs in to application console. First, a new Ignite instance will be created and it will join the new cluster. In cluster console, you should see the logs as follows.

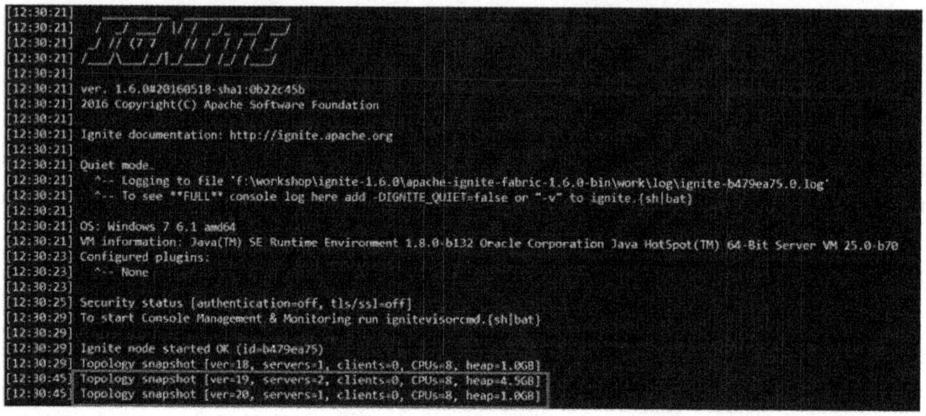

Figure 1.6

Let's examine the cluster with visor administration console. Open the visor with command.

```
ignitevisorcmd.sh
```

Run the following command in visor console.

```
cache -a
```

It should return you the details of the cache statistics for our cache called *testCache* as shown in figure 7.

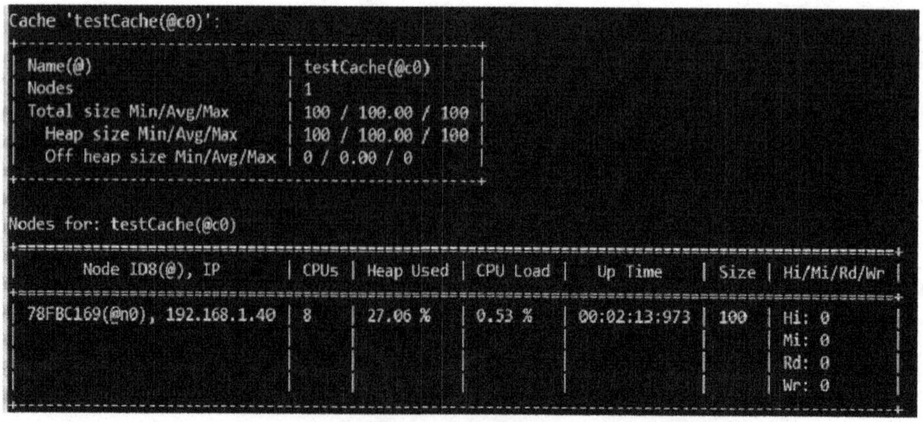

Figure 1.7

Total cache size is 100 entries, as we expected. For simplicity, we didn't use any **spring configuration** in the above example.

SQL client

Apache Ignite provides SQL queries execution on the caches, SQL syntax is an ANSI-99 compliant. Therefore, you can execute SQL queries against any caches from any SQL client which supports *JDBC thin client*. This section is for those, who feels comfortable with SQL rather than execute a bunch of code to retrieve data from the cache. Apache Ignite out-of-the-box is shipped with JDBC driver that allows you to connect to Ignite caches and retrieve distributed data from the cache using standard SQL queries.

Next section of this chapter will describe how to connect the SQL IDE (Integrated Development Environment) to Ignite cache and executes some SQL queries to play with cache entries. SQL IDE or SQL editor can simplify the development process and allow you to get productive much quicker.

Most database vendors have their own front-end specially developed IDE for their database. Oracle has SQL developer and Sybase has Interactive SQL and so on. Unfortunately, Apache Ignite doesn't provide any SQL editor to work with Ignite caches, however, GridGain (commercial version of the Apache Ignite) provides a commercial GridGain web console[6] web console application to connect to the Ignite cluster and run SQL queries against cache entries. As far as I work with the multi-platform database in my daily works, for the last couple of years, I have used Dbeaver[7] for working with different databases. A couple of words about Dbeaver: it's an open-source multi-platform database tool for Developers, Analytics or Database administrators. It supports a huge range of Databases and also lets you connect to any Database with JDBC thin client (if the database supports JDBC). Anyway, you can also try SQuirrel SQL client or Jetbrains DataGrip to connect to Ignite cluster, they all supports JDBC.

> **Note:**
> Cache updates are not supported by SQL queries in version 1.6, you can only use SELECT queries. Since 1.8 version, SQL DML queries also supported by the Ignite.

To run SQL queries against caches, we already added a complete Java application (**HelloIgniteSpring**) in the *installation* chapter. You can run the application by executing the following command.

```
java -jar .\target\HelloIgniteSpring-runnable.jar
```

At this moment, we are not going into details about all the concepts of Ignite cache queries here. We will have a detailed look at Ignite SQL queries on **chapter four**. For now, after running the HelloIgniteSpring application, it will put a few Person objects into the cache named **testCache**. Object *Person* has attributes like *name* and *age* as follows:

---

[6] http://ignite.apache.org/addons.html#web-console
[7] http://dbeaver.jkiss.org/

№	Property Name	Property Age
1	Shamim	37
2	Mishel	2
3	Scott	55
4	Tiger	5

After completing the configuration of the Dbeaver SQL client, we will run a few SQL queries against the above objects. Now it's the time to download the Dbeaver and complete the JDBC configuration on it.

Step 1:

Download the Dbeaver Enterprise edition (it's free but not an open source product) for your operating system from the following url:

```
http://dbeaver.jkiss.org/download/enterprise/
```

Step 2:

Install the Dbeaver (please refer to the install section of the Dbeaver site, if you encounter any problems during the installation).

Step 3:

Compile the maven `chapter-installation` project, if you didn't do it before.

Step 4:

Run the `HelloIgniteSpring` application with the following command:

```
java -jar ./target/HelloIgniteSpring-runnable.jar
```

You should have the following output in your console:

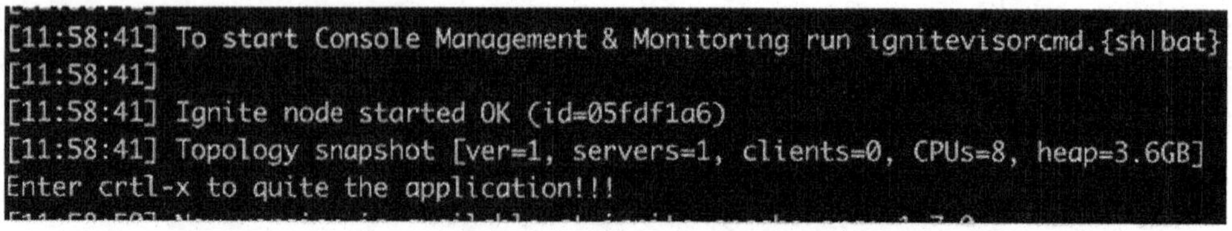

```
[11:58:41] To start Console Management & Monitoring run ignitevisorcmd.{sh|bat}
[11:58:41]
[11:58:41] Ignite node started OK (id=05fdf1a6)
[11:58:41] Topology snapshot [ver=1, servers=1, clients=0, CPUs=8, heap=3.6GB]
Enter crtl-x to quite the application!!!
```

Figure 1.8

If you are curious about the code, please refer to the chapter-installation[8].

Step 5:

Now, let's configure the JDBC driver for the Dbeaver. Go to Database -> Driver Manager -> New

---
[8] https://github.com/srecon/ignite-book-code-samples/tree/master/chapters/chapter-installation

In the **Settings** section, fill the requested information as follows:

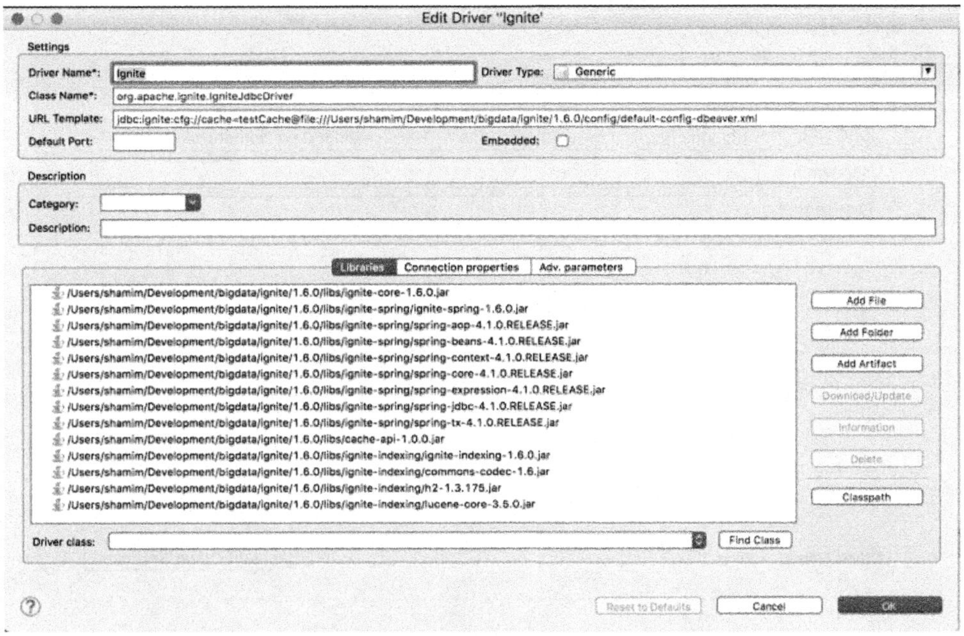

Figure 1.9

Add all the *libraries* shown in the above screenshot. Copy and rename the file `~/ignite-book-code-samples/chapters/chapter-installation/src/main/resources/default-config.xml` into *default-config-dbeaver.xml* somewhere in your file system. Change the *clientMode* properties value to *true* in the default-config-dbeaver.xml file. Add the file path to the URL template as shown in the above screenshot and click ok.

Step 6:

Create a New connection based on the Ignite Driver manager. Go to the Database->New Connection. Select Ignite drive manager from the drop down list and click next. You should have the following screen before you.

Chapter one: Installation and the first Ignite application

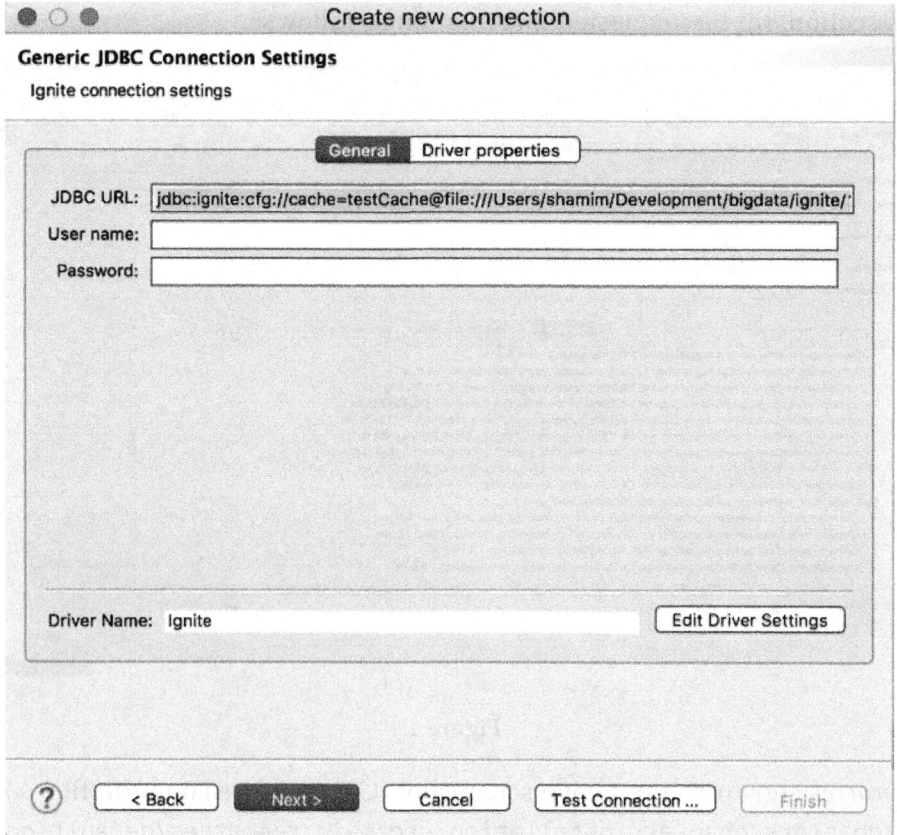

Figure 1.10

Click the **Test connection** button for quick test. If everything done properly, you should have the next screenshot with the success notification.

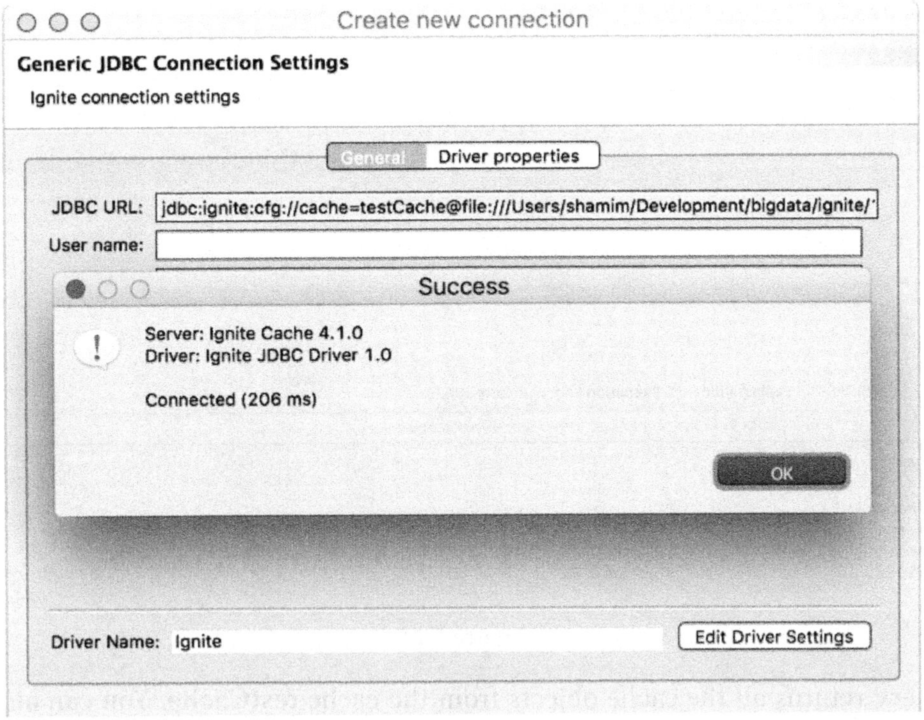

Figure 1.11

Click *ok* button and go through all the next step to complete the connection.

Step 7:

Create a new SQL editor tab and enter the following SQL query on Dbeaver.

```
SELECT name FROM Person;
```

Step 8:

Run the script by pressing the button command+x and you should have the following result.

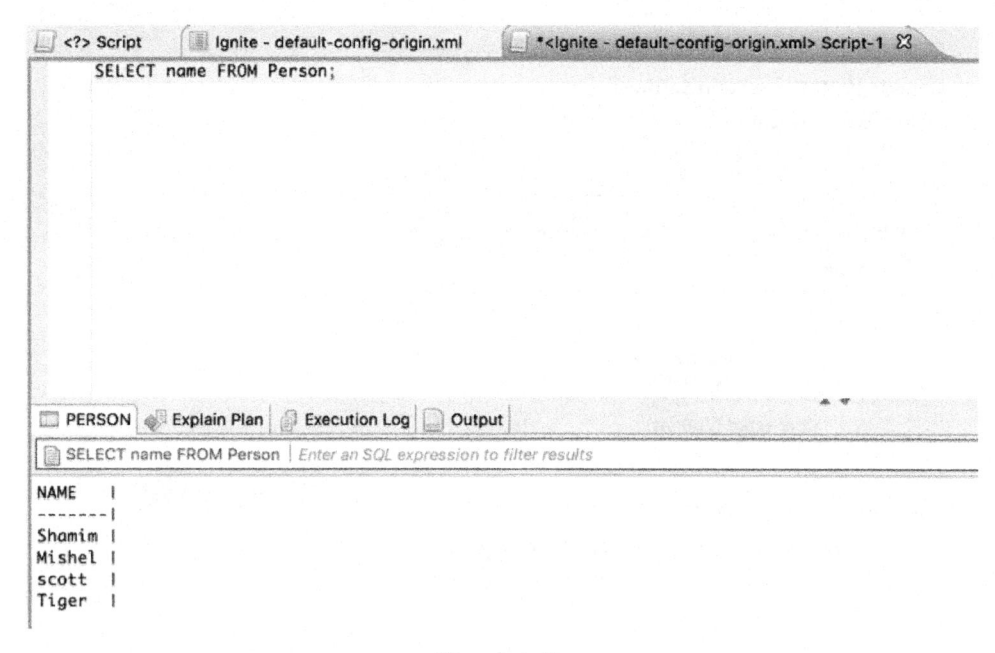

Chapter one: Installation and the first Ignite application

Figure 1.12

The above query returns all the cache objects from the cache **testCache**. You can also execute the following query:

```
SELECT name FROM Person p WHERE p.age BETWEEN 30 AND 60;
```

It should return the result with the following names:

```
Shamim
Scott
```

Ignite SQL engine is fully **ANSI-99** compliant and let you run any SQL query like analytical or Ad-hoc queries. It's enough for now for a quick start with Apache Ignite.

Conclusion

In this chapter, we discussed only the basic, most commonly used configuration option to get up and running with Ignite cluster. Also, you have already covered a lot of ground:

1. Obtaining and installing Ignite.
2. Launching Ignite instance on single-host and on a cluster.
3. Use Ignite RestFull API to manipulates with the cache.
4. Develop a *HelloWorld* application to write to and read from the Ignite cache.
5. Install Dbeaver SQL IDE and run a few SQL queries.
6. Some key concepts, such as **IgniteVisor** to management and monitoring Ignite cache.

What's Next

In the next chapter, we will move away from the short code examples you have seen so far, and we will make an architecture overview of the Apache Ignite.

Chapter two: Architecture overview

To better understand the functionality of Apache Ignite and use cases, it's very important to understand its architecture and topology. By getting a better understanding of Ignite's architecture, you can decide the topology or cache mode to solve different problems in your enterprise architecture landscape and get the maximum benefits from in-memory computing. Unlike master-slave designs, Ignite makes use of an entirely peer-to-peer architecture. Every node in the Ignite cluster can accept read and write, no matter where the data is being written. In this chapter we are going to cover the following topics:

- Apache Ignite functional overview.
- Different cluster topology.
- Cluster topology.
- Caching strategy.
- Clustering.
- Data model.
- Multi-datacenter replication.
- Asynchronous support.
- How SQL queries works in Ignite.
- Resilience.

Functional overview

The Ignite architecture has sufficient flexibility and advanced features that can be used in a large number of different architectural patterns and styles. You can view Ignite as a collection of independent, well-integrated, in-memory components geared to improve the performance and scalability of your application. The following schematic represents the basic functionalities of Apache Ignite.

Chapter two: Architecture overview

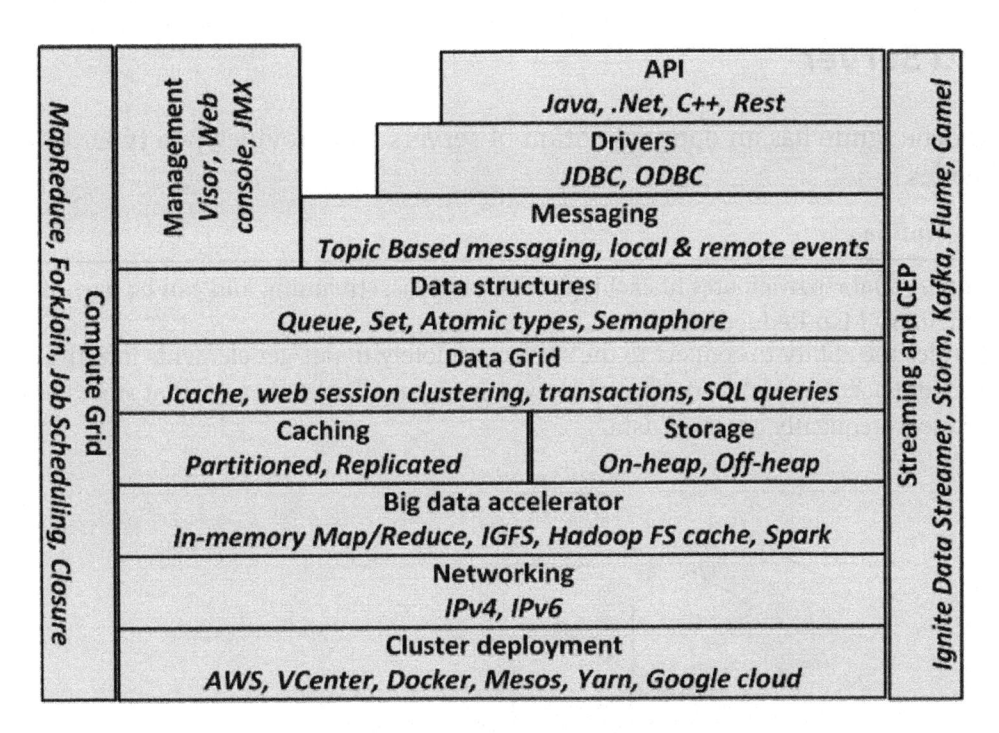

Compute Grid MapReduce, ForkJoin, Job Scheduling, Closure	Management Visor, Web console, JMX	**API** Java, .Net, C++, Rest	Streaming and CEP Ignite Data Streamer, Storm, Kafka, Flume, Camel
		Drivers JDBC, ODBC	
		Messaging Topic Based messaging, local & remote events	
	Data structures Queue, Set, Atomic types, Semaphore		
	Data Grid Jcache, web session clustering, transactions, SQL queries		
	Caching Partitioned, Replicated	**Storage** On-heap, Off-heap	
	Big data accelerator In-memory Map/Reduce, IGFS, Hadoop FS cache, Spark		
	Networking IPv4, IPv6		
	Cluster deployment AWS, VCenter, Docker, Mesos, Yarn, Google cloud		

Figure 2.1. Functional architecture

Note that Apache Ignite contains a lot of features not shown in the above figure due to lack of space. Ignite is organized in a modular fashion and provides a single jar (library) for each functionality. You only have to apply the desired library into your project to use Ignite.

Cluster Topology

Ignite design implies that the entire system itself is both inherently available and massively scalable. Ignite internode communication allows all nodes to receive updates without the need for a **master coordinator** quickly. Nodes can be added or removed non-disruptively to increase the amount of *RAM* available. Ignite data fabrics are fully resilient, allowing non-disruptive automated detection and recovery of a single server or multiple servers.

> **Note:**
> In contrast to the monolithic and master-slave architectures, there are no special nodes in Ignite. All nodes are identical in the Ignite cluster.

Client and Server

However, Apache Ignite has an optional notion of servers and provides two types of nodes: Client and Server nodes.

Node	Description
Server	Contains Data, participates in caching, computations, streaming and can be part of the in-memory Map-Reduce tasks.
Client	Provides the ability to connect to the servers remotely to put/get elements into the cache. It can also store portions of data (near cache), which is a smaller local cache that stores most recently and most frequently accessed data.

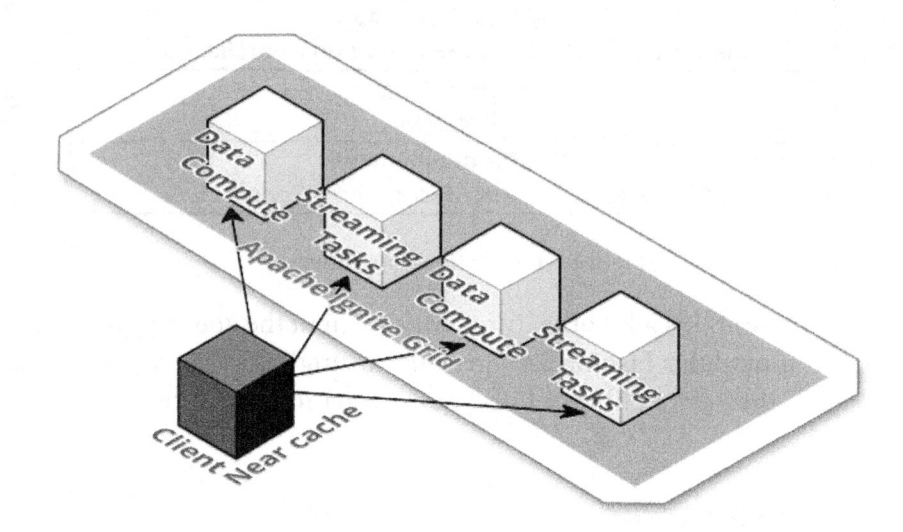

Figure 2.2. Ignite client and servers

The server node also can be grouped together in a cluster to perform work. Within a cluster, you can limit job execution, service deployment, streaming and other tasks to run only within cluster group. You can create a cluster group based on any predicate. For instance, you can create a cluster group from a group of nodes, where all the nodes are responsible for caching data for **testCache**. We shall discuss the clustering in more detail in the subsequent section of this chapter. By default, all nodes are started as server nodes. Client mode needs to be explicitly enabled. Note that you can't physically separate data nodes from compute nodes. In Apache Ignite, servers that contain data, are also used to execute computations.

Apache Ignite client nodes also participate in job executions. The concept might seem complicated at first glance, but let's try to clarify the concept.

Server nodes always store data and **by default** can participate in any computation task. On the other hand, the *Client* node can manipulate the server caches, store *local* data and participate in **computation tasks**. Usually, client nodes are used to put or retrieve data from the caches. This type of hybrid client nodes gives flexibility when developing a massive Ignite grid with many nodes. Both clients and server nodes are located in one grid, in some cases (as for example, high volume acid transactions in data node) you just do not want to execute any computation on a data node. In this case, you can choose to execute jobs only on client nodes by creating a corresponding cluster group. This way, you can separate the data node from the compute node in one grid. Compute on clients can be performed with the following pseudo code.

```
ClusterGroup clientGroup = ignite.cluster().forClients();
IgniteCompute clientCompute = ignite.compute(clientGroup);
// Execute computation on the client nodes.
clientCompute.broadcast(() -> System.out.println("sum of: " + (2+2)));
```

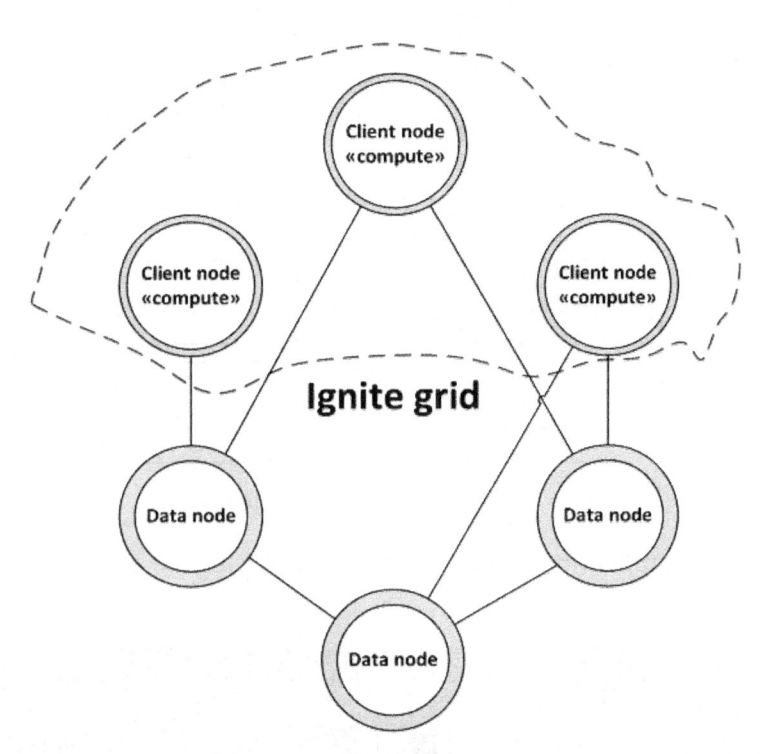

Figure 2.3. Client cluster group

There is one downside of this approach. With this approach, data will be allocated to separate nodes and for the computation of this data, all client nodes will need to retrieve the data from the server nodes. It can produce a lot of network connections and create latency. However, you can always run client and server nodes in separate JVM on one single host to decrease the network latency. We will discuss the different deployment approaches in more detail later in this chapter.

From the deployment point of view, Apache Ignite servers can be divided into the following groups.

- Embedded with application.
- Server in separate JVM.

Embedded with the application

With this approach, Apache Ignite node runs on the same JVM with the application. It can be any web application running on an application server or with standalone Java application. For example, our standalone **HelloIgnite** application from the chapter one – is an embedded Ignite server. Ignite server run along with the application in the same JVM and joins with other nodes of the grid. If the application dies or is taken down, Ignite server will also shut down. This topology approach is shown in the following diagram:

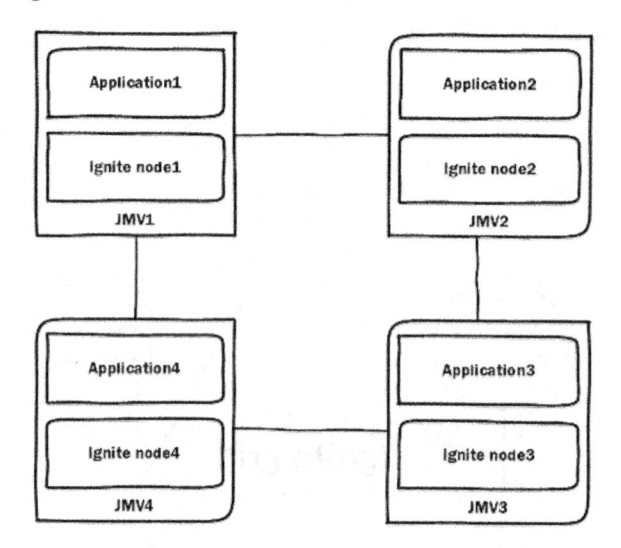

Figure 2.4. Embedded with the application

If you run the HelloIgnite application again and examine the logs of the server, you should find the following:

```
[18:36:05] Ignite node started OK (id=3113ed1e)
[18:36:05] Topology snapshot [ver=8, servers=1, clients=0, CPUs=8, heap=1.0GB]
[21:26:12] Topology snapshot [ver=9, servers=2, clients=0, CPUs=8, heap=4.5GB]
[21:26:13] Topology snapshot [ver=10, servers=1, clients=0, CPUs=8, heap=1.0GB]
```

Figure 2.5. Ignite log

HelloIgnite application run and joins to the cluster as a server. After completing the task, the application exits with the Ignite server from the Ignite grid.

Server in separate JVM (real cluster topology)

In this approach, server nodes will run in a separate JVM and client nodes remotely connects to the servers. Server nodes participate in caching, compute executions, streaming and much more. The client can also use REST API to connect to any individual node. By default, all Ignite nodes are started as server nodes; client nodes need to be explicitly enabled.

Chapter two: Architecture overview 38

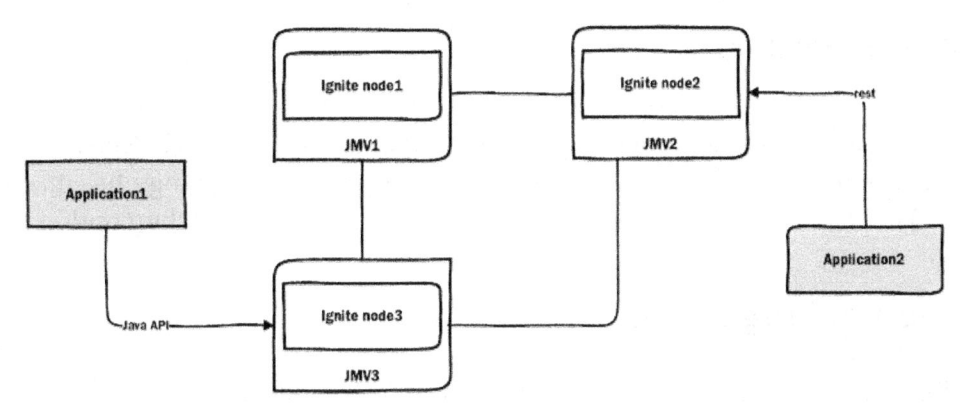

Figure 2.6. Real cluster topology

This is the most common approach, as it provides greater flexibility in terms of cluster mechanics. Ignite servers can be taken down and restarted without any impact to the overall application or cluster.

Client and Server in separate JVM on single host

You can consider this approach whenever you have a high volume of transactions on your data nodes and planning to perform some computations on this node. You can execute client and server in a separate JVM within a container such as Docker or OpenVZ. Containers can be located in the single host machine. The container will isolate the resources (cpu, ram, network interface, etc.) and the JVM will only use isolated resources assigned to this container.

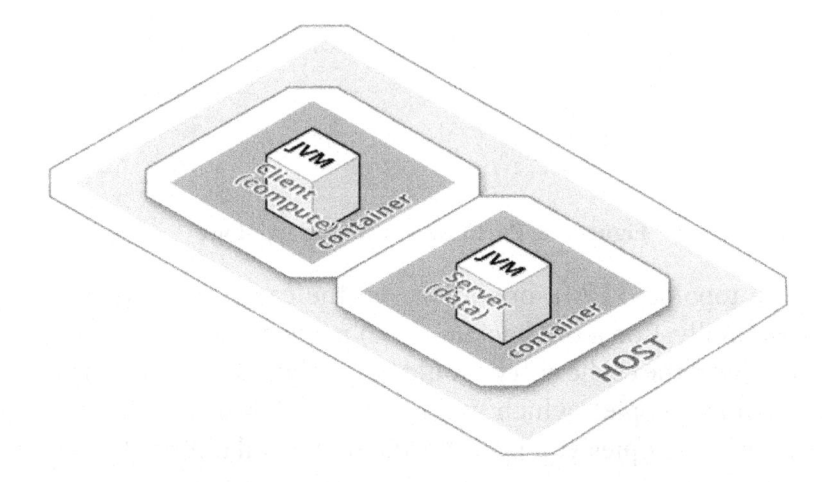

Figure 2.7. Client and server in separate JVM

This approach also has its own downside. During execution, the client (compute) node can retrieve data from any other data node that reside on other hosts and it can increase the network latency.

Caching Topology

Ignite provides three different approaches to caching topology: *Partitioned, Replicated* and *Local*. A *cache mode* is configured for each cache individually. Every caching topology has its own goal with pros and cons. The default cache topology is *partitioned*, without any backup option.

Partitioned caching topology

The goal of this topology is to get extreme *scalability*. In this mode, the Ignite cluster transparently **partitions** the cached data to distribute the load across an entire cluster evenly. By partitioning the data evenly, the size of the cache and the processing power grows linearly with the size of the cluster. The responsibility for managing the data is automatically shared across the cluster. Every node or server in the cluster contains its primary data with a backup copy if defined.

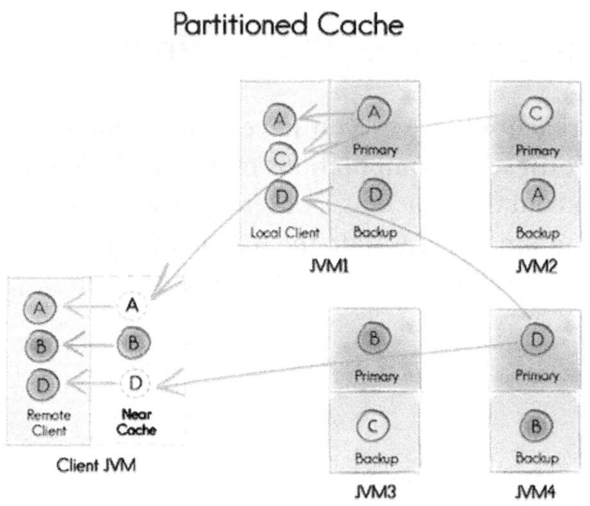

Figure 2.8. Partitioned caching topology

With partitioned cache topology, DML operations on the cache are extremely fast, because only one primary node (optionally 1 or more backup node) needs to be updated for every key. For high availability, a backup copy of the cache entry should be configured. The backup copy is the redundant copy of one or more primary copies, which will live in another node. There is a simple formula to calculate, how many backups copies you need for the high availability of your cluster.

Number of backup copies = N-1, where N is the total number of the nodes in the cluster.

Assume, you have a total number of 3 nodes in the cluster. If you always want to get a response from your cluster (when some of your nodes are unavailable), the number of backup copies should be not less than 2. In this case, 3 copies of the cache entry exist, 2 backup copies and 1 primary.

Partitioned caches are ideal when working with large datasets and updates are very frequent. The backup process can be synchronous or asynchronous. In synchronous mode, the client should wait for the responses from the remote nodes, before completing the commit or write.

Replicated caching topology

The goal of this approach is to get extreme **performance**. With this approach, cache data is *replicated* to all members of the cluster. Since the data is replicated to each cluster node, it is available for use without any waiting. This provides highest possible speed for read-access; each member accesses the data from its own memory. The downside is that frequent writes are very expensive. Updating a replicated cache requires pushing the new version to all other cluster members. This will limit the scalability if there are a high frequency of updates.

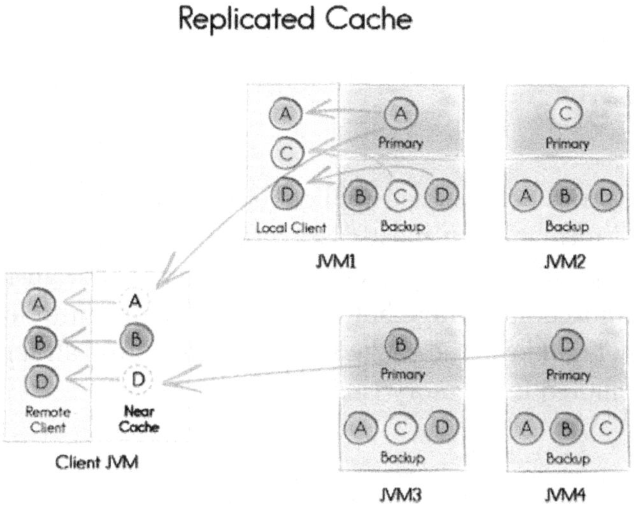

Figure 2.9. Replicated caching topology

In the above diagram, the same data is stored in all cluster nodes; the size of a replicated cache is limited by the amount of memory available on each node with the smallest amount of RAM. This mode is ideal for scenarios where cache reads are a lot more frequent than cache writes, and the data sets are small. The scalability of replication is inversely proportional to the number of members, the frequency of updates per member, and the size of the updates.

Local mode

This is a very primitive version of cache mode; with this approach, no data is distributed to other nodes in the cluster. As far as the Local cache does not have any replication or partitioning process, data fetching is very inexpensive and fast. It provides zero latency access to recently and frequently used data. The local cache is mostly used in read-only operations. It also works very well for read/write-through behavior, where data is loaded from the data sources on cache misses. Unlike a

Chapter two: Architecture overview 41

distributed cache, local cache still has all the features of distributed cache; it provides query caching, automatic data eviction and much more.

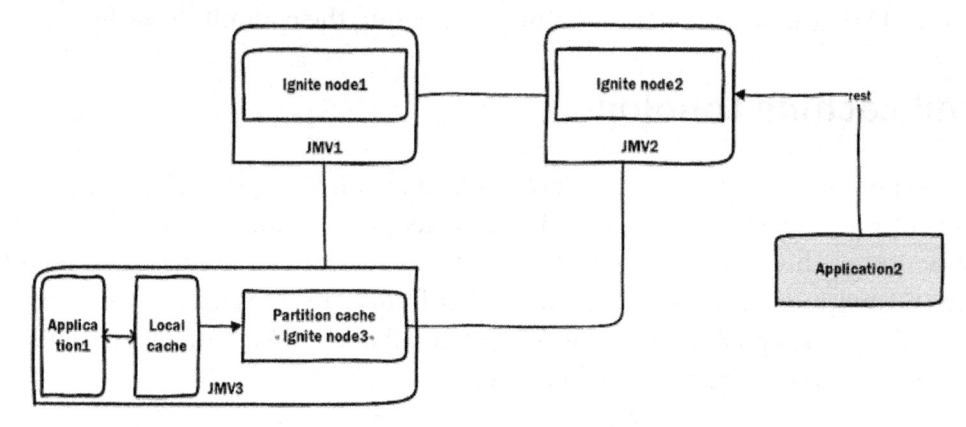

Figure 2.10. Local mode

Caching strategy

With the explosion of high transactions web applications and mobile apps, data storage has become the main bottleneck of performance. In most cases, persistence stores such as relational databases cannot scale out perfectly by adding more servers. In this circumstance, in-memory distributed cache offers an excellent solution to data storage bottleneck. It extends multiple servers (called a grid) to pool their memory together and keep the cache synchronized across all servers. There are two main strategies to use in a distributed in-memory cache:

Cache-aside

In this approach, an application is responsible for reading and writing from the persistence store. The cache doesn't interact with the database at all. This is called *cache-aside*. The cache behaves as a fast scaling in-memory data store. The application checks the cache for data before querying the data store. Also, the application updates the cache after making any changes to the persistence store.

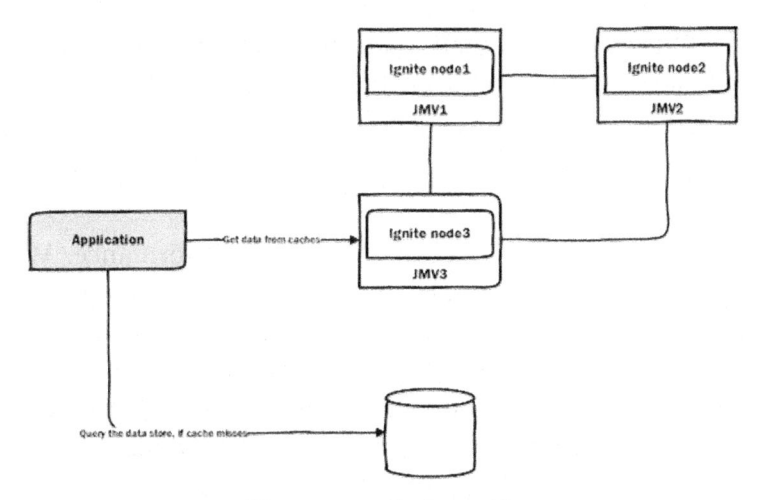

Figure 2.11. Cache-aside

However, even though cache-aside is very fast, there are quite a few disadvantages with this strategy. Application code can become complex and may lead to code duplication if multiple applications deal with the same data store. When there are cache data misses, the application will query the data store, update the caches and continue processing. This can result in multiple data store visits if different application threads perform this processing at the same time.

Read-through and Write-through

This is where application treats in-memory cache as the main data store, and reads data from it and writes data to it. In-memory cache is responsible for propagating the query to the data store on cache misses. Also, the data will be updated automatically whenever it is updated in the cache. All read-through and write-through operations will participate in the overall cache transaction and will be committed or rolled back as a whole.

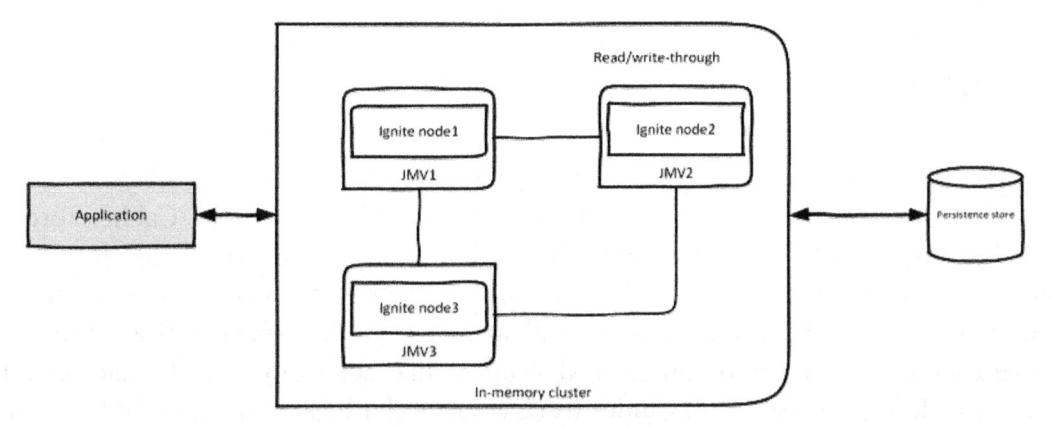

Figure 2.12. Read/Write-through

Read-through and write-through have numerous advantages over cache-aside. First of all, it simplifies application code. Read-through allows the cache to reload objects from the database when it expires automatically. This means that your application does not have to hit the database in peak hours because the latest data is always in the cache.

Write behind

It is also possible to use write-behind to get better write performance. Write-behind lets your application quickly update the cache and return. It then aggregates the updates and asynchronously flushes them to persistence store as a bulk operation. Also with Write-behind, you can specify throttling limits, so the database writes are not performed as fast as the cache updates and therefore the pressure on the database is lower. Additionally, you can schedule the database writes to occur during off-peak hours, which can minimize the pressure on the Database.

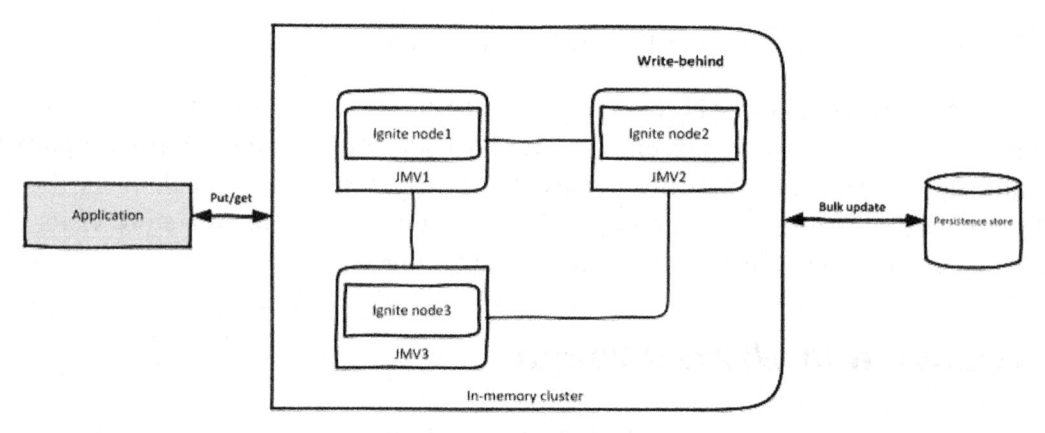

Figure 2.13. Write behind

Apache Ignite provides all the above caching strategies by implementing the Java JCache specification. In addition, Ignite provides Ignite *Cassandra* module, which implements persistent store for Ignite caches by utilizing Cassandra as a persistent storage for expired cache entries.

Data model

Apache Ignite implements a Key-Value data model, especially **JCache (JSR 107)** specification. JCache provides a common way for Java application to interact with the Cache. Terracotta has played the leading role in JSR107 development, acting as a specification lead. The JCache final specification was released on 18th March 2014. On September that year, Spring 4.1 was released with an implementation of the JSR107. Why did we need another specification of Java? Because open source caching projects and commercial vendors like Terracotta and Oracle have been out there over a decade. Each project and vendor use a very similar hash table like API for basic storage. With the JSR107 specification, at last developers can program to a standard API instead of being tied to a single vendor.

From a design point of view, JCache provides a very simple key-value store. A key-value store is a simple Hashtable or Map, primarily used when you access the database table via a primary key. You can take a key-value as a simple table in a traditional RDBMS with two columns such as key and value. The data type of the value column can be any primitive data type such as String, Integer or any complex Java object (or Blob – in Oracle Terms). The application can provide a Key and Value and persist the pair. If the Key already exists, the value will be overwritten, otherwise, a new Value will be created. For clarity, we can compare the key-value store with Oracle terminology.

Oracle	Apache Ignite
Database Instance	Apache Ignite server
Table	Cache
Row	Key-value
RowID	Key

Key-value stores are the simplest data store in NoSQL world. It has very primitive operations like *put*, *get* or *delete* the value from the store. Since it always uses primary key access, they generally have a great performance and scalability.

Since 2014, JCache supports the following platforms:

JCache Delivery	Target Platform
Specification	Java 6+ (SE or EE)
Reference Implementation	Java 7+ (SE or EE)
Technology Compatibility kit	Java 7+ (SE or EE)
Demos and Samples	Java 7+ (SE or EE), Java 8+ (SE or EE)

Currently most caching projects and vendors implement the JCache specification as follows:

- Oracle Coherence
- Hazelcast
- Terracotta Ehcache
- Apache Ignite
- Infinispan

The Java caching API defines five core interfaces: CachingProvider, CacheManager, Cache, Entry and Expiry.

- A CachingProvider defines the mechanism to establish, configure, acquire, manage and control zero or more CacheManagers.
- A CacheManager defines the mechanism to establish, configure, acquire, manage and control zero or more uniquely named Caches all within the context of a CacheManager
- A Cache is a hash table like data structure that allows the temporary storage of key-based values. A Cache is owned by a single CacheManager.
- An entry is a single key-value pair stored in a Cache.

Chapter two: Architecture overview 45

A Key-value pair can be easily illustrated in a diagram. Consider the following figure of an entry in Cache.

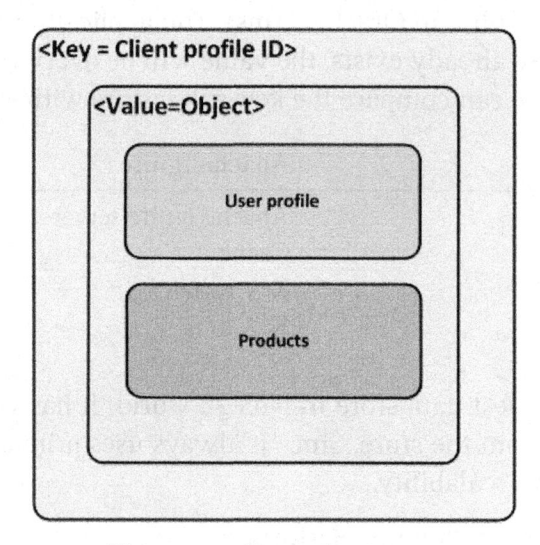

Figure 2.14. Key-value entry

With the key-value store, Java caching API also provides the following additional features:

- Basic Cache operations
- atomic operations, similar to java.util.ConcurrentMap
- read-through caching
- write-through caching
- Entry processor
- cache event listeners
- statistics
- caching annotations
- full generics API for compile time safety
- storage by reference (applicable to on heap caches only) and storage by value

In addition to JCache, Apache Ignite provides ACID transaction, SQL query capability, data loading, Asynchronous mode and various memory models. Apache Ignite provides the **IgniteCache** interface, which extends the Java Cache interface for working with the Cache. In the previous chapter, we already saw some basic operations of IgniteCache. Here is the pseudo code of the HelloWorld application from the previous chapter.

```java
IgniteCache<Integer, String> cache = ignite.getOrCreateCache("testCache");
// put some cache elements
for(int i = 1; i <= 100; i++){
    cache.put(i, Integer.toString(i));
}
// get them from the cache and write to the console
for(int i =1; i<= 100; i++){
    System.out.println("Cache get:"+ cache.get(i));
}
```

Apache Ignite also provides the JCache entry processor functionality for eliminating the network round trips across the network when doing puts and updates in the cache. JCache *EntryProcessor* allows for processing data directly on primary nodes, often transferring only the **deltas** instead of the full state.

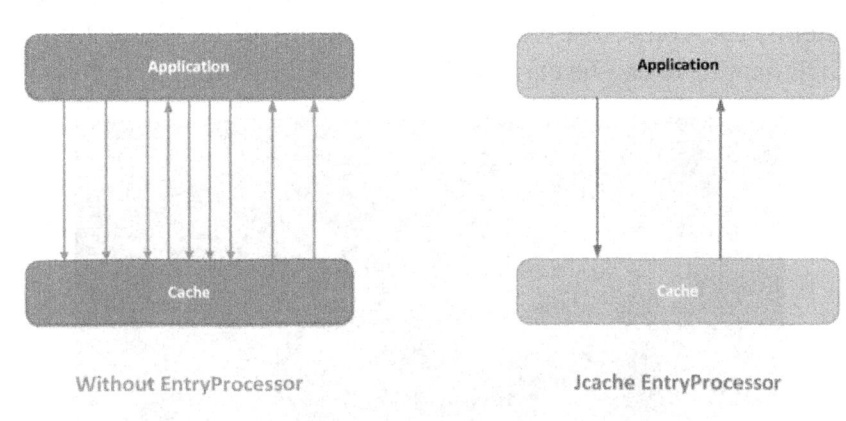

Figure 2.15. EntryProcessor

Moreover, you can add your own logic into EntryProcessors, for example, taking the previously cached value and incrementing it by 1.

```java
IgniteCache<String, Integer> cache = ignite.jcache("mycache");
// Increment cache value 10 times.
for (int i = 0; i < 10; i++)
  cache.invoke("mykey", new EntryProcessor<String, Integer, Void>() {
    @Override
    public Object process(MutableEntry<Integer, String> entry, Object... args) {
      Integer val = entry.getValue();
      entry.setValue(val == null ? 1 : val + 1);
      return null;
    }
  });
```

CAP theorem and where does Ignite stand in?

When I first started working with Apache Ignite, I wondered how on the one hand Ignite supports ACID transactions, and on the other hand, Ignite is also a highly available distributed system. Supporting ACID transactions and at the same time providing high availability is a challenging feature in any NoSQL data store. To scale horizontally, you need strong network partition tolerance which requires giving up either consistency or availability. NoSQL system typically accomplishes this by relaxing relational availability or transactional semantics. A lot of popular NoSQL data stores like Cassandra and Riak still do not have transaction support and are classified as an AP system. The word AP comes from the famous CAP theorem[9] and means availability and partition tolerance, which are generally considered more important in NoSQL systems than consistency.

In 2000, Eric Brewer[10] in his keynote speech at the ACM Symposium said that one could not guarantee consistency in a distributed system. This was his conjecture based on his experience with the distributed systems. This conjecture was later formally proved by Nancy Lynch and Seth Gilbert in 2002. Each NoSQL data store can be classified by the CAP theorem as follows.

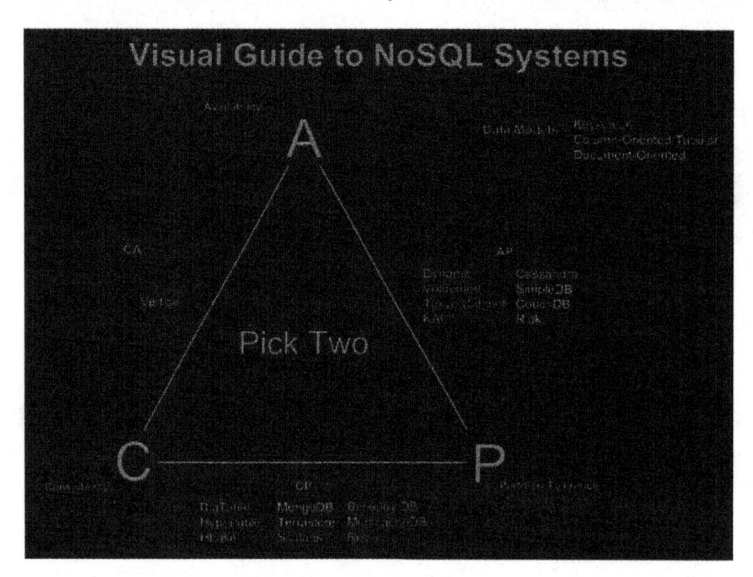

Figure 2.16. CAP theorem

The above illustration is taken from the blog post[11] of the Nathan Hurst. As you can see, a distributed system can only have two of the following three properties:

- Partition tolerance: meaning, if you chop the cable between two nodes, the system still works.
- Consistency: each node in the cluster has the same data.
- Availability: a node will always answer the queries if possible.

---

[9] https://en.wikipedia.org/wiki/CAP_theorem
[10] https://en.wikipedia.org/wiki/Eric_Brewer_(scientist)
[11] http://blog.nahurst.com/visual-guide-to-nosql-systems

So, let us see how choosing two out of three options affects the system behavior as follows:

CA system: In this approach, you sacrifice partition tolerance for getting consistency and availability. Your database system offers transactions, and the system is highly available. Most of the relational databases are classified as CA systems. This system has serious problems with scaling.

CP system: the opposite of the CA system. In CP system availability is sacrificed for consistency and partition-tolerance. In the event of the node failure, some data will be lost.

AP system: This system is always available and partitioned. Also this system scales easily by adding nodes to the cluster. Cassandra is a good example of this type of system.

Now, we can return back to our question, where does Ignite stand in the CAP theorem? At first glance, Ignite can be classified by CP, because Ignite is fully ACID compliant distributed transactions with partitioned tolerance. But this is half part of the history. Apache Ignite can also be considered an AP system. But why does Ignite have two different classifications? Because it has two different transactional modes for cache operations, transactional and atomic.

In transactional mode, you can group multiple DML operations in one transaction and make a commit into the cache. In this scenario, Ignite will lock data on access by a pessimistic lock. If you configure backup copy for the cache, Ignite will use 2p commit protocol for its transaction. We will look at transactions in detail in chapter four.

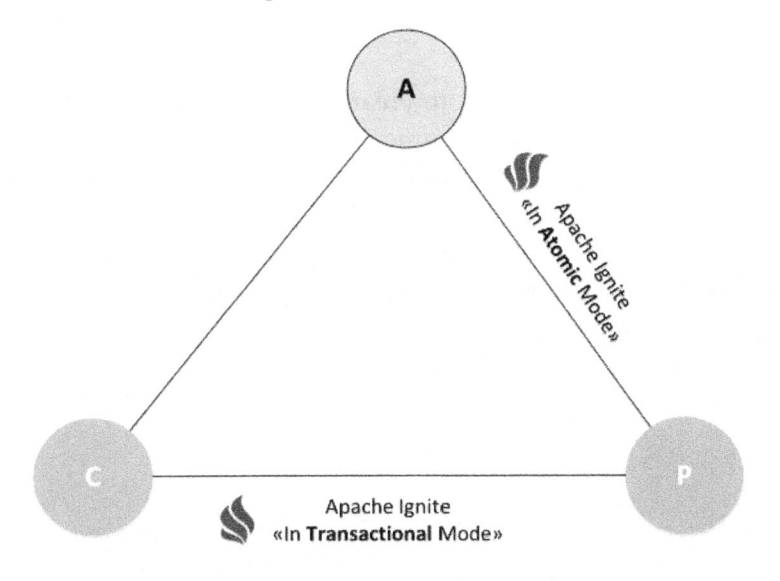

Figure 2.17. Ignite position in CAP theorem

On the other hand, in atomic mode Ignite supports multiple atomic operations, one at a time. In the atomic mode, each DML operation will either succeed or fail and neither Read nor Write operation will lock the data at all. This mode gives a higher performance than the transactional mode. When you make a write in Ignite cache, for every piece of data there will be a master copy in primary node and a backup copy (if defined). When you read data from Ignite grid, you always read from the Primary node, unless the Primary node is down, at which time data will be read from the backup. From this point of view, you gain the system availability and the partition-tolerance of the entire system as an AP system. In the atomic mode, Ignite is very similar to Apache Cassandra.

However, real world systems rarely fall neatly into all of these above categories, so it's more helpful to view CAP as a continuum. Most systems will make some effort to be consistent, available, and partition tolerant, and many can be tuned depending on what's most important.

Clustering

The design goal of the Apache Ignite is to handle high workloads across multiple nodes within a cluster. A cluster is arranged as a group of nodes. Clients can send read/write requests to any node in the cluster. Ignite nodes can automatically discover each other and data is distributed among all nodes in a cluster. This helps scale the cluster when needed, without restarting the entire cluster at a time. Ignite provides an easy way to create logical groups of cluster nodes within your grid and also collocate the related data into similar nodes to improve performance and scalability of your application. In the next few subsections, we will discover a few very important and yet unique features of Apache Ignite such as cluster group, data allocation (sometimes calls *affinity collocation*) and ability to scale and zero single points of failure.

Cluster group

Ignite `ClusterGroup` provides a simple way to create a logical group of nodes within a cluster. By design, all nodes in an Ignite cluster are the same. However, Ignite allows to logically group nodes of any application for a specific purpose. For instance, you can cluster all nodes together that service the cache with name *myCache*, or all client nodes that access the cache *myCache*. Moreover, you may wish to deploy a service only on remote nodes. You can limit job executions, service deployment, messaging, events, and other tasks to run only within some cluster groups.

Chapter two: Architecture overview

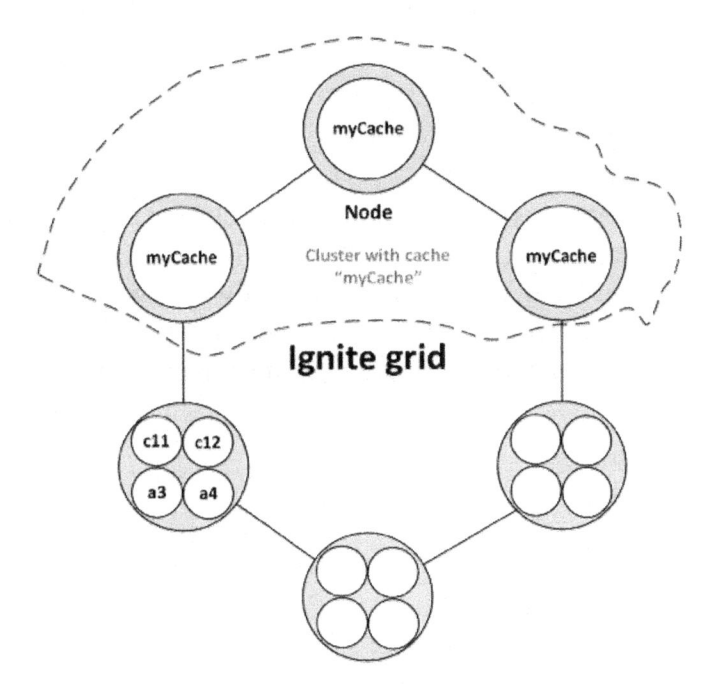

Figure 2.18. Cluster group

Ignite provides the following three ways to create a logical cluster into Ignite Grid:

Predefined cluster group. Ignite provides predefined implementations of ClusterGroup of an interface to create cluster group based on any predicate. Predicates can be Remote Node, Cache Nodes, Node with specified attributes and so on. Here is an example cluster group with all nodes caching data for cache *myCache*.

```
IgniteCluster cluster = ignite.cluster();
// All the data nodes responsible for caching data for "myCache".
ClusterGroup dataGroup = cluster.forDataNodes("myCache");
```

Cluster group with Node Attributes. Although every node into the cluster is same, a user can configure nodes to be master or worker and data nodes. All cluster nodes on startup automatically register all environment and system properties as node attributes. However, users can choose to assign their own node attributes through configuration:

```
IgniteConfiguration cfg = new IgniteConfiguration();
Map<String, String> attrs = Collections.singletonMap("ROLE", "master");
cfg.setUserAttributes(attrs);
// Start Ignite node.
Ignite ignite = Ignition.start(cfg);
```

After stating the node, you can group the nodes with the attribute master as follows:

```
IgniteCluster cluster = ignite.cluster();
ClusterGroup workerGroup = cluster.forAttribute("ROLE", "master");
Collection<GridNode> workerNodes = workerGroup.nodes();
```

Custom cluster group. Sometimes it also calls dynamic cluster group. You can define dynamic cluster groups based on some predicate; predicates can be based on any metrics such as CPU utilization or free heap space. Such cluster groups will always only include the nodes that pass the predicate. Here is an example of a cluster group over nodes that have less than 256 MB heap memory used. Note that the nodes in this group will change over time based on their heap memory used.

```
IgniteCluster cluster = ignite.cluster();
// Nodes with less than 256MB heap memory used
ClusterGroup readyNodes = cluster.forPredicate((node) -> node.metrics().getHeapMemoryUsed(\
) < 256);
```

Data collocation

Term *data collocation* means, allocation of same related data into the same node. For instance, if we have one cache for Clients profile and another cache for Clients transactions. We can allocate the same clients profile and its transactions records in the same node. In this approach, network roundtrips for the related data decrease and the client application can get the data from a single node. In this case, multiple caches with the same set of fields are allocated to the same node.

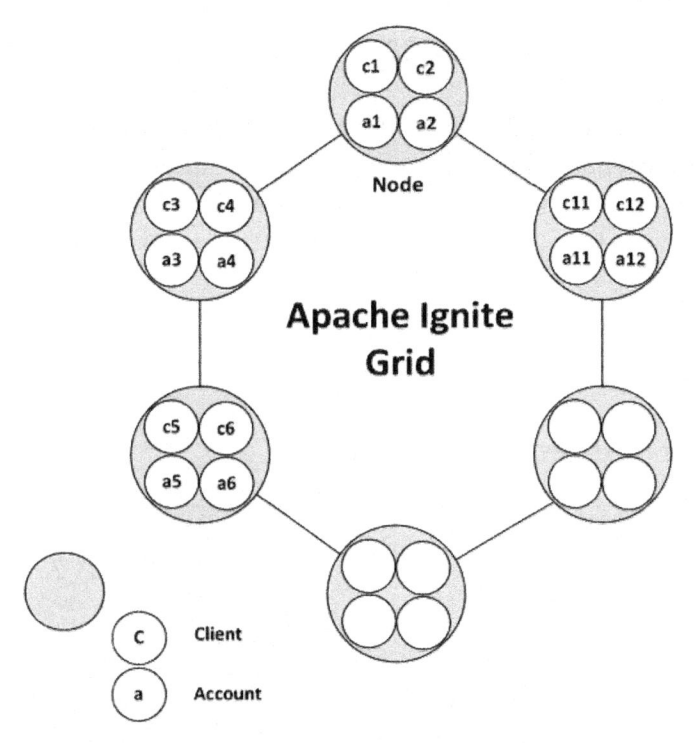

Figure 2.19. Data collocation

For example, the client and its account information are located on the same Ignite host. To achieve that, the cache key used to cache Client objects should have a field or method annotated with `@AffinityKeyMapped` annotation, which will provide the value of the account key for collocation. For convenience, you can also optionally use *AffinityKey* class as follows:

```
Object clientKey1 = new AffinityKey("Client1", "accId");
Object clientKey2 = new AffinityKey("Client2", "accId ");

Client c1 = new Client (clientKey1, ...);
Client c2 = new Client (clientKey2, ...);

// Both, the client and the account information objects will be cached on the same node.
cache.put("accId ", new Account("credit card"));
cache.put(clientKey1, c1);
cache.put(clientKey2, c2);
```

To calculate the affinity function, you can use any set of fields, it is not necessary to use any kind of unique key. For example, to calculate the Client account affinity function, you can use the field *client ID* that owns the account id. We will briefly describe the topics with a complete example in chapter seven.

Compute collocation with Data

Apache Ignite also provides the ability to route the data computation unit of work to the nodes where the desired data is cached. This concept is known as Collocation Of Computations And Data. It allows routing whole units of work to a certain node. To collocate computation with data you should use `IgniteCompute.affinityRun(...)` and `IgniteCompute.affinityCall(...)` methods.

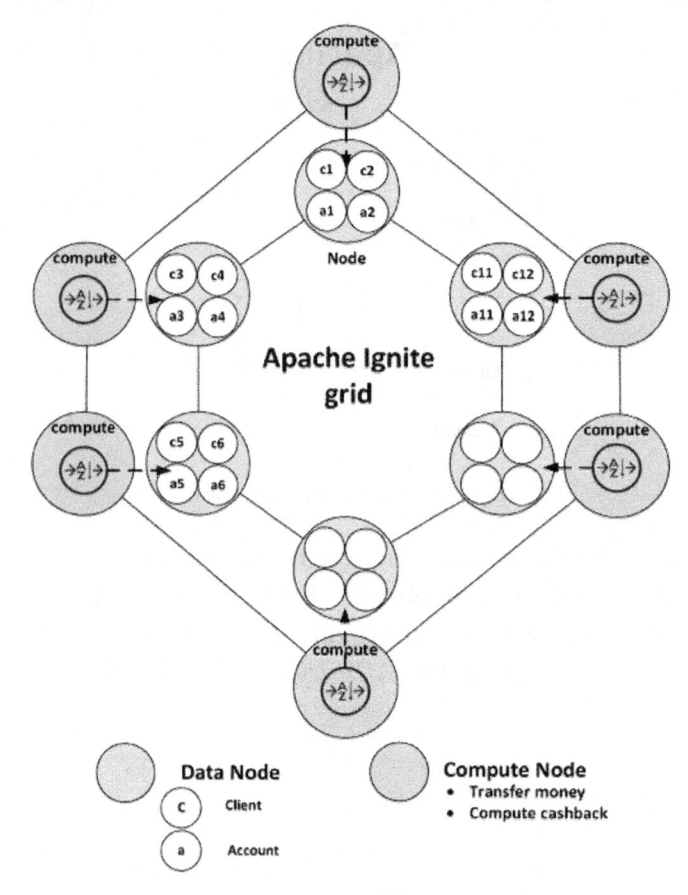

Figure 2.20. Compute collocation with Data

Here is how you can collocate your computation in the same cluster node on which the Client and its account information are allocated.

```
String accId = "acountId";
// Execute Runnable on the node where the key is cached.
ignite.compute().affinityRun("myCache", accId, () -> {
Account account = cache.get(accId);
Client c1 = cache.get(clientKey1);
Client c2 = cache.get(clientKey2);
    ...
});
```

Here, the computation unit accesses to the Client data as local, this approach highly decreases the network roundtrip of the data across the cluster and increases the performance of data processing.

Apache Ignite out of the box ships with two affinity function implementations:

RendezvousAffinityFunction[12] - This function allows a bit of discrepancy in partition-to-node mapping (i.e. some nodes may be responsible for a slightly larger number of partitions than others). However, it guarantees that when topology changes, partitions are migrated only to a joined node or only from a left node. No data exchange will happen between existing nodes in a cluster. This is the default affinity function used by the Apache Ignite.

FairAffinityFunction - This function tries to make sure that partition distribution among cluster nodes is even. This comes at a price of a possible partition migration between existing nodes in a cluster.

Later in this book, we will provide a complete real life example with the explanation in chapter seven.

Zero SPOF

In any distributed system, node failure should be expected, particularly as the size of the cluster grows. The Zero Single Point of Failure (SPOF) design pattern ensures that no single part of a system can stop the entire cluster or system from working. Sometimes, the system using master-slave replication or the mixed master-master system falls into this category. Prior to Hadoop 2.0.0, the Hadoop NameNode was an SPOF in an HDFS cluster. Netflix has calculated the revenue loss for each ms of downtime or latency, and it is not small at all. Most businesses do not want single points of failure for the obvious reason.

Apache Ignite, as a horizontally scalable distributed system, is designed in such way that all nodes in the cluster are equal, you can read and write from any node in the cluster. There are no master-slave communications in the Ignite cluster.

---

[12] https://en.wikipedia.org/wiki/Rendezvous_hashing

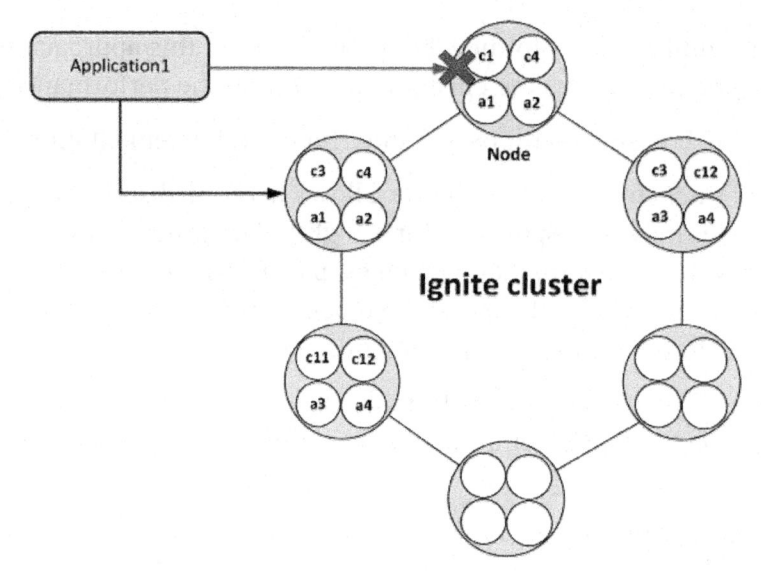

Figure 2.21. Zero SPOF

Data is backed up or replicated across the cluster so that failure of any node doesn't bring down the entire cluster or the application. This way Ignite provides a dynamic form of **High Availability**. Another benefit of this approach is the ease at which new nodes can be added. When new nodes join the cluster, they can take over a portion of data from the existing nodes. Because all nodes are the same, this communication can happen seamlessly in a running cluster.

How SQL queries works in Ignite

In chapter one, we introduced Ignite SQL query feature very superficially. In chapter four, we will go into more details about Ignite SQL queries. It's interesting to know how a query processes under the hood of Ignite. There are two main approaches to process SQL queries in Ignite:

- In-memory Map-Reduce: If you are executing any SQL query against a Partitioned cache, Ignite under the hood splits the query into in-memory map queries and a single reduce query. The number of map queries depends on the size of the partitions and number the partitions in the cluster. Then all map queries are executed on all data nodes of the participating caches, providing results to the reducing node, which will, in turn, run the reduce query over these intermediate results. If you are not familiar with the Map-Reduce pattern, you can imagine it as a Java Fork-join process.
- H2 SQL engine: if you are executing SQL queries against Replicated or Local cache, Ignite knows that all data is available locally and runs a simple local SQL query in the H2 database engine. Note that, in replicated caches, every node contains a replica data for other nodes. H2 database is a free database written in Java and can work in an embedded mode. Depending on the configuration, every Ignite node can have an embedded H2 SQL engine.

Multi-datacenter replication

In the modern world, multi-datacenter replication is one of the main requirements for any Database, including RDBMS and NoSQL. In simple terms, multi-datacenter replication means the replication of data between different data centers. Multiple datacenter replications can have a few scenarios.

Geographical location scenario. In this scenario, data should be hosted in different data centers depending on the user location in order to provide a responsive exchange. In this case, data centers can be located in different geographical locations such as in different regions or in different countries. Data synchronization is completely transparent and bi-directional within data centers. The logic that defines which datacenter a user will be connected to resides in the application code.

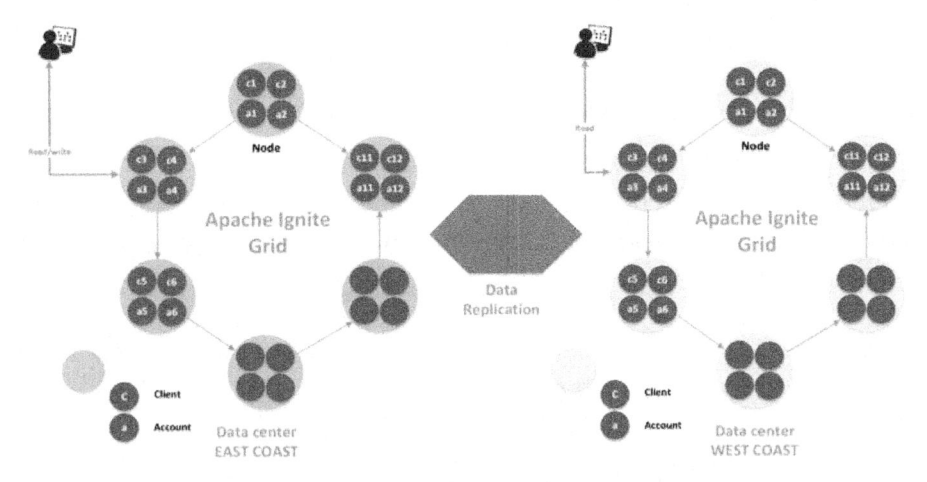

Figure 2.22. Geolocational data replication

Live backup scenario. In this scenario, most users use different datacenter as a live backup that can quickly be used as a fallback cluster. This use case is very similar to disaster recovery. Sometimes it's also called passive replication. In passive replication, replication occurs in one direction: from master to the replica. Clients can connect to the master database in one data center and perform all the CRUD operation on the database.

Chapter two: Architecture overview

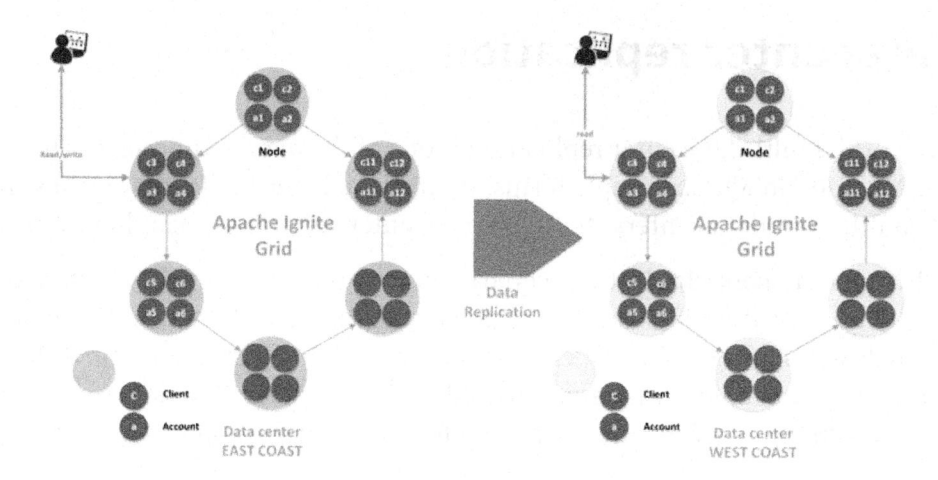

Figure 2.23. Realtime backup

To ensure consistency between the two databases, the replica is started as a read-only database, where only transactions replicated from the master can modify the database contents.

Unfortunately, out of the box, Apache Ignite doesn't support multi-data center replication. However, you can span Ignite nodes in different data centers (for instance, 10 nodes in one data center and other 10 nodes in another).

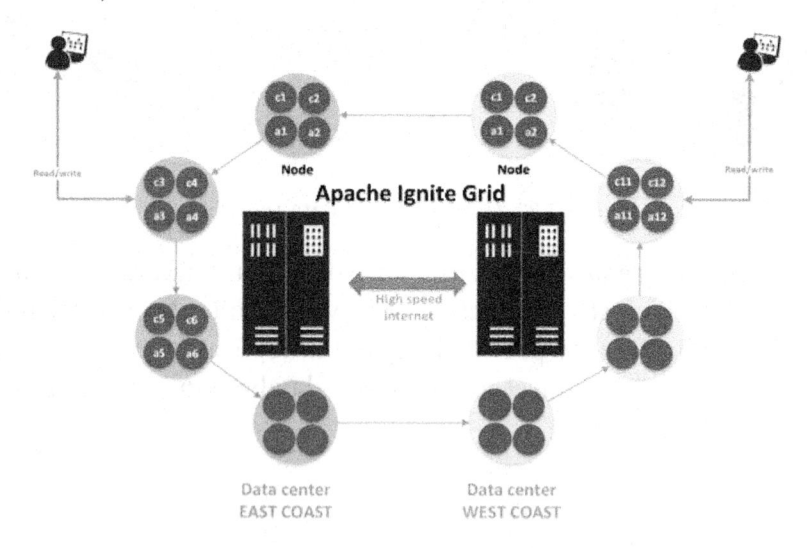

Figure 2.24. Span Ignite grid into multiple DC

Span Ignite grid into multiple data center can introduce a few issues:

- Latency: this is going to hinder performance quite a bit on the server side. If any nodes from different datacenter have a backup copy of your master data, transaction time can be very high. In the long run, you could have a problem with data consistency also.
- Clients connected to different datacenters is going to face very different latency for client operations.

However, GridGain[13] (commercial version of Ignite) provides full functionality Data center replication in different geographical location. It also supports bi-directional, active-active data replication between data centers. You can read a more detail here in GridGain site.

Asynchronous support

Usually, any plain(synchronous) put/get or execute call blocks the execution of the application until the result is available from the server. Afterward, the result can be iterated and consumed as needed by the client. This is probably the most common way to deal with any persistence store. However, asynchronous method execution can provide significant benefits and is a requirement of the modern system. Apache Ignite provides a flexible paradigm of using asynchronous and synchronous method call on all distributed APIs. It could be put/get any entries from the store or executes a job in a compute grid. Ignite asynchronous method execution is a non-blocking operation, and return an IgniteFuture object instead of the actual result. You can later get the result by calling IgniteFuture.get() method.

> **Note:**
> Any asyncCache.future() call returns the IgniteFuture object immediately. IgniteFuture is general concurrency abstraction, also known as a promise, which promises to return a result in the near future.

Here is a very simple example of using asynchronous invocation for getting entries from the Ignite cache (see the github project-installation[14] for the complete example).

```
// get or create cache
IgniteCache<Integer, String> cache = ignite.getOrCreateCache("testCache");
// get an asynchronous cache
IgniteCache<Integer, String> asynCache = cache.withAsync();

// put some cache elements
for(int i = 1; i <= 100; i++){
    cache.put(i, Integer.toString(i));
}

//get the first entries asynchronously
asynCache.withAsync().get(1);
// get the future promise
```

---

[13] https://gridgain.readme.io/docs/data-center-replication
[14] https://github.com/srecon/ignite-book-code-samples/tree/master/chapters/chapter-installation

```
IgniteFuture<String> igniteFuture = asynCache.future();
// java 8 lamda expression
igniteFuture.listen(f-> System.out.println("Cache Value:" + f.get()));
```

In the above pseudo code, we have inserted 100 entries synchronously into the Ignite cache *testCache*. After that, asynchronously request the first entry and got future for the invocation. Next, we asynchronously listen for the operation to complete (see the GitHub project-installation for the complete example). Note that, the main thread of the Java main() method doesn't wait for the task to complete, rather it hands over the task to another thread and moves on.

Resilience

Ignite client node is completely resilient in nature. The word resilience means the ability of a server or system to recover quickly and continue operating when there has been a failure. Ignite client node can disconnect from the cluster in several cases:

- In the case of a network problem.
- Host machine dies or is restarted.
- Slow clients can be disconnected by the server.

When the client determines that a node disconnected from the cluster, it tries to re-establish the connection with the server. This time it assigns to a new node ID and tries to reconnect to the cluster.

Security

Apache Ignite is an open source project and does not provide any security features. However, the commercial version of Ignite has this functionality. The commercial version is called **GridGain Enterprise Edition**. GridGain enterprise edition provides extensible and customizable authentication and security features to satisfy a variety of security requirements for Enterprise.

Key API

Apache Ignite provides a rich set of different API's to work with the Data Fabrics. The APIs are implemented in the form of native libraries for major languages and technologies as Java, .NET and C++. A very short list of some useful APIs is described below.

Name	Description
org.apache.ignite.IgniteCache	The main cache interface, the entry point for all Data Grid API's. The interface extends javax.cache.Cache interface.
org.apache.ignite.cache.store.CacheStore	Interface for cache persistence storage for read-through and write-through behavior.
org.apache.ignite.cache.store.CacheStoreAdapter	The cache storage convenience adapter, implements interface CacheStore. It's provides default implements for bulk operations, such as writeAll and readAll.
org.apache.ignite.cache.query.ScanQuery	Scan query over cache entries.
org.apache.ignite.cache.query.TextQuery	Query for Lucene based fulltext search.
org.apache.ignite.cache.query.SqlFieldsQuery	SQL Fields query. This query can return specific fields of data based on SQL clause.
org.apache.ignite.transactions.Transaction	Ignite cache transaction interface, have a default 2PC behavior and supports different isolation levels.
org.apache.ignite.IgniteFileSystem	Ignite file system API, provides a typical file system view on the particular cache. Very similar to HDFS, but only on in-memory.
org.apache.ignite.IgniteDataStreamer	Data streamer is responsible for streaming external data into the cache. This streamer will stream data concurrently by multiple internal threads.
org.apache.ignite.IgniteCompute	Defines compute grid functionality for executing tasks and closures over nodes ClusterGroup.
org.apache.ignite.services.Service	An instance of the grid managed service. Whenever a service is deployed, Ignite will automatically calculate how many instances of this service should be deployed on each node within the cluster.
org.apache.ignite.IgniteMessaging	An interface that provides functionality for topic-based message exchange among nodes defined by ClusterGroup.

Conclusion

We covered the foundational concepts of the in-memory data grid. We first briefly described the Ignite functional overview and various caching strategies with different topologies. We also presented some techniques based on standard data access patterns such as caching-aside, read-through, and write-through. We went through the Ignite data collocation technics and briefly explained the Ignite key-value data store.

What's next

In the next chapter, we will look at the Ignite data grid implementations such as 2nd level cache, web session clustering and so on.

Chapter three: In-memory caching

So far we have covered the basic functionalities of the Apache Ignite and its architecture. Now it is time to deep drive into the implementations of the Apache Ignite functionalities and observe how it can boost your application performance. In the previous chapters, we have talked a lot about Ignite features and architecture, now we will go through all of the most important Ignite in-memory data grid features and explain the use cases to understand how and when you should use such features. The main goal of this chapter is to demonstrate the use of Apache Ignite for accelerating applications performance without changing code.

IMDG or In-memory data grid is not an in-memory relational database, a NoSQL database or a relational database. However, it is a distributed key-value store, which can be imagined as a distributed partitioned hash map, where every node in a cluster has its own portions of data. The data model is distributed across many servers in a single location or across multiple locations. This distribution is known as a data fabric. This distributed model is also known as a *shared nothing* architecture. IMDG has the following characteristics:

1. All servers can be active on each site.
2. All data is stored in the RAM of the servers.
3. Servers can be added or removed non-disruptively to increase the amount of RAM available.
4. The data model is non-relational and is object-based.
5. Distributed applications are written in the platform independent language.
6. The data fabric is resilient, allowing non-disruptive automated detection and recovery of a single server or multiple servers.

As we discussed earlier, Apache Ignite implements JCache specification to develop in-memory data grid. However, Ignite provides a lot of advanced functionalities for the in-memory data grid. In this chapter we are going to cover the following topics:

- Apache Ignite as a 2nd level cache.
- Java method caching.
- Web sessions clustering.
- Apache Ignite as a big memory, off-heap memory.

Apache Ignite as a 2nd level cache

Let's start with the definition of 2nd level cache.

> A 2nd level cache is a local or distributed data store of entity data managed by the persistence provider to improve *application performance.*

A second level cache can improve application performance by avoiding expensive database calls, keeping the data local to the application. A 2nd level cache is fully managed by the persistence provider and typically transparent to the application. That is, application reads, writes and commits data through entity manager without knowing about the cache.

There is also Level 1 cache based on the persistence provider, such as MyBatis or Hibernate. Level 1 is used to cache objects retrieved from the database within the *current database session.* When front-side (web page or web service) invokes a service, an HTTP session is opened and reused until the service method returns. All operations performed until the service method return will share the L1 cache, so the same object will not retrieve twice from the database. After finishing the database session, objects retrieved from the database will not be available. In most persistence providers, Level 1 cache is always enabled by default.

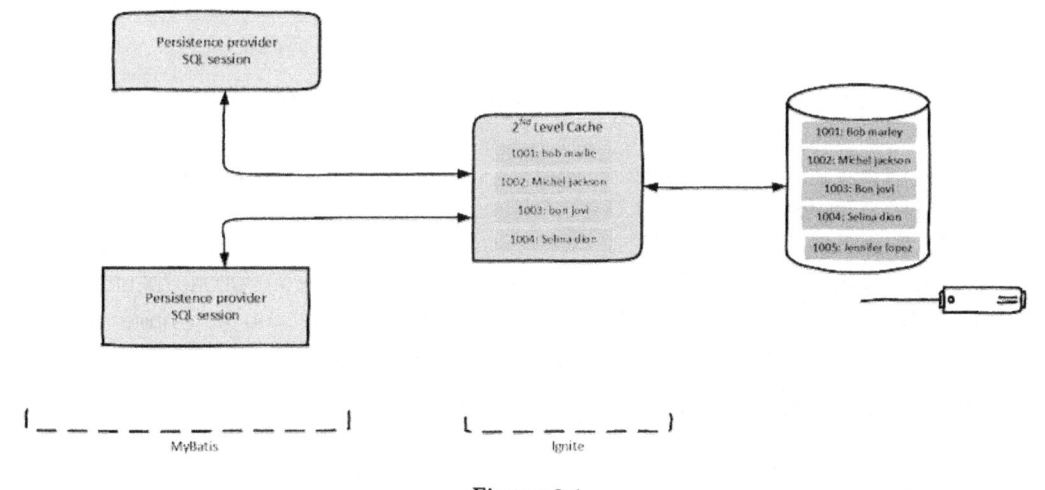

Figure 3.1

Unlike the 1st level cache, a 2nd level cache is able to span across database sessions and stores database objects and result of the queries (Query cache). It sits between the persistence provider and the database (see figure 3.1). Persistence context shares the cache, making the second level cache available throughout the application. Therefore, database traffic is reduced considerably because entities are loaded into the shared cache and made available from there. So, in a nutshell, the 2nd level cache provides the following benefits.

1. Boost performance by avoiding expensive database calls.

Chapter three: In-memory caching 63

2. Data are kept transparent to the application.
3. CRUD operation can be performed through normal persistence manager functions.
4. By using 2nd level cache, you can accelerate applications performance without changing code.

MyBatis 2nd level cache

In Ignite, the 2nd level cache for MyBatis stores the entity data, but NOT the entities or objects themselves. The data is stored in a *serialized* format, which looks like a hashmap where the key is the entity Id, and the value is a list of primitive values. Here is an example how the cache entries look like in Apache Ignite:

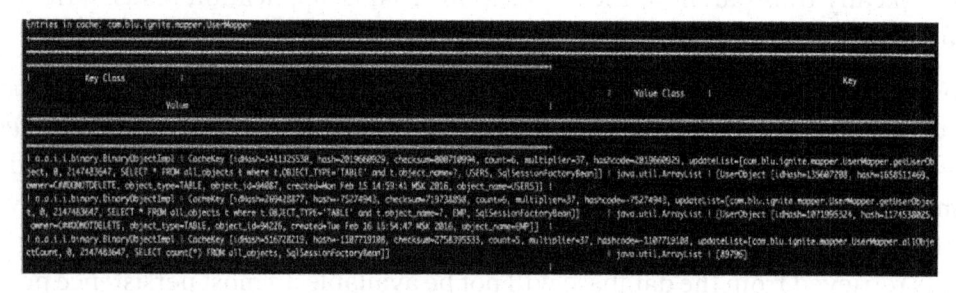

Figure 3.2

Where,

```
Cache Key: CacheKey [idHash=1499858, hash=2019660929, checksum=800710994, count=6, multipl\
ier=37, hashcode=2019660929, updateList=[com.blu.ignite.mapper.UserMapper.getUserObject, 0\
, 2147483647, SELECT 1 FROM all_objects t where t.OBJECT_TYPE='TABLE' and t.object_name=?,\
 USERS, SqlSessionFactoryBean]]
Value class: java.util.ArrayList
Cache Value: [UserObject [idHash=243119413, hash=1658511469, owner=CDONOTDELETE, object_ty\
pe=TABLE, object_id=94087, created=Mon Feb 15 13:59:41 MSK 2016, object_name=USERS]]
```

As for example, I selected the *all_objects* tables and the following query from the Oracle Database.

```
SELECT count(*) FROM all_objects;
SELECT * FROM all_objects t where t.OBJECT_TYPE='TABLE' and t.object_name='EMP';
SELECT * FROM all_objects t where t.OBJECT_TYPE='TABLE';
```

In my case, the following query executed in 600 ms on average.

```
SELECT count(*) FROM all_objects;
```

And the next following query execution time is more than 700ms.

```
SELECT t.object_type, count(*) FROM all_objects t group by t.OBJECT_TYPE;
```

Here, our goal is to minimize the query execution times. Next, we will develop an application with MyBatis and Ignite to calculate the performance gain. If you want to know how to install and configure Apache Ignite with spring, please refer to **chapter one: installation**. All the source code of our example application you can find in GitHub repo[15] (chapter-caching/mybatis).

Step 1:

Create a maven project

$mvn archetype:create –DgroupId=com.blu.ignite –DartifactId=ignite-mybatis

Step 2:

Add the following maven dependencies in the current project.

```
<dependency>
   <groupId>org.apache.ignite</groupId>
   <artifactId>ignite-core</artifactId>
   <version>${ignite.version}</version>
</dependency>
<dependency>
   <groupId>org.apache.ignite</groupId>
   <artifactId>ignite-spring</artifactId>
   <version>${ignite.version}</version>
</dependency>
<!-- myBatis -->
<dependency>
   <groupId>org.mybatis.caches</groupId>
   <artifactId>mybatis-ignite</artifactId>
   <version>1.0.0-beta1</version>
</dependency>
<dependency>
   <groupId>org.mybatis</groupId>
   <artifactId>mybatis-spring</artifactId>
   <version>1.2.4</version>
</dependency>
<dependency>
   <groupId>org.mybatis</groupId>
   <artifactId>mybatis</artifactId>
   <version>3.3.1</version>
</dependency>
```

---

[15] https://github.com/srecon/ignite-book-code-samples

Chapter three: In-memory caching

```xml
<!-- PostgresSQL-->
<dependency>
  <groupId>postgresql</groupId>
  <artifactId>postgresql</artifactId>
  <version>9.1-901.jdbc4</version>
</dependency>
```

In this project, we are going to use spring framework, so you must add a few spring related dependencies. Also, we add a MyBatis core library and `mybatis-Ignite` library to integrate with Apache Ignite as a 2nd level cache. At compile time, Maven uses this information to look up all these above libraries in the Maven repository. Maven first looks in the repository on your local computer. If the libraries aren't there, it will download them from the public Maven repository and store them in the local repository. Note that, I am going to use *Postgres version 9* database as a persistence store.

Step 3:

Now, we have to add our spring context XML file in resources directory of the project to add it to java classpath. The full version of the spring context file will be similar. Let's have a detailed look at the `spring-core.xml` file.

Chapter three: In-memory caching 66

Figure 3.3

- 1–> In this section we declared all the necessary XML namespaces, which we will use in this XML configuration file. All of this namespaces and URI are the standard spring namespaces.
- 2–> We have declared our *soap service bean* and *user mapper bean*, the source code of this classes and interface will be explained a little bit later.
- 3–> This is the Main configuration part of the Ignite node. Here we declared the cache name called *myBatisCache*, configured the cache mode to **partitioned**. Note that, cache mode can be replicated too. Also, we configured one backup copy for the cache and enabled the cache statistics. Property name="backups" value="1" indicates that always there will be one redundant copy of a cache entry on another node. Later in this configuration, we added SPI

Chapter three: In-memory caching

discovery to find node members in the cluster. In our case, we are using multicast TCP/IP finder. If you have your own Ignite cluster running, don't forget to add or update the IP address in the configuration file as follows.

```
<list>
  <!-- In distributed environment, replace with the actual host IP address. -->
  <value>127.0.0.1:47500..47509</value>
</list>
```

- 4-> In this section, we have setup JDBC data source for PostgreSQL server. We also added standard data source connection with JDBC URL, username and password, without any *connection pool*.
- 5-> Next, we have configured MyBatis SQL mapper bean. Indicate the mapper interface with SQL session factory, also add the classpath of all the SQL mapper files in the XML.

Step 4:

Now, we are going to add `UserMapper.xml` to the *classpath*. Note that, this following xml file is located in the absolute classpath (/resources/com/blu/imdg/mapper/UserMapper.xml).

```
<?xml version="1.0" encoding="UTF-8" ?>
<!DOCTYPE mapper
        PUBLIC "-//mybatis.org//DTD Mapper 3.0//EN" "http://mybatis.org/dtd/mybatis-3-mapp\
er.dtd">
<mapper namespace="com.blu.imdg.mapper.UserMapper">
    <cache type="org.mybatis.caches.ignite.IgniteCacheAdapter" />
    <select id="getEmploee" parameterType="String" resultType="com.blu.imdg.dto.Employee" \
useCache="true">
        SELECT * FROM emp WHERE ename = #{ename}
    </select>
</mapper>
```

The mapper namespace and the cache type is most important part of the configuration. Note that, for every mapper namespace, one replicated cache will be created in the Ignite cluster. In this case, cache name will be `com.blu.imdg.mapper.UserMapper`. With the cache type, we have declared the interface of the Ignite cache adapter. Next, we added our SQL query, it's parameter type and the type of the return value. We are using very simple SQL query to get the employee by employee name. Here we have completed all our declarative configuration through XML. Now we are ready to add business logic to our application.

Step 5:

Execute the following DDL and DML scripts from the folder *scripts* to create the database tables and insert a few rows into the tables. For simplicity, we are using famous `emp` and `dept` entity from the Oracle database. I have slightly modified the DDL/DML scripts to run them into PostgreSQL. The structure of the department (dept) and employee (emp) table is very simple, they are related to each other with one-to-many relationships.

```
create table dept(
  deptno   integer,
  dname    text,
  loc      text,
  constraint pk_dept primary key (deptno)
);
create table emp(
  empno    integer,
  ename    text,
  job      text,
  mgr      integer,
  hiredate date,
  sal      integer,
  comm     integer,
  deptno   integer,
  constraint pk_emp primary key (empno),
  constraint fk_deptno foreign key (deptno) references dept (deptno)
);
```

Step 6:

Now that you've set up the project and the build system, you can proceed to create your web service. At this moment, the soap web service contains only one web method, getEmployee.

```
@WebService(name = "BusinessRulesServices",
        serviceName="BusinessRulesServices",
        targetNamespace = "http://com.blu.rules/services")
public class WebServices {
    private UserServices userServices;
    @WebMethod(exclude = true)
    public void setDao(UserServices userServices){
        this.userServices = userServices;
    }
    @WebMethod(operationName = "getEmploee")
    public Employee getEmploee (String ename) {return userServices.getEmploee(ename);}
}
```

All other supplementary classes such as DTO you can obtain from the source code.

Step 7:

To run the web service, we are going to use *one-jar plugin* with maven build. Build the project by the following command.

Chapter three: In-memory caching

```
mvn clean install
```

Step 8:

Run the web service from the folder `chapter-caching/mybatis` by the following command.

```
java -jar ./target/mybatis-1.0-SNAPSHOT.one-jar.jar
```

If everything goes fine, you should see the following logs on your console.

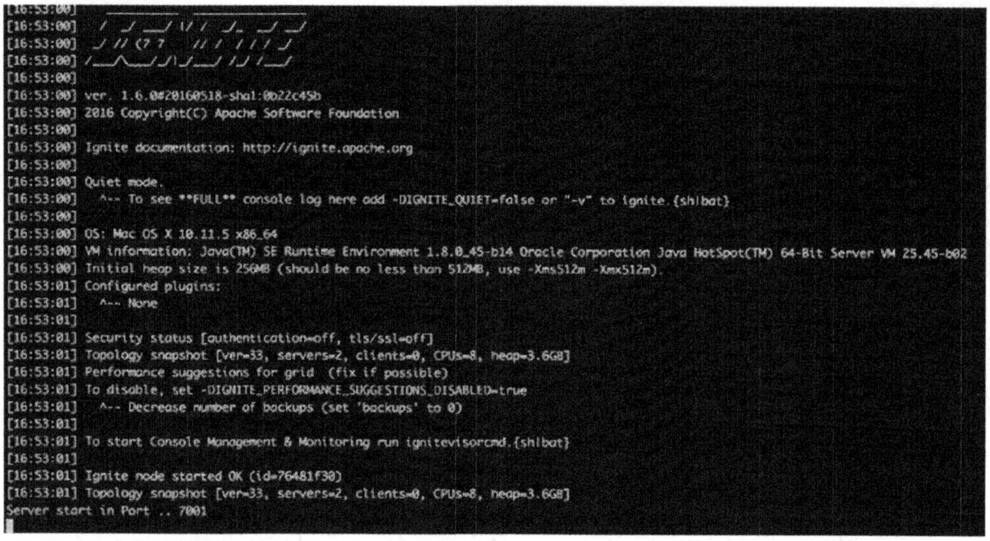

Figure 3.4

Web service running on port 7001 on localhost. You can discover the web service WSDL by this URL Web service WSDL[16]. Now you can use your favorite soap client to invoke the web service, I will go with my soapUI to test the service. When I invoked the service first time, the invoke time is approximately 178 ms (see Figure 3.5), because the query result is not in the cache yet.

---

[16] http://localhost:7001/invokeRules?wsdl

Chapter three: In-memory caching 70

Figure 3.5

Let's, invoke the web method again.

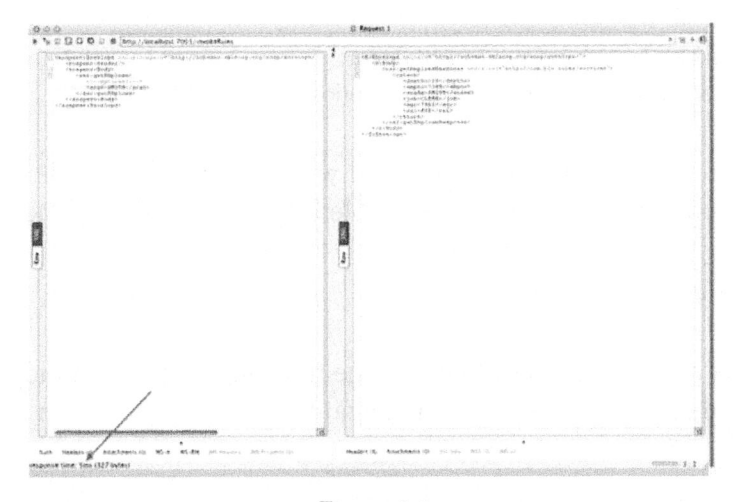

Figure 3.6

This time, response time is 5 ms, that is what we expected. MyBatis just return the result from the Ignite cache. It's almost near real-time (< 10ms) response. Let's, take a look at the cache entries in the Ignite cache. `Ignitevisor` command *scan* can help you to find all the entries in the cache.

Chapter three: In-memory caching

Figure 3.7

Where,

Cache Key = org.apache.ibatis.cache.CacheKey [idHash=1538632341, hash=872929822, checksum=\
2936898376, count=6, multiplier=37, hashcode=872929822, updateList=[com.blu.imdg.mapper.Us\
erMapper.getEmploee, 0, 2147483647, SELECT * FROM emp WHERE ename = ?, KING, SqlSessionFac\
toryBean]]
Key Value = [com.blu.imdg.dto.Employee [idHash=545458831, hash=342167489, date=null, ename\
=KING, mgr=null, empno=7839, job=PRESIDENT, deptno=10, sal=5000]]

We have a few rows (total 12) in the emp table and we don't have any index on field *ename*. Let's create a unique index on the field *ename* of the table *emp* and re-execute the service invocation.

CREATE UNIQUE INDEX ename_idx ON emp (ename);

It creates a *btree* index on field ename. Now, change the *ename* of the employee in SOAP message, for example, *FORD* and execute the web method again.

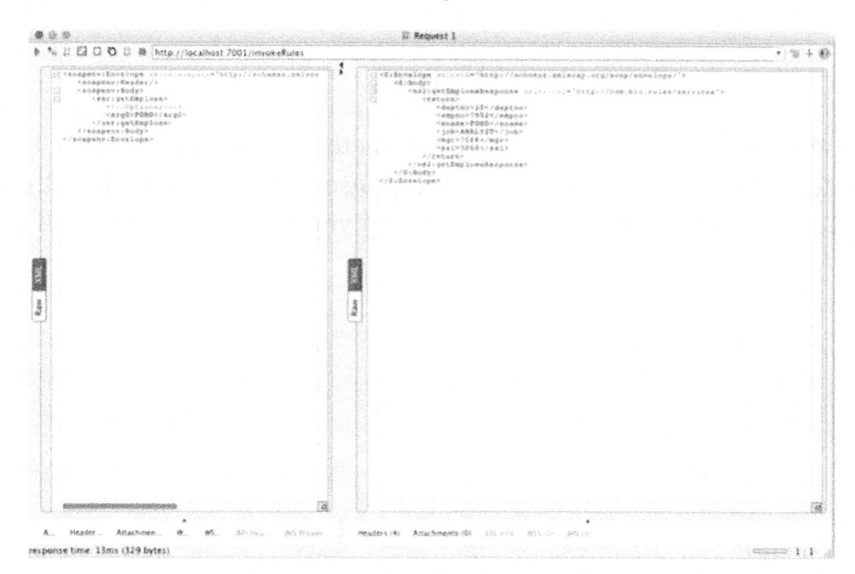

Figure 3.8

The response time is now **13 ms**, you might think that the difference is not so much. But in the production system, you will have millions of rows, rather than 13 rows in your database tables. Also, when you have an index on your tables, your DML operations will re-index the database table every time, and this will also decrease the performance of your application. Most of the time, the response time from Ignite cache will not vary because there is no extra overhead of consuming connection of DB, soft/hard parsing of SQL queries.

Calculate application speedup:

You can use Amdhal's law[17] to calculate the application speedup.

> **Note:**
>
> *Amdhal's law*, after Gene Amdhal, is used to find the system speed up from a speed up in part of the system.
>
> 1/((1 - Proportion speed up) + Proportion speed up / speed up)

$$\frac{1}{(1-P) + \frac{P}{S}}$$

Amdhal's law

Where,

- P is proportional speed up, and
- S is speed up.

Also, note that for a web application the *system* should include browser render time and network latency.

When you are using *Cache*, an application performance depends on a minimum of these two following factors:

- how many times a cached piece of data retrieved by the application;
- and the proportion of the response time that is alleviated by caching.

Assume, we have a web application and uncached full page rendering time is 3 seconds. Now, let's calculate the speed up from a database level cache. In our case:

---

[17] https://en.wikipedia.org/wiki/Amdahl%27s_law

Chapter three: In-memory caching

- Uncached page time : 3 seconds
- Database time : 13 ms. (see figure 3.8)
- Cache retrieval time : 5 ms (see figure 3.6)
- Proportion : 13/3*1000 $\sim$ 0.43%

The expected system speedup should be:

1/((1-0.0043) + 0.0043/(13/5)) = 1/(0.995 + 0.00156) $\sim$ 1 times system speed up.

Although 1 times system speed up is not very impressive, in the production environment the result will be very much different from the current result. This is the end of the section MyBatis 2nd level cache, in the next section, we are going to learn about another 2nd level cache using Hibernate.

Hibernate 2nd level cache

In this chapter, we are going to develop a CRUD application in Hibernate and use the Apache Ignite as an in-memory caching layer between hibernate and the database. Unlike MyBatis, Hibernate provides 3 types of caching:

First-level or Session Cache:

First level cache is the session cache, it's enabled by default, and every request to the database must pass through this level. The scope of this level is the session. Its cached objects are within the current session. This session level cache is very similar to MyBatis first level cache.

2nd level cache:

The 2nd level cache is responsible for caching objects across sessions. When it's turned on, objects will be first searched in the cache and if they are not found, a database query will be executed. Note that the second level cache will be used when the objects are loaded using their primary key. As like MyBatis, Hibernate 2nd level cache stores the entity data, not the entity or POJO itself. The data is stored in serialized format, where the key is the entity id and the value is the list of primitive types.

Query Cache:

The query cache is used to cache the result of a query, it can be Hibernate SQL query or Hibernate named query (HQL) with property `setCacheable(true)`. When the query cache is enabled, the results of the query are stored in the cache with a combination of the query and parameters. Every time the query executes, the cache manager checks for the query result and the associated parameter in the cache, if they are found in the caches, cache manager returns the result from the cache. Otherwise, the cache manager propagated the query to the database.

As for example, we have the following SQL query from the application.

```
Select * from emp e where e.ename=:ename
```

Where, *:ename* is the parameter of the query parameter. In this case, Ignite will generate a hash string from the above SQL query with the parameter and when any SQL query executes, Ignite will first check the hash value from the caches. If it's found in the cache, Ignite will return the value. MyBatis 2nd level cache is exactly same as the hibernate query cache.

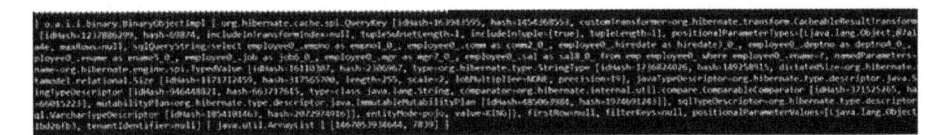

Figure 3.9

The Hibernate query cache feature is **optional** and requires a few additional physical cache regions that hold the cached query results and the timestamps when a table (or cache) was last updated (see the Figure 3.10).

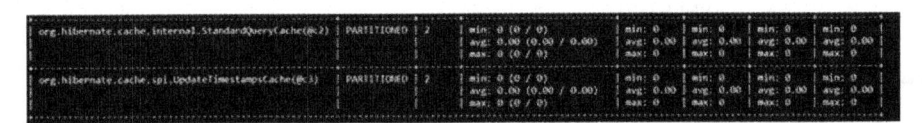

Figure 3.10

This feature is very useful for queries that are frequently run with the same parameters. Let's, get started developing Hibernate CRUD application in full swing. We will use the same tables *emp* and *dept* from the previous chapter.

Now, we are going to add the following features to our application:

1. Add a new employee to appropriate department.
2. Query all the employees.
3. Query employees by the employee name.

The result of these basic operations will be a simple CRUD-style web service (only without an update or delete). After that, we will configure hibernate 2nd level and *query cache* to the application and measure the performance. The full source code is available at GitHub repository (**chapter-caching/hibernate**).

Step 1:

Add the following dependencies to the maven project.

Chapter three: In-memory caching

```xml
<dependency>
    <groupId>org.apache.ignite</groupId>
    <artifactId>ignite-core</artifactId>
    <version>${ignite.version}</version>
</dependency>
<dependency>
    <groupId>org.apache.ignite</groupId>
    <artifactId>ignite-spring</artifactId>
    <version>${ignite.version}</version>
</dependency>
<!-- Spring orm-->
<dependency>
    <groupId>org.springframework</groupId>
    <artifactId>spring-orm</artifactId>
    <version>4.1.0.RELEASE</version>
</dependency>
<!-- Hibernate libs-->
<dependency>
    <groupId>org.apache.ignite</groupId>
    <artifactId>ignite-hibernate</artifactId>
    <version>1.2.0-incubating</version>
</dependency>
<dependency>
    <groupId>org.hibernate</groupId>
    <artifactId>hibernate-core</artifactId>
    <version>${hibernate.version}</version>
</dependency>
<dependency>
    <groupId>org.hibernate</groupId>
    <artifactId>hibernate-entitymanager</artifactId>
    <version>${hibernate.version}</version>
</dependency>
<dependency>
    <groupId>javassist</groupId>
    <artifactId>javassist</artifactId>
    <version>3.12.1.GA</version>
</dependency>
<!-- PostgresSQL-->
<dependency>
    <groupId>postgresql</groupId>
    <artifactId>postgresql</artifactId>
    <version>9.1-901.jdbc4</version>
</dependency>
```

Note that, we are using hibernate version 4.2.6-final and the Ignite version of 1.6.0 or above.

Step 2:

To keep things simple, we start with a tiny well-known domain: **Employee** with following attributes:

```java
@Entity
@Table( name = "emp" )
@Cacheable
@Cache(usage = CacheConcurrencyStrategy.READ_WRITE)
public class Employee implements Serializable{
    @Id
    @Column(name = "empno")
    private Integer empno;
    @Column(name = "ename")
    private String ename;
    @Column(name = "job")
    private String job;
    @Column(name = "mgr")
    private Integer mgr;
    @Column(name = "hiredate")
    private Date    date;
    @Column(name = "sal")
    private Integer sal;
    @Column(name = "deptno")
    private Integer deptno;
    @Column(name = "comm")
    private Integer comm;

    public Employee() { }
// ... methods omitted
}
```

- First, we've annotated the class with `@Entity`, which tells Hibernate that this class represents an object that we can persist. Any entity class can extend either entity class or a non-entity user defined class. It can contain constructors, methods, fields and nested types with any access modifier.
- The `@Table(name = "emp")` annotation allows you to specify the details of the table that will be used to persist the entity in the database. Any additional table also might be specified by the annotation SecondaryTable.
- The `@Column(name = "empno")` annotation is used to map this property to the EMPNO column in the emp table.
- The `@Cacheable` annotation enables caching for the given entity.
- The `@Cache(usage = CacheConcurrencyStrategy.READ_WRITE)` annotation defines the concurrent caching strategy, in our case it's READ_WRITE. Depends on the entity manager, a strategy can be TRANSACTIONAL, READ_ONLY etc.

- The `@Id` annotation is used to define unique identifier of the entity instances, similar to a primary key. Primary key values are unique per entity class.

Step 3:

Let's add the code for Employee data manipulation. So we are going to create a simple DAO with the following three operations:

```
public interface EmpDao {
    List<Employee> getAllEmployees();
    void create(Integer empno, String ename, String job, Integer mgr);
    List<Employee> getEmpByName(String ename);
}
```

- getAllEmployees () – this method will return all the Employee records from the tables.
- create(Integer empno, String ename, String job, Integer mgr) – will create a new employee with a new employee number, employee name. Note that, empno will always be unique to create a new Employee.
- getEmpByName(String ename) – returns Employee entity by employee name.

Similarly, we have a web service with three web methods to invoke from the end user.

```
@WebMethod(operationName = "addEmployee")
public void addEmployee(Integer empno, String ename, String job, Integer mgr ) {
    empDao.create(empno, ename, job, mgr);
}
@WebMethod(operationName = "getEmpByName")
public List<Employee> getEmpByName(String ename) {
    return empDao.getEmpByName(ename);
}
```

All three above web methods delegates the calls to the implementation of the DAO class. Let's take a look at the DAO implementation methods from class *EmpDaoImpl*.

```
public List<Employee> getAllEmployees() {
    Session session = sessionFactory.openSession();
    Query query = session.createQuery("from Employee e");
    List<Employee> employees = query.list();
    session.close();
    if(employees != null && !employees.isEmpty()){
        return employees;
    }
    return Collections.emptyList();
}
```

We first open the session from the session factory, then create an HQL (Hibernate Query) query from this session. Then run the query by call the query.list() method and returns the query result.

So far so good. At this stage, let's add the spring configurations, *spring-conf.xml*. This file is too large to fit in an entire page. So, I will split the configurations into a few blocks for simplicity. Note that, spring configurations can be very compact and can import other spring configuration files. First, we will ship the data source configuration:

```
<bean id="dataSource" class="org.springframework.jdbc.datasource.DriverManagerDataSource">
    <property name="driverClassName" value="${jdbc.driver}"/>
    <property name="url" value="${jdbc.url}"/>
    <property name="username" value="${jdbc.username}"/>
    <property name="password" value="${jdbc.password}"/>
</bean>
```

Very straight forward, we defined all the data source configurations from the `jdbc.properties` files. Now, add the hibernate session factory configuration bean.

```
<bean id="sessionFactory" class="org.springframework.orm.hibernate4.LocalSessionFactoryBea\
n">
    <property name="dataSource" ref="dataSource" />
    <property name="packagesToScan">
        <list>
            <value>com.blu.imdg.dto</value>
        </list>
    </property>
    <property name="hibernateProperties">
        <props>
            <prop key="hibernate.cache.use_second_level_cache">true</prop>
            <!-- Generate L2 cache statistics. -->
            <prop key="hibernate.generate_statistics">true</prop>
            <!-- Specify ignite as L2 cache provider. -->
            <prop key="hibernate.cache.region.factory_class">org.apache.ignite.cache.hiber\
```

```xml
nate.HibernateRegionFactory</prop>
            <!-- Specify the name of the grid, that will be used for second level caching.\
 -->
            <prop key="org.apache.ignite.hibernate.grid_name">hibernate-grid</prop>
            <!-- Set default L2 cache access type. -->
            <prop key="org.apache.ignite.hibernate.default_access_type">READ_WRITE</prop>
            <!-- Enable query cache. prefix hibernate is necessary here.-->
            <prop key="hibernate.cache.use_query_cache">true</prop>
            <prop key="show_sql">true</prop>
        </props>
    </property>
</bean>
```

Take a moment to read through the code comments to understand how this works. In the above configuration, we first include our data source properties bean. Then we make sure the packages to scan for Hibernate entity classes are available. Next, we enable the hibernate 2nd level cache and set the cache provider. In our case, the cache provider is Ignite `HibernateRegionFactory`.

We also specify the name of the Ignite cache grid, which will be used for the second level cache and set the cache access type to READ_WRITE. We also enable the **query cache** here. Note that, to enable query cache you have to use the hibernate prefix. Next, we will define our **DAO implementation** bean and the web service bean.

```xml
<bean id="empDAO" class="com.blu.imdg.EmpDaoImpl">
    <property name="sessionFactory" ref="sessionFactory"/>
</bean>
<!-- Service-->
<bean id="serviceBean" class="com.blu.imdg.ws.WebService">
    <property name="empDao" ref="empDAO"/>
</bean>
```

We also provide the Ignite configuration bean to bring everything together.

```xml
<bean id="ignite.cfg" class="org.apache.ignite.configuration.IgniteConfiguration">
    <!-- Set true to enable distributed class loading, default is false. -->
    <property name="peerClassLoadingEnabled" value="false"/>

    <property name="gridName" value="hibernate-grid"/>
    <!-- Enable client mode. -->
    <property name="clientMode" value="false"/>

    <property name="cacheConfiguration">
        <list>
            <!--
```

```xml
                Configurations for entity caches.
            -->
            <bean parent="transactional-cache">
                <property name="name" value="com.blu.imdg.dto.Employee"/>
            </bean>
            <!-- Query cache (refers to atomic cache defined in above example). -->
            <bean parent="atomic-cache">
                <property name="name" value="org.hibernate.cache.internal.StandardQueryCac\
he"/>
            </bean>
            <!-- Configuration for update timestamps cache, it's also necessary for query \
cache-->
            <bean parent="atomic-cache">
                <property name="name" value="org.hibernate.cache.spi.UpdateTimestampsCache\
"/>
            </bean>
        </list>
    </property>
<!--discovery spi property omitted -->
</bean>
```

Here, we first set the grid name property to `hibernate-grid`, then we disable the client mode. Finally, we set the transactional cache for our Employee entity. We also defined the query cache to *atomic cache* and enable the update timestamp cache to store (the time, when the cache has been updated). There is a basic configuration for transactional cache and atomic cache. The configuration is shown below.

```xml
<bean id="atomic-cache" class="org.apache.ignite.configuration.CacheConfiguration" abstrac\
t="true">
    <property name="cacheMode" value="PARTITIONED"/>
    <property name="atomicityMode" value="ATOMIC"/>
    <property name="writeSynchronizationMode" value="FULL_SYNC"/>
</bean>
<bean id="transactional-cache" class="org.apache.ignite.configuration.CacheConfiguration" \
abstract="true">
    <property name="cacheMode" value="PARTITIONED"/>
    <property name="atomicityMode" value="TRANSACTIONAL"/>
    <property name="writeSynchronizationMode" value="FULL_SYNC"/>
</bean>
```

At this moment, we are ready to compile and run our application. To compile the project, type the following command into your terminal.

Chapter three: In-memory caching   81

```
mvn clean install
```

To run the application, apply the following command.

```
java -jar ./target/hibernate-1.0-SNAPSHOT.one-jar.jar
```

Now, we can use any soap client like soapUI to invoke our web service. Let's invoke the `getAllEmployee` web method to observe the response time.

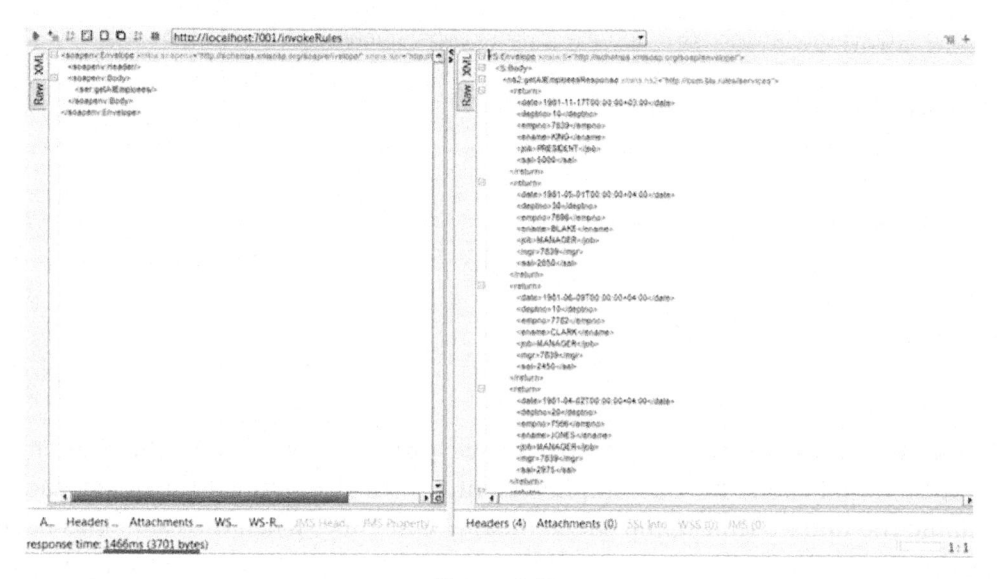

Figure 3.11

Let's make a deep drive to the Ignite cache for looking Hibernate 2nd level cache. Run the `ignitevisorcmd.sh/bat` and check the cache by the command *cache -a*.

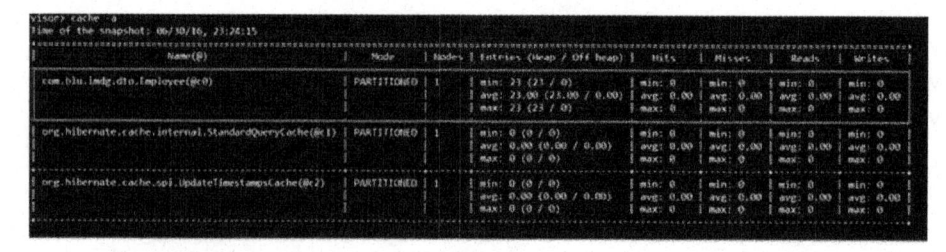

Figure 3.12

We should notice that 23 cache entries are now in Employee cache. Let's scan the cache Employee for further details.

Chapter three: In-memory caching   82

Figure 3.13

Although, the output of the console is not very readable, but it's clear that Ignite store all the Employees serialized instance in the cache. Next time, if we will run the above web method again, Hibernate entity manager will return the result from the cache and the response time will be very small. What will happen, if we add an Employee through our web method? Theoretically, it will add a new Employee entry into the Ignite cache and also commit the Employee instance into the database. Let's invoke the web method *addEmployee* to create an Employee.

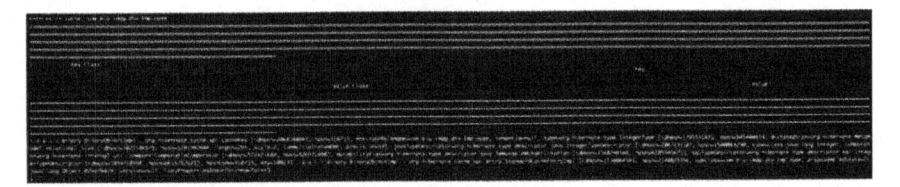

Figure 3.14

Exactly what we expected, one new cache entry for Employee now allocated into the Ignite cache. We can reformat the cache entry to take a better look on it.

```
| o.a.i.i.binary.BinaryObjectImpl | org.hibernate.cache.spi.CacheKey
[idHash=2068160447, hash=310713, entityOrRoleName=com.blu.imdg.dto.Employee, tenantId=null\
, type=org.hibernate.type.IntegerType
[idHash=1795331831, hash=945408619, dictatedSize=org.hibernate.metamodel.relational.Size
[idHash=1022186575, hash=1281942644, length=255, scale=2, lobMultiplier=NONE, precision=19\
], javaTypeDescriptor=org.hibernate.type.descriptor.java.IntegerTypeDescriptor
[idHash=2067231107, hash=1580083290, type=class java.lang.Integer, comparator=org.hibernat\
e.internal.util.compare.ComparableComparator
[idHash=572421684, hash=526971408], mutabilityPlan=org.hibernate.type.descriptor.java.Immu\
tableMutabilityPlan
[idHash=1348240344, hash=610554567]], sqlTypeDescriptor=org.hibernate.type.descriptor.sql.\
IntegerTypeDescriptor
[idHash=1059718958, hash=661575262]], hashCode=310713, key=10023] | o.a.i.i.binary.BinaryO\
bjectImpl | org.hibernate.cache.spi.entry.StandardCacheEntryImpl
[idHash=2136064545, hash=2140825356, subclass=com.blu.imdg.dto.Employee, disassembledState\
=[Ljava.lang.Object;@2eafb429, version=null, lazyPropertiesAreUnfetched=false] |
```

Chapter three: In-memory caching

From the above logs, it's clear the definitions of the cache entry for the Employee instance. Also if we query the table *emp* now, we will also find the newly added Employee entry. If we take a closer look at our cache into the Ignite, we will have found a very interesting thing (see, Figure 3.15).

```
visor> cache -scan
Time of the snapshot: 07/01/16, 11:28:32
+---+----------------------------------------------------+-------------+---------------------------+
| # |                       Name(@)                      |    Mode     |   Size (Heap / Off heap)  |
+---+----------------------------------------------------+-------------+---------------------------+
| 0 | <default>(@c0)                                     | PARTITIONED | min: 0 (0 / 0)            |
|   |                                                    |             | avg: 0.00 (0.00 / 0.00)   |
|   |                                                    |             | max: 0 (0 / 0)            |
+---+----------------------------------------------------+-------------+---------------------------+
| 1 | com.blu.imdg.dto.Employee(@c1)                     | PARTITIONED | min: 0 (0 / 0)            |
|   |                                                    |             | avg: 0.50 (0.50 / 0.00)   |
|   |                                                    |             | max: 1 (1 / 0)            |
+---+----------------------------------------------------+-------------+---------------------------+
| 2 | org.hibernate.cache.internal.StandardQueryCache(@c2)| PARTITIONED | min: 0 (0 / 0)            |
|   |                                                    |             | avg: 0.00 (0.00 / 0.00)   |
|   |                                                    |             | max: 0 (0 / 0)            |
+---+----------------------------------------------------+-------------+---------------------------+
| 3 | org.hibernate.cache.spi.UpdateTimestampsCache(@c3) | PARTITIONED | min: 0 (0 / 0)            |
|   |                                                    |             | avg: 0.50 (0.50 / 0.00)   |
|   |                                                    |             | max: 1 (1 / 0)            |
+---+----------------------------------------------------+-------------+---------------------------+
```

Figure 3.15

UpdateTimestampCache also has a cache entry for it. Let's scan the cache to observe the cache entry.

```
Entries in cache: org.hibernate.cache.spi.UpdateTimestampsCache
+=================================================================+
|   Key Class        | Key | Value Class      | Value             |
+=================================================================+
| java.lang.String   | emp | java.lang.Long   | 1467361013819     |
+-----------------------------------------------------------------+
```

Entries of this cache contain the timestamp value in milliseconds, which indicate the time when the table has been updated. If we convert the timestamp value to date, it will show the exact time of the cache entry time, in my case, it's `Friday, July 1, 2016, 8:16:53 AM GMT`.

Step 4:

We have reached out the end of this section, this time we will discover the QueryCache and its overall performance. When we have configured our `spring-core.xml`, we have explicitly enabled the Hibernate Query cache with Ignite by this following property.

```
<!-- Enable query cache, prefix hibernate is necessary here.-->
<prop key="hibernate.cache.use_query_cache">true</prop>
```

Chapter three: In-memory caching

> **Note:**
> *UpdateTimeStampCache* is the required bean for query cache, without *UpdateTimeStampCache* bean, query cache will not work.

To enable query cache, we have to explicitly set the *query.setCacheable(true)* property in Query or Criteria instance as follows:

```java
public List<Employee> getEmpByName(String ename) {
    Session session = sessionFactory.openSession();
    Query query = session.createQuery("from Employee e where e.ename=:ename");
    query.setParameter("ename", ename);
    query.setCacheable(true);
    List<Employee> employees =  query.list();
    return employees;
}
```

Now, let's invoke our third web method, getEmpByName. We are looking for the employee *Robin* by his name.

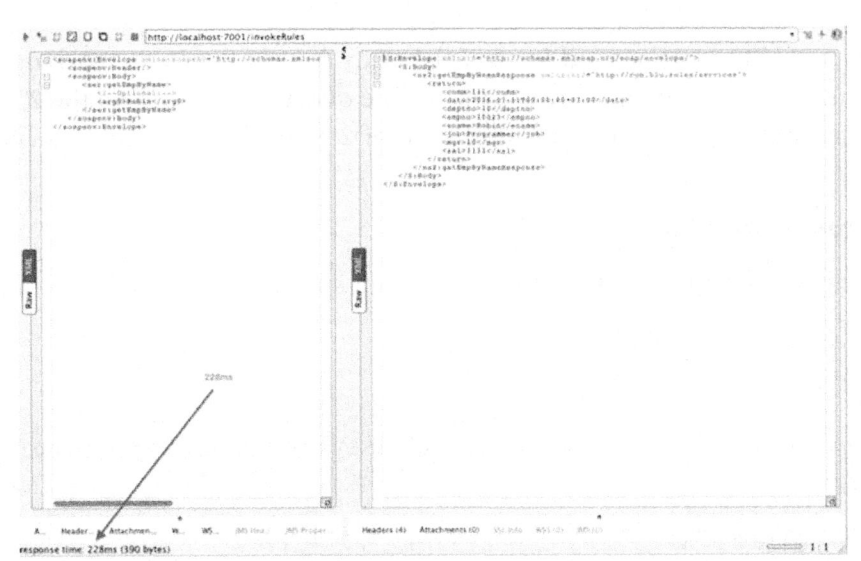

Figure 3.16

The query returns within 228 ms of time. Let's run the web method again, and monitor the response time.

Chapter three: In-memory caching   85

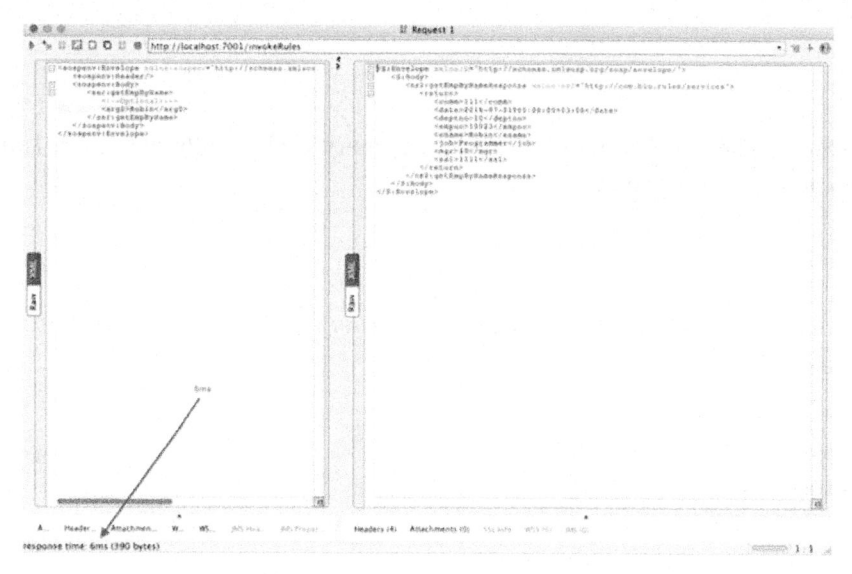

Figure 3.17

As we expected, it took only 6 ms of time to get a response. If we take a look at the cache, we should find the cache entry for our database query with parameter `ROBIN`.

Figure 3.18

So, it's clear that our Hibernate second level cache with Apache Ignite is working fine and we are getting maximum low latency of executing time for the query. By setting up the 2nd level cache into the in-memory cache we reduce the execution time of 228 ms to 6 ms, this is a huge performance boost.

Calculate application speedup:

You can use Amdhal's law[18] to calculate the application speedup.

> **Note:**
>
> *Amdhal's law*, after Gene Amdhal, is used to find the system speed up from a speed up in part of the system.
>
> 1/((1 - Proportion speed up) + Proportion speed up / speed up)

---

[18] https://en.wikipedia.org/wiki/Amdahl%27s_law

$$\frac{1}{(1-P) + \frac{P}{S}}$$

Amdhal's law

Where,

- P is proportional speed up, and
- S is speed up.

Also, note that, for a web application the *system* should include browser render time and network latency.

When you are using *Cache*, an application performance depends on a minimum of two of the following factors:

- how many times a cached piece of data is retrieved by the application;
- and the proportion of the response time that is alleviated by caching.

Assume, we have a web application and uncached full page rendering time is 3 seconds. Now, let's calculate the speed up from a database level cache. In our case:

- Uncached page time : 3 seconds
- Database time : 228 ms. (see figure 3.16)
- Cache retrieval time : 6 ms (see figure 3.17)
- Proportion : 228/3*1000 $\sim$ 7.6%

The expected system speedup should be:

1/((1-0.076) + 0.076/(228/6)) = 1/(0.924 + 0.002) $\sim$ 1.07 times overall system speed up.

Overall speed up time is $\sim$ 1.

In the next section, we will study the Java method caching, which can also improve the performance of your application.

Java method caching

As far as we have learned about the only second level cache, which can reduce database call to speed up application performance. However, there could be one more caching tier between java method and persistence manager. Assume, you have a method that takes time to execute, and method result can only depend on its input parameters. In this situation, you can cache the result of the function, which will return the same result for the same input.

For instance, suppose you have a function, which returns the current U.S dollar rate for any given regions of Russia (U.S dollar exchange rate is different in every region of Russia). All the exchange rates are stored in the database or somewhere in Microsoft excel file. With the Java method cache, the cache manager will immediately return the value from the cache by region, the function will not start computing business logic at all. Very straight forward, yeah! Rather than reprocessing all the business logics, returning the previously cached response can save lots of CPU resources. Thus, you can increase the economy of your functions execution time up to 2-3 milliseconds.

Maybe you are wondered, why this 2-3 ms is so important? In the end of 2014 in Russia, when the dollar exchange rate was changed on every hour, a few Russian bank website was not able to handle the high traffic. People rushed to the bank website to know the exchange rate.

> **Note:**
> Java method caching is useful, when your Java procedure or function is doing some heavy CPU/IO intensive operation such as calculating tax, grace period, compute Fibonacci number or complex OLAP query on the database.

Java provides a few different approaches to solving this problem, one of them is Java Temporary caching API, Guava from google and the Spring cache abstraction from Spring. Apache Ignite supports and shipped with an implementation of the Spring Cache abstraction. It provides support for transparently adding caching into spring application, which will store the cache into Ignite. Since Spring 4.1, cache abstraction is significantly improved and even supports annotations. The cache abstraction provides a set of java annotations:

- `@Cacheable` - triggers cache population
- `@CacheEvict` - triggers cache eviction
- `@CachePut` - updates the cache without interfering with the method execution
- `@Caching` - regroups multiple cache operations to be applied on a method
- `@CacheConfig` - shares some common cache-related settings at class-level.

Enable caching the result of a Java method

To enable the spring cache, we need two spring configurations bean in spring context file.

Chapter three: In-memory caching

```xml
<cache:annotation-driven/>
<!-- Ignite-->
<bean id="cacheManager" class="org.apache.ignite.cache.spring.SpringCacheManager">
    <property name="configuration" ref="ignite.cfg" />
</bean>
```

Annotation-driven enables the caching, and the *SpringCacheManager* will be the cache manager for the spring application. For every Java function, the cache manager will create an entire new cache.

```
Entries in cache: exchangeRate
+===================================================================+
|    Key Class       |   Key     |   Value Class      | Value |
+===================================================================+
| java.lang.String   | Moscow    | java.lang.String   | 65    |
| java.lang.String   | Vladimir  | java.lang.String   | 71    |
+-------------------------------------------------------------------+
```

Figure 3.19

How does it work?

The approach is very primitive. There is a distributed hash map, where the key is the function parameters and the values are the function *results*. The Key consists of the parameter type and the name of the parameters. In the above example, the key is the state Moscow or Vladimir and the value are the 65 or 71. Once we have configured our spring bean, let's create the appropriate java class to add spring cache. We will use our previous example from the chapter-caching/hibernate, and will add a few more methods for spring cache annotations.

Step 1:

Let's create the table *Exchangerate* with a few rows in it.

```sql
create table exchangerate(
   ratedate         date,
   usdollar   decimal,
   euro             decimal,
   gbp              decimal,
   region           text,
   primary key (ratedate, region)
);
INSERT INTO public.exchangerate (ratedate,usdollar,euro,gbp,region) VALUES (
TO_DATE('2015-05-01','YYYY-MM-DD'),69.7,75.9,103.01,'Vladimir');
INSERT INTO public.exchangerate (ratedate,usdollar,euro,gbp,region) VALUES (
TO_DATE('2015-05-02','YYYY-MM-DD'),71.7,77.1,102.03,'Tver');
INSERT INTO public.exchangerate (ratedate,usdollar,euro,gbp,region) VALUES (
TO_DATE('2015-05-02','YYYY-MM-DD'),71.7,77.1,102.03,'Moscow');
INSERT INTO public.exchangerate (ratedate,usdollar,euro,gbp,region) VALUES (
```

Chapter three: In-memory caching

```
                TO_DATE('2015-05-02','YYYY-MM-DD'),71.7,77.1,102.03,'Vladimir');
INSERT INTO public.exchangerate (ratedate,usdollar,euro,gbp,region) VALUES (
                TO_DATE('2015-05-03','YYYY-MM-DD'),71.9,77.4,101.03,'Tver');
INSERT INTO public.exchangerate (ratedate,usdollar,euro,gbp,region) VALUES (
                TO_DATE('2015-05-03','YYYY-MM-DD'),70.3,76.1,103.07,'Moscow');
INSERT INTO public.exchangerate (ratedate,usdollar,euro,gbp,region) VALUES (
                TO_DATE('2015-05-03','YYYY-MM-DD'),71.1,77.4,101.01,'Vladimir');
commit;
```

You can find the DDL and DML file in the scripts directory of the `chapter-caching\hibernate` project. The above script will create a new table and inserts a few rows for our next example.

Step 2:

Create a simple Hibernate entity.

```java
@Entity
@Table( name = "emp" )
public class ExchangeRate {
    @Id
    @Column(name = "region")
    private String region;
    @Column(name = "ratedate")
    private Date rateDate;
    @Column(name = "usdollar")
    private double usdollar;
    @Column(name = "euro")
    private double euro;
    @Column(name = "gbp")
    private double gbp;

    public ExchangeRate() {
    }
// ... getter and setter methods omitted
    @Override
    public boolean equals(Object o) {
        if (this == o) return true;
        if (o == null || getClass() != o.getClass()) return false;

        ExchangeRate that = (ExchangeRate) o;

        if (!rateDate.equals(that.rateDate)) return false;
        if (!region.equals(that.region)) return false;

        return true;
    }
```

```java
    @Override
    public int hashCode() {
        int result = region.hashCode();
        result = 31 * result + rateDate.hashCode();
        return result;
    }
}
```

Note that, for ExchangeRate entity we will also need the *equals* and *hash* method to identify our entity.

Step 3:

Now, we are going to create two new DAO service methods as follows:

```java
String getExchangeRateByRegion(String region);
void updateExchange(ExchangeRate e);
```

Implementations:

```java
@Override
@Cacheable(value = "exchangeRate")
public String getExchangeRateByRegion(String region) {
    Session session = sessionFactory.openSession();
    // in real life, it should be current date time
    SQLQuery query = session.createSQLQuery("select * from exchangerate e where e.ratedate\
 = TO_DATE('2015-05-02','YYYY-MM-DD') and e.region=:region");
    query.setParameter("region", region);
    query.addEntity(ExchangeRate.class);
    ExchangeRate res = (ExchangeRate)query.uniqueResult();
    session.close();
    return String.valueOf(res.getUsdollar());
}

@Override
@CacheEvict(value = "exchangeRate", key = "#e.region")
public void updateExchange(ExchangeRate e) {
    Session session = sessionFactory.openSession();
    session.getTransaction().begin();
    SQLQuery query = session.createSQLQuery("update exchangerate \n" +
            " set usdollar = :usdollar" +
            " where region = :region and ratedate = TO_DATE('2015-05-02','YYYY-MM-DD')") ;

    query.setParameter("region", e.getRegion());
    query.setParameter("usdollar", e.getUsdollar());
```

Chapter three: In-memory caching

```
    query.addEntity(ExchangeRate.class);
    query.executeUpdate();
    session.getTransaction().commit();
    session.close();
}
```

First, in DAO interface, we have declared two new interfaces, *getExchangeRateByRegion* and *updateExchange*. Implementations of this interface are very simple. We are using Hibernate native SQL query feature to query the database. The interesting part of the above code is the annotations. Let's take a closer look at the annotations. `@Cacheable(value = "exchangeRate")` – creates a new cache with name exchangeRate, if cache already exists, spring cache manager will reuse the cache. In the preceding code above, method,

- `getExchangeRateByRegion` is associated with the cache name exchangeRate. Each time the method is invoked, the cache is checked to see whether the invocation has been already executed and doesn't have to repeat the execution block of the method. By default, only one cache is declared, but this annotation allows multiple names of the cache to be specified. As for example:

`@Cacheable({"exchangeRate", "dollars"})`

In this case, each of the caches will be checked before executing the method. If at least one entry is found in any of the caches, then the associated value will be returned.

- `@CacheEvict(value = "exchangeRate", key = "#e.region")` – allows eviction of the particular cache. This process is very useful to remove the unused or stale cache from the Ignite. There are two flavors of this eviction process. With this annotation, you can either evict the entire cache or evict only the cache entry that is stalled. In the snipped code, only the cache entry with the appropriate region will be deleted.

Note that, here, we are using, Spring *SpEL* to declare the cache key. To explicitly specify what is used for cache key, we used the key parameter of the annotation. Spring SpEL indicate that we have to get the value from the ExchangeRate entity and use its code region to delete the cache entry.

To delete the entire cache, you can use the following annotation:

`@CacheEvict(value = "exchangeRate", allEntries=true)`

> **Note:**
> It's not recommended to evict the entire cache because when your cache is empty, every method call will execute the business logic, which can decrease the performance of your application for a

Chapter three: In-memory caching 92

> while.

Step 4:

For now, we need two more methods for SOAP services and we are ready to go for the test.

```java
@WebMethod(operationName = "getExchangeRateByRegion")
public String getExchangeRateByRegion(String str){
    return empDao.getExchangeRateByRegion(str);
}
@WebMethod(operationName = "updateExchangeRate")
public void updateExchangeRate(String region, Date rateDate, double usdollar, double euro,\
 double gbp){
    ExchangeRate e = new ExchangeRate();
    e.setRegion(region);
    e.setUsdollar(usdollar);
    e.setEuro(euro);
    e.setGbp(gbp);
    e.setRateDate(rateDate);

    empDao.updateExchange(e);
}
```

In getExchangeRateByRegion web method, we have just delegated the method call to our DAO, and the web method updateExchangeRate creates a new Exchange instance and delegate the method call to the *updateExchange* method.

Step 5:

To call the above web methods, I used my favorite soapUI. Let's invoke the method getExchangeRateByRegion a few times with different region name, Moscow/Vladimir/Tver.

Chapter three: In-memory caching

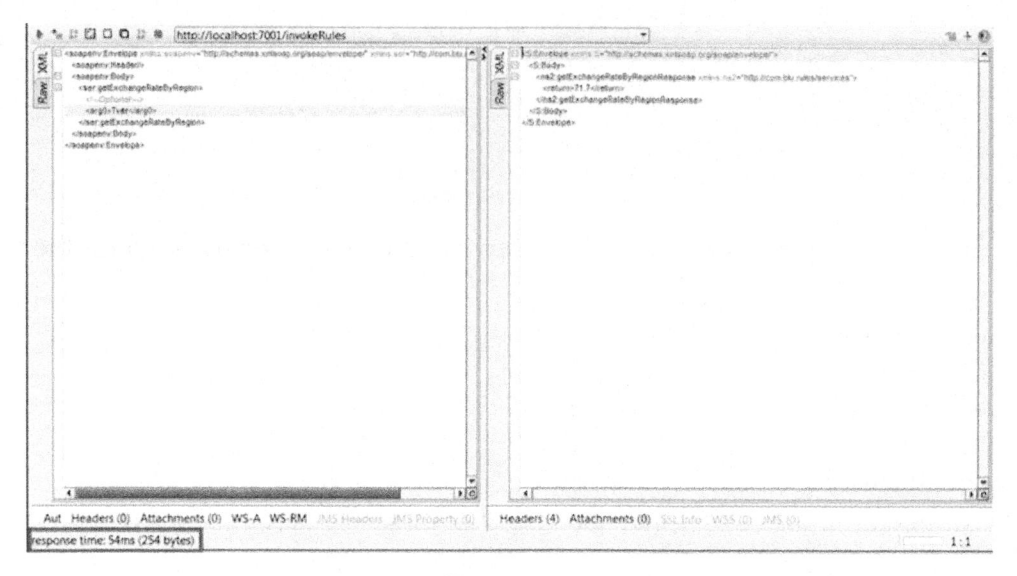

Figure 3.20

At this moment the execution time is 54 ms. Let's check the cache entries by the command `cache -scan` in IgniteVisor.

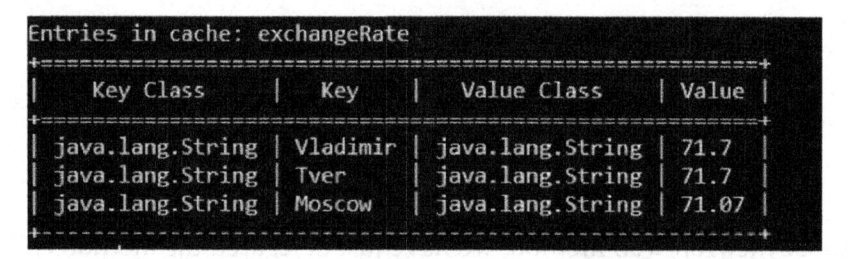

Figure 3.21

You can see that all the exchange rates of the U.S. dollar are moved into the cache now. If we will re-invoke our web method again, spring cache manager will return the value from the cache.

Chapter three: In-memory caching 94

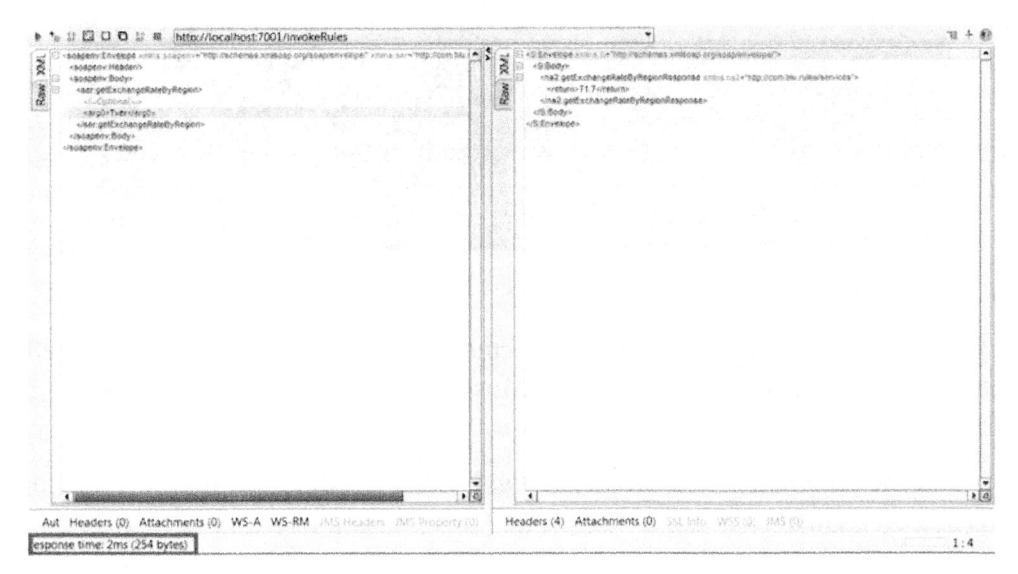

Figure 3.22

Please note that the response time of the web method is closer to **2 ms**. The execution time is almost real time.

Step 6:

This is the last part of this section. We are going to update a few exchange rates and observe how it will affect the cache into Ignite. So far we have 3 entries in Ignite cache. Let's call the method `updateExchangeRate` web method with the following parameters:

```
<ser:updateExchangeRate>
    <arg0>Moscow</arg0>
    <arg1>2015-05-02</arg1>
    <arg2>71.081</arg2>
    <arg3>78.3</arg3>
    <arg4>101,5</arg4>
</ser:updateExchangeRate>
```

The above invocation will update the database table row.

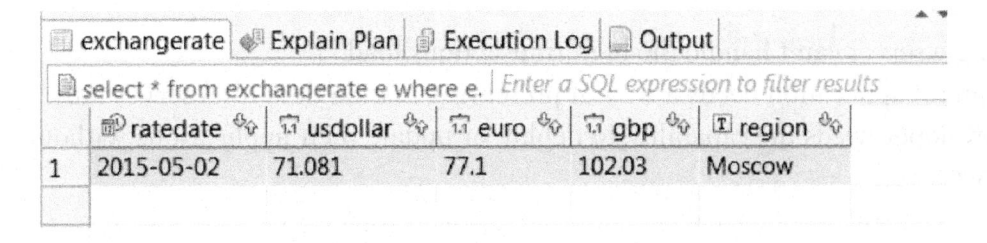

Figure 3.23

If we scan the cache `exchangeRate` into Ignite, we should find the following entries as follows:

Chapter three: In-memory caching

```
Entries in cache: exchangeRate
+==================================================================+
|    Key Class     |   Key    |   Value Class    | Value |
+==================================================================+
| java.lang.String | Vladimir | java.lang.String | 71.7  |
| java.lang.String | Tver     | java.lang.String | 71.7  |
+------------------------------------------------------------------+
```

Figure 3.24

The cache for the Moscow region has been evicted. Next time when the web method getExchangeRateByRegion will call again for region Moscow, the cache entry will appear in the cache exchangeRate.

This is the end of the section *Java method caching*. Next, we will go through a very import feature of Ignite - WebSession clustering.

Web session clustering with Apache Ignite

In Microservice era, web session clustering is a headache for every programmer and for any architects. Breaking down a monolith into a collection of microservices has some wonderful benefits, but also has a few nasty downsides. One of them is session management.

Not only microservice but session management had also always been a problem for enterprise Java. Native session management from application servers such as Oracle WebLogic, IBM WebSphere or Tomcat was error prone. Any of them could not replicate session very well to provide high availability of applications because always there is room for server maintenance.

Web session clustering is designed to provide a higher scalable solution for synchronizing session data across a cluster of web application servers. That means any web application can grow beyond a single server, in an application cluster. Apache Ignite in-memory data grid provides an excellent way to store sessions from the servlet containers to scale your web applications and handle extreme transaction load.

However, term session clustering can look like a complicated topic, but the basics are very simple. In the computer world, clustered architecture is used to solve one or more of the following problems:

- A single server can't handle the high transactions load.
- A stateful application needs a way of preserving session data if its server fails.
- A developer needs the capability to deploy or update their applications without interrupting services.

A clustered architecture solves these above problems using a combination of load balancer and some kind of session replication. A classical cluster architecture is shown below.

Chapter three: In-memory caching

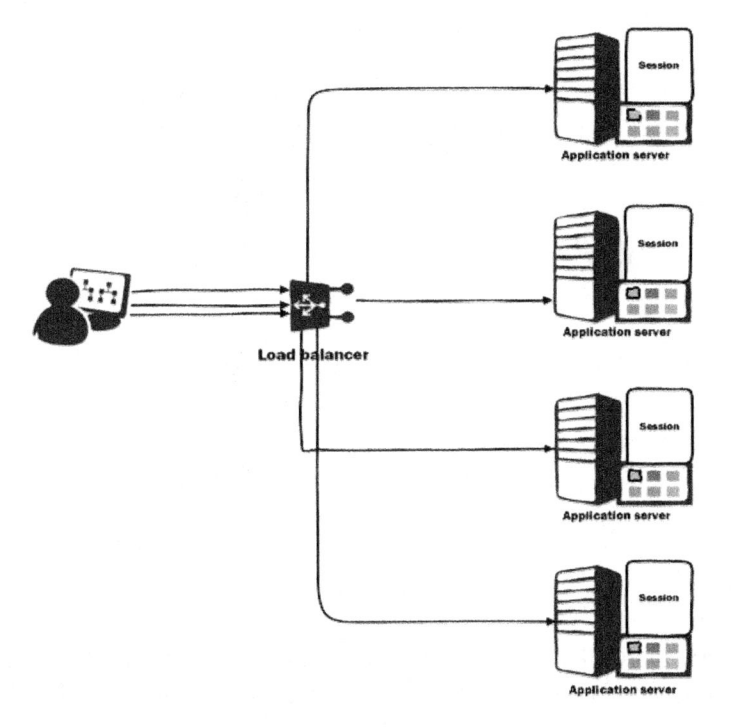

Figure 3.25

> **Note:**
> We are talking about only standalone servlet containers such as tomcat, jetty etc. However, Oracle WebLogic cluster, IBM WebSphere provides session clustering and session replications. But when you redeploy or update your application or doing service maintenance, you can lose session data.

In the above architecture, a load balancer distributes requests between multiple application server instances or servlet containers with algorithms such as round robin, reducing the load on each instance. The problem here is web session availability. A web session keeps an intermediate logical state between requests by using cookies and is normally bound to a particular application instance. There are a few classic solutions to solve this problem.

Classic solution, using sticky session.

Sticky session or session affinity ensures that request from the same user is handled by the same application server instance. Most of all web server, such as Nginx, Apache web server can provide multiple algorithms and modules to provide such functionality. However, if the instance fails or halt (worst case), the session is lost, and the user will face an unexpected result or error. Moreover, the sticky session is also unresponsive and can be slow.

Chapter three: In-memory caching

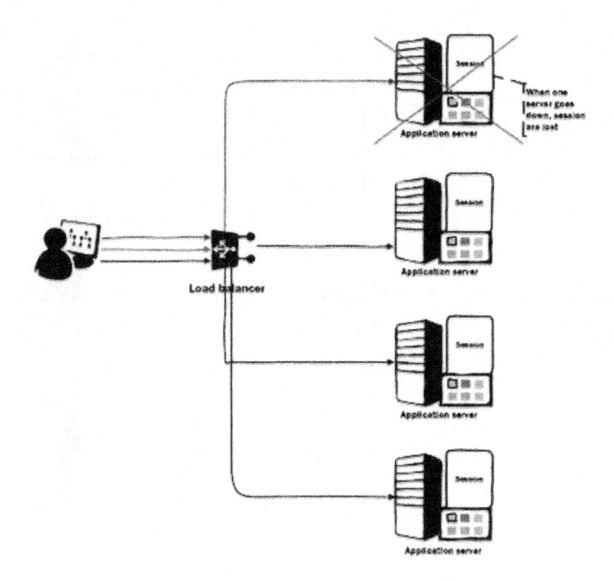

Figure 3.26

In all of these cases, even for a given period of time, an application server that is still up and running may not accept new connections or handle new requests, or is entirely down and will never handle them. Under these scenarios, a client may be redirected to an alternate application server. The session affinity or sticky session mechanism will resume from that endpoint, but the original one will be abandoned. The sticky session is usually an optimization and not a replacement for long-lived connections.

Classic solution, store sessions in DB.

In this approach, the database can become both a bottleneck and a single point of failure. Servlet containers such as a jetty or tomcat can take steps to reduce the load on the database. But in a high loaded environment, it is highly recommended not to use such solution, because, in every request, the servlet container will query the database.

Chapter three: In-memory caching 98

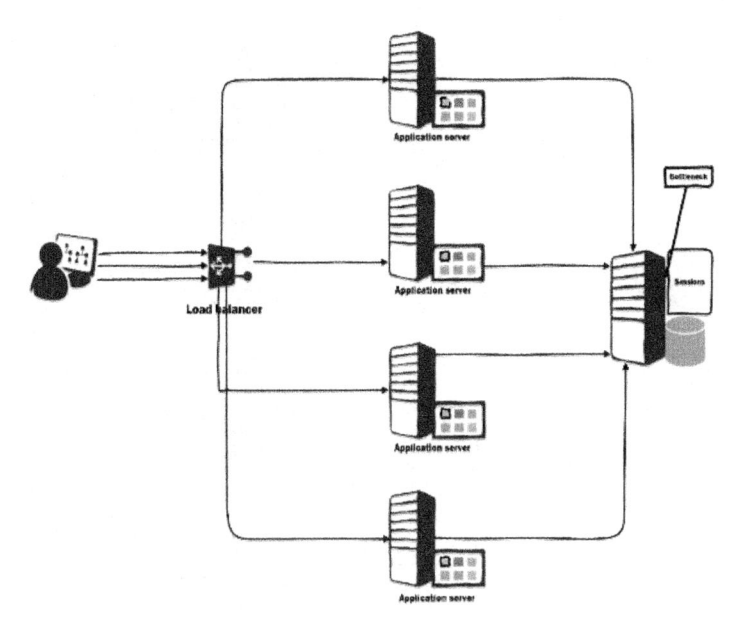

Figure 3.27

Classic solution, use only stateless service.

In the real world, it is almost not possible to do all services stateless. For a simple e-commerce site, having a shopping cart or a simple captcha in your web form will force you to use stateful service.

Distributed web session clustering.

A solution here is to use distributed Ignite in-memory web session clustering, that will maintain and store a copy of each created session, sharing them between all application server instances, by using multiple copies of redundancy (depends on replication strategy). In the event of an application server failure, the load balancer redirects to a new application server which has access to the user session in the Ignite cluster. The handoff to the new application server is seamless for the user.

Chapter three: In-memory caching   99

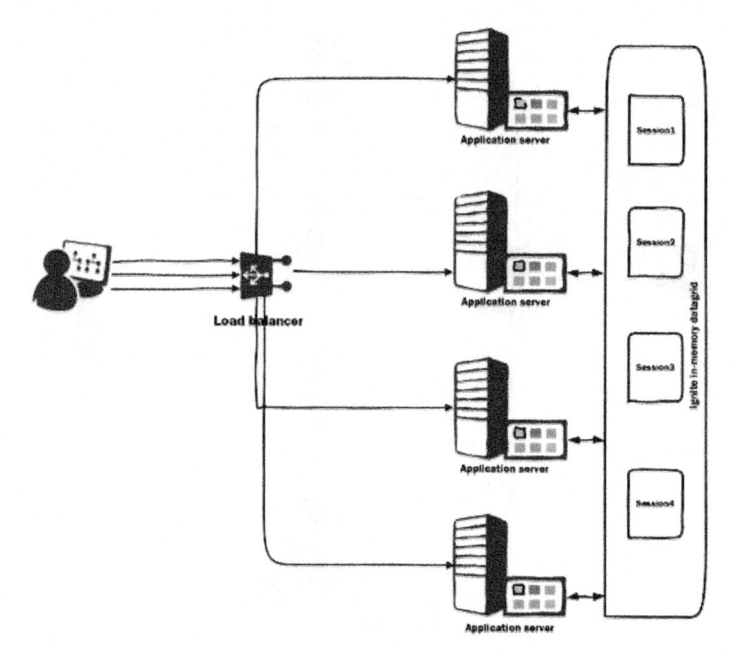

Figure 3.28

The above approach provides the highest level of high availability of a system and a good customer experience. Since Ignite is an in-memory solution, the performance of this web session clustering and replication mechanism of user web session is very high. In addition, Ignite need no modification to your application tier, so you can apply Ignite web session clustering without modifying existing application (only a few modifications in web.xml).

So far in this chapter, we have got a very basic idea about web session clustering and how it could make our life easier in web development. Next, we are going to build a spring MVC web application, that allows us to save some user session information in a **web session** stored in the Ignite in-memory cluster. Before we move on to start coding, let's have a detailed look at how the HTTP session works in a servlet container.

HttpSession

When a client visits the web application for the first time, the servlet container will create a new Http Session object, generate a long and unique id and stores it in server's memory. The servlet container will also set a Cookie in the Set-Cookie header of the HTTP response with JSESSIONID as cookie name and the unique session id as a cookie value.

The HTTP session lives until it has not been used for more than the sessions time, a setting you can specify in web.xml, which default to 30 minutes. So, when a client doesn't visit the web application anymore for 30 minutes, then the servlet container will remove the session from memory. Every subsequent request, even though with the cookie specified, will not have access to the same session anymore. The servlet container will create a new session.

In a nutshell,

- The HttpSession lives as long as the client is interacting with the web app with the same

browser instance and the session hasn't timed out at the server side yet. It's been shared among all requests in the same session.
- The HttpServletRequest and HttpServletResponse live as long as the client has sent it until the complete response (the web page) arrives. It is not being shared elsewhere.
- Any Servlet, Filter, and Listener live as long as the web app lives. They are being shared among all requests in all sessions.

Let's prepare the sandbox for our web application. In this application we are going to use the following components:

1. Spring 4.1.0.RELEASE
2. Jetty-9.2.11
3. Ignite-1.6.0 version

To enable web session clustering in our web application with Ignite, we need the following Ignite libraries:

1. ignite.jar
2. ignite-web.jar
3. ignite-log4j.jar
4. ignite-spring.jar

Step 1:

Add this following library to the maven project.

```
<dependencies>
    <dependency>
        <groupId>org.springframework</groupId>
        <artifactId>spring-webmvc</artifactId>
        <version>${springframework.version}</version>
    </dependency>
    <dependency>
        <groupId>javax.servlet</groupId>
        <artifactId>javax.servlet-api</artifactId>
        <version>3.1.0</version>
    </dependency>
    <dependency>
        <groupId>javax.servlet.jsp</groupId>
        <artifactId>javax.servlet.jsp-api</artifactId>
        <version>2.3.1</version>
    </dependency>
```

Chapter three: In-memory caching

```xml
<dependency>
    <groupId>javax.servlet</groupId>
    <artifactId>jstl</artifactId>
    <version>1.2</version>
</dependency>
<!-- Ignite dependencies-->
<dependency>
    <groupId>org.apache.ignite</groupId>
    <artifactId>ignite-core</artifactId>
    <version>${ignite.version}</version>
</dependency>
<dependency>
    <groupId>org.apache.ignite</groupId>
    <artifactId>ignite-web</artifactId>
    <version>${ignite.version}</version>
</dependency>
<dependency>
    <groupId>org.apache.ignite</groupId>
    <artifactId>ignite-log4j</artifactId>
    <version>${ignite.version}</version>
</dependency>
<dependency>
    <groupId>org.apache.ignite</groupId>
    <artifactId>ignite-spring</artifactId>
    <version>${ignite.version}</version>
</dependency>
</dependencies>
```

In the above maven project dependencies, we also add spring MVC library. To keep things simple, we will use embedded jetty servlet container. Also, our web app will be very simple, without any web form. In this web application, we will have two HTTP methods (`/putperson`), one for put session data into user session and another HTTP method (`/getperson`) to get the session data from the cache. If you are curious about the code, it's available at GitHub project[19] (chapter-caching\web-session-clustering).

Step 2:

Next, create the java class `Person`, which will be our session data.

---
[19] https://github.com/srecon/ignite-book-code-samples

```
public class Person implements Serializable{
    private String firstName;
    private int    age;
        // setter and getter are omitted
}
```

Also create the MVC controller as follows:

```
@Controller
@RequestMapping("/")
@SessionAttributes("personObj")
public class WebSessionController {
        @RequestMapping(value="/putperson", method = RequestMethod.GET)
        public String putSession(ModelMap model, HttpServletRequest request) {
        model.addAttribute("person", "Add Person to user session");
        String fName = request.getParameter("name");
        int age = Integer.valueOf(request.getParameter("age"));
        Person person = new Person();
        person.setFirstName(fName);
        person.setAge(age);
        // set user session data
                request.getSession().setAttribute(fName, person);
        // return to the welcome.jsp view
                return "welcome";
        }
        @RequestMapping(value="/getperson", method = RequestMethod.GET)
        public String getSession(ModelMap model, HttpServletRequest request) {
        String fName = request.getParameter("name");
        // get session data
                model.addAttribute("person", request.getSession().getAttribute(fName) != null ? "Age: "
+ ((Person) request.getSession().getAttribute(fName)).getAge() : " Unknown");
                // view welcome.jsp
        return "welcome";
        }
}
```

Let's have a detailed look at the above preceding code. The first annotation *@Controller* says that the given class is a Spring MVC controller. Next, the annotation *@RequestMapping* allows us to map web request into our specific controller. Another interesting method annotation is *@RequestMapping*, which provides a very simple way to mapping web requests into specific handler methods. The HTTP method `putSession` simply parse the HTTP get parameters (name, age) from the URL and add the parameters values into the session. Similarly, HTTP method `getSession` parse the parameter from the URL and prints the age of the Person into the web page.

Now, that we have dipped our toes into web session, it's time to configure the Ignite cluster to store the web session.

> **Note:**
> We didn't add any Ignite related code in the web application, web session clustering in Ignite is fully **transparent** to the web application.

Step 3:

Now, we have to add our spring-servlet.xml to configure our MVC application.

```xml
<context:component-scan base-package="com.blu.imdg.wsession.controller" />
<mvc:annotation-driven />
<bean class="org.springframework.web.servlet.view.InternalResourceViewResolver">
    <property name="prefix">
        <value>/WEB-INF/views/</value>
    </property>
    <property name="suffix">
        <value>.jsp</value>
    </property>
</bean>
```

In the above *spring-servlet.xml* configuration file, we have defined a tag <context:component-scan>. This will allow Spring to load all the components from the package com.blu.imdg.wsession.controller and all its child packages. Also, we defined a bean *viewResolver*. This bean will resolve the view and add prefix string */WEB-INF/jsp/* and suffix *.jsp* to the view in *ModelAndView*. Note that in our WebSessionController class, we have returned a View object with view name welcome. This will be resolved to the path /WEB-INF/jsp/welcome.jsp.

Step 4:

Create new file *spring-ignite-cache.xml* and place it into the folder */resources/META-INF*.

```xml
<beans xmlns="http://www.springframework.org/schema/beans"
    xmlns:context="http://www.springframework.org/schema/context"
    xmlns:xsi="http://www.w3.org/2001/XMLSchema-instance"
    xmlns:cache="http://www.springframework.org/schema/cache"
    xmlns:mvc="http://www.springframework.org/schema/mvc"
    xsi:schemaLocation="
      http://www.springframework.org/schema/beans
      http://www.springframework.org/schema/beans/spring-beans.xsd
      http://www.springframework.org/schema/cache
      http://www.springframework.org/schema/cache/spring-cache-3.1.xsd
      http://www.springframework.org/schema/mvc
      http://www.springframework.org/schema/mvc/spring-mvc-4.0.xsd
```

```xml
            http://www.springframework.org/schema/context
            http://www.springframework.org/schema/context/spring-context.xsd ">

    <bean id="ignite.cfg" class="org.apache.ignite.configuration.IgniteConfiguration">
        <property name="peerClassLoadingEnabled" value="false" />
        <property name="gridName" value="session-grid" />
        <!-- Enable client mode. -->
        <property name="clientMode" value="false" />
        <property name="cacheConfiguration">
            <list>
                <bean class="org.apache.ignite.configuration.CacheConfiguration">
                    <!-- Cache mode. -->
                    <property name="cacheMode" value="PARTITIONED" />
                    <property name="backups" value="1" />
                    <!-- Cache name. -->
                    <property name="name" value="session-cache" />
                    <!-- Setup LRU eviction policy with 10000 sessions limit. -->
                    <property name="evictionPolicy">
                        <bean class="org.apache.ignite.cache.eviction.lru.LruEvictionPolicy">
                            <property name="maxSize" value="10000" />
                        </bean>
                    </property>
                </bean>
            </list>
        </property>
        <!-- Explicitly configure TCP discovery SPI to provide list of initial nodes. -->
        <property name="discoverySpi">
            <bean class="org.apache.ignite.spi.discovery.tcp.TcpDiscoverySpi">
                <property name="ipFinder">
                    <bean class="org.apache.ignite.spi.discovery.tcp.ipfinder.multicast.TcpDi\
scoveryMulticastIpFinder">
                        <property name="addresses">
                            <list>
                                <!-- In distributed environment, replace with actual host IP \
address. -->
                                <value>127.0.0.1:47500..47509</value>
                                <value>192.168.15.150:47500..47509</value>
                            </list>
                        </property>
                    </bean>
                </property>
            </bean>
        </property>
    </bean>
</beans>
```

Chapter three: In-memory caching   105

File location of the above file is very *crucial*, for Ignite to start the cache instance the path to the configuration file can be absolute, or relative to either **IGNITE_HOME**. Nothing new in the above file except eviction policy. We have set the eviction policy to LRU and the maximum size of the cache to 10000 entries.

Step 5:

This is the last and final step to configure the Ignite web session clustering. Here, we add **web.xml** file into WEB-INF folder.

```xml
<web-app id="WebApp_ID" version="2.4" xmlns="http://java.sun.com/xml/ns/j2ee" xmlns:xsi="h\
ttp://www.w3.org/2001/XMLSchema-instance" xsi:schemaLocation="http://java.sun.com/xml/ns/j\
2ee     http://java.sun.com/xml/ns/j2ee/web-app_2_4.xsd">
    <display-name>Ignite web session clustering example</display-name>
    <listener>
        <listener-class>org.apache.ignite.startup.servlet.ServletContextListenerStartup</l\
istener-class>
    </listener>
    <servlet>
        <servlet-name>dispatcher</servlet-name>
        <servlet-class>
                    org.springframework.web.servlet.DispatcherServlet
            </servlet-class>
        <init-param>
            <param-name>contextConfigLocation</param-name>
            <param-value>/WEB-INF/spring-servlet.xml</param-value>
        </init-param>
        <load-on-startup>1</load-on-startup>
    </servlet>
    <servlet-mapping>
        <servlet-name>dispatcher</servlet-name>
        <url-pattern>/</url-pattern>
    </servlet-mapping>
    <!-- Ignite -->
    <filter>
        <filter-name>IgniteWebSessionsFilter</filter-name>
        <filter-class>org.apache.ignite.cache.websession.WebSessionFilter</filter-class>
    </filter>
    <filter-mapping>
        <filter-name>IgniteWebSessionsFilter</filter-name>
        <url-pattern>/*</url-pattern>
    </filter-mapping>
    <!-- Ignite config from META-INF folder-->
    <context-param>
        <param-name>IgniteConfigurationFilePath</param-name>
        <param-value>spring-ignite-cache.xml</param-value>
```

```
        </context-param>
        <!-- Specify the name of Ignite cache for web sessions. -->
        <context-param>
            <param-name>IgniteWebSessionsCacheName</param-name>
            <param-value>session-cache</param-value>
        </context-param>
        <context-param>
            <param-name>IgniteWebSessionsGridName</param-name>
            <param-value>session-grid</param-value>
        </context-param>
</web-app>
```

The above configuration in *web.xml* file will map `DispatcherServlet` the URL with pattern */welcome.jsp*. One thing to note is the name of the servlet in the <servlet-name> tag in web.xml. Once the DispatcherServlet is initialized, it will look for a file name *[servlet-name]-servlet.xml* in WEB-INF folder of web application. In this example, the framework will look for a file called *spring-servlet.xml*.

We also initialized the Ignite servlet listener `ServletContextListenerStartup` into the web.xml listener section. Once the application starts, the listener will start an Ignite node within the web application, which will connect to the other nodes in the network, forming a distributed cluster. In this preceding web.xml file, there is three most import configuration parameter (context param) relies on Ignite cluster as follows:

Parameter name	Description	Value
IgniteConfigurationFilePath	The path to Ignite configuration file (relative to META_INF folder or IGNITE_HOME). Make sure that, you have already put the file in META-INF folder	spring-ignite-cache.xml
IgniteWebSessionsCacheName	Name of the Ignite cache to use for web session caching. The name should be same as the Ignite cache name in spring-ignite-cache.xml.	session-cache
IgniteWebSessionsGridName	Name of the Ignite grid to use for web session caching. The name should be same as the Ignite cache name in spring-ignite-cache.xml.	session-grid

If you got the following error during application startup,

> Failed to find Spring configuration file path provided should be either absolute, relative to IGNITE_HOME, or relative to META-INF folder.

please, recheck your configuration in the `web.xml` file twice.

Step 6:

Chapter three: In-memory caching 107

Finally, we are ready to launch our web application. Let's run the web application in two separate terminals with different ports.

```
mvn -Djetty.port=8080 jetty:run
mvn -Djetty.port=8081 jetty:run
```

The following screenshot shows it in action.

Figure 3.29

Let's open the browser and go to the following URL.

```
http://localhost:8080/test-session/putperson?name=shamim&age=38
```

This will put a user defined session in the Ignite cluster. If you open the network tab for developer view in Chrome/Firefox, you can also see the JSESSIONID of this request.

Figure 3.30

Now, check the entries in Ignite cache with *Ignitevisior*.

Chapter three: In-memory caching

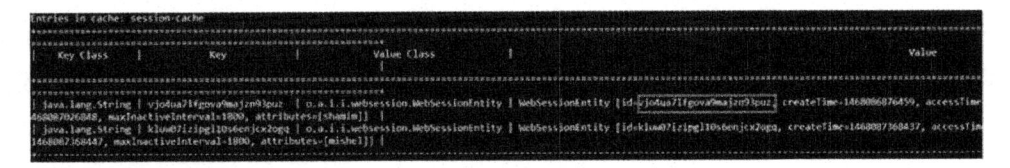

Figure 3.31

Impressing! Ignite stored the cache entity with the JSESSIONID and the value into the cache. We have two servlet container up and running, now, if we go to the next URL to get the value from the session as follows:

`http://localhost:8081/test-session/getperson?name=shamim`

It will print the Age: 38 in the web page. Note that, it's another instance of the servlet container, which doesn't hold our user session for Person Shamim. Our first web application looks for the session entries in local session, whenever it doesn't find the entries locally, it queries the Ignite cluster and gets the result from the cluster.

We can also install a Nginx load balancer to load balancing request between this two servlet container, and the result will be same. If one of the servlet containers will go down, no session data will lose.

This is the end of the current section of this chapter. Here we learned that session Clustering is used in currently most high traffic web applications. The feature offers an easy way to scale your application. Also, session clustering offers a way to handle failing server instances and provides a way for high availability of the application.

Apache Ignite as a big memory, off-heap memory

To cut a long story short, Off-heap or Heap off memory is:

- Memory outside the Java heap.
- Off-heap memory stores serialized objects.
- No overhead of GC pause.
- Unlimited storage.

During execution, objects and arrays created by the Java application get their space allocated in the Java Heap memory. For every java application, java Heap size is limited. The total amount of the heap memory for a JVM is determined by the value set to *-Xmx* parameter when starting the java application. When object allocated is released by Java application, the correspondent memory is made available for later use by the JVM GC collector.

Although modern Garbage collector such as GC1 is a low pause, regionalized and generational, the overhead of the GC pause time exists in current days. If a Java application requires large memory (in GBs), the time it takes to complete the GC process will be detrimental to its performance. If the application is performance sensitive, then large heap memory size can adversely impact its performance. So,

$$\text{Big heap} == \text{Slow GC}$$

In order to mitigate this, one can try to use memory outside Java heap and hence reduce the Java heap memory use and its size. Anyway, there are a few disadvantages of using off-heap memory:

- Objects are serialized first and stored in the off-heap memory.
- Retrieving objects are slower than retrieving objects from Java heap but much faster than disk.

Solutions:

There are a few solutions in the market from different vendors for working with off-heap memory. Most popular of them are:

- Terracotta bigMemory
- Infinispan
- Hazelcast
- Apache direct memory
- and Apache Ignite.

In this chapter, we are going to try Ignite off-heap memory feature. Also, we will study the best use cases, where it will be fit well to increase the performance of the application.

Use Cases:

There are a lot of use cases, where caching in off-heap memory is very useful and can gain the application performance.

1. Store expensive large objects - storing expensive large objects in on-heap memory is not so efficient if these objects are frequently used. This types of objects can take a huge place in the heap. In such case, storing objects in off-heap is an ideal solution.
2. Storing data dictionaries - in some cases, storing data dictionary in off-heap is less expensive than storing in the database or into the file system.
3. User activity data - for computing real user measurement, we have to store user activity data somewhere in the system. The data model of such types is not suitable for RDBMS. If you don't have any NoSQL DB in your system, an off-heap memory of Ignite cache is the idle place to store and compute user activity data.

Apache Ignite off-heap design principle is very straightforward.

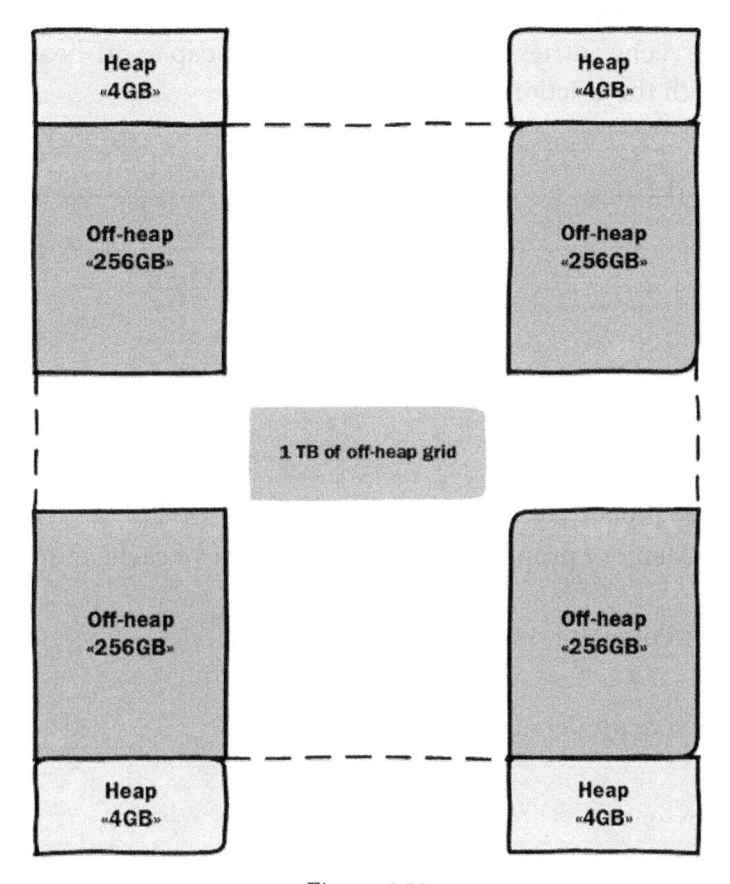

Figure 3.32

The configuration of the off-heap memory for Ignite cache is fully transparent, no programming or Java code needed to initialized the off-heap memory process. You only have to configure it in a declarative way in Spring or in Java Ignite configuration. Apache Ignite also stores query indexes of the off-heap caches in off-heap memory. Ignite provides three different types of memory model of off-heap memory storage.

Memory mode	Description
ONHEAP_TIERED	Stores cache entries in on-heap and remove the entries to off-heap. This is the default memory mode.
OFFHEAP_TIERED	Stores entries only in off-heap native memory, bypassing on-heap and optionally moving to swap.
OFFHEAP_VALUES	Stores keys into on-heap and values into off-heap memory.

Ignite cache can be configured to use any of this above memory modes by using the *memorymode* configuration property of the *cacheconfiguration*. Next, we will examine all the preceding memory modes in details.

ONHEAP_TIERED:

Chapter three: In-memory caching   111

This is the Ignite default memory mode. In this memory mode, all the cache entries are stored in JVM heap memory. Cache entries can traverse from the JVM heap to off-heap memory and later to swap storage. Note that, cache entries will traverse from on-heap to off-heap, if off-heap memory is explicitly configured with the eviction policy.

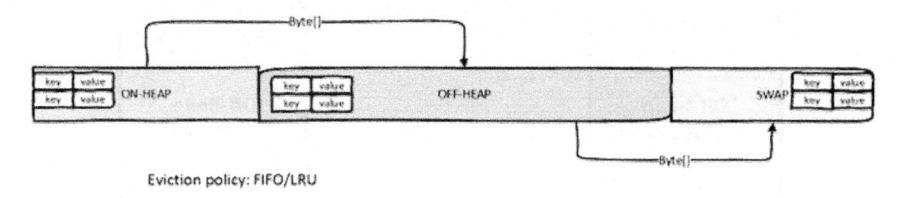

Figure 3.33

Configuration:

- Add memoryMode property of CacheConfiguration to ONHEAP-TIERED;
- Add offHeapMaxMemory properties, if you want to move cache entries from on-heap to off-heap;
- Configure evictionPolicy for on-heap memory.

Below is an example of *onheap-tiered* spring configuration.

```
<bean class="org.apache.ignite.configuration.CacheConfiguration">
    <!-- ommited -->
    <!-- Stores entries in on-heap memory -->
    <property name="memoryMode" value="ONHEAP_TIERED" />
    <!-- Enable Off-Heap memory with max size of 1 Gigabytes (0 for unlimited). -->
    <property name="offHeapMaxMemory" value="#{1 * 1024L * 1024L * 1024L}" />
    <!-- Configure eviction policy. -->
    <property name="evictionPolicy">
        <bean class="org.apache.ignite.cache.eviction.fifo.FifoEvictionPolicy">
            <!-- Evict to off-heap after cache size reaches maxSize. -->
            <property name="maxSize" value="100" />
        </bean>
    </property>
</bean>
```

Next, we are going to create a simple java console application to store cache entries and observe the cache entries into Ignite cache. You can grab the whole application from the GitHub repository[20] (chapter-caching\offheap).

---

[20] https://github.com/srecon/ignite-book-code-samples

Chapter three: In-memory caching

```
public class PutElementstoOffHeap {
    public static void main(String[] args) throws Exception{
        System.out.println("Put elements to Off Heap Memory!");
        // Start Ignite cluster
        Ignite ignite = Ignition.start("spring-onheap-tiered.xml");
        // get or create cache
        IgniteCache<Integer, String> cache =  ignite.getOrCreateCache("offheap-cache");
        for(int i = 1; i < 1000; i++){
            cache.put(i, Integer.toString(i));
        }
        Thread.sleep(Integer.MAX_VALUE);
        ignite.close();
    }
}
```

The preceding code creates a cache called off-heap-cache and enters **999** cache entries into it. Cache entry type is primitive, the key is the type of Integer, and the value is the type of String. Run the application from the root of the maven project as follows:

```
java -jar .\target\offheap-1.0-SNAPSHOT.one-jar.jar spring-onheap-tiered.xml
```

Where spring-onheap-tiered.xml is the Ignite configuration file. You can find three different spring configuration files for different memory modes. In the above preceding codes, we have entered 999 elements, where last 100 cache entries will be in on-heap and the rest of entries should be allocated to off-heap. Let's take a look at the Ignite cache with the following Ignite visor command.

cache -a

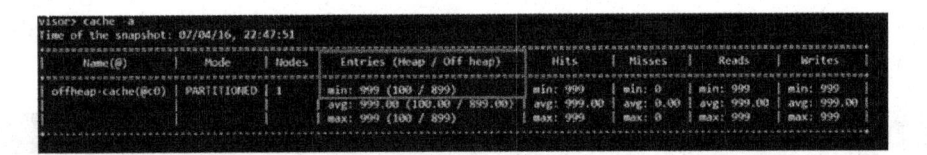

Figure 3.34

We have configured FIFO eviction policy for the cache and the result is what we expected. Thereby, we can configure the size and the eviction policy of the *off-heap memory*. If we continue entering new elements into the cache, there will **always be 100 elements** into on-heap memory and the *rest of all entries* will be into the off-heap memory until the size of cache is more than 1GB. There is another version of eviction policy LRU also available to be used instead of FIFO.

OFFHEAP_TIERED

In this approach, all the cache entries store into the native off-heap memory. Configure eviction policy is redundant here, entries store into off-heap memory by-passing the on-heap memory.

Default eviction policy will be LRU (Least Recently Used – the oldest element is the less recently used element) if eviction to swap file is enabled.

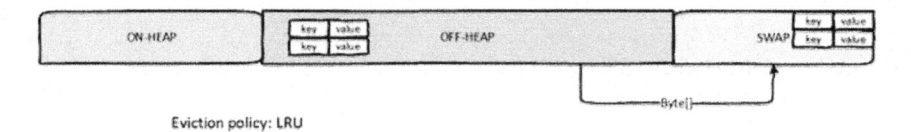

Figure 3.35

Configuration:

- Add *memoryMode* property of CacheConfiguration to ONHEAP-TIERED.
- Add *offHeapMaxMemory* properties to 0 for unlimited space – not recommended.

Offheap-tiered configuration in Spring will look like this:

```xml
<bean class="org.apache.ignite.configuration.CacheConfiguration">
    <!-- ommited -->
    <!-- Stores entries in off-heap memory -->
    <property name="memoryMode" value="OFFHEAP_TIERED" />
    <!-- Enable Off-Heap memory with max size of 1 Gigabytes (0 for unlimited). -->
    <property name="offHeapMaxMemory" value="#{1 * 1024L * 1024L * 1024L}" />
</bean>
```

Next, run our previous java application with the new **spring off-heap** configuration as follows:

```
java -jar .\target\offheap-1.0-SNAPSHOT.one-jar.jar spring-offheap-tiered.xml
```

The above application will add 1000 entries into the offheap-memory of the Ignite cache. Let's go back to *igniteivsor* command console and run the command `cache -a`, which will show the details of our off-heap cache.

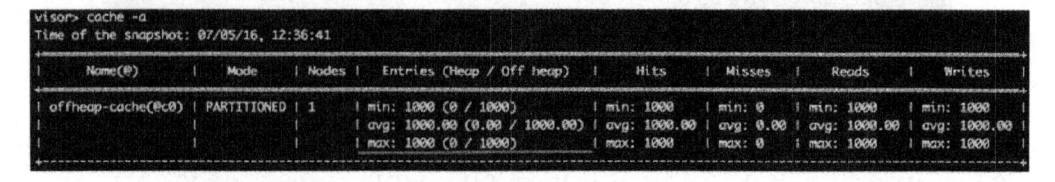

Figure 3.36

As we expected, all entries of the cache located in the off-heap memory.

OFFHEAP_VALUES

You can manually force to store keys and values into different memory mode. This memory mode provides for storing cache keys into on-heap memory and the values of the caches into the off-heap memory. This memory mode is very useful when the keys are small, and the values are large.

Chapter three: In-memory caching   114

For example, in one of our web application, we have to save a draft of a few web forms (forms, that users didn't complete), but a user can get back later and continue to work with an uncompleted web form. In such use case, we used Ignite `offheap-values` to keep all the drafts into the cache in JSON format.

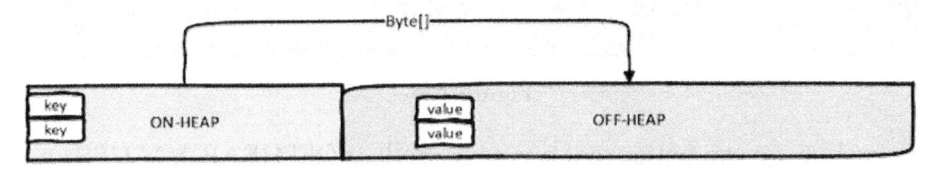

Figure 3.37

Configuration:

Very similar to the previous memory mode configuration.

- Add `memoryMode` property of CacheConfiguration to OFFHEAP-VALUES.
- Add `offHeapMaxMemory` properties, 0 for unlimited space – not recommended.
- Eviction policy is optional.

Spring configuration is also very similar to the previous memory mode with little difference.

```xml
<bean class="org.apache.ignite.configuration.CacheConfiguration">
    <!-- ommited -->
    <!-- Stores entries in off-heap memory -->
    <property name="memoryMode" value="OFFHEAP_VALUES" />
    <!-- Enable Off-Heap memory with max size of 1 Gigabytes (0 for unlimited). -->
    <property name="offHeapMaxMemory" value="#{1 * 1024L * 1024L * 1024L}" />
</bean>
```

Let's run our java application again with the following Spring configuration file:

```
java -jar .\target\offheap-1.0-SNAPSHOT.one-jar.jar spring-offheap-values.xml
```

The preceding command will run the application and enter 1000 elements into the cache, where on-heap will store only the keys of entries, and the values will be stored into the off-heap memory. Let's see the statistics of the cache with the following command in *ignitevisor.sh*

```
cache -i
```

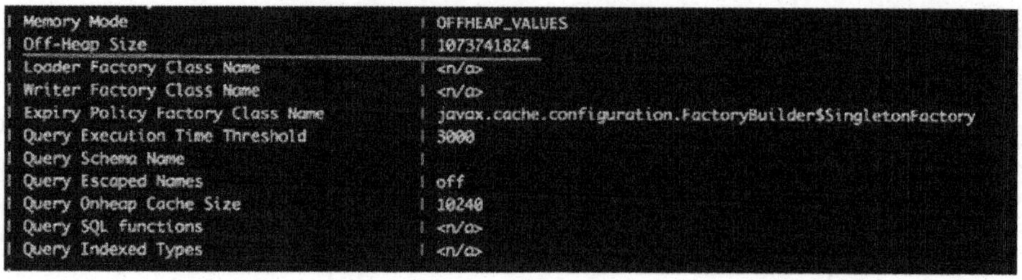

```
| Memory Mode                      | OFFHEAP_VALUES
| Off-Heap Size                    | 1073741824
| Loader Factory Class Name        | <n/a>
| Writer Factory Class Name        | <n/a>
| Expiry Policy Factory Class Name | javax.cache.configuration.FactoryBuilder$SingletonFactory
| Query Execution Time Threshold   | 3000
| Query Schema Name                |
| Query Escaped Names              | off
| Query Onheap Cache Size          | 10240
| Query SQL functions              | <n/a>
| Query Indexed Types              | <n/a>
```

Figure 3.38

In the above screenshot, we can notice that memory mode is OFFHEAP_VALUES and the maximum size of the off-heap is 1 GB.

Swap space

We highly discourage you not to use swap memory to store cache entries. Since swap files always allocated on disk, it is significantly slower than on-heap or off-heap memory.

Conclusion

We have covered a lot of ground in this chapter by examples. We have covered:

- The concept of the 2nd level cache and how to implement it with Ignite.
- Java method caching, which can improve the function execution time to 2 ms.
- Web session clustering for high availability of the application.
- Apache Ignite as an off-heap memory to store long living objects into the cache and increase the performance of the application.

What's next

In the next chapter, we will continue our study with Ignite DataGrid features such as transactions and query cache.

Chapter four: Persistence

In-memory approaches can achieve blazing speed by putting the working set of the data into the system memory. When all data is kept in memory, the need to deal with issues arising from the use of traditional spinning disks disappears. This means, for instance, there is no need to maintain additional cache copies of data and manage synchronization between them. But there is also a downside to this approach because the data is in memory only, it will not survive if the whole cluster gets terminated. Therefore, this types of data stores are not considered persistence at all.

In most cases, you can't (should not) store the whole data set in memory for your application, most often you should store relatively small hot or active subset of data to increase the performance of the application. The rest of the data should be stored somewhere in low-cost disks or tape for archiving. There are two main in-memory database storage requirements available:

- Permanent media, to store committed transactions, thereby maintaining durability and for recovery purpose if the in-memory database needs to be reloaded into the memory.
- Permanent storage, to hold a backup copy of the entire in-memory database.

Permanent storage or media can be any distributed or local file system, SAN, NoSQL database or even RDBMS like Postgres or Oracle. Apache Ignite provides an elegant way to connect persistence data stores such as RDBMS or NoSQL DB like mongo DB or Cassandra.

Another outstanding must-have feature for any enterprise class system is the transaction. Support of ACID transactions guaranty you that, once changes to a record set are made, the data is correct, and no data is lost. With the ability of transaction, the modern enterprise often needs low latency transactional system with analytical capabilities on one single system. This type of Hybrid transactional processing often called HTAP (Hybrid transactional and analytical processing). HTAP enable you to process real-time analysis of your most recent data. In HTAP, data doesn't need to move from the operational database to separated data marts to support analytics. In such system, SQL support plays a vital role. De facto SQL is a natural language for data analysis and a productive language for writing Query. In this chapter we are going to explore the following topics:

1. Persistence Ignite data grid cache.
2. Transactions in Apache Ignite.
3. Running SQL queries against Ignite caches.
4. using JPA with Apache ignite.
5. Way to update Ignite cache, eviction, and expiration policy.

Moreover, before you start, you may find out it helpful to know that:

- Each application presented in this chapter can be downloaded from the GitHub[21] repository.

---

[21] https://github.com/srecon/ignite-book-code-samples/tree/master/chapters/chapter-persistence

Chapter four: Persistence

- There is no need for you to reconstruct each application as you read unless you want to.

Persistence Ignite's cache

Before starting the chapter in details, it's important to clear the concept of word **persistence**. In the context of storing data in the computer system, this means that the data survives after the process with which it created has ended. In other words, for the data store to be considered persistence, it must write to non-volatile storage. While using an in-memory database to store data, you might consider a few things:

- Every piece of data of your system has its own life cycle. Data can be hot, active or historical. It's unnecessary to store a high volume of historical data in-memory. Storing historical data in memory will be very expensive and a waste of resources.
- In the case of any node failure, it may cause the loss of any data in that node.

Let's consider an example from the online banking system. The online banking system can store their client profile and related products information in memory as a hot subset of data. The client last 100 transactions can be considered as active pieces of data and can also be located in memory for calculating dynamic pricing or something like that. The rest of the subset of data related to the client such as client audit data and transactions older than one month can be considered as cold or historical data. A subset of cold data can ambitiously store into any non-volatile storage such as tape as shown in figure 4.1.

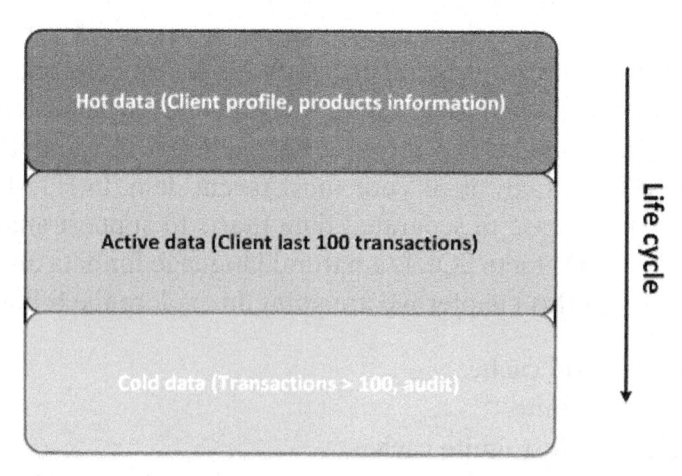

Figure 4.1

Unlike a 2nd level cache, the in-memory data store is the primary data store for an application. To support persistence data store, Apache Ignite implements the JCache interface for CacheLoader and CacheWriter, which are used for read-through and write-through to and from any underlying persistence media. In chapter two (architecture overview), we described the concept of read-through and write-through briefly. For simplicity, Ignite provides org.apache.ignite.cache.store.CacheStore interface, which extends both *CacheLoader* and *CacheWriter* interface. Apache ignite out-of-the-box supports external persistence store such as Oracle, Postgres and NoSQL databases like MongoDB or Cassandra.

> **Note:**
>
> You can implements the `org.apache.ignite.cache.store.CacheStore` interface yourself (custom) to store cache entries to any external resources such as *local file system, SAN/NAS or Hadoop HDFS*.

Moreover, Ignite CacheStore is fully transactional and automatically merges into the ongoing cache transaction.

There is a tradeoff when using the write-through approach. For every single transaction, Ignite tries to save or update the data into persistence store or on-disk database and therefore the overall duration of the cache update time might be relatively high. In this case, Ignite is same as an on-disk database.

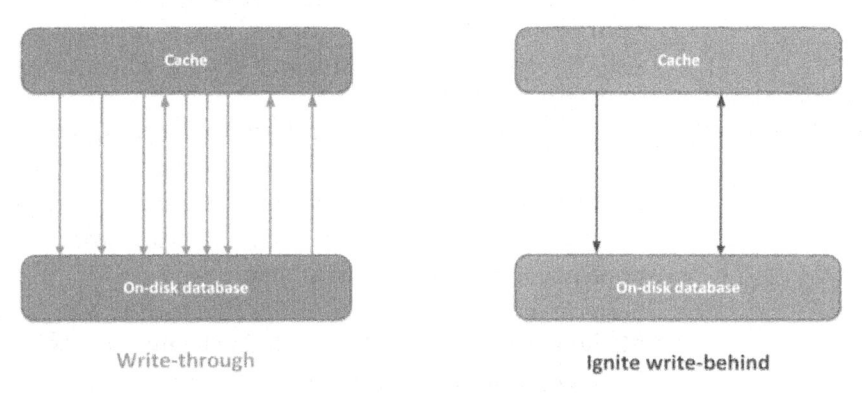

Figure 4.2

Additionally, an intensive cache update rate can cause an extremely high storage load on the on-disk database. For such cases, Ignite offers a bulk update option to update in an asynchronous way named write-behind as shown in figure 4.2. The main idea behind this approach is to aggregate updates and asynchronously flush it into the persistence store. Ignite write-behind implementation is very similar to JCache entry processor which we described in chapter two. Ignite can flush the aggregated data with different criteria:

- **Time-based events**: the maximum time that data entry can reside in the queue
- **Queue-size events**: the queue is flushed when it's size reaches some particular point
- Both of them in combination.

Chapter four: Persistence

> **Note:**
> With the write-behind approach, only the last update of an entry will be written to the underlying storage. If the cache entry with key key1 is sequentially updated with values value1, value2, and value3 respectively, then only a single store request for (key1, value3) pair will be propagated to the persistent storage.

In addition to JCache cache storing and loading method, Ignite `CacheStore` interface provides the ability to bulk store and load caches from the persistence store. Also, Ignite offers cache storage convenience adapter named `CacheStoreAdapter` which implements the CacheStore, interface and provides a default implementation for bulk operations. Abstract class *CacheStoreAdapter* has the following methods, which you have to implement for working with persistence store:

Method names	Descriptions
load(), write(), delete()	Methods inherited from interfaces JCache.CacheLoader and JCache.CacheWrite which allows you to put, get or delete cache entries from the persistence store. These methods are used to enable *read-through* and *write-through* behavior when working with individual cache,entries.
loadAll(), writeAll(), deleteAll()	Methods inherited from the interfaces JCache.CacheLoader and JCache.CacheWriter allows you to perform bulk operations. These methods are used to enable write-through and read-through behavior when working with multiple cache entries. These methods should be implemented for batch operation on persistence store to get better performance.
loadCache()	Method inherited from the Ignite.CacheStore interface and used to loads all values from underlying persistence storage. It is generally used for hot-loading the cache on startup but can also be called at any point after the cache has been started.
sessionEnd()	An optional method which provides default empty implementation for ending transactions. Ignite uses this method to store session which may span through more than one cache store operation. This method is useful when working with transaction.

Class `CacheConfiguration` defines Ignite grid cache configuration and offers a set of methods to enable write/read-through and write-behind caching.

Methods	Descriptions	default
setCacheStoreFactory()	Set factory for persistence storage. Cache store factory should be implementation of the CacheStoreAdapter abstract class.	
setReadThrough(boolean)	Enables the read-through persistence approach.	False
setWriteThrough(boolean)	Enables the write-through persistence approach.	False
setWriteBehindEnabled(boolean)	Enables the write-behind persistence approach.	False
setWriteBehindFlushSize(int)	The maximum size of the write-behind cache. If cache size exceeds this value, all cached items are flushed to the cache store and write cache is cleared. If this value is 0, then flush is performed according to the flush frequency interval. Note that you cannot set both flush size and flush frequency to 0.	10240
setWriteBehindFlushFrequency(long)	The frequency with which write-behind cache is flushed to the cache store in milliseconds. This value defines the maximum time interval between object insertion/deletion from the cache and the moment when corresponding operation is applied to the cache store. If this value is 0, then flush is performed according to the flush size. Note that, you cannot set both flush size and flush frequency to 0.	5 seconds
setWriteBehindFlushThreadCount(int)	The number of threads that will perform cache flushing.	1
setWriteBehindBatchSize(int)	The maximum batch size for write-behind cache store operations.	512

This is the end of the theoretical part of persistence approach for Apache Ignite. In the next few subsection, we will explore how to store cache entries into Postgres database and MongoDB.

Persistence in RDBMS (PostgreSQL)

So far, we have introduced you why to use persistence store and explored a few basics for quick starts. In this section, we are going to store Apache Ignite cache entries into the relational database such as PostgreSQL. As we mentioned before, you can use any RDBMS such as Oracle, MySQL or even Teradata to store Ignite cache entries; the persistence process is identical for all RDBMS.

Chapter four: Persistence   121

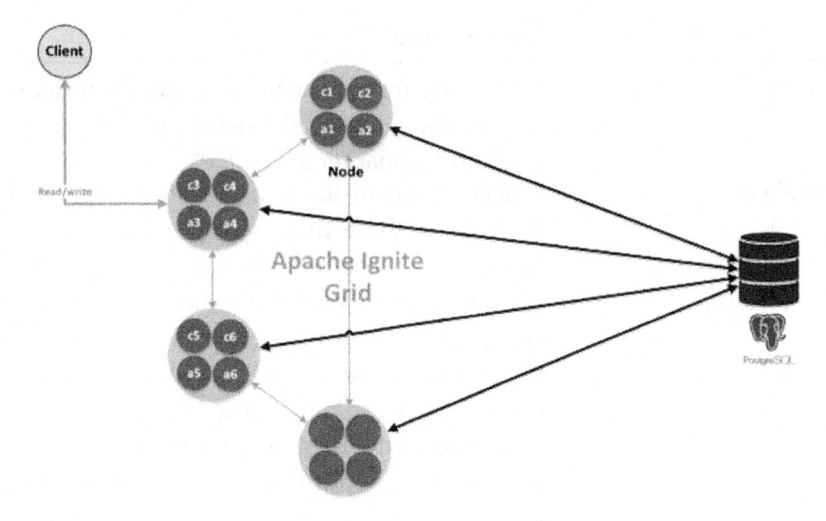

Figure 4.3

In our case, persistence store will be PostgreSQL[22], an open source very popular enterprise class RDBMS.

In this section we are going to populate the following sceneries:

- Write-through: write cache entries into PostgreSQL.
- Read-through: read from the persistence store, when cache entries are not found in the cache.
- Write-behind: aggregate the updates into a single operation to update the stores.

To accomplished the above sceneries, we have to fulfill a few prerequisites:

1. Install and configure the PostgreSQL server.
2. Create a new schema or use the default (public).
3. Create tables according to the cache entries.

There a few different versions and distributions offers from the PostgreSQL. You can download PostgreSQL distribution from the PostgreSQL download page by yours choose. In our case, I am going to use Postgres.app[23]: a simple, native Mac OS app without any installation of PostgreSQL server. The full table of the pre-requires are as follows:

N	Name	Value
1	PostgreSQL	9.6.1.0
2	Java	1.8
3	Dbeaver	3.6.7
4	Apache Ignite	1.6
5	A favorite IDE or text editor	

---

[22] https://www.postgresql.org/download/macosx
[23] http://postgresapp.com/

Chapter four: Persistence

If you didn't skip chapter one, you're probably familiar with the Dbeaver. Instead of Dbeaver, you can use any of your favorite SQL clients. In my daily life, I use Dbeaver, because, it's all-in-one tools to work with a wide range of Databases such as Cassandra, MongoDB, Hive, and RDBMS. The full source of the current section you can download from the GitHub[24] repositories. To start from the scratch, do the following:

Step 1:

Create the table posts into the PostgreSQL public schema as follows:

```
DROP TABLE IF EXISTS POSTS;
CREATE TABLE POSTS (
    id           VARCHAR(150),
    title        VARCHAR(255),
    description  TEXT,
    creationDate DATE,
    author       VARCHAR(150)
);
DROP INDEX IF EXISTS posts_id_uindex;
CREATE UNIQUE INDEX posts_id_uindex ON POSTS (id);
ALTER TABLE POSTS
    ADD CONSTRAINT posts_id_pk PRIMARY KEY (id);
ALTER TABLE POSTS
    ALTER COLUMN id SET NOT NULL;
```

The structure of the table POSTS is very simple, mostly used by the twitter domain model. The table contains unique ID of the post, name of the title, author of the post and the post creation date. Column ID is the primary key of the table. The structure of the table should be as follows as figure 4.4.

#	Column Name	Data type	Length	Precision	Scale	Not Null	Default	Description
1	id	varchar	150	150		✓		
2	title	varchar	255	255		☐		
3	description	text				☐		
4	creationdate	date		13		☐		
5	author	varchar	150	150		☐		

Figure 4.4

You can download the ddl script from this url[25].

Step 2:

Configure the JDBC URL for the PostgreSQL server in the file jdbc.properties. jdbc.properties file also located in the same directory with the file create-db-schema.ddl in directory resources.

---

[24] https://github.com/srecon/ignite-book-code-samples/tree/master/chapters/chapter-persistence/persistence-store

[25] https://github.com/srecon/ignite-book-code-samples/blob/master/chapters/chapter-persistence/persistence-store/src/main/resources/create-db-scheme.ddl

Chapter four: Persistence

```
jdbc.driver=org.postgresql.Driver
jdbc.url=jdbc:postgresql://localhost:5432/postgres
jdbc.username=postgres
jdbc.password=postgres
```

Change JDBC URL and the username/password properties of the above file.

Step 3:

Specify the following maven dependencies in the maven project.

```xml
<dependency>
    <groupId>org.apache.ignite</groupId>
    <artifactId>ignite-core</artifactId>
    <version>1.6</version>
</dependency>
<dependency>
    <groupId>org.apache.ignite</groupId>
    <artifactId>ignite-spring</artifactId>
    <version>1.6</version>
</dependency>
<dependency>
    <groupId>org.postgresql</groupId>
    <artifactId>postgresql</artifactId>
    <version>9.4.1209</version>
</dependency>
```

Step 4:

Let's create the DTO for the table posts. Class com.blu.imdg.jdbc.model.Post will map the row for the table Posts. Class **Post** will have the following properties:

```java
public class Post implements Serializable {
    private static final long serialVersionUID = 0L;

    private String id;
    private String title;
    private String description;
    private LocalDate creationDate;
    private String author;
// rest of the setter and getter are omitted
}
```

Step 5:

Here, we are going to create a simple implementation of Ignite CacheStore. The class com.blu.imdg.jdbc.Postgres extends the Ignite abstract class CacheStoreAdapter and also implements the interface LifecycleAware. If a component implements the interface LifecycleAware, then method start will be called during node startup. We are also using Spring JdbcTemplate to simplify the PostgreSQL native JDBC call.

```java
public class PostgresDBStore extends CacheStoreAdapter<String, Post> implements LifecycleA\
ware {
    @Autowired
    private NamedParameterJdbcTemplate jdbcTemplate;

    @Override
    public Post load(String key) throws CacheLoaderException {
        Map<String, Object> inputParam = new HashMap<>();
        inputParam.put("id", key);
        return jdbcTemplate.queryForObject("SELECT * FROM POSTS WHERE id=?", inputParam, n\
ew RowMapper<Post>() {
            @Override
            public Post mapRow(ResultSet rs, int i) throws SQLException {
                return new Post(rs.getString(1), rs.getString(2), rs.getString(3), rs.getD\
ate(4).toLocalDate(), rs.getString(5));
            }
        });

    }

    @Override
    public void write(Cache.Entry<? extends String, ? extends Post> entry) throws CacheWri\
terException {
        com.blu.imdg.jdbc.model.Post post = entry.getValue();
        Map<String, Object> parameterMap = new HashMap<>();
        parameterMap.put("ID", post.getId());
        parameterMap.put("TITLE", post.getTitle());
        parameterMap.put("DESCRIPTION", post.getDescription());
        parameterMap.put("CREATIONDATE", post.getCreationDate());
        parameterMap.put("AUTHOR", post.getAuthor());
        jdbcTemplate.update("INSERT INTO POSTS(ID,TITLE,DESCRIPTION,CREATIONDATE,AUTHOR) V\
ALUES (:ID,:TITLE,:DESCRIPTION,:CREATIONDATE,:AUTHOR);", parameterMap);

    }

    @Override
    public void delete(Object key) throws CacheWriterException {
        Map<String, String> deleteMap = new HashMap<>();
        deleteMap.put("ID", (String) key);
```

Chapter four: Persistence

```
            jdbcTemplate.update("DELETE FROM POSTS WHERE ID= ?", deleteMap);

    }

    @Override
    public void start() throws IgniteException {
        ConfigurableApplicationContext context = new ClassPathXmlApplicationContext("postg\
res-context.xml");
        jdbcTemplate = context.getBean(NamedParameterJdbcTemplate.class);
    }

    @Override
    public void stop() throws IgniteException {

    }
}
```

The `PostgresDBStore` is concise and simple, but there's plenty going on. Let's break it down step by step.

The `load()` method queries the table **Posts** by the id (post) and loads the entries into the cache if found. The method `write()` is intended to store entries into table posts. This method gets the instance of the DTO **post** as an input parameter and inserts the post data into the table posts. In the method `delete()`, we delete the entry from the table by the key. The method start() will be invoked when the node starts for the first time. In the `start()` method, we initialize the spring context from the classpath and get the `JdbcTemplete` from the spring context.

Step 6:

To store and load the data to and from the PostgreSQL, we configure the Ignite cacheConfiguration in a programmatic fashion. Another way is to use Spring XML configuration to configure the Ignite cacheConfiguration. We provide a `com.blu.imdg.CacheStoreSample` example to store and load the entries from the cache. The given class is used for the PostgreSQL and for MongoDB also. For now, we will explore the Postgres part of this class. Let's take a closer look at the cache configuration for the PostgreSQL as follows.

```
IgniteConfiguration cfg = new IgniteConfiguration();

CacheConfiguration configuration = new CacheConfiguration();
configuration.setName("dynamicCache");
configuration.setAtomicityMode(CacheAtomicityMode.TRANSACTIONAL);

configuration.setCacheStoreFactory(FactoryBuilder.factoryOf(PostgresDBStore.class));
configuration.setReadThrough(true);
configuration.setWriteThrough(true);
```

```
configuration.setWriteBehindEnabled(true);
cfg.setCacheConfiguration(configuration);
```

First, we create the Ignite CacheConfiguration instance and set the cache name to dynamicCache. Set the atomicity mode to transactional. We will explore the transaction in the next section. Next, we set our PostgresDBStore as the caching factory and enable the Readthrough and WriteThrough features.

Step 7:

Now that, we have our project done, we can compile and run the application. Compile the project with the following maven command.

```
mvn clean install
```

The above command will compile and creates an executable jar to run the application.

Step 8:

Start the application from the command line. Go to the folder **persistence-store** and run the command below.

```
java -jar ./target/cache-store-runnable.jar postgresql
```

The above command will run the application and add 10 new unique posts into the Ignite cache. Cache entries will also be stored into the table Posts. Let's take a look at the console log.

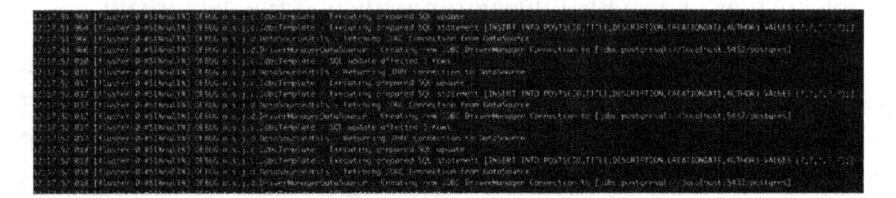

Figure 4.5

Ignite CacheStore factory executes the SQL statements to store the entries into the table. With ignitevisior command line tools you can also look for the cache entries into the cache dynamicCache.

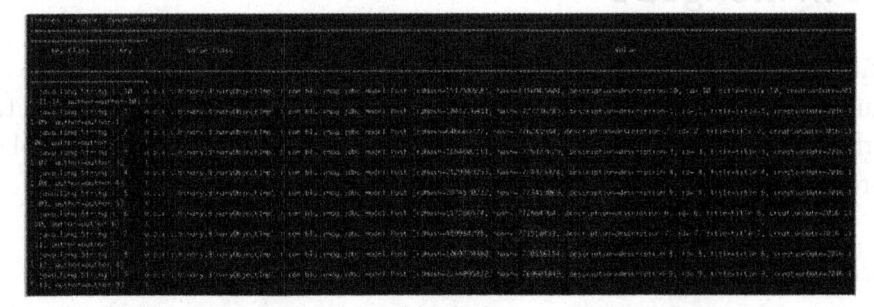

Figure 4.6

Let's query the table Posts by executing the following SQL query.

```
Select * from the posts;
```

The above SQL statement should return you the following figure.

id	title	description	creationdate	author
_1	title-1	description-1	2016-11-05	author-1
_3	title-3	description-3	2016-11-07	author-3
_5	title-5	description-5	2016-11-09	author-5
_6	title-6	description-6	2016-11-10	author-6
_8	title-8	description-8	2016-11-12	author-8
_2	title-2	description-2	2016-11-06	author-2
_4	title-4	description-4	2016-11-08	author-4
_7	title-7	description-7	2016-11-11	author-7
_9	title-9	description-9	2016-11-13	author-9
_10	title-10	description-10	2016-11-14	author-10

Figure 4.7

This is the very primitive way to store the entries into database tables. One thing I have to mention is that every entry from the each Ignite node will write to the database table. If any entry already exists in the table, it will be updated or escaped (depends on the configuration). With high density, write into the Ignite cache can create a serious load on the database. To overcome the situation, you should carefully configure the JDBC **connection pool** of the database. There is one drawback of using RDBMS as a persistence store: RDBMS are hard to scale out. However, you can use scalable PostgreSQL-XL[26] to overcome the problem. Using RDBMS also gives some advantages: you can use any existing BI tools such as Oracle BI, Tableau for analyzing the data easily.

To remove the complexity of creating database tables and maps with Java DTO, Apache Ignite offers database schema mapping wizard application, which provides automatic support for integrating with persistence store. This wizard automatically connects to the underlying database and creates all the required XML OR-mapping configuration and Java domain model POJOs. Apache Ignite documentation[27] briefly describe the entire process, so we have decided not to cover those topics in this book.

Persistence in MongoDB

The main benefit of using NoSQL or MongoDB as a persistence store is that they are very suitable for scaling out. By using MongoDB, you can store the cold or historical data directly to the presentation tier as JSON without any conversion of data. The persistence approach with MongoDB is very much similar to the previous section.

---

[26] http://www.postgres-xl.org/
[27] https://apacheignite.readme.io/docs/automatic-persistence

Chapter four: Persistence   128

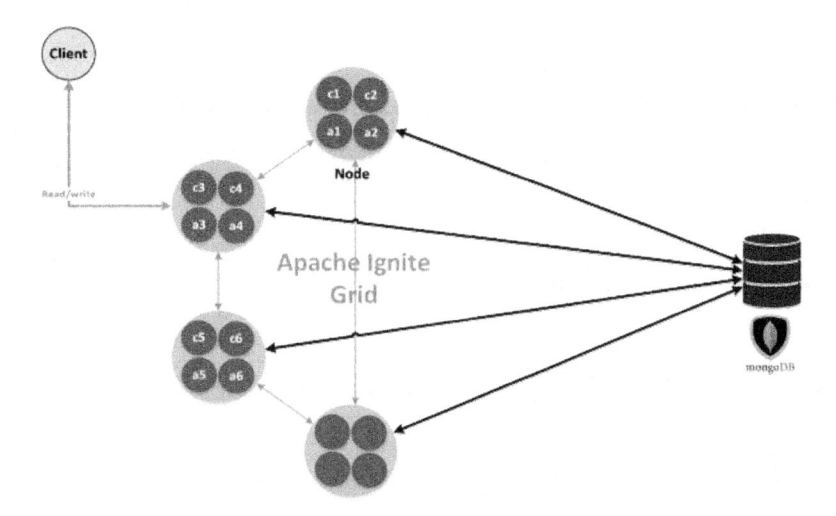

Figure 4.8

Figure 4.8 shows a conceptual architecture of using MongoDB as a persistence store. A few words about MongoDB: MongoDB is an open source schemaless database. MongoDB is a document-oriented database and stores all the data in BSON or binary JSON format. This gives MongoDB the flexibility to access his functionalities through javascript, making the integration of data in certain types easier and faster. MongoDB also supports data **sharding** through the configuration of shared cluster; it means you can scale MongoDB vertically and horizontally seamlessly. Typically, MongoDB is used for real-time analytics, where latency is low, and availability is very high.

The complete example of using MongoDB as a persistence store can be downloaded from the GitHub[28] repository.

What we are going to use here shown in the next table.

N	Name	Value
1	MongoDB	3.2.10
2	Java	1.8
3	Dbeaver	3.6.7
4	Apache Ignite	1.6
5	spring-data-mongodb library	1.9.2.RELEASE
6	A favorite IDE or text editor	

To accomplished the persistence of cache entries in MongoDB, we are going install the MongoDB first and prepare the maven project. If you already have installed and configured the MongoDB database in your system, you can skip the first step and continue from the step 4.

Step 1:

Download the MongoDB distribution from here[29]. I am going to using community edition and downloaded the distribution for the MacOS.

---
[28] https://github.com/srecon/ignite-book-code-samples/tree/master/chapters/chapter-persistence/persistence-store
[29] https://www.mongodb.com/download-center?jmp=nav#community

Chapter four: Persistence

Step 2:

Unarchive the distribution somewhere in your operating system as follows.

```
tar -xvf mongodb-osx-ssl-x86_64-3.2.10.tgz
```

Create folder /data/db in your local file system.

Step 3:

Run the MongoDB server with the following command into your favorite command console.

```
./mongod --dbpath PATH_TO _YOUR_DATA/DB_FOLDER
```

If everything goes fine, you should see the following output into the console.

Figure 4.9

MongoDB has been started and running on port 27017.

Step 4:

Create a maven project or modify the downloaded project from the GitHub and add all the dependencies in pom.xml file as shown below.

```xml
<dependency>
    <groupId>org.apache.ignite</groupId>
    <artifactId>ignite-core</artifactId>
    <version>1.6</version>
</dependency>
<dependency>
    <groupId>org.apache.ignite</groupId>
    <artifactId>ignite-spring</artifactId>
    <version>1.6</version>
</dependency>
<dependency>
    <groupId>org.springframework.data</groupId>
    <artifactId>spring-data-mongodb</artifactId>
    <version>1.9.2.RELEASE</version>
```

```xml
</dependency>
<dependency>
    <groupId>org.springframework.data</groupId>
    <artifactId>spring-data-jpa</artifactId>
    <version>1.10.3.RELEASE</version>
</dependency>
<dependency>
    <groupId>org.springframework</groupId>
    <artifactId>spring-tx</artifactId>
    <version>4.3.2.RELEASE</version>
</dependency>
```

Step 5:

We are using the same data model (Post) from the previous example. In JSON format, the data model will appear as follows.

```
{
    _id:"_1",
    _class:"com.blu.imdg.nosql.model.MongoPost",
    title:"title-1",
    description:"description-1",
    creationDate:"Sat Nov 05 00:00:00 MSK 2016",
    author:"author-1"
}
```

Let's create the `com.blu.imdg.nosql.model.MongoPost` class corresponding the data model in MongoDB.

```java
public class MongoPost {
    @Id
    private String id;
    private String title;
    private String description;
    private LocalDate creationDate;
    private String author;
    // setter and getter methods are omitted
}
```

Step 6:

We are going to use the `spring-data-MongoDB` library from spring framework for working with MongoDB. The given library is a façade and makes your life easier to work with MongoDB. We also made a spring context file to configure the MongoDB factory.

Chapter four: Persistence

```xml
<?xml version="1.0" encoding="UTF-8"?>
<beans xmlns="http://www.springframework.org/schema/beans"
       xmlns:xsi="http://www.w3.org/2001/XMLSchema-instance"
       xmlns:mongo="http://www.springframework.org/schema/data/mongo"
       xmlns:context="http://www.springframework.org/schema/context"
       xsi:schemaLocation="http://www.springframework.org/schema/data/mongo http://www.spr\
ingframework.org/schema/data/mongo/spring-mongo.xsd
            http://www.springframework.org/schema/beans http://www.springframework.org/schema/beans\
spring-beans.xsd http://www.springframework.org/schema/context http://www.springframework.\
org/schema/context/spring-context.xsd">

    <context:annotation-config/>

    <mongo:mongo id="mongo" host="localhost" port="27017"/>

    <mongo:db-factory id="mongoDbFactory" dbname="test" mongo-ref="mongo" />

    <mongo:repositories base-package="com.blu.imdg.nosql" mongo-template-ref="mongoTemplat\
e"/>
    <bean id="mongoTemplate" class="org.springframework.data.mongodb.core.MongoTemplate">
        <constructor-arg ref="mongoDbFactory" />
    </bean>
    <bean class="org.springframework.dao.annotation.PersistenceExceptionTranslationPostPro\
cessor"/>

</beans>
```

Let's a closer look at the above spring context file. The above XML file instructs the Spring to do following:

1. Specified the MongoDB `host` and `port`. You have to change the configuration if you have another host name or port.
2. Set the MongoDB factory database name to `test`.
3. Convert the MongoPost DTO to mongo `Bson`.
4. Set the MongoDB template to factory.

Step 7:

Now that we have our DTO, spring application context in place. It's time to implement the Ignite CacheStore. Create a new Java class named `MongoDBStore`, which will extend the Ignite CacheStoreAdapter and implements the LifecycleAware interface.

Chapter four: Persistence   132

```java
public class MongoDBStore extends CacheStoreAdapter<String, MongoPost> implements Lifecycl\
eAware {

    @Autowired
    private PostRepository postRepository;
    @Autowired
    private MongoOperations mongoOperations;

    private static Logger logger = LoggerFactory.getLogger(MongoDBStore.class);

    @Override public MongoPost load(String key) throws CacheLoaderException {

        logger.info(String.valueOf(postRepository));
        return postRepository.findOne(key);
    }

    @Override public void write(Cache.Entry<? extends String, ? extends MongoPost> entry) \
throws CacheWriterException {
        MongoPost post = entry.getValue();
        logger.info(String.valueOf(postRepository));
        postRepository.save(post);
    }

    @Override public void delete(Object key) throws CacheWriterException {
        logger.info(String.valueOf(postRepository));
        postRepository.delete((String)key);
    }

    @Override public void start() throws IgniteException {
        ConfigurableApplicationContext context = new ClassPathXmlApplicationContext("mongo\
-context.xml");
        postRepository = context.getBean(PostRepository.class);
        logger.info(String.valueOf(postRepository));
        mongoOperations = context.getBean(MongoOperations.class);
        if (!mongoOperations.collectionExists(MongoPost.class))
            mongoOperations.createCollection(MongoPost.class);

    }

    @Override public void stop() throws IgniteException {}
}
```

Here, we implements and override the three CacheStore methods: load(), write() and delete(). In load() method, we look for the documents in MongoDB by the given key and return the MongoPost instance. Write() method saves the single cache entry into the MongoDB test database. Delete()

Chapter four: Persistence

method deletes the bson documents from the MongoDB by the given key.

Step 8:

To store and load the data to and from the MongoDB database, we configure the Ignite `cacheConfiguration` in a programmatic fashion. We provide a `com.blu.imdg.CacheStoreSample` class to store and load the entries from the cache. Let's take a closer look at the cache configuration for the MongoDB as follows.

```
IgniteConfiguration cfg = new IgniteConfiguration();

CacheConfiguration configuration = new CacheConfiguration();
configuration.setName("mongoDynamicCache");
configuration.setAtomicityMode(CacheAtomicityMode.TRANSACTIONAL);

configuration.setCacheStoreFactory(FactoryBuilder.factoryOf(MongoDBStore.class));
configuration.setReadThrough(true);
configuration.setWriteThrough(true);

configuration.setWriteBehindEnabled(true);
cfg.setCacheConfiguration(configuration);
```

First, we create the Ignite CacheConfiguration instance and set the cache name to mongoDynamic-Cache. Set the atomicity mode to transactional. We will explorer the transaction in the next section. Next we set our `MongoDBStore` as the caching factory and enable the Readthrough and WriteThrough features.

Step 9:

Let's compile the project through maven and run the application to store some entries into MongoDB from the Ignite cache.

```
mvn clean install
```

Run the application with the following command.

```
java -jar ./target/cache-store-runnable.jar mongodb
```

The application will produce a lot of logs into the console as shown bellows.

Chapter four: Persistence   134

Figure 4.10

Now, if we connect to the MongoDB test database with the Dbeaver, we should see the following output.

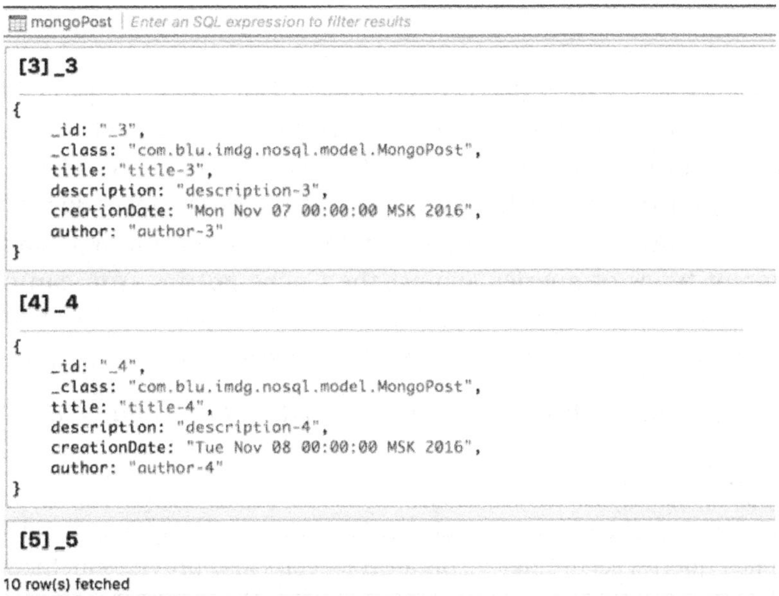

Figure 4.11

The above screen shot shows that 10 documents have been stored in the MongoDB database. We can also share documents by author or blog post creation time. You can modify or extends the project to your use case to store cache entries in the MongoDB database. In the next section, we will explore cache queries and runs a few example to see how it works in Ignite.

Cache queries

Apache Ignite provides a powerful Query API which supports Predicate-base Scan Queries, ANSI-99 compliant SQL queries, Text search queries and Continuous queries.

Suppose your cache contains Company objects as follows:

Chapter four: Persistence

```
public class Company {
    private Long id;
    private String companyName;
    private String email;
    private String address;
    private String city;
    private String state;
    private String zipCode;
    private String phoneNumber;
    private String faxNumber;
    private String webAddress;
}
```

Cache with the entries company will be partitioned and spread across the Ignite Data grid. Definitely, you can iterate over the Cache entries and look for certain entries that you are interested in as we have done in Chapter one. But iterating over the whole cache is not very efficient because you will have to fetch the entire entry set and iterate locally. If the entry set is large, it will increase the network traffic. On the contrary, Apache Ignite provides a programming interface, which allows you to execute different types of queries against the Cache entries. You can choose API by your application requirements, for instance, if you want to execute text search of the companies which address is similar to *BLEECKER ST APT 51*, Ignite *Text queries* is the best choice for you.

Apache Ignite delivers two main abstractions of Query API: *Query* and *QueryCursor* interface.

Name	Description
Query	Base class for all Ignite cache queries. You have to use SqlQuery and TextQuery for SQL and text queries accordingly. This abstract class also provides methods such as *setLocal()* and *setPageSize()* to executes queries in local node and set the page size for the returned cursor.
QueryCursor	Interface, which represents the query result with page-by-page iteration. When pagination is not needed, you can use *QueryCursor.getAll()* method which will fetch the whole query result and store it in a collection. Note that, you must close the cursor explicitly, whenever iterating over the cursor in a for loop or explicitly getting Iterator.

> **Note:**
> QueryCursor interface is not thread safe, you should use it from single thread only.

Scan queries

Ignite `Scan queries` allow you to run distributed queries over cache entries. If no predicate is specified, queries return all the entries of the cache. You can define any predicate based on objects stored in the cache.

> **Note:**
> A predicate is a specialized expression, which always returns a Boolean type.

The query will apply the predicates to all of the entries to find matches. For demonstrating the power of the scan queries, we are going to use the following data set.

ID	CAT	COMPANY_NAME	EMAIL	ADDRESS	CITY	STATE	ZIPCODE	PHONE_NUMBER	FAX_NUMBER
230001	M	Medical-ID.com	bcourt@aol.com	115 Cooper Dr	VAILS GATE	NY	12584	null	null
230002	W	WEINBERG; KEITH	keith@groupdigital.com	272 BLEECKER ST APT 51	NEW YORK	NY	10013	null	null
230003	M	Maccio Physical Therapy	Maccio@macciophysicaltherapy.com	1 New Hampshire Ave	Troy	NY	12180-1754	5182730701	5182732121
230004	P	Prudential Douglas Elliman Re	thomas.uhlinger@prudentialelliman.com	10200 Main Rd / Po Box 1410	Mattituck	NY	11952	63129880000	-
230005	F	Fragomen Del Rey Bernsen & Low	sanfranciscoinfo@fragomen.com	515 Madison Ave # 15	New York	NY	10022-5493	9494400119	2126888555

Figure 4.12

where,

- ID: Serial Number
- CAT: CAT (Company Name starting letter)
- COMPANY_NAME: Name of the company
- EMAIL: email used by company or individuals
- ADDRESS: Street address or area
- CITY: City name
- STATE: State Name
- ZIPCODE: Zipcode details
- PHONE_NUMBER: Phone number used by company or individuals
- FAX_NUMBER: Fax number used by company or individuals

The dataset contains all the companies contact information located in the state of New York. We downloaded the above resource from the Internet. We are going to load the entries from the CSV file into the cache and apply some predicate to scan query over the cache entries. You can download the full source code from the GitHub repository[30] (chapter persistence/text query).

---
[30] https://github.com/srecon/ignite-book-code-samples/tree/master/chapters/chapter-persistence/textquery

Chapter four: Persistence

Step 1:

Create a new Maven project with the following dependencies.

```xml
<dependency>
    <groupId>org.apache.ignite</groupId>
    <artifactId>ignite-core</artifactId>
    <version>1.6.0</version>
</dependency>
<dependency>
    <groupId>org.apache.ignite</groupId>
    <artifactId>ignite-spring</artifactId>
    <version>1.6.0</version>
</dependency>
```

Step 2:

First of all, create a new Java class *com.blu.imdg.model.Company* in the `src\main\java\com\blu\imdg\model` directory which will represent the dataset.

```java
public class Company implements Serializable {

    private Long id;
    private String cat;
    private String companyName;
    private String email;
    private String address;
    private String city;
    private String state;
    private String zipCode;
    private String phoneNumber;
    private String faxNumber;
    // setter and getter are omitted
}
```

Note that, the above Java class is a plain old Java class without any annotations.

Step 3:

Now, you can create another Java class and add a method to load the data from the CSV file into the Ignite cache. Create a new Java class named `com.blu.imdg.scanQueryExample` in the directory `/src/main/java/com/blu/imdg`. Add a method named initialized() and use the following contents:

Chapter four: Persistence

```
private static void initialize() throws InterruptedException, IOException {
    IgniteCache<Long, Company> companyCache = Ignition.ignite().getOrCreateCache (COMPANY_\
CACHE_NAME);
    // Clear caches before start.
    companyCache.clear();
    // Companies
    try (
            Stream<String> lines = Files.lines(Paths.get(TextQueryExample.class.getClassLo\
ader().getResource("USA_NY_email_addresses.csv").toURI()));
    ) {
        lines
                .skip(1)
                .map(s1 -> s1.split("\",\""))
                .map(s2 -> new Company(Long.valueOf(s2[0].replaceAll("\"", "")), s2[1], s2\
[2], s2[3], s2[4], s2[5], s2[6], s2[7], s2[8], s2[9], s2[10], s2[11], s2[12].replaceAll("\\
"", "")))
                .forEach(r -> companyCache.put(r.getId(), r));
    } catch (URISyntaxException | IOException e) {
        log(e.getMessage());
    }
    // Wait 1 second to be sure that all nodes processed put requests.
    Thread.sleep(1000);
}
```

Take a moment to read through the code to understand how this works. Actually, the code is very straight forward. First, we create an Ignite cache with name companyCache, which will store all the entries of the company. Then we use Java 8 Stream API to read and gets the content of the file *USA_NY_email_addresses.csv* as a stream. Next, we skip the CSV file first line, split every row by ',' and creates new Company objects to store into the Ignite cache. The last line of the above code forces the application to wait for a second to be sure that all nodes of the cluster processed the put requests.

Step 4:

Let's apply the Ignite *Scan queries* to the cache. Add a new Java method named scanQuery() in the class **scanQueryExample** as follows:

Chapter four: Persistence

```java
private static void scanQuery() {
    IgniteCache<Long, Company> companyCache = Ignition.ignite().cache(COMPANY_CACHE_NA\
ME);

        // Query for all companies which the city 'NEW YORK' - State NewYork.
        QueryCursor cursor = companyCache.query(new ScanQuery<Long, Company>((k, p) -> p.g\
etCity().equalsIgnoreCase("NEW YORK")));

        for(Iterator ite = cursor.iterator(); ite.hasNext();)
        {
            CacheEntryImpl company = (CacheEntryImpl) ite.next();

            log(((Company)company.getValue()).getCompanyName());
        }
        cursor.close();
}
```

In the above pseudo code, we first get the Ignite cache for the *company* and create a new ScanQuery with the Java 8 lambda expression. We also pass the following predicates expression:

```
p.getCity().equalsIgnoreCase("NEW YORK")
```

Where we are looking for the company objects which city name equals to NEW YORK. Ignite will apply the above predicates to all of the cache entries and return QueryCursor of that cache entry, which city name equals to NEW YORK. Next, we simply iterate through the query cursor and print the *company name* on the console.

> **Note:**
> After processing the cursor, we explicitly close the cursor by invoking the method **cursor.close()**.

Step 5:

To compile and execute the application, run:

```
mvn clean install && java -jar target/textquery-runnable.jar scanquery
```

You should see a lot of output like this.

```
09:21:33.241 [main] INFO  c.b.i.TextQueryExample - Yes Network
09:21:33.242 [main] INFO  c.b.i.TextQueryExample - Launch Photography
09:21:33.242 [main] INFO  c.b.i.TextQueryExample - ekstra design inc
09:21:33.242 [main] INFO  c.b.i.TextQueryExample - New York Times
09:21:33.242 [main] INFO  c.b.i.TextQueryExample - Lewis Brisbois
09:21:33.242 [main] INFO  c.b.i.TextQueryExample - CafeCleo.com
09:21:33.242 [main] INFO  c.b.i.TextQueryExample - Canfield media and arts; inc
09:21:33.242 [main] INFO  c.b.i.TextQueryExample - DKO New York
09:21:33.242 [main] INFO  c.b.i.TextQueryExample - Wedding Ring Originals
09:21:33.242 [main] INFO  c.b.i.TextQueryExample - Slater
09:21:33.242 [main] INFO  c.b.i.TextQueryExample - Text query example finished.
```

Figure 4.13

Figure 4.13 shows that Ignite scan query found all the company with the city name New York. You can combine a few predicates expression in one statement. Check the following pseudo code:

```
new ScanQuery<Long, Company>((k, p) -> p.getCity().equalsIgnoreCase("NEW YORK") && p.getEm\
ail().equalsIgnoreCase("abc@yescompany.com") )
```

Here, we are looking for the companies, which city name belongs to the New Work and e-mail address equals abc@yescompany.com.

Sometimes, you need to work with a few *properties* of the cache entries rather than the entire cache objects. This is useful, for example, when you want to fetch only several fields out of a large object and want to minimize the network traffic. Scan query provides optional transformer closure, which can transform the object in server node and returns the transformed object. For example, if we need only the *company Id* which is situated in the city New York, we can do this as follows:

```
List<Long> companyName = companyCache.query(new ScanQuery<Long, Company>(
  // Remote filter.
  new IgniteBiPredicate<Long, Company>() {
      @Override public boolean apply(Long k, Company p) {
          return p.getCity().equalsIgnoreCase("NEW YORK");
      }
  }),
  // Transformer.
  new IgniteClosure<Cache.Entry<Long, Company>, Long>() {
      @Override public Long apply(Cache.Entry<Long, Company> e) {
          return e.getValue().getId();
      }
  }
).getAll();
```

The above pseudo code will return the List of the companies Id which will match the predicate expression getCity==New York.

Next, we are going to explore another very interesting feature of the **full-text search** of the Apache Ignite.

Text queries

Text queries in Apache Ignite let you run full-text queries against character-based cache entries. Let's define why we need full-text search queries and how it differs from the Scan queries. For example, my spouse asked me to find a list of the `beauty salon` in New York. With scan queries, I can run the following queries:

```
QueryCursor cursor = companyCache.query(new ScanQuery<Long, Company>((k, p) -> p.getCompan\
yName.contains("beauty salon") ));
```

The above query will return me the list of companies whose company name contains `beauty salon`. But this approach has a few downsides:

1. It will scan the entire cache, which is very inefficient if the cache contains a large range of datasets.
2. To run the query, I have to know the properties of the company's object. In my case, it's is the name of the company.
3. When used with complex predicates based on different properties, scan query gets complicated. For instance, I have to look for companies, which are located in `New York city`, the address is something like `abc street`` and an `index is 4356`" etc.

In daily life, we perform a lot of text search on the Web: Google or Bing. Most of the search engine works in principle of full-text search. We enter search items into the search box of the Google; Google search engine returns the list of the websites or resources that contain the search item.

Apache Ignite supports **text-based queries** based on Lucene indexing. Lucene is an open source full-text search library in Java, which makes it easy to add search functionality to any application. Lucene does it by adding content to a full-text **index**. It then allows you to perform queries on this index. This type of index is called an inverted index because it inverts a page-centric data structure (page->words) to a keyword-centric data structure (word->pages). You can imagine it as an index at the back of the book.

In Lucene, a *Document* is the unit of index and search. An index can contain one or more documents. A Lucene document doesn't have to be a document in Microsoft word. For instance, if you are creating a Lucene index of *companies*, then each and every company will be representing a document in Lucene index. Lucene search can retrieve documents from the index via a Lucene *IndexSearcher*.

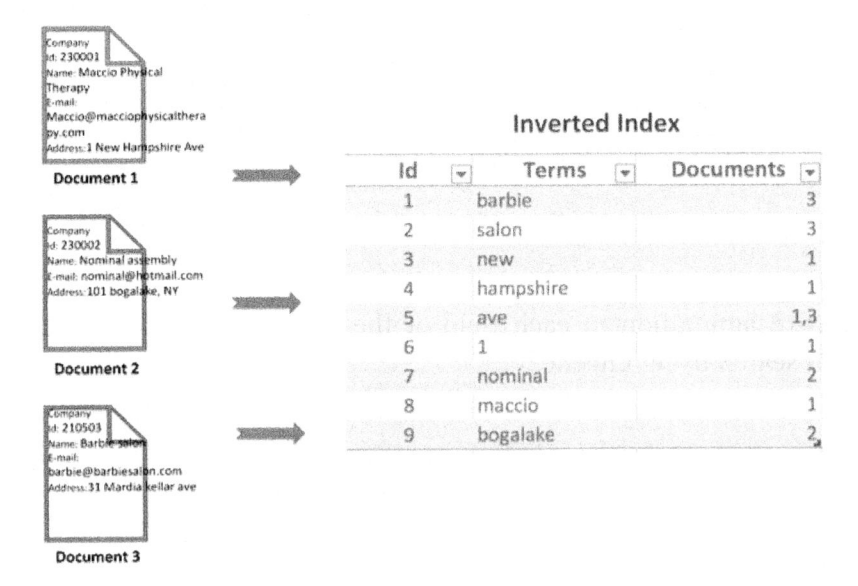

Figure 4.14

In Apache Ignite, each node contains a local Lucene engine that stores the index in memory that reference in local cache entries. When any distributed full-text queries are executed, each node performs the search in local index via IndexSearcher and send the result back to the client node, where the result is aggregated.

> **Note:**
>
> The Ignite cache doesn't contain the Lucene index, instead, Ignite provides an in-memory `GridLuceneDirectory` directory, which is the memory-resident implementation to store the Lucene index in memory. GridLuceneDirectory is very much similar to the Lucene `RAMDirectory`.

We are going to use the same data set from the previous subsection and extend the application to perform text search in Ignite cache. Let's modify the maven project slightly to add full-text search functionality. Please refer to the GitHub repository[31] (chapter-persistence/textquery) for downloading the full source code of the project.

Step 1:

Add the following maven dependencies as follows:

---

[31] https://github.com/srecon/ignite-book-code-samples/tree/master/chapters/chapter-persistence/textquery

Chapter four: Persistence

```xml
<dependency>
    <groupId>org.apache.ignite</groupId>
    <artifactId>ignite-indexing</artifactId>
    <version>1.6.0</version>
</dependency>
```

Step 2:

Add `@QueryTextField` annotation to each field of the `com.blu.imdg.model.Company` class to be indexed for full text search using Lucene.

```java
public class Company implements Serializable {

    private Long id;
    private String cat;
    @QueryTextField
    private String companyName;
    @QueryTextField
    private String email;
    @QueryTextField
    private String address;
    @QueryTextField
    private String city;
    @QueryTextField
    private String state;
    @QueryTextField
    private String zipCode;
    private String phoneNumber;
    private String faxNumber;
    private String sicCode;
    private String sicDescription;
    @QueryTextField
    private String webAddress;
}
```

> **Note:**
> You can also use the annotation to *getter method* of the class. Field or getter method that doesn't have the annotation will not be indexed.

Step 3:

Create a new static method called **textQuery** with the following contents:

Chapter four: Persistence

```
private static void textQuery() {
    IgniteCache<Integer, Company> cache = Ignition.ignite().cache(COMPANY_CACHE_NAME);

    // Query for all companies which has a text "John".
    TextQuery<Integer, Company> john = new TextQuery<>(Company.class, "John");

    // Query for all companies which has a text "beauty salon".
    TextQuery<Integer, Company> primavera = new TextQuery<>(Company.class, "beauty salon");

    log("==So many companies with information about 'John'==", cache.query(john).getAll());
    log("==A company which name is starting with 'Beauty salon'==", cache.query(primavera)\
.getAll());
}
```

The above pseudo code is very much similar to the scanQuery method. First, we retrieve the cache *company* and creates two text queries with text *John* and *beauty salon*. Then executes the query with the texts which returns the list of the companies and prints the results into the console.

Step 4:

Compile and run the application with the following command:

```
mvn clean install && java -jar target/textquery-runnable.jar textquery
```

You should see the following output as shown in figure 4.15

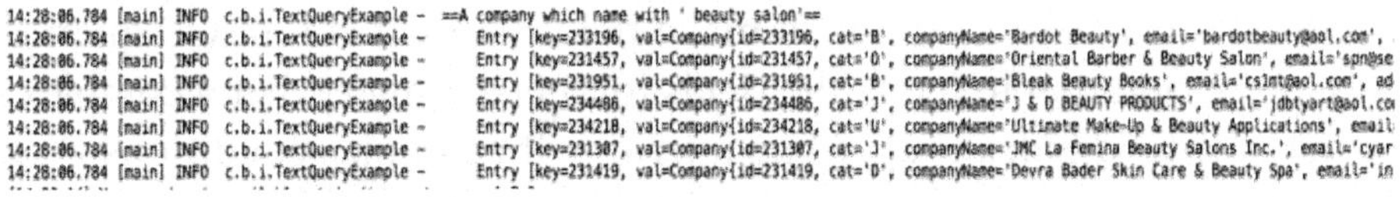

Figure 4.15

You can edit the text query application with different search criteria. In normal use cases, the Ignite built-in text queries should be sufficient to perform the full-text search.

In the next subsection, we are going to study the Ignite SQL capabilities and will run a few examples to perform SQL queries.

SQL queries

Apache Ignite provides SqlQuery and SqlFieldsQuery API to support SQL queries against caches. SQL syntax is a fully **ANSI-99** complaint, means you can execute an aggregate function like AVG(), COUNT(), grouping or ordering. Apache Ignite also includes distributed SQL joins (collocated and non-collocated) for querying in-memory data, whenever data resided into the different caches.

Supporting ANSI-99 SQL queries is one the unique features of the Apache Ignite than others in-memory vendors like Hazelcast or Infinispan.

Historically, distributed *JOINS* against large dataset was very challenging because the overhead of an individual key lookup in different tables or caches is relatively large. Thus, most of the NoSQL or in-memory cache vendor doesn't support for query JOINS. In this case, the user performs joins manually by combining multiple query results. However, Apache Ignite solves the problem of JOINS in a different fashion. Ignite versions earlier than **1.7** perform the query only on **local** data, and for getting reliable query result, data should be **collocated** on the same node.

Anyway, Apache Ignite version of 1.7 or later provides a new approach of distributed joins named **non-collocated distributed joins**, where data collocation is no longer need for the SQL JOINS. There are other possibilities of cross joins of data from different datasets defined as *Cross-cache queries*. In cross-join queries, your data should be residing on the same node. Otherwise, you might get non-reliable query results.

To help explain what we have discussed earlier, we have to return back to our caching topology of Ignite again (chapter two). Caches are distributed in Ignite in two fashions: Replicated and Partitioned. In Replicated mode, all the nodes contain its primary dataset and the backup copy. In the Partitioned mode, datasets are replicated through the Ignite cluster. All the complexity of distributed JOINS comes in, whenever you are using the partitioned topology of the Ignite cluster. In the partitioned mode, if you are executing any cross-join queries, Apache Ignite cannot give you the guarantee of getting a reliable query result. For getting proper query result you should have to collocate the related dataset in the same node or use the non-collocated distributed joins when it's extremely difficult or impossible to collocate all the data but you still need to execute a number of SQL queries such as ad-hoc queries over non-collocated caches.

Apache Ignite also offers Java annotations to make fields accessible for SQL queries. Additionally, you can use the same annotation to Index the fields for a faster query. For a complex query, Apache Ignite also offers a multi-field index to speed up queries with complex conditions. Apache Ignite also provides a Java API for SQL projection. With *SqlFieldsQuery* you can choose only specified fields rather than the whole objects.

With the Ignite SQL core concepts under your belt, you can tackle most of the SQL problems with the Ignite. There are still more to cover, though, in this current subsection, we are going to cover the following topics:

- Projection and indexing with annotations.
- Query API.
- Collocated, non-collocated distributed joins.
- Performance tuning SQL queries.

Dataset:

The dataset that we are going to be using is *Employee* and *Department* entity from the Oracle Database. The structure of the department (dept) and Employee (emp) entity is very simple, they are

Chapter four: Persistence 146

related with a one-to-many relationship with each other (see figure 4.16). This simple data structure will help us to cover all of our topics on SQL queries.

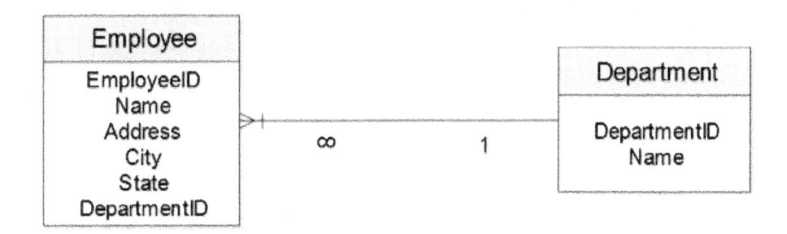

Figure 4.16

Source code for this subsection can be found at GitHub repository[32] (chapter-persistence/sqlqueries).

Disclaimer:

Figure 4.18, 4.19 and two performance tips have been taken from the Ignite documentation.

Projection and indexing with annotations

First thing first, in order to use SQL queries against cache entries, you have to make the entity fields accessible for the SQL queries. You can achieve this in the two following ways:

Name	Description
org.apache.ignite.cache.query.annotations.QuerySqlField	Java class property annotation.
org.apache.ignite.cache.QueryEntity	Entity description class, composed of key and value. Usually used for XML configuration with XML.

> **Note:**
> @QuerySqlField is equivalent to use QueryEntity because property annotations are converted into query entities internally. Do not use the two approaches at the same time, because spring configuration will overwrite all the other configuration through annotations.

Next pseudo code will show the use of @QuerySqlField annotation.

---
[32] https://github.com/srecon/ignite-book-code-samples/tree/master/chapters/chapter-persistence/sqlqueries

```
public class Employee implements Serializable {
    private static final AtomicInteger GENERATED_ID = new AtomicInteger();
    @QuerySqlField
    private Integer empno;
    @QuerySqlField
    private String ename;
    @QueryTextField
    private LocalDate hiredate;
    private Integer sal;
    @QuerySqlField
    private Integer deptno;
// rest of the code is omitted
}
```

Let's have a detailed look at the above code. With the `@QuerySqlField` annotation, we have enabled the empno, ename, hiredate and sal properties to be used by the SQL queries. Note that, property or field *sal* is not enabled for SQL queries. There are two predefined fields for every entity: _key and _val, which represents links to the whole key and value of the cache entries. This is useful, for example, when cache entry value is primitive, and you want to filter by its value. To do this, execute a query like SELECT * FROM Employee WHERE _key = 100. Additionally, for every cache with primitive (Boxed) types already have this above predefined fields for SQL query. Assume, we have the following cache in Ignite.

```
IgniteCache<Integer, String> myCache = Ignition.ignite().cache(CACHE_NAME);
```

You can also execute query like Select * from myCache where _key=101.

For now, with our Employee entity, we can execute any of the following SQL queries.

```
select e.ename ,e.sal, m.ename, m.sal from Employee e, (select ename, empno, sal from Empl\
oyee) m where e.mgr = m.empno and e.sal > m.sal
```

If you are curious about the code and want to execute a few queries, run the following command in the console.

```
mvn clean install && java -jar ./target/sql-query-employees-runnable.jar
```

You can also use the `@QuerySqlField` annotation to index the field values to speedup the query execution. To create a single column index you can annotate field with `@QuerySqlField(index = true)`. This will create an index value for the entity field. Let's see an example as follows:

```java
public class Employee implements Serializable {
    private static final AtomicInteger GENERATED_ID = new AtomicInteger();
    @QuerySqlField(index = true)
    private Integer empno;
    @QuerySqlField
    private String ename;
    @QueryTextField
    private String job;
    @QuerySqlField
    private Integer mgr;
    @QuerySqlField
    private LocalDate hiredate;
    @QuerySqlField
    private Integer sal;
    @QuerySqlField(index = true)
    private Integer deptno;
// rest of the code is ommitted
}
```

In the above fragment of the code, we have created an index for fields *empno* and *deptno*.

> **Note:**
> Indexes in Ignite has also consumed places in memory, it can be off-heap on on-heap memory. Also, each index needs to be updated separately, thus your cache update can be slower if you have more indexes. You should Index fields, that are participating in the *where clause* of the SQL query.

It is also possible to combine one or more indexes in one group to speedup the queries execution with a complex condition. In this case, you have to use `@QuerySqlField.Group` annotation. It is possible to put multiple `@QuerySqlField.Group` annotations into orderedGroups, if you want the field to participate in more than one group index.

```java
public class Employee implements Serializable {
  /** Indexed in a group index with " hiredate  and salary". */
  @QuerySqlField(orderedGroups={@QuerySqlField.Group(
    name = "hiredate_salary_idx", order = 0, descending = true)})
  private LocalDate hireDate;
  /** Indexed separately and in a group index with "age". */
  @QuerySqlField(index = true, orderedGroups={@QuerySqlField.Group(
    name = " hiredate _salary_idx", order = 3)})
  private Integer sal;
}
```

Chapter four: Persistence

With the above configurations, you can execute SQL queries like

```
select e.ename ,e.sal, m.ename, m.sal from Employee e, (select ename, empno, sal from Empl\
oyee) m where e.mgr = m.empno and (e.sal > m.sal and e.hiredate >='DATE_TIME');
```

Now that, we have got the basics, and run some single cache queries, it's time to go for the distributed joins. In the next subsection, we are going to dip our toes into the distributed joins.

Query API

Apache Ignite provides two different `Query API` to execute SQL queries over cache entries.

Name	Description
org.apache.ignite.cache.query.SqlQuery	Class that always returns the whole key and the value of the objects. It's very much similar to the Hibernate HQL. For example, you can run the following query to get all the employees with salaries between 1000 and 2000. `SqlQuery qry = new SqlQuery<>(Employee.class, "sal > 1000 and sal <= 2000");`
org.apache.ignite.cache.query.SqlFieldsQuery	This query can return specific fields of data based on SQL `select` clause. You can choose to select only specific fields in order to minimize network and serialization overhead. Also it is useful when you want to execute some aggregate query. For example, `SqlFieldsQuery qry = new SqlFieldsQuery(,"select avg(e.sal), d.dname " +,"from Employee e, \"" + DEPARTMENT_CACHE_NAME + "\".Department d " +,"where e.deptno = d.deptno " +,"group by d.dname " +,"having avg(e.sal) > ?");`

Collocated distributed Joins

As far as we discussed the topics caching topology of the Apache Ignite. Let's explore another important topic in depth: data collocation. In the partitioned mode, the dataset will be partitioned and located in different Ignite nodes. It means an *Employee* related to the specified *Department* can be located in the different nodes and vice-versa. In runtime, if we want to execute any business logics, where we need to find out the Employee related to their department will be very time-consuming. To resolve this issue, Apache Ignite provides affinity key concept, where related dataset can be located on the same node. For instance, by the affinity key `AffinityKey(int empNo, int deptNo)` of Employee id and the Department id, Ignite will make sure that all the employee's data will reside with their department's data on the same single node. Let's explain all the details in an example.

Step 1:

Chapter four: Persistence   150

Add the Department plain old Java class into the project as follows:

```java
public class Department implements Serializable {
    private static final AtomicInteger GENERATED_ID = new AtomicInteger();
    @QuerySqlField(index = true)
    private Integer deptno;
    @QuerySqlField
    private String dname;
    @QuerySqlField
    private String loc;
    public Department(String dname, String loc) {
        this.deptno = GENERATED_ID.incrementAndGet();
        this.dname = dname;
        this.loc = loc;
    }
// setter and getter are omitted here
}
```

In the above Java class, deptno is the Department ID and this value will be used as a cache key in the Cache. We will also have a separate cache for Department entity. We can initialize the cache for a department and store the department entities as follows:

```java
IgniteCache<Integer, Department> deptCache = Ignition.ignite().cache(DEPARTMENT_CACHE_NAME\
);
// create instance of Departments
Department dept1 = new Department("Accounting", "New York");
deptCache.put(dept1.getDeptno(), dept1);
```

Also note that the key value will be used as a primary key at the time of SQL execution.

Next, add another Java class for the Employee entity as follows:

```java
public class Employee implements Serializable {
    private static final AtomicInteger GENERATED_ID = new AtomicInteger();
    @QuerySqlField(index = true)
    private Integer empno;
    @QuerySqlField
    private String ename;
    @QueryTextField
    private String job;
    @QuerySqlField
    private Integer mgr;
    @QuerySqlField
    private LocalDate hiredate;
```

Chapter four: Persistence   151

```
    @QuerySqlField
    private Integer sal;
    @QuerySqlField(index = true)
    private Integer deptno;
    private transient EmployeeKey key;
    //Affinity employee key
    public EmployeeKey getKey() {
        if (key == null) {
            key = new EmployeeKey(empno, deptno);
        }
        return key;
    }
// rest of the part ommited here
}
```

Most of the part is very similar to the Department class except the field `deptno` and `key`. The field deptno identified the Employee's department, and the field key with type EmployeeKey is the AffinityKey. Let's take a closer look at its definition.

```
public class EmployeeKey implements Serializable {
    private final int empNo;
    @AffinityKeyMapped
    private final int deptNo;
    public EmployeeKey(int empNo, int deptNo) {
        this.empNo = empNo;
        this.deptNo = deptNo;
    }
}
```

Instead of `empno`, `key` (type `EmployeeKey`) will be the cache key. `EmployeeKey` class is the key mapped to the Employee id and the Department Id, where department id (deptno) will be the Employee's affinity key. The following code will be used to add Employee on the cache.

```
IgniteCache<EmployeeKey, Employee> employeeCache = Ignition.ignite().cache(EMPLOYEE_CACHE_\
NAME);
// Employees
Employee emp1 = new Employee("King", dept1, "President", null, localDateOf("17-11-1981"), \
5000);
// Note that, we use custom affinity key for Employee objects
// to ensure that all persons are collocated with their departments.
employeeCache.put(emp1.getKey(), emp1);
```

So, the Employee *King* will be located with the Department *Accounting* on the same node. Now, if we will execute the method `sqlFieldsQueryWithJoin` from the class `SqlQueryEmployees`, the following SQL query should run:

```
select e.ename, d.dname from Employee e, departments.Department d where e.deptno = d.deptn\
o;
```

Note that, you can also run the class `SqlQueryEmployees` from the command line as follows:

```
java -jar ./target/sql-query-employees-runnable.jar
```

The output of the method should be as follows:

```
c.b.i.SqlQueryEmployees -    ==Names of all employees and departments they belong to (SQL join)==
c.b.i.SqlQueryEmployees -    [King, Accounting]
c.b.i.SqlQueryEmployees -    [Clark, Accounting]
c.b.i.SqlQueryEmployees -    [Miller, Accounting]
c.b.i.SqlQueryEmployees -    [Jones, Research]
c.b.i.SqlQueryEmployees -    [Scott, Research]
c.b.i.SqlQueryEmployees -    [Ford, Research]
c.b.i.SqlQueryEmployees -    [Smith, Research]
c.b.i.SqlQueryEmployees -    [Adams, Research]
c.b.i.SqlQueryEmployees -    [Blake, Sales]
c.b.i.SqlQueryEmployees -    [Allen, Sales]
c.b.i.SqlQueryEmployees -    [Ward, Sales]
c.b.i.SqlQueryEmployees -    [Martin, Sales]
c.b.i.SqlQueryEmployees -    [Turner, Sales]
c.b.i.SqlQueryEmployees -    [James, Sales]
```

Figure 4.17

The above SQL query returns all the Employees belongs to their departments. The following dataflow (figure 4.18) will explain what's going under the hood when you are executing the SQL.

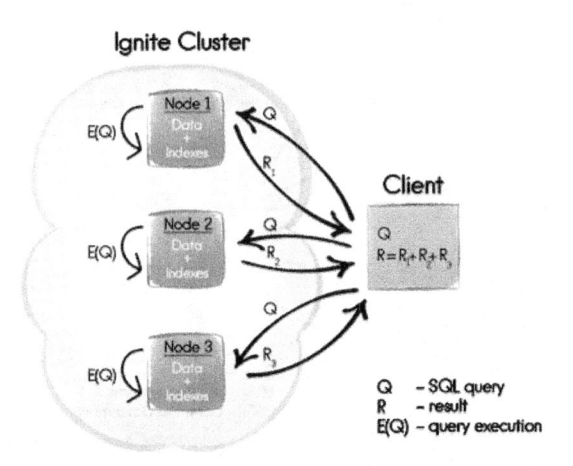

Figure 4.18

Let's details the execution flow:

1. *Phase Q*: Ignite Client node initialize the SQL queries and sends the SQL query to all the node.
2. *Phase E(Q)*: All the Ignite nodes that receive the SQL query runs the query against local data. So far we are using the affinity key, local data will contain employees with their departments.
3. *Phase R1-3*: All the nodes send their execution result set to the Ignite Client node.

Chapter four: Persistence

4. *Phase R*: Ignite Client node will appear as a reducer and aggregates all the result set in a single result set. In our case, it will print the result into the console.

Note that, the name of the cache act as *schema* names in regular SQL. This means all caches can be referred by the cache names in quotes. The cache on which the query was created acts as the default schema and does not need to be explicitly specified. In the above SQL query, *Employee* is the default schema name and we explicitly define the cache name for the department *(departments.Department d)*.

Non-collocated distributed joins

In real life, it's not always possible to collocated all the data together in the same node. Most often, when you are doing some analytics on hot data by an ad-hoc query. In such a situation, from Ignite version 1.7.0 or later you can use non-collocated distributed joins over non-collocated caches. You can enable the non-collocated SQL joins for the specified query by setting the `SqlQuery.setDistributedJoins(true)` parameter. When this parameter is enabled, then the node to which the query was mapped will request for the missing data (data that are not presented locally) from the remotes nodes by sending either a broadcast or unicast request. The execution flow is illustrated in the figure 4.19.

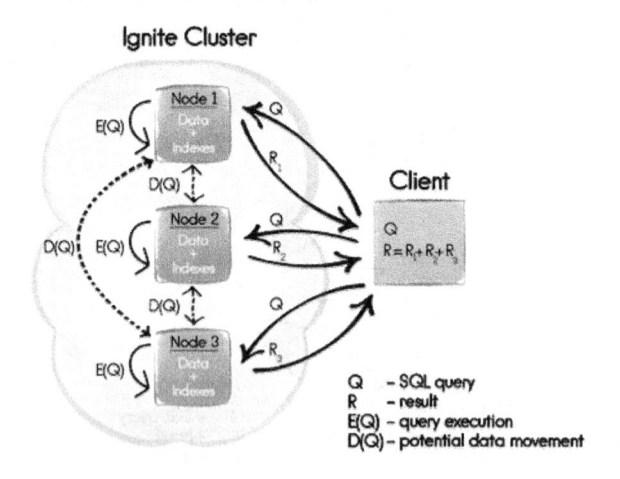

Figure 4.19

With this approach, we can use Employee's `empno` field as the cache key instead of `EmployeeKey(empno, deptno)` affinity key. So, we should have the following change in our code as follows:

```
// Employees
Employee emp1 = new Employee("King", dept1, "President", null, localDateOf("17-11-1981"), \
5000);
employeeCache.put(emp1.getEmpno(), emp1);
```

Now we can execute the following query as follows:

```
select e.ename, d.dname from Employee e, departments.Department d where e.deptno = d.deptno
```

Even after this above modification, we will still get a complete result regardless of the fact that Employee is no longer collocated with its department data. In this case, a broadcast request will be sent from the node to all other nodes. If you want to use unicast request, we have to change our above SQL query slightly as follows:

```
select e.ename, d.dname from Employee e, departments.Department d where e.deptno = d._key
```

Note that, we are using `_key` predefined index instead of `d.deptno` field in SQL joins. Let's details the execution flow from the figure 4.19.

1. Phase Q: Ignite Client node initialize the SQL query and sends the SQL query to all the node.
2. Phase E(Q): All the Ignite nodes that receive the SQL query runs the query against local data.
3. Phase D(Q): If any data is missing locally it will be requested from the remote node by multicast or unicast request.
4. Phase R1-3: All the nodes send their execution result set to the Ignite Client node.
5. Phase R: Ignite Client node will appear as a reducer and aggregate all the result set in a single result set. In our case, it will print the result into the console.

> **Note:**
> There is a serious impact on query performance, whenever you use non-collocated distributed joins. With non-collocated distributed query, there will be much more network roundtrip and data movement between the nodes during query execution.

Performance tuning SQL queries

There are a few principles you should follow or consider when using SQL queries against Ignite cache.

- Carefully use the index, Indexes also consumes memory (on-heap/off-heap). Also, each index needs to be updated separately. If you have a huge update on a cache, index update can seriously decrease your application performance.
- Index only **fields**, that are participating in SQL **WHERE** clause.
- Do not overuse the non-collocated distributed joins approach in practice because the performance of this type of joins is worse than the performance of the affinity collocation-based joins due to the fact that there will be much more network round-trips and data movement between the nodes to fulfill a query.
- In SQL projection statement, select fields that you exactly needs. Extra fields often increase the data roundtrip over the network.
- If the query is using operator OR then it may use indexes in a way you not would expect. For example, for query `select name from Person where sex='M' and (age = 20 or age = 30)` index on field age will not be used even if it is obviously more selective than index on field sex and thus is preferable. To workaround this issue you have to rewrite the query with `UNION ALL` (notice that UNION without ALL will return DISTINCT rows, which will change query semantics and introduce additional performance penalty) like `select name from Person where sex='M' and age = 20 UNION ALL select name from Person where sex='M' and age = 30`. This way indexes will be used correctly.
- If query contains operator IN then it has two problems: it is impossible to provide variable list of parameters (you have to specify the exact list in query like where id in (?, ?, ?), but you can not write it like where id in ? and pass array or collection) and this query will not use index. To work around both problems, you can rewrite the query in the following way: select p.name from Person p join table(id bigint = ?) i on p.id = i.id. Here you can provide object array (Object[]) of any length as a parameter, and the query will use an index on field id. Note that primitive arrays (int[], long[], etc..) can not be used with this syntax, you have to pass an array of boxed primitives.

Apache Ignite with JPA

Often the first step to developing an Enterprise information system is creating the domain model, that is, listing the entities in the domain and defining the relationships between them. A domain model is a conceptual image of the problem your system is trying to solve. Domain model elements can be linked by relationships. Usually, relational objects are represented in a tabular format, while application object model is represented in an interconnected graph of the object format. While storing and retrieving an object model from the relational database, a few mismatch occurs such as Granularity, SubTypes, etc. To solve the mismatches between relational and object model, JPA provides a collection of APIs and methods to manipulates with the persistence store. The JPA specification only defines relational database access, but its API and many of its annotations are not relational specific. There are a few factors we have to take into account before applying JPA into any NoSQL database:

- Pure relational concepts may not be apply well in NoSQL.
    - Table, Column, Joins.
- JPA queries may not be suitable for NoSQL. NoSQL data modeling is typically driven by application-specific access patterns.

> **Note:**
> If your dataset is by nature `non-domain model` centric, then JPA is not for you.

Anyway, Apache Ignite provides in-memory KeyValue store, and it's quite well fit for using JPA. Other NoSQL vendor like Infinspan, Oracle NoSQL, Ehcache also supported by JPA persistence as well. There are a few NoSQL/JPA solutions available in today's market.

1. Kundera
    - One of the first JPA implementations for NoSQL databases.
    - Supports Cassandra, MongoDB, HBase, Redis, Oracle NoSQL DB, etc.
2. DataNucleus
    - Persistence layer behind Google App engine
    - Supports MongoDB, Cassandra, Neo4J
3. Hibernate OGM
    - Using Hibernate ORM engine to persists entities in NoSQL database.
    - Supports MongoDB, Cassandra, Neo4j, Infinspan, Ehcache
    - `Experimental` support for Apache Ignite.

Hibernate OGM talks to NoSQL database via store-specific dialects. Hibernate OGM or Hibernate Object Grid Mapper also supports several ways for searching entities and returning them as Hibernate managed objects:

1. JP-QL queries.
2. Datastore specific native queries.
3. Full-text queries, using Hibernate Search as indexing engine.

Chapter four: Persistence

So, for Apache Ignite we are going to give a try to use JPA by Hibernate OGM framework. Note that, Apache Ignite support by Hibernate OGM is still in development stage and not recommended for use in production. The project is available at Github repositories[33] and any contributions are welcome. Anyway, you can also contribute to code review of this project with others through this URL[34]. A high-level view of the Hibernate OGM is shown below:

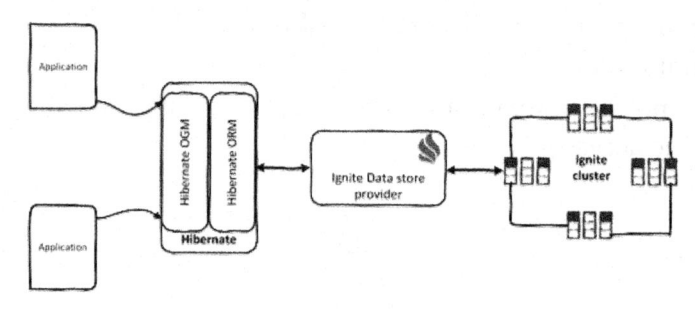

Figure 4.20

In the next few subsections we will cover the following topics:

- Clone and build the *Ignite module* for Hibernate OGM framework.
- Create a new maven project for using Hibernate OGM with Ignite.
- Persisting a few entities into Ignite caches through JPA.

Before we start, make sure the prerequisites of the project are installed in your workstation:

1. Java JDK 1.8
2. Ignite version 1.7.0
3. Apache Maven version >3.0.3

Step 1:

Let's setup the sandbox first. Clone or download the Hibernate OGM framework source code from the Github repositories[35].

```
git clone git@github.com:Z-z-z-z/hibernate-ogm.git hibernate-ogm
```

Step 2:

Modify the pom.xml, delete the following modules as follows:

---

[33] https://github.com/Z-z-z-z/hibernate-ogm
[34] https://github.com/hibernate/hibernate-ogm/pull/628
[35] https://github.com/Z-z-z-z/hibernate-ogm

Chapter four: Persistence

```
<module>infinispan</module>
<module>infinispan-remote</module>
<module>mongodb</module>
<module>neo4j</module>
<module>couchdb</module>
<module>cassandra</module>
<module>redis</module>
```

We donot need these above modules in our project. Make sure that, you have the `ignite module` on pom.xml file.

Step 3:

Build the project with the following command:

```
mvn clean install -Dmaven.test.skip=true -DskipDocs -DskipDistro
```

If everything goes fine, you should have all the necessary libraries in your local maven repositories.

Step 4:

Clone or download the `ignite-jpa` repository from the GitHub[36]. If you create your own maven project, add these dependencies into your pom.xml.

```xml
<dependency>
    <groupId>org.hibernate.ogm</groupId>
    <artifactId>hibernate-ogm-ignite</artifactId>
    <version>5.1.0-SNAPSHOT</version>
</dependency>
<dependency>
    <groupId>org.hibernate.javax.persistence</groupId>
    <artifactId>hibernate-jpa-2.1-api</artifactId>
    <version>1.0.0.Final</version>
</dependency>
```

The dependencies are:

1. The hibernate OGM Ignite module for working with Apache Ignite cache. This maven dependency will pull all other required modules such as Hibernate OGM core and so on.
2. Hibernate JPA API to working with JPA.

---
[36] https://github.com/srecon/ignite-jpa

Chapter four: Persistence

The domain model:

Our example domain model consists of two main entities: Breed and Dog.

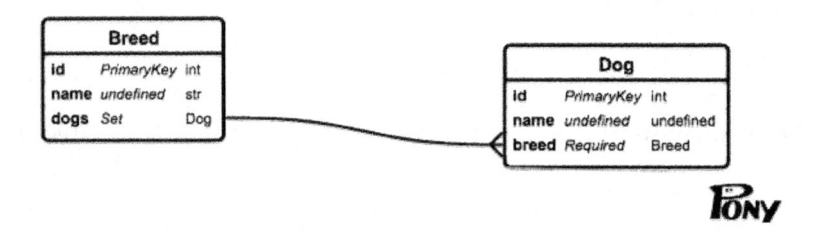

Figure 4.21

The association between Breed and Dog is a *ManyToOne*. One Dog can have only one breed and so on.

Step 5:

Now let's map the domain model by creating the entity Java classes and annotating them with the required meta-information. Let's strat with the Breed class.

```java
@Entity(name = "BREED")
public class Breed {
    @Id
    @GeneratedValue(generator = "uuid")
    @GenericGenerator(name="uuid", strategy="uuid2")
    private String id;

    private String name;

    public String getId() { return id; }
    public void setId(String id) { this.id = id; }

    public String getName() { return name; }
    public void setName(String name) { this.name = name; }

    @Override
    public String toString() {
        return "Breed{" +
                "id='" + id + '\'' +
                ", name='" + name + '\'' +
                '}';
    }
}
```

Chapter four: Persistence

The entity is marked as a JPA annotation of @Entity, while other properties such as ID are annotated by the `@ID`. By the @ID annotation, Hibernate will take care to generate the primary key or the key value for the entity object. `@GeneratedValue` UUID will generate a UUID value as an entity identifier.

```
@Entity
public class Dog {
    @Id
    @GeneratedValue(strategy = GenerationType.TABLE, generator = "dog")
    public Long getId() { return id; }
    public void setId(Long id) { this.id = id; }
    private Long id;

    public String getName() { return name; }
    public void setName(String name) { this.name = name; }
    private String name;

    @ManyToOne
    public Breed getBreed() { return breed; }
    public void setBreed(Breed breed) { this.breed = breed; }
    private Breed breed;

    @Override
    public String toString() {
        return "Dog{" +
                "id=" + id +
                ", name='" + name + '\'' +
                ", breed=" + breed +
                '}';
    }
}
```

We annotated the Dog entity with @Entity and @ID annotation as well. Also, we add `@ManyToOne` annotation to make the association with Breed entity.

Step 6:

Let's create the cache configuration class and the `persistence.xml`. Create an Ignite cache configuration class with name `ConfigurationMaker` as follows:

```java
public class ConfigurationMaker implements IgniteConfigurationBuilder {
    @Override
    public IgniteConfiguration build() {
        IgniteConfiguration config = new IgniteConfiguration();
        config.setPeerClassLoadingEnabled(true);
        config.setClientMode(false);
        TcpDiscoverySpi discoSpi = new TcpDiscoverySpi();
        TcpDiscoveryMulticastIpFinder ipFinder = new TcpDiscoveryMulticastIpFinder();
        ArrayList<String> addrs = new ArrayList<>();
        addrs.add("127.0.0.1:47500..47509");
        ipFinder.setAddresses(addrs);
        discoSpi.setIpFinder(ipFinder);
        config.setDiscoverySpi(discoSpi);

        CacheConfiguration accountCacheCfg = new CacheConfiguration()
                .setName("BREED")
                .setAtomicityMode(TRANSACTIONAL)
                .setIndexedTypes(
                        String.class, Breed.class
                );

        config.setCacheConfiguration(accountCacheCfg);
        return config;
    }
}
```

The above class represented the Ignite Cache configuration, instead of using spring configuration. We have explained the cache configurarion in chapter one. Let's create the persistence.xml file in the /ignite-jpa/src/main/resources/META-INF/persistence.xml directory.

```xml
<?xml version="1.0"?>
<persistence xmlns="http://java.sun.com/xml/ns/persistence"
            xmlns:xsi="http://www.w3.org/2001/XMLSchema-instance"
            xsi:schemaLocation="http://java.sun.com/xml/ns/persistence http://java.sun.co\
m/xml/ns/persistence/persistence_2_0.xsd"
            version="2.0">

    <persistence-unit name="ogm-jpa-tutorial" transaction-type="RESOURCE_LOCAL">
        <provider>org.hibernate.ogm.jpa.HibernateOgmPersistence</provider>
        <properties>

            <property name="com.arjuna.ats.jta.jtaTMImplementation" value="com.arjuna.ats.\
internal.jta.transaction.arjunacore.TransactionManagerImple"/>
            <property name="com.arjuna.ats.jta.jtaUTImplementation" value="com.arjuna.ats.\
internal.jta.transaction.arjunacore.UserTransactionImple"/>
```

```xml
            <property name="hibernate.ogm.datastore.provider" value="IGNITE_EXPERIMENTAL"/>
            <property name="hibernate.ogm.ignite.configuration_class_name" value="com.blu.\
imdg.exampleOgm.ConfigurationMaker"/>
        </properties>
    </persistence-unit>
</persistence>
```

If you have familiar with JPA before, this persistence definition unit should look very common to you. The main difference to using the classic Hibernate ORM on top of a relational database is the specific provider class we need to specify for Hibernate OGM: org.hibernate.ogm.jpa.HibernateOgmPersiste Also, note that we are using RESOURCE_LOCAL instead of JTA. If you want to use JTA, you should have provided a particular JTA implementation such as JBoss. In addition, we have also specified the following configurations:

- DataStore provide: **IGNITE_EXPERIMENTAL**
- Configuration_class_name : Ignite configuration (ConfigurationMaker)

Step 7:

Let's persist a set of entities and retrieve them from the Ignite caches. Create a class with name TestOgm and add the following content:

```java
public class TestOgm {
    public static void main(String[] args) throws SystemException, NotSupportedException, \
HeuristicRollbackException, HeuristicMixedException, RollbackException {
        EntityManagerFactory emf = Persistence.createEntityManagerFactory("ogm-jpa-tutoria\
l");

        EntityManager em = emf.createEntityManager();
        em.getTransaction().begin();

        Breed collie = new Breed();
        collie.setName("breed-collie");
        em.persist(collie);

        Dog dina = new Dog();
        dina.setName("dina");
        dina.setBreed(collie);
        //persis dina
        em.persist(dina);
        em.getTransaction().commit();
        //get ID dina
        Long dinaId = dina.getId();
```

Chapter four: Persistence

```
        // query
        Dog ourDina =  em.find(Dog.class, dinaId);
        System.out.println("Dina:" + ourDina);

        em.close();

    }

    private static TransactionManager extractJBossTransactionManager(EntityManagerFactory \
factory) {
        SessionFactoryImplementor sessionFactory = (SessionFactoryImplementor) ( (Hibernat\
eEntityManagerFactory) factory ).getSessionFactory();
        return sessionFactory.getServiceRegistry().getService( JtaPlatform.class ).retriev\
eTransactionManager();
    }
}
```

First, we have created an `EntityManagerFactory` instance with parameter `ogm-jpa-tutorial`. Next, we derived our EntityManager from the factory; this EntityManager will be our entry point for persistence entities. We opened a transaction from the EntityManager and created an instance of the *Breed* with name *breed-collie*. Persisted the `breed-collie` instance with the entityManager's persist() method. Also created an another instance of Dog: **dina** and associated it with the breed-collie instance. Next, we persisted the dog instance *dina* in the cache with the same method persist() and retrieve the instance by the find() method.

Step 8:

Let's build and run the application. Before running the class `TestOgm`, we have to run an instance of the Ignite node. Run the following command to start an instance of Ignite node.

```
mvn exec:java -Dexec.mainClass=com.blu.imdg.StartCacheNode
```

Now run the following command to execute the TestOgm class as follows:

```
mvn exec:java -Dexec.mainClass=com.blu.imdg.exampleOgm.TestOgm
```

You should find a lot of log messages into the console:

Chapter four: Persistence 164

Figure 4.22

The log messages confirm that two entries (dina and breed-collie) has been flushed into the Ignite cache and retrieves the dog Dina from the cache. Let's explorer the cache through *ignitevisor*.

Figure 4.23

Two different caches have been created for the entities: Breed and Dog. If we scan the cache entries of the cache *Dog*, we should find the following entities on it.

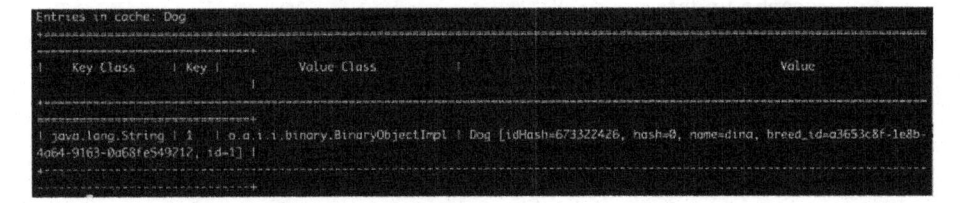

Figure 4.24

Entity Dina has been persisted into the cache with the key of the Breed *breed-collie*. Unfortunately, Hibernate HQL or Search is not working on this experimental version of this Hibernate OGM Ignite module. All the hibernate features are under development and will be supported soon.

Expiration & Eviction of cache entries in Ignite

Apache Ignite caches are very powerful and can be configured and tuned to suit the needs of most applications. Apache Ignite provides two different approaches for data refreshing, which refers to an aspect of a copy of data (e.g,. entries in a cache) being up-to-date with the source version of the data. A stale copy of the data is considered to be out of use. Expiration and Evictions of cache entries is one of the key aspects of caching.

Expiration

Usually, the purpose of a cache is to store short-lived data that needs to refresh regularly. You can use Apache Ignite expiry policy to store entry only for a certain period of time. Once expired, the entry is automatically removed from the cache. For instance, the cache could be configured to expire entries ten seconds after they are put in. Sometimes, it is called Time-to-live or TTL. Or to expire 20 seconds after the last time the entry was accessed or retrieve from the cache. Apache Ignite provides five differents predefined expire policy as follows:

Policy name	Description	Creation time	Last access time	Last update time
CreatedExpiryPolicy	Defines the expiry of a Cache Entry based on when it was created. An update does not reset the expiry time.	Used		
AccessedExpiryPolicy	Defines the expiry of a Cache Entry based on the last time it was accessed. Accessed does not include a cache update.	Used	Used	
ModifiedExpiryPolicy	Defines the expiry of a Cache Entry based on the last time it was updated. Updating includes created and changing (updating) an entry.	Used		Used
TouchedExpiryPolicy	Defines the expiry of a Cache. Entry based on when it was last touched. A touch includes creation, update or,access.	Used	Used	Used

Policy name	Description	Creation time	Last access time	Last update time
EternalExpiryPolicy	Specifies that Cache Entries won't expire. This, however, doesn't mean they won't be evicted if an underlying implementation needs to free-up resources whereby it may choose to evict entries that are not due to expire.			
CustomExpiryPolicy	Implements javax.cache.expiry interface, which defines functions to determine when cache entries will, expire based on creation, access and modification operations			

> **Note:**
> There is no default expiry policy in Apache Ignite, you can configure expiry policy manually based on your business requirements.

Each cache `ExpirePolicy` provides `factoryOf()` method with *Duration* (expect EternalExpiryPolicy) parameter to construct cache entry expiration. Class *Duration* defines the duration of time before the cache entry will be expired. Expiry policy can be setup in *CacheConfiguration**. This policy will be used for all entries in the cache.

Take a look at the following pseudo code to configure `CreatedExpirePolicy`.

```
Ignite ignite = Ignition.start(CLIENT_CONFIG);
CacheConfiguration cacheConfiguration = new CacheConfiguration("myCacheConfig");
cacheConfiguration.setExpiryPolicyFactory(CreatedExpiryPolicy.factoryOf(Duration.FIVE_MINU\
TES));
ignite.getOrCreateCache(cacheConfiguration);
```

The above configuration will expire each cache entry after five minutes from their creation time.

Also, it is possible to change or set Expiry Policy for individual operations on the cache. Take a look at the next fragment of the code below:

```
IgniteCache<Object, Object> cache = cache.withExpiryPolicy(new CreatedExpiryPolicy(new Dur\
ation(TimeUnit.SECONDS, 5)));
```

This policy will be used for each operation invoked on the returned cache instance. Also, you can implement your own custom ExpiryPolicy.

> **Note:**
>
> In order to implement custom expiry policy, you have to implement the `javax.cache.expiry` interface, which defines functions to determine when cache entries will expire based on creation, access or modification operations.

As an alternative to Java configuration, you can use spring configuration for expiring cache entries in Ignite. Let's take a look at the next example of using spring configuration:

```
<bean id="ignite.cfg" class="org.apache.ignite.configuration.IgniteConfiguration">
    ....
    <property name="cacheConfiguration">
      <list>
          <bean class="org.apache.ignite.configuration.CacheConfiguration">
              <property name="name" value="testCache"/>
              <property name="atomicityMode" value="ATOMIC"/>
              <property name="expiryPolicyFactory">
                  <bean id="expiryPolicy" class="javax.cache.expiry.CreatedExpiryPolicy" fac\
tory-method="factoryOf">
                      <constructor-arg>
                          <bean class="javax.cache.expiry.Duration">
                              <constructor-arg value="MILLISECONDS"/>
                              <constructor-arg value="20000"/>
                          </bean>
                      </constructor-arg>
                  </bean>
              </property>
          </bean>
      </list>
    </property>
</bean>
```

Chapter four: Persistence   168

We used the `expiryPolicyFactory` property to configure the expiry policy. In the above example, we defined `createdExpiryPolicy` with 20 seconds duration. Each entry will live 20 seconds before it is removed from the cache. Full source code of the example is available at chapter-persistence of the GitHub repository[37].

Let's run the application and see what will happen after 20 seconds. Execute the following command from the directory `/chapter-persistence/expiry`:

```
mvn clean install && java -jar ./target/ignite-expiry.jar
```

Open the `ignitevisior` into another console by the following command:

```
./ignitevisorcmd.sh
```

Print the cache statistics of the cache `testCache` as follows:

```
cache -a
```

You should be presented with the following statistics of the cache as shown below.

```
Cache 'testCache(@c0)':
+------------------------------------------------------+
| Name(@)                   | testCache(@c0) |
| Nodes                     | 1              |
| Total size Min/Avg/Max    | 4 / 4.00 / 4   |
|   Heap size Min/Avg/Max   | 4 / 4.00 / 4   |
|   Off heap size Min/Avg/Max | 0 / 0.00 / 0 |
+------------------------------------------------------+

Nodes for: testCache(@c0)
+=====================================================================================+
|    Node ID8(@), IP     | CPUs | Heap Used | CPU Load |    Up Time   | Size | Hi/Mi/Rd/Wr |
+=====================================================================================+
| 186B4E2F(@n0), 192.168.1.37 | 8 | 6.24 %  | 0.33 %   | 00:00:19:310 |  4   | Hi: 0       |
|                        |      |          |          |              |      | Mi: 0       |
|                        |      |          |          |              |      | Rd: 0       |
|                        |      |          |          |              |      | Wr: 0       |
+=====================================================================================+
```

Figure 4.25

The size of the cache is **4** because we have just entered 4 entries into the cache. Check the cache statistics after a while, exactly after 20 seconds. You should have found that the cache is empty. Take a look at the following screenshot:

---

[37] https://github.com/srecon/ignite-book-code-samples/tree/master/chapters/chapter-persistence/expiry

```
Cache 'testCache(@c0)':
+------------------------------------------------------+
| Name(@)                     | testCache(@c0)         |
| Nodes                       | 1                      |
| Total size Min/Avg/Max      | 0 / 0.00 / 0           |
|   Heap size Min/Avg/Max     | 0 / 0.00 / 0           |
|   Off heap size Min/Avg/Max | 0 / 0.00 / 0           |
+------------------------------------------------------+

Nodes for: testCache(@c0)
+===============================================================================================+
|       Node ID8(@), IP       | CPUs | Heap Used | CPU Load |   Up Time    | Size | Hi/Mi/Rd/Wr |
+===============================================================================================+
| 186B4E2F(@n0), 192.168.1.37 | 8    | 7.33 %    | 0.17 %   | 00:07:10:229 | 0    | Hi: 0       |
|                             |      |           |          |              |      | Mi: 0       |
|                             |      |           |          |              |      | Rd: 0       |
|                             |      |           |          |              |      | Wr: 0       |
+===============================================================================================+
```

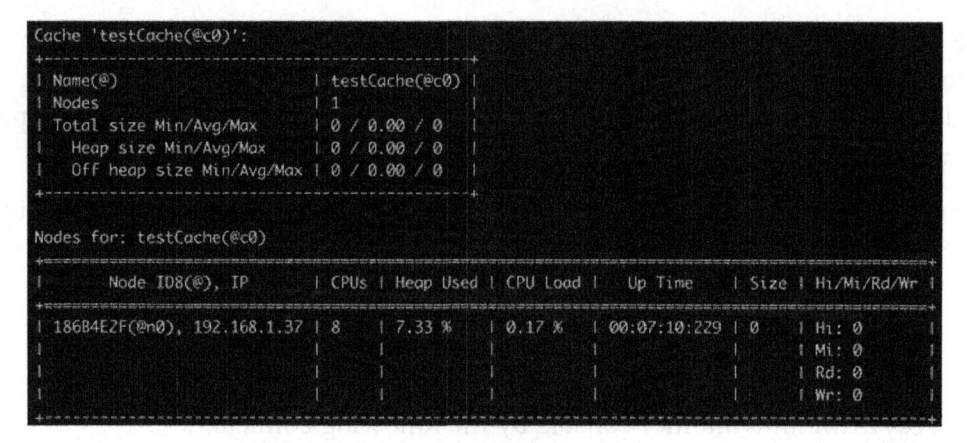

Figure 4.26

The expiration configuration that would be most appropriate for your cache (if any) would be a mixture of a business and technical decision based upon the requirements and assumptions of your application.

Eviction

Usually, caches are unbounded, i.e. they grow indefinitely and it is up to the application to removed unneeded cache entries. A cache eviction algorithm is a way of deciding which entries to evict (removed) when the cache is full. However, when maximum on-heap memory is full, entries are evicted into the off-heap memory, if one is enabled.

Some eviction policies support batch eviction and eviction by memory size limit. If a batch eviction is enabled then eviction starts when cache size (batchSize) is greater than the maximum cache size. In this cases, **batchSize** entries will be evicted. If eviction by memory size limit is enabled, then eviction starts when the size of cache entries in bytes becomes greater than the maximum memory size.

> **Note:**
> Batch eviction is supported only if maximum memory limit isn't set.

In 1966 Laszlo Belady showed that the most efficient caching algorithm would always be to discard the information that will not be needed for the longest time in the future. This it a theoretical result that is unimplementable without domain knowledge. Apache Ignite provides EvictionPolicy interface to control eviction process of entries in the Ignite cache. There is four predefined eviction policy provides by the Apache Ignite.

LRU (Least Recently Used):

This eviction policy is based on LRU algorithm. The oldest element is the Less Recently Used (LRU) element gets evicted first. The last used timestamp is updated when an element is put into the cache, or an element is retrieved from the cache with a get call. This algorithm takes a random sample of the Elements and evicts the smallest. Using the sample size of 15 elements, empirical testing shows that an Element in the lowest quartile of use is evicted 99% of the time. This eviction policy supports batch eviction and eviction by memory size limits. This eviction policy is suitable for most of all applications and recommended by Apache Ignite. This eviction policy can be configured by Java and spring configuration. Take a look at the Java configuration as shown below.

```
CacheConfiguration cacheCfg = new CacheConfiguration();
cacheCfg.setName("cacheName");
// Set the maximum cache size to 1 million (default is 100,000).
cacheCfg.setEvictionPolicy(new LruEvictionPolicy(1000000));
IgniteConfiguration cfg = new IgniteConfiguration();
cfg.setCacheConfiguration(cacheCfg);
// Start Ignite node.
Ignition.start(cfg);
```

For complete spring configuration, please check the chapter three, section *Apache Ignite as a big memory, off-heap memory.*

FIFO (First In First Out):

Elements are evicted in the same order as they come in. When a put call is made for a new element (and assuming that the max limit is reached for the memory store), the element that was placed first (First-In) in the store is the candidate for eviction (First-Out).

This algorithm is used if the use of an element makes it less likely to be used in the future. An example here would be an authentication cache. It takes a random sample of the Elements and evicts the smallest. Using the sample size of 15 elements, empirical testing shows that an Element in the lowest quartile of use is evicted 99% of the time.

This implementation is very efficient since it does not create any additional table-like data structures. The ordering information is maintained by attaching ordering metadata to cache entries. This eviction policy supports batch eviction and eviction by memory size limit. This eviction policy is implemented by `FifoEvictionPolicy` and can be configured via `CacheConfiguration`.

Chapter four: Persistence

```
CacheConfiguration cacheCfg = new CacheConfiguration();

cacheCfg.setName("cacheName");

// Set the maximum cache size to 1 million (default is 100,000).
cacheCfg.setEvictionPolicy(new FifoEvictionPolicy(1000000));

IgniteConfiguration cfg = new IgniteConfiguration();

cfg.setCacheConfiguration(cacheCfg);

// Start Ignite node.
Ignition.start(cfg);
```

Sorted:

Sorted eviction policy is similar to FIFO eviction policy with the difference that the entries order is defined by default or user defined comparator and ensures that the minimal entry (i.e. the entry that has integer key with the smallest value) gets evicted first.

Default comparator uses cache entries keys for comparison that imposes a requirement for keys to implementing Comparable interface. The user can provide own comparator implementation which can use keys, values or both for entries comparison. Supports batch eviction and eviction by memory size limit. This eviction policy is implemented by SortedEvictionPolicy and can be configured via *CacheConfiguration.*

```
CacheConfiguration cacheCfg = new CacheConfiguration();

cacheCfg.setName("cacheName");

// Set the maximum cache size to 1 million (default is 100,000).
cacheCfg.setEvictionPolicy(new SortedEvictionPolicy(1000000));

IgniteConfiguration cfg = new IgniteConfiguration();

cfg.setCacheConfiguration(cacheCfg);

// Start Ignite node.
Ignition.start(cfg);
```

Random:

This cache eviction policy selects random cache entry for eviction if cache size exceeds the **getMaxSize** parameter. This implementation is extremely light weight, lock-free, and does not create any data structures to maintain any order for eviction. Random eviction will provide the best performance over any key queue in which every key has the same probability of being accessed.

Chapter four: Persistence

This eviction policy implementation doesn't support near cache and doesn't work on client nodes. This eviction policy is mainly used for debugging and benchmarking purposes. This eviction policy is implemented by `RandomEvictionPolicy` and can be configured via CacheConfiguration as follows:

```java
CacheConfiguration cacheCfg = new CacheConfiguration();

cacheCfg.setName("cacheName");

// Set the maximum cache size to 1 million (default is 100,000).
cacheCfg.setEvictionPolicy(new RandomEvictionPolicy(1000000));

IgniteConfiguration cfg = new IgniteConfiguration();

cfg.setCacheConfiguration(cacheCfg);

// Start Ignite node.
Ignition.start(cfg);
```

> **Note:**
> Note that, Random eviction policy is deprecated since 1.5 version and not recommended for use in production environment.

As we mentioned before, if any off-heap memory enabled, you can evict cache entries into off-heap memory. The configuration of the eviction policy into off-heap memory can be achieved by the spring configuration. Here is an example of such a spring configuration:

```xml
<bean class="org.apache.ignite.configuration.CacheConfiguration">
    <!-- Set a cache name. -->
    <property name="name" value="offheap-cache"/>
    <!-- Set cache mode. -->
    <property name="cacheMode" value="PARTITIONED"/>
    <property name="backups" value="1"/>
    <property name="statisticsEnabled" value="true" />
    <!-- Stores entries in on-heap memory -->
    <property name="memoryMode" value="ONHEAP_TIERED"/>
    <!-- Enable Off-Heap memory with max size of 1 Gigabytes (0 for unlimited). -->
    <property name="offHeapMaxMemory" value="#{1 * 1024L * 1024L * 1024L}"/>
    <!-- Configure eviction policy. -->
    <property name="evictionPolicy">
        <bean class="org.apache.ignite.cache.eviction.fifo.FifoEvictionPolicy">
```

```
        <!-- Evict to off-heap after cache size reaches maxSize. -->
        <property name="maxSize" value="100"/>
      </bean>
    </property>
</bean>
```

For a full complete example, please refer to the chapter three *Apache Ignite as a big memory, off-heap memory.*

Transaction

To explain what transaction are, let's take a look at an example from a real world scenario. A classic example of the transaction is transferring money from one bank account to another. To do that you have to first withdraw an amount from one account and then deposit the money to the destination account. The operation either has to completed fully or not at all. If something goes wrong in halfway, the money will be lost. Another common example of transactions is purchasing goods (books etc.) online. This seems like an everyday scenario but can be fairly complex series of events. Whenever you are purchasing books online, you have to put the book in the shopping cart first; you must fill the shipping and credit/debit card details before you can confirm the purchase. If your credit/debit card is declined, the purchase will not be confirmed. The result of this operations is either of two states: either the purchase was confirmed, or the purchase was declined, leaving your bank card balance unchanged. Same with the money transfer scenario, transaction guarantee that there will NOT be a situation where money is withdrawn from one account, but not deposit to another.

Ignite provides two different modes for cache operations:

- transactional and
- atomic.

The smallest set of operations (withdraw an amount from one account or fill the shipping details) we described above is atomic, guaranteed to be either completely fully or not at all. The series of events (a group of operations) to fulfill the whole operation described before is the transaction, in a transactional term, they either commit or rollback; either they all are completed or they all fail –it's all or nothing. Let's make comparisons between atomic and transactional modes:

Atomic	Transactional
Supports atomic-only cache behavior, doesn't provides distributed transaction and distributed locking.	Supports fully ACID-compliant transactions.
Supports multiple atomic operations, one at a time.	Support multiple cache operations in a transaction.

Atomic	Transactional
Bulk operations such as putAll(..), removeAll(..) and transformAll(..) methods can partially fail.	Supports bulk operations in a transaction.
Extremly fast, because explicit locking is not needed.	Doesn't allow high-performance and throughput because of distributed locking.
Ignite default atomicity mode.	Should be explicitly enabled.

> **Note:**
> If you are not familiar with ACID transactions, the Wikipedia[a] page is a good place to start learning about it.
>
> [a]http://en.wikipedia.org/wiki/ACID

The above atomicity modes are defined in Ignite `CacheAtomicityMode` enum. Cache atomicity mode controls whatever cache should maintain fully transactional semantics or more light-weight atomic behavior. Cache atomicity mode may be set via `org.apache.ignite.configuration.CacheConfiguration.getA` configuration property.

An example of atomicity mode configuration is shown below:

```
<bean class="org.apache.ignite.configuration.IgniteConfiguration">
    ...
    <property name="cacheConfiguration">
        <bean class="org.apache.ignite.configuration.CacheConfiguration">
            <!-- Set a cache name. -->
            <property name="name" value=" clientLoyalties "/>
            <!-- Set atomicity mode, can be ATOMIC or TRANSACTIONAL.
                ATOMIC is default. -->
            <property name="atomicityMode" value="TRANSACTIONAL"/>
        </bean>
    </property>
</bean>
```

To help explain the difference between two transaction modes in Ignite, let's consider the following pseudo code:

Chapter four: Persistence

Atmoic mode	Transactional mode

try (Ignite ignite = Ignition.start(cfg)) {
 	
   BankAccount bankAccount = cacheAccount.get(accountNumber);
 	
   // Deposit into account.
 	
   bankAccount.deposit(amount);
 	
   // Store updated account in cache.
 	
   cacheAccount.put(accountNumber, bankAccount);
 	
   cacheAudit.put(accountNumber, bankAccount);
}
 	
In atomic mode, the two above cache operations can partialy fail.
	try (Transaction tx = Ignition.ignite().transactions().txStart()) {
	
	   BankAccount bankAccount = cacheAccount.get(accountNumber);
	
	   // Deposit into account.
	
	   bankAccount.deposit(amount);
	
	   // Store updated account in cache.
	
	   cacheAccount.put(accountNumber, bankAccount);
	
	   cacheAudit.put(accountNumber, bankAccount);
	
	   tx.commit();
	}
	
	In transactional mode, the two above cache operations will either commit or rollback.

Figure 4.27

Ignite transactions

IgniteTransactions façade provides ACID compliant semantic whenever working with caches. You can create transaction when working with one cache or across multiple caches. Caches with different cache mode like PARTITIONED or REPLICATED can also participate in a single transaction. An example of a transaction in Ignite are shown below:

```
Transaction tx = Ignition.ignite().transactions().txStart();
try{
   Account acct = cache.get(acctId);

   // Current balance.
   double balance = acct.getBalance();

   // Deposit $100 into account.
   acct.setBalance(balance + 100);

   // Store updated account in cache.
   cache.put(acctId, acct);

   tx.commit();
}
```

Ignite `IgniteTransactions` are *autoclosable*, so they will automatically rollback if any exceptions occur. However, you always can explicitly rollback any transaction. Here is an example of transaction rollback.

```
Transaction tx = Ignition.ignite().transactions().txStart();
try{
   Account acct = cache.get(acctId);
   // Current balance.
   double balance = acct.getBalance();
   // Deposit $100 into account.
   acct.setBalance(balance + 100);
   // Store updated account in cache.
   cache.put(acctId, acct);
   tx.commit();
} catch(){
   tx.rollback();
}
```

Ignite `IgniteTransactions` interface provides three different overloaded methods to start transactions:

- **txStart()** - Starts transaction with default isolation, concurrency, timeout, and invalidation policy.
- **txStart(TransactionConcurrency concurrency, TransactionIsolation isolation)** - Starts new transaction with the specified concurrency and isolation.
- **txStart(TransactionConcurrency concurrency, TransactionIsolation isolation, long timeout, int txSize)** - Starts transaction with specified isolation, concurrency, timeout, invalidation flag, and a number of participating entries.

There are two transaction concurrencies available in Ignite: PESSIMISTIC or OPTIMISTIC.

Transactional isolation can be

- READ_COMMITTED - Read committed isolation level
- REPEATABLE_READ - Repeatable read isolation level
- SERIALIZABLE - Serializable isolation level

We will have a detailed look at the transaction concurrency a little bit later.

Chapter four: Persistence

Transaction commit protocols

Ignite provides two types of commit protocols for utilizing transactions: One-phase commit (1p), Two-phase commit (2p). Ignite automatically decides when to use 1-phase commit or 2-phase commit protocol. At first glance, it may appear too hard to understand. The decision mainly depends on Ignite cache mode configuration: Partitioned or Replicated and data co-allocation. Later we are going to explore, how and when Ignite uses this above commit protocols to utilize transactions. To help explain the commit protocols, let's imagine the following conditions:

1. We have three nodes Ignite cluster with 150 entries in the cache.
2. Cache mode will be either Replicated or Partitioned.

1-phase commit:

1-phase commit or 1p commit usually used in one system or database and doesn't span through multiple systems or DBs. A high-level view of the 1p commit will look like follows:

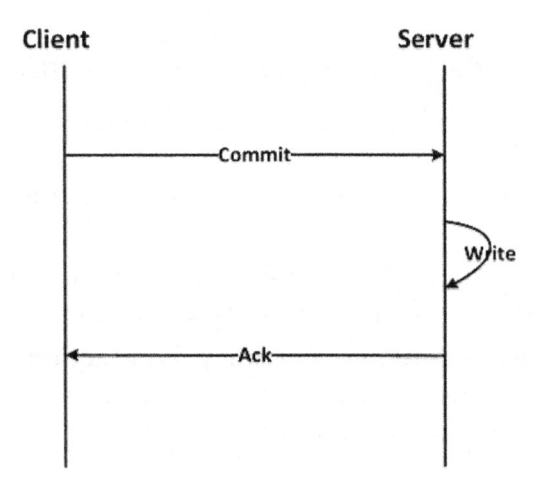

Figure 4.28

A client sends requests for commit and waiting for the acknowledgment from the server. The server on his side, either commit the transaction or rollback the data. Things are getting complicated when it comes to the distributed database like Ignite. In Ignite, whenever you use REPLICATED cache mode with more than 2 nodes, the commit protocol will always 2p commit. Because in Ignite replicated caches are implemented using Partitioned cache where every key has a primary copy and is also backed up on all other nodes in the cluster. If you have 2 nodes Ignite cluster with replicated cache mode, Ignite should use 1p commit protocol for utilizing transaction. This time 1p commit process will look like follows:

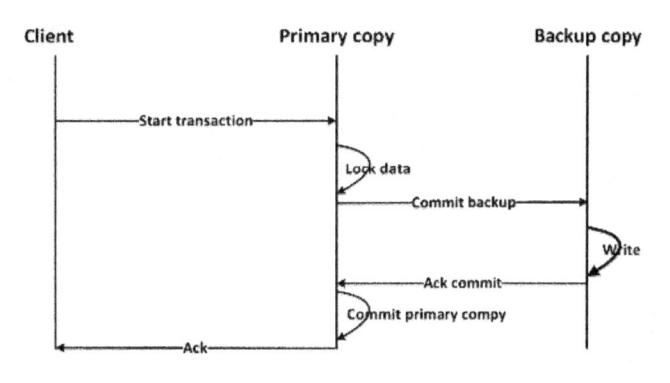

Figure 4.29

In the partitioned cache, every key-value pair is assigned to a specific node within the cluster. In our case (3 nodes with 150 cache entries), every node will cache 150/3 = 50 entries. In real life scenario, we will also have to backup our cache, so we will have 1 primary copy and few more backup copies. If we will have more than 1 backup copy, then Ignite will use 2p commit protocol in the transaction. For using 1p commit protocol in Partitioned mode, we have to fulfill the following condition:

1. Backup copy must be *1*
2. Cache entries participate in a transaction must reside in the *same partition.*

We can use affinity key to co-allocated cache entries to satisfy the second condition. Assuming we have bank clients profiles and transactions which are in different cache, we can use the clientID as an affinity key to bind the two different data sets. With the affinity key, Client with his transactions with the same cleintID will reside in the same partition on the same node. The diagram below illustrates the 1p commit protocol in the partitioned cache.

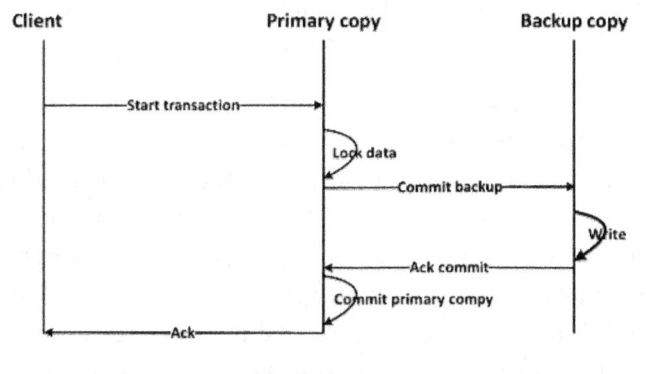

Figure 4.30

2-phase commit:

Typically, a 2p commit is initialized whenever you have more than *1* backup copy of your primary data in Ignite cluster. In 2p commit there is one more phase *prepare* appeared in the transaction process. The 2p commit protocol phases are shown in figure 4.31.

Chapter four: Persistence 179

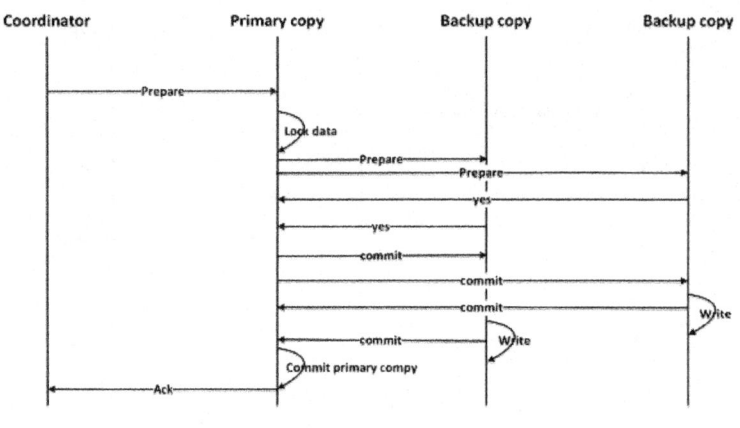

Figure 4.31

Whenever a client initiates a commit request to Ignite node, the coordinator node sends a prepare message to the primary nodes of the data, primary node after acquiring the proper locks, synchronously send the prepare message to all the nodes holding the backup copy of the data. Every backup copy nodes reply with the messages **yes** on prepare request. Once every *yes* vote is collected from the backup nodes, a commit message is sent, and the transaction gets committed.

Next two subsections (optimistic transaction & pessimistic transaction) we obtained from the Ignite documentation because we didn't want to change the meaning and the contexts. If you are already familiar with optimistic & pessimistic lock, you can skip the next two subsections.

Optimistic Transactions

In **OPTIMISTIC** transactions, entry locks are acquired on primary nodes during the prepare step, then promoted to backup nodes and released once the transaction is committed. The locks are never acquired if the transaction is rolled back by the user and no commit attempt was made. The following isolation levels can be configured with OPTIMISTIC concurrency mode:

- READ_COMMITTED - Changes that should be applied to the cache are collected on the originating node and applied upon the transaction commit. Transaction data is read without a lock and is never cached in the transaction. The data may be read from a backup node if this is allowed in the cache configuration. In this isolation you can have so-called Non-Repeatable Reads because a concurrent transaction can change the data when you are reading the data twice in your transaction. This mode combination does not check if the entry value has been modified since the first read or write access and never raises an optimistic exception.
- REPEATABLE_READ - Transactions at this isolation level work similar to OPTIMISTIC READ_COMMITTED transactions with only one difference - read values are cached on the originating node and all subsequent reads are guaranteed to be local. This mode combination does not check if the entry value has been modified since the first read or write access and never raises an optimistic exception.

- SERIALIZABLE - Stores an entry version upon first read access. Ignite will fail a transaction at the commit stage if the Ignite engine detects that at least one of the entries used as part of the initiated transaction has been modified. This is achieved by internally checking the version of an entry remembered in a transaction to the one actually in the grid at the time of commit. In short, this means that if Ignite detects that there is a conflict at the commit stage of a transaction, we fail such a transaction throwing TransactionOptimisticException & rolling back any changes made. The user should handle this exception and retry the transaction.

Pessimistic Transactions

In **PESSIMISTIC** transactions, locks are acquired during the first read or write access (depending on the isolation level) and held by the transaction until it is committed or rolled back. In this mode, locks are acquired on primary nodes first and then promoted to backup nodes during the prepare stage. The following isolation levels can be configured with PESSIMISTIC concurrency mode:

- READ_COMMITTED - Data is read without a lock and is never cached in the transaction itself. The data may be read from a backup node if this is allowed in the cache configuration. In this isolation you can have the so-called Non-Repeatable Reads because a concurrent transaction can change the data when you are reading the data twice in your transaction. The lock is only acquired at the time of first write access (this includes EntryProcessor invocation). This means that an entry that has been read during the transaction may have a different value by the time the transaction is committed. No exception will be thrown in this case.
- REPEATABLE_READ - Entry lock is acquired and data is fetched from the primary node on the first read or write access and stored in the local transactional map. All consecutive access to the same data is local and will return the last read or updated transaction value. This means no other concurrent transactions can make changes to the locked data, and you are getting Repeatable Reads for your transaction.
- SERIALIZABLE - In the PESSIMISTIC mode, this isolation level works the same way as REPEATABLE_READ.

Note that in PESSIMISTIC mode, the order of locking is important. Moreover, Ignite will acquire locks sequentially and exactly in the order provided by a user.

Performance impact on transaction

The following factors impacts on transactions in Apache Ignite:

1. *Number of the backup nodes*: number of the backup nodes directly impact on the transaction performance. The more you have (backup node), the more time it will take to complete the transaction process.

Chapter four: Persistence

2. *Data co-allocation*: if all the related datasets are located on the same partition or on the same node, a transaction on such datasets will be faster than other datasets.
3. *Backup update mode (synchronous and asynchronous)*: write synchronization mode tells Ignite whether the client node should wait for responses from remote nodes, before completing a commit. This can also increase the transaction wait time on the client side. However, you can choose, FULL_ASYNC mode. In this case, client node does not wait for responses from participating nodes, in which case remote nodes may get their state updated slightly after any of the caches write methods complete or after `Transaction.commit()` method completes.

Thus, you have to choose your cluster configuration carefully and transaction modes to get desired performance.

Conclusion

In this chapter we have explored the following topics:

- Persistence Ignite cache entries in RDBMS and NoSQL.
- Cache queries, SQL, and text query by example.
- HibernOGM and learned how to use JPA with Ignite.
- Ignite cache eviction & expiration policies.
- Ignite transaction on depth.

What's next

In the next chapter, we focus on more advanced features and extensions to the Ignite platform. We will discuss the main problems of the Hadoop ecosystems and how Ignite can help to improve the performance of the existing Hadoop jobs.

Chapter five: Accelerating Big Data computing

Hadoop has quickly become the standard for business intelligence on huge data sets. However, it's batch scheduling overhead, and disk-based data storage have made it unsuitable for use in analyzing live, real-time data in a production environment. One of the main factors that limit performance scaling of Hadoop and Map/Reduce is the fact that Hadoop relies on a file system that generates a lot of input/output (I/O) files. I/O adds latency that delays the Map/Reduce computation. An alternative is to store the needed distributed data within the memory. Placing Map/Reduce in-memory with the data it needs, eliminates file I/O latency.

Apache Ignite has offered a set of useful components allowing in-memory Hadoop job executing and file system operations. Even, Apache Ignite provides an implementation of Spark RDD which allows sharing state in-memory across Spark applications.

In this chapter, we are going to explore how big data computing with Hadoop/Spark can be performed by combining an in-memory data grid with an integrated, standalone Hadoop Map/Reduce execution engine, and how it can accelerate the analysis of large, static data sets.

Hadoop accelerator

Ignite in-memory Map/Reduce engine executes Map/Reduce programs in seconds (or less) by incorporating several techniques. By avoiding Hadoop's batch scheduling, it can start up jobs in milliseconds instead of tens of seconds. In-memory data storage dramatically reduces access times by eliminating data motion from the disk or across the network. This is the Ignite approach to accelerating Hadoop application performance without changing the code. The main advantages are, all the operations are highly transparent and that it is accomplished without changing a line of MapReduce code.

Ignite Hadoop in-memory plug and play accelerator can be grouped by into three different categories:

- **In-memory Map/Reduce:** It's an alternative implementation of Hadoop Job tracker and task tracker, which can accelerate job execution performance. It eliminates the overhead associated with job tracker and task trackers in a standard Hadoop architecture while providing low-latency, HPC-style distributed processing.
- **Ignite in-memory file system (IGFS):** It's also an alternate implementation of Hadoop file system named *IgniteHadoopFileSystem*, which can store data sets in-memory. This in-memory file system minimizes disk I/O and improves performances.

Chapter five: Accelerating Big Data computing 183

- **Hadoop file system cache**: This implementation works as a caching layer above HDFS, every read and write operations would go through this layer and can improve Map/Reduce performance. See chapter two for more about read-write behind cache strategy.

Conceptual architecture of the Ignite Hadoop accelerator is shown in figure 5.1:

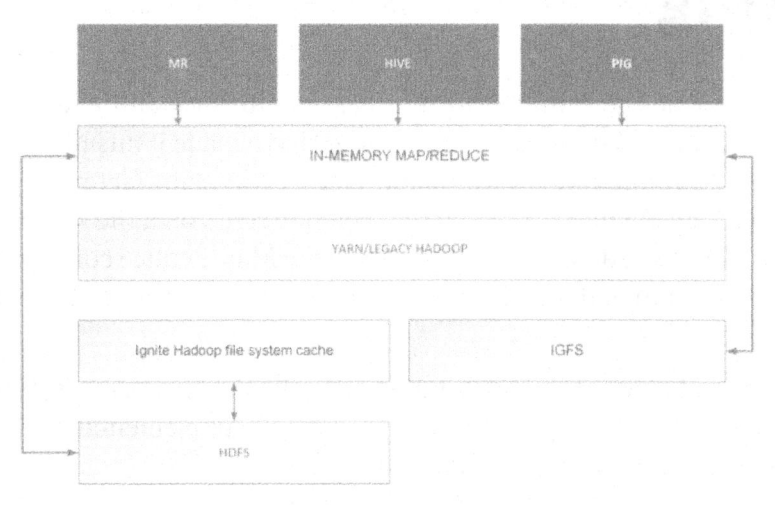

Figure 5.1

The apache Ignite Hadoop accelerator tool is especially very useful when you already have an existing Hadoop cluster up and running and want to get more performance with minimum efforts. I can still remember my first Hadoop project in the summer of the year 2011. After a few months of use of our 64 nodes Hadoop cluster, we stuck were with the problem of data motion between Hadoop nodes it was very painful to overcome. This time, Spark was not so much matured to use. In the long run, we made a serious change in our infrastructure, replaced most of the hard drive to SSD. As a consequence, it was very costly.

> **Note:**
> Hadoop running on commodity hardware is a *myth*. Most of the Hadoop process is I/O intensive and requires homogenous and mid-end servers to perform well.

When running Map/Reduce using one of the most popular open source distribution of Hadoop, Hadoop Map/Reduce introduces numerous I/O overhead that extends analysis times to minutes.

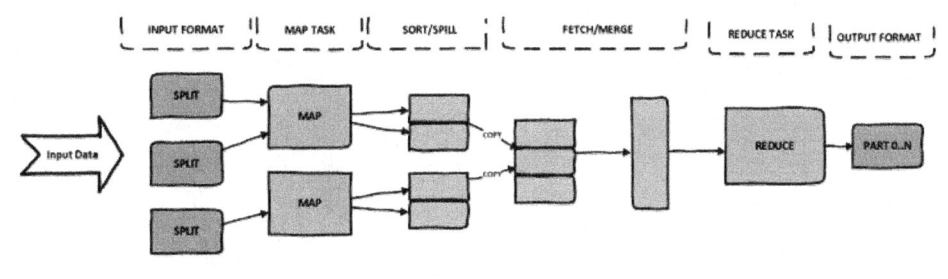

Chapter five: Accelerating Big Data computing   184

Figure 5.2

The generic phases of Hadoop job are shown in figure 5.2, phase sort, merge or shuffle are highly I/O intensive. These overheads are prohibitive when running real-time analytics that returns the result in milliseconds or seconds. With Ignite IGFS, you can replace the Hadoop HDFS and eliminate the I/O overhead, which can boost Map/Reduce performance. Because in-memory data grid hosts fast-changing data in memory, Map/Reduce application can input data directly from the grid and output results back to the grid. This speeds up the analysis by avoiding the delay in accessing HDFS during real-time analysis.

However, to decrease the access time for reading data into Hadoop from HDFS, the input data set can be cached within the Ignite cache storage. Ignite Hadoop file system (IGFS) cache provides a distributed caching feature that speeds access times by capturing data from HDFS or other data sources during Map/Reduce processing and working as a second level cache for HDFS. Ignite Hadoop accelerator is compatible with the latest versions of the most popular Hadoop platforms, including Apache, Cloudera and Horton. This means that you can run fully compatible MapReduce applications for any of these platforms on Ignite in-memory Map/Reduce engine.

Next, we are going to explore the details of the Hadoop accelerator tools.

In-memory Map/Reduce

This is the Ignite in-memory Map/Reduce engine, which is 100% compatible with Hadoop HDFS and Yarn. It reduces the startup and the execution time of the Hadoop Job tracker and the Task tracker. Ignite in-memory Map/Reduce provides dramatic performance boosts for CPU-intensive tasks while requiring an only minimal change to existing applications. This module also provides an implementation of weight based Map/Reduce planner, which assigns mappers and reducers based on their weights. Weight describes how much resources are required to execute the particular map and reduce task. This planning algorithm assigns mappers so that, total resulting weight on all nodes as minimal as possible. Reducers are assigned slightly different.

This approach minimizes the expensive data motion over the network. Reducer assigned to a node with mapper are called local. Otherwise, it is considered as remote. High-level architecture of the Ignite in-memory Map/Reduce is shown below:

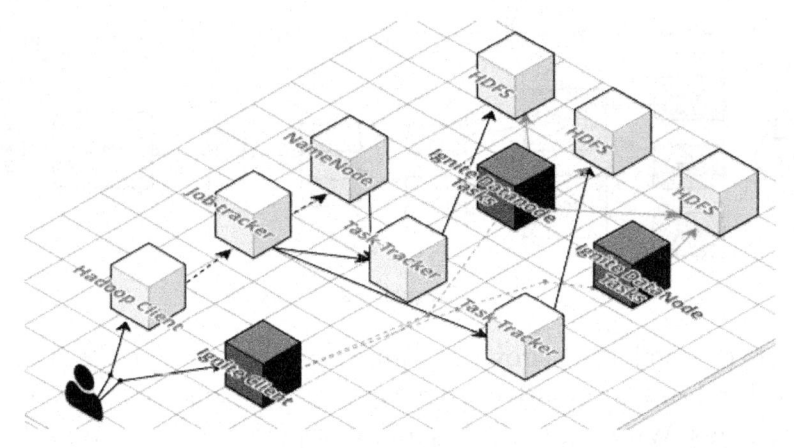

Figure 5.3

Ignite in-memory grid has pre-stage java based execution environment on all grid nodes and reuse it for multiple data processing. This execution environment consists of a set of Java virtual machines one on each server within the cluster. This JVM's forms the Ignite Map/Reduce engine as shown in figure 5.2. Also, the Ignite in-memory data grid can automatically deploy all necessary executable programs or libraries for the execution of the Map/Reduce across the grid, this greatly reduces the startup time down to milliseconds.

Now that, we have got the basics, let's try to configure the sandbox and execute a few Map/Reduce jobs in Ignite Map/Reduce engine.

For simplicity, we are going to install a Hadoop *Pseudo-Distributed* cluster in a single virtual machine and will run Hadoop famous *word count* example as a Map/Reduce job and then we will complicate our example to study the other features of the Ignite Hadoop accelerator tool.

> **Note:**
> Hadoop `Pseudo-Distributed` cluster means, Hadoop datanode, namenode, tasktracker/jobtracker, everything will be on one virtual (Host) machine.

Let's have a look at our sandbox configuration as shown below.

Sandbox configuration:

VM	VMWare
OS	RedHat enterprise Linux
CPU	2
RAM	2 Gb
JVM version	1.7_60
Ignite version	1.6, single node cluster

Chapter five: Accelerating Big Data computing

First of all, we are going to install and configure Hadoop and will proceed to Apache Ignite. Assuming that, Java has been installed, and JAVA_HOME is in the environment variables.

Step 1:

Unpack the Hadoop distribution archive and set the JAVA_HOME path in the `etc/hadoop/hadoop-env.sh` file as follows. This step is optional if your JAVA_HOME is properly configured in Linux box.

```
export JAVA_HOME=JAVA_HOME_PATH
```

Step 2:

Add the following configuration in the `etc/hadoop/core-site.xml` file.

```
<configuration>
    <property>
        <name>fs.defaultFS</name>
        <value>hdfs://localhost:9000</value>
    </property>
</configuration>
```

Also append the following data replication strategy into the `etc/hadoop/hdfs-site.xml` file.

```
<configuration>
    <property>
        <name>dfs.replication</name>
        <value>1</value>
    </property>
</configuration>
```

Step 3:

Setup password less or passphrase less ssh for your operating system.

```
$ ssh-keygen -t dsa -P '' -f ~/.ssh/id_dsa
$ cat ~/.ssh/id_dsa.pub >> ~/.ssh/authorized_keys
$ chmod 0600 ~/.ssh/authorized_keys
```

Try the following command into your console.

```
$ ssh localhost
```

It shouldn't ask you for input password.

Step 4:

Format the Hadoop HDFS file system.

Chapter five: Accelerating Big Data computing 187

```
$ bin/hdfs namenode -format
```

Next, start the *namenode/datanode* daemon by the following command:

```
$ sbin/start-dfs.sh
```

Also, I would like to suggest you to add the HADOOP_HOME environmental variable to operating system.

Step 5:

Make a few directories in HDFS file system to run Map/Reduce jobs.

```
bin/hdfs dfs -mkdir /user
bin/hdfs dfs -mkdir /input
```

The above command will create two folder user and input in HDFS file system. Insert some text files in directory *input*.

```
bin/hdfs dfs -put $HADOOP_HOME/etc/hadoop /input
```

Step 6:

Run the Hadoop native Map/Reduce application to count the words of the file.

```
$ bin/hadoop jar $HADOOP_HOME/share/hadoop/mapreduce/hadoop-mapreduce-examples-2.7.2.jar w\
ordcount /input/hadoop output
```

You can view the result of the words count by the following command:

```
bin/hdfs dfs -cat output/*
```

In my case, the file is huge with words and its number of count, let's see the fragment of the file.

```
want 1
warnings. 1
when 9
where 4
which 7
while 1
who 6
will 23
window 1
window, 1
with 62
within 4
without 1
work 12
writing, 27
```

At this stage, our Hadoop pseudo cluster is configured and ready to use. Now let's start configuring the Apache Ignite.

Step 7:

Unpack the distribution of the Apache Ignite somewhere in your sandbox and add the *IGNITE_HOME* path to the root directory of the installation. For getting *statistics about tasks and executions*, you have to add the following properties in your /config/default-config.xml file.

```xml
<bean id="ignite.cfg" class="org.apache.ignite.configuration.IgniteConfiguration">
  ....
  <property name="includeEventTypes">
    <list>
      <util:constant static-field="org.apache.ignite.events.EventType.EVT_TASK_FAILED"/>
      <util:constant static-field="org.apache.ignite.events.EventType.EVT_TASK_FINISHED"/>
      <util:constant static-field="org.apache.ignite.events.EventType.EVT_JOB_MAPPED"/>
    </list>
  </property>
</bean>
```

Above configuration will enable the event task for statistics.

> ⚠ **Warning:**
> By default, all events are disabled. Whenever these above events are enabled, you can use the command "tasks" in *ignitevisor* to get statistics about tasks executions.

IgniteVisor **tasks** command is very useful to get aggregated results of all executed tasks for a given

Chapter five: Accelerating Big Data computing

period of time. Check the *chapter-bigdata/src/main/config/ignite-inmemory* directory from GitHub repository[38] for complete configuration of the `defult-config.xml` file.

Step 8:

Add the following libraries in the `$IGNITE_HOME/libs` directory.

```
asm-all-4.2.jar
ignite-hadoop-1.6.0.jar
hadoop-mapreduce-client-core-2.7.2.jar
hadoop-common-2.7.2.jar
hadoop-auth-2.7.2.jar
```

Note that, *asm-all-4.2.jar* library version is dependent on your Hadoop version.

Step 9:

We are going to use the Apache Ignite default configuration, `config/default-config.xml` file to start the Ignite node. Start the Ignite node with the following command.

```
bin/ignite.sh
```

Step 10:

Add a few more staffs to use Ignite job tracker instead of Hadoop. Add the `HADOOP_CLASSPATH` to the environmental variables as follows.

```
export HADOOP_CLASSPATH=$HADOOP_CLASSPATH:$IGNITE_HOME/libs/ignite-core-1.6.0.jar:$IGNITE_\
HOME/libs/ignite-hadoop-1.6.0.jar:$IGNITE_HOME/libs/ignite-shmem-1.0.0.jar
```

Step 11:

In this stage, we are going to override the Hadoop `mapred-site.xml` file. For a quick start, add the following fragment of xml to the mapred-site.xml.

---

[38] https://github.com/srecon/ignite-book-code-samples

Chapter five: Accelerating Big Data computing   190

```xml
<property>
  <name>mapreduce.framework.name</name>
  <value>ignite</value>
</property>
<property>
  <name>mapreduce.jobtracker.address</name>
  <value>127.0.0.1:11211</value>
</property>
```

Note that, we explicitly added the Map/Reduce framework to Ignite. Port *11211* is the default port to listening for the task.

> **Note:**
> You don't need to restart the Hadoop processes after making any change to `mapred-site.xml`.

Step 12:

Run the above example of the word count Map/Reduce example again.

```
$bin/hadoop jar $HADOOP_HOME/share/hadoop/mapreduce/hadoop-mapreduce-examples-2.7.2.jar wo\
rdcount /input/hadoop output2
```

The output should be very similar as shown in figure 5.4.

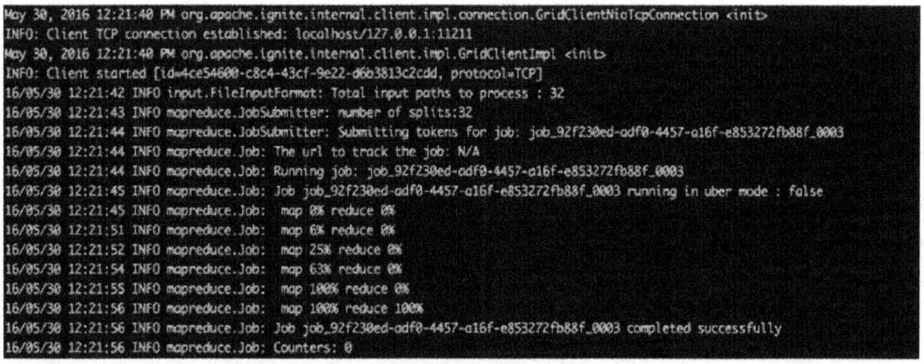

Figure 5.4

Now Execution time is faster than last time whenever we have used Hadoop task tracker. Let's examine the Ignite task execution statistics through Ignite visor:

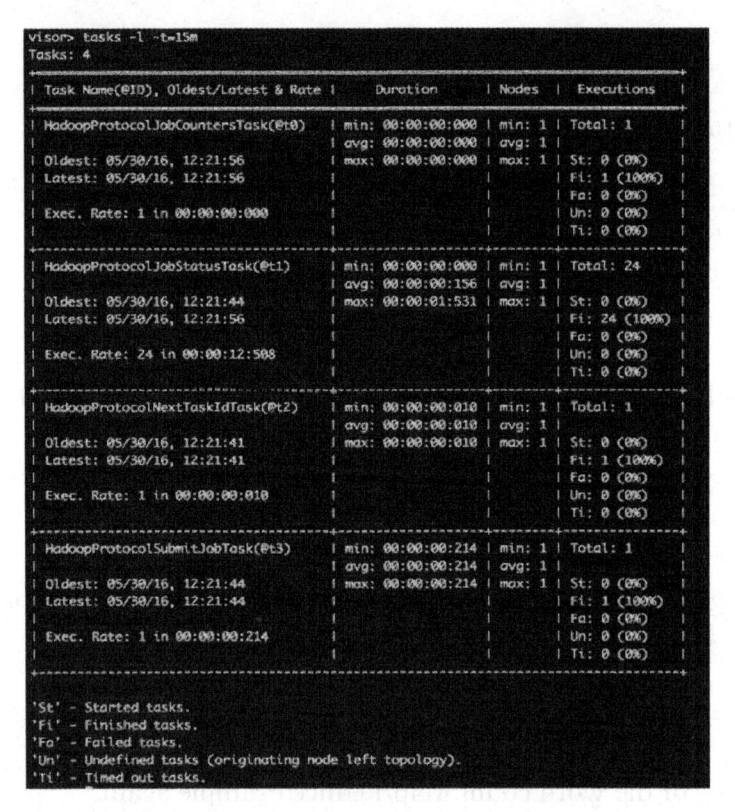

Chapter five: Accelerating Big Data computing   191

Figure 5.5

From the figure 5.5, we should notice that, the total executions and the durations times of the in-memory task tracker. In our case, total executions task (*HadoopProtocolJobStatusTask(@t1)*) is 24 and the execution rate are 12 second.

Benchmark

To demonstrate the performance advantage of the Ignite Map/Reduce engine, measurements were made of the familiar Hadoop WordCount and PI sample application. This program was run both on the standard Apache Hadoop distribution and on an Ignite grid that included a built-in Hadoop MapReduce execution engine.

The Hadoop distribution comes with a number of benchmarks, which are bundled in hadoop-*test*.jar and hadoop-*examples*.jar. The two benchmarks we are going to use are `WordCount` and `PI`. The full list of available options for hadoop-*examples*.jar are shown bellow:

```
$ bin/hadoop jar hadoop-*examples*.jar
An example program must be given as the first argument.
Valid program names are:
  aggregatewordcount: An Aggregate based map/reduce program that counts the words in the i\
nput files.
  aggregatewordhist: An Aggregate based map/reduce program that computes the histogram of \
the words in the input files.
  dbcount: An example job that count the pageview counts from a database.
  grep: A map/reduce program that counts the matches of a regex in the input.
  join: A job that effects a join over sorted, equally partitioned datasets
  multifilewc: A job that counts words from several files.
  pentomino: A map/reduce tile laying program to find solutions to pentomino problems.
  pi: A map/reduce program that estimates Pi using monte-carlo method.
  randomtextwriter: A map/reduce program that writes 10GB of random textual data per node.
  randomwriter: A map/reduce program that writes 10GB of random data per node.
  secondarysort: An example defining a secondary sort to the reduce.
  sleep: A job that sleeps at each map and reduce task.
  sort: A map/reduce program that sorts the data written by the random writer.
  sudoku: A sudoku solver.
  teragen: Generate data for the terasort
  terasort: Run the terasort
  teravalidate: Checking results of terasort
  wordcount: A map/reduce program that counts the words in the input files.
```

The wordcount example, for instance, will be used to count the word from the The Complete Works of William Shakespeare file. On the other hand, we are going to use the PI example to calculate the digit of pi using Monte-Carlo method. However, it's not recommended to use Hadoop pseudo-distributed server for benchmarking. We will do it for academic purposes.

Sandbox for the benchmark:

VM	VMWare
OS	RedHat enterprise Linux
CPU	2
RAM	2 Gb
JVM version	1.7_60
Ignite version	1.6, single node cluster
Hadoop version	2.7.2, pseudo cluster

First of all, we are going to use the wordcount example to count words from the *The Complete Works of William Shakespeare* file.

Step 1:

Create another input directory in HDFS to store the file t8.shakespeare.txt. You can download the file from the *input* directory of the GitHub project chapter-bigdata/src/main/input/t8.shakespeare.txt.

Chapter five: Accelerating Big Data computing

The file size is approximately 5,5 MB.

```
hdfs dfs -mkdir /wc-input
```

Step 2:

Store the file into the HDFS *wc-input* directory.

```
hdfs dfs -put /YOUR_PATH_TO_THE_FILE /t8.shakespeare.txt /wc-input
```

Step 3:

Comment the following fragment of the properties into the mapred-site.xml.

```xml
<property>
        <name>mapreduce.framework.name</name>
        <value>ignite</value>
</property>
<property>
        <name>mapreduce.jobtracker.address</name>
        <value>localhost:11211</value>
</property>
```

Step 4:

And before we start, here's a nifty trick for your tests: When running the benchmarks described in the following sections, you might want to use the Unix `time` command to measure the elapsed time. This saves you the hassle of navigating to the Hadoop *JobTracker* web interface to get the (almost) same information. Simply prefix every Hadoop command with `time` command as follows:

```
time hadoop jar $HADOOP_HOME/share/hadoop/mapreduce/hadoop-mapreduce-examples-2.7.2.jar wo\
rdcount /wc-input/ output6
```

Run the above job a few times. You should get the relevant value (real) into the console as shown below:

Chapter five: Accelerating Big Data computing

```
16/09/05 16:05:56 INFO mapred.LocalJobRunner: 2 / 2 copied.
16/09/05 16:05:56 INFO mapred.Task: Task attempt_local1864495227_0001_r_000000_0 is allowe\
d to commit now
16/09/05 16:05:56 INFO output.FileOutputCommitter: Saved output of task 'attempt_local1864\
495227_0001_r_000000_0' to hdfs://localhost:9000/user/user/output20/_temporary/0/task_loca\
l1864495227_0001_r_000000
16/09/05 16:05:56 INFO mapred.LocalJobRunner: reduce > reduce
16/09/05 16:05:56 INFO mapred.Task: Task 'attempt_local1864495227_0001_r_000000_0' done.
16/09/05 16:05:57 INFO mapreduce.Job:  map 100% reduce 100%
16/09/05 16:05:57 INFO mapreduce.Job: Job job_local1864495227_0001 completed successfully
16/09/05 16:05:57 INFO mapreduce.Job: Counters: 35
        File System Counters
                FILE: Number of bytes read=2948198
                FILE: Number of bytes written=5833532
                FILE: Number of read operations=0
        Map-Reduce Framework
                Map input records=128803
                Map output records=926965
                Map output bytes=8787114
                Map output materialized bytes=1063186
                Input split bytes=219
        Shuffle Errors
                BAD_ID=0
                CONNECTION=0
                IO_ERROR=0
                WRONG_LENGTH=0
                WRONG_MAP=0
                WRONG_REDUCE=0
        File Input Format Counters
                Bytes Read=5596513
        File Output Format Counters
                Bytes Written=724175
real    0m25.732s
user    0m14.582s
sys     0m0.616s
```

Step 5:

Next, run the Ignite version of the Map/Reduce for wordcount example. Uncomment or add the following fragment of the xml into `mapred-site.xml` file.

Chapter five: Accelerating Big Data computing

```
<property>
        <name>mapreduce.framework.name</name>
        <value>ignite</value>
</property>
<property>
        <name>mapreduce.jobtracker.address</name>
        <value>localhost:11211</value>
</property>
```

Execute the same command a few times as follows.

```
time hadoop jar $HADOOP_HOME/share/hadoop/mapreduce/hadoop-mapreduce-examples-2.7.2.jar wo\
rdcount /wc-input/ output7
```

In the console, you should get the following output.

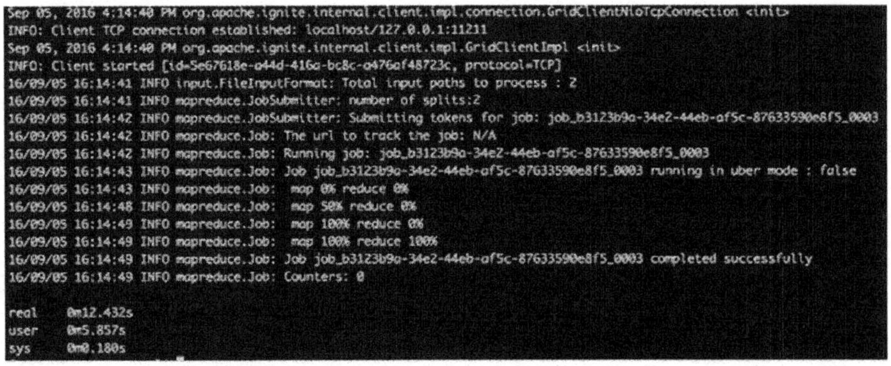

Figure 5.6

Step 6:

For the second benchmark test, we executes the PI example with 16 maps and 1000000 sample per map. Run the following command for Hadoop and Ignite Map/Reduce as follows:

```
time hadoop jar $HADOOP_HOME/share/hadoop/mapreduce/hadoop-mapreduce-examples-2.7.2.jar pi\
 16 1000000
```

The output should be the same as shown below:

Chapter five: Accelerating Big Data computing   196

Figure 5.7

After running the benchmark test, we can demonstrate the performance gain of the Ignite in-memory Map/Reduce. Two different test were run with same data sets 3 times and Ignite demonstrates a 1.7% performance gain on both tests as shown in figure 5.7 below.

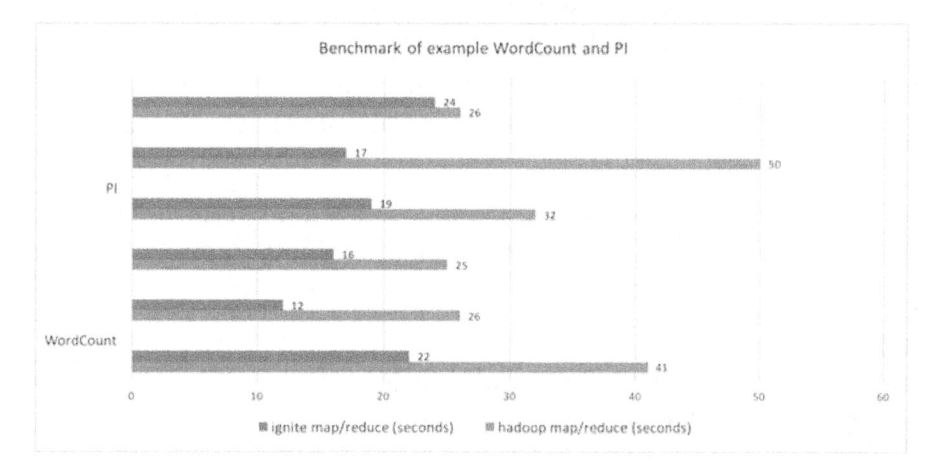

Figure 5.8

Note that, both of the tests executes on single node machine, and the result will be varying on real cluster. Anyway, we have seen how the Ignite can enable significant speed reduction in analysis time. Ignite also allows the input data set to be updated while the MapReduce analysis is in progress. Using the standard Hadoop MapReduce distribution, live updates are not possible since data in HDFS can only be appended and not updated.

Here, we are going to finish this section. In the next section, we will use Apache Pig for data analysis.

Using Apache Pig for data analysis

Apache Pig provides a platform for analyzing a very large-scale data set. With Apache Pig you can easily analyze your data from Hadoop HDFS. Apache Pig compiles instruction to sequences of Map/Reduce programs which will run on a Hadoop cluster. Apache Pig provides `PigLatin` scripting

Chapter five: Accelerating Big Data computing   197

language, which can perform operations like ETL or AdHoc data analysis. The Apache Pig was built to make programming Map/Reduce easier, before Pig, Java was the only way to process the data stored in HDFS.

Apache Ignite provides a transparent way to run PigLatin scripts in Ignite in-memory Map/Reduce. You have almost nothing to configure to run PigLatin script. Our setup from the previous section is enough to run in-memory Map/Reduce through PigLatin script. We just have to install Apache Pig in our environment to execute the PigLatin script.

Let's have a look at the features of Pig. Apache Pig comes with the following features:

- **Ease of programming** – PigLatin script is very much similar to SQL script. It's very easy to write a script in Pig if you are good at SQL.
- **Analytical functions** – Pig provides a lot of functions and operators to perform operations like `Filter`, `GroupBy`, `Sort`, etc.
- **Extensibility** – With existing operators, a user can develop their custom functions to read, write or process data. For example, we have developed a Pig function to parse XML and validate XML documents from HDFS.
- **Handles all kinds of Data** - Apache Pig can process or handle any kind of data, both structured or semi-structured. It can store the result into HDFS, Cassandra or Hbase.

Usually, Apache Pig is used by the data scientist or data analyst for performing `ad-hoc` scripting and quick prototyping. Apache Pig is hugely used in batch processing, such as

- Processing time sensitive data.
- Data analysis through sampling, for example weblogs.
- Data processing for search platform.

Although Map/Reduce is a powerful programming model, there is a significant difference between Apache Pig and Map/Reduce. The major difference between Pig and the Map/Reduce are shown below:

Pig	MapReduce
Apache Pig is a data flow language.	Map/Reduce is a data processing paradigm.
Apache Pig is a high-level language.	Map/Reduce is a low-level language, almost written in java or Python.
During execution of the PigLatin script, every Pig operator is converted internally into a Map/Reduce job.	Map/Reduce job have a long compilation process.

Now, we are going to use two different datasets for our examples, one of them are `Shakespeare all works` in a text file, and another one is the `movies_data.csv` CSV file, which contains a list of movies name, release year, rating, etc. Both of them reside in the directory */chapter-bigdata/src/main/input*.

Next, we explains how to install, setup and run PigLatin scripts in-memory Map/Reduce.

It is essential that you have Java and Hadoop installed and configured in your sandbox to get up and running with Pig. Check the previous section to configure Hadoop and Ignite into your system.

Let's have a look at our sandbox configuration as shown below.

VM	VMWare
OS	RedHat enterprise Linux
CPU	2
RAM	2 Gb
JVM version	1.7_60
Ignite version	1.6, single node cluster
Hadoop version	2.7.2, pseudo cluster
Pig version	0.16.0

Next, we will download and install Apache Pig in our sandbox.

Step 1:

Download the latest version of the Apache Pig from the following link[39]. In our case, the Pig version is 0.16.0.

Step 2:

Untar the gz archive anywhere in your sandbox.

```
tar xvzf pig-0.16.0.tar.gz
```

And rename the folder for easier access as follows:

```
mv pig-0.16.0 pig
```

Step 3:

Add */pig/bin* to your path. Use export (bash, sh) or setenv (csh).

```
export PATH=/<my-path-to-pig>/pig/bin:$PATH
```

Step 4:

Test the pig installation with the following simple command.

---

[39] https://github.com/srecon/ignite-book-code-samples

```
pig --help
```

That's it, now you are ready to run PigLatin scripts. Apache Pig scripts can be executed in three different ways: an `interactive` mode, `batch` mode and, `embedded` mode.

1. Interactive mode or Grunt shell – In this shell, you can enter the PigLatin statements and get the output or results.
2. Batch mode or script mode – You can run Apache Pig scripts in batch mode by writing the Pig Latin scripts in a single file with extension *pig*.
3. Embedded mode - Apache Pig provides the provision of defining our own functions (User Defined Functions) in programming languages such as Java, and using them in your script.

You can run the Grunt shell in desired mode (local/cluster) using the –x option as follows:

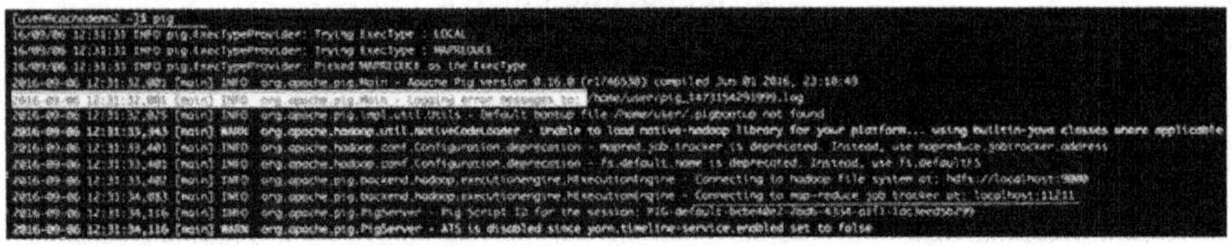

Figure 5.9

With –x option, Grunt shell will start in cluster mode as above. In figure 5.9 we can notice that Pig is connected to Ignite in-memory job tracker at port 11211. Now, we execute the example of classic wordcount application with Apache Pig. For that, we are going to use our previously inserted `t8.shakespeare.txt` file from the Hadoop HDFS.

Step 5:

Use the following command to load the data from HDFS.

```
A = load '/wc-input/t8.shakespeare.txt';
```

The above statement is made up of two parts. The part to the left of "=" is called the relation or alias. It looks like a variable but you should notice that this is not a variable. When this statement is executed, no Map/Reduce task is executed. On the other hand, all the data loads from the HDFS to variable A.

Step 6:

Let's generate data transformation based on the column of data. Sometimes, we want to eliminate nesting, this can be accomplished by `flattening` keywords.

```
B = foreach A generate flatten(TOKENIZE((chararray)$0)) as word;
```

Step 7:

Using the `group` keyword, we can group together all the tuples that have the same group key.

Chapter five: Accelerating Big Data computing   200

```
C = group B by word;
```

Step 8:

Use the count function to compute the number of elements in the bags.

```
D = foreach C generate COUNT(B), group;
```

That's is. Only four lines of code and the wordcount example is ready to go. At this moment, we can dump the results into the console or store the result into the HDFS file. Let's dump the output into the console.

```
E = limit D 100;
dump E;
```

Before dumping the result, we limit it to 100 rows for demonstration purpose. Whenever you execute the DUMP command, in-memory Map/Reduce will run and compute the count of all words in the text file and output the result to the console as shown below.

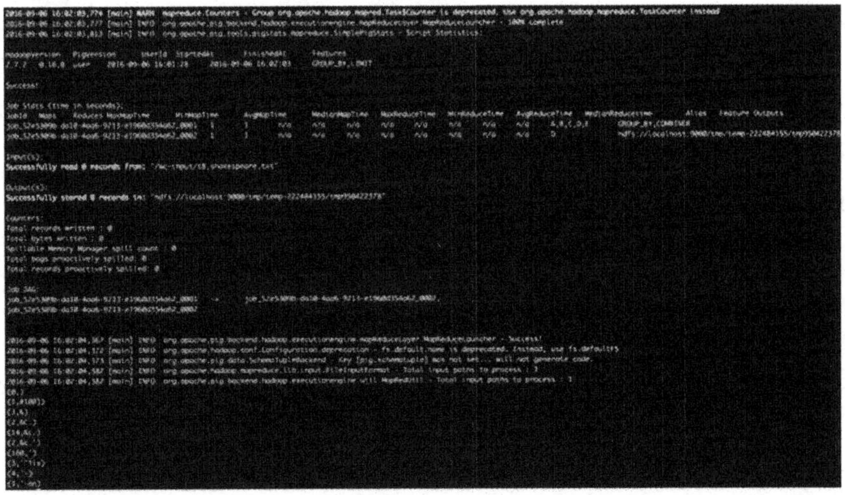

Figure 5.10

Let's have a look at the Ignite task statistics through *ignitevisor* as follows:

Chapter five: Accelerating Big Data computing

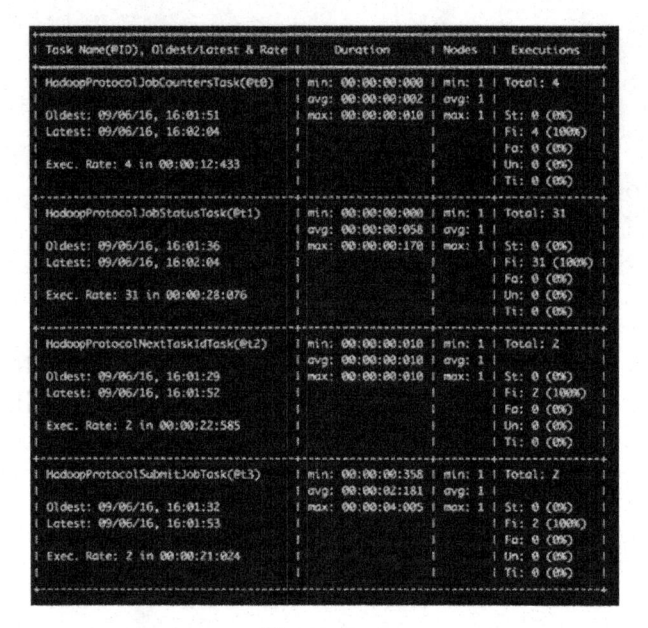

```
+-------------------------------------+------------------------+---------+------------------+
| Task Name(@ID), Oldest/Latest & Rate |       Duration         |  Nodes  |    Executions    |
+-------------------------------------+------------------------+---------+------------------+
| HadoopProtocolJobCountersTask(@t0)  | min: 00:00:00:000      | min: 1  | Total: 4         |
|                                     | avg: 00:00:00:002      | avg: 1  |                  |
| Oldest: 09/06/16, 16:01:51          | max: 00:00:00:010      | max: 1  | St: 0 (0%)       |
| Latest: 09/06/16, 16:02:04          |                        |         | Fi: 4 (100%)     |
|                                     |                        |         | Fa: 0 (0%)       |
| Exec. Rate: 4 in 00:00:12:433       |                        |         | Un: 0 (0%)       |
|                                     |                        |         | Ti: 0 (0%)       |
+-------------------------------------+------------------------+---------+------------------+
| HadoopProtocolJobStatusTask(@t1)    | min: 00:00:00:000      | min: 1  | Total: 31        |
|                                     | avg: 00:00:00:058      | avg: 1  |                  |
| Oldest: 09/06/16, 16:01:36          | max: 00:00:00:170      | max: 1  | St: 0 (0%)       |
| Latest: 09/06/16, 16:02:04          |                        |         | Fi: 31 (100%)    |
|                                     |                        |         | Fa: 0 (0%)       |
| Exec. Rate: 31 in 00:00:28:076      |                        |         | Un: 0 (0%)       |
|                                     |                        |         | Ti: 0 (0%)       |
+-------------------------------------+------------------------+---------+------------------+
| HadoopProtocolNextTaskIdTask(@t2)   | min: 00:00:00:010      | min: 1  | Total: 2         |
|                                     | avg: 00:00:00:010      | avg: 1  |                  |
| Oldest: 09/06/16, 16:01:29          | max: 00:00:00:010      | max: 1  | St: 0 (0%)       |
| Latest: 09/06/16, 16:01:52          |                        |         | Fi: 2 (100%)     |
|                                     |                        |         | Fa: 0 (0%)       |
| Exec. Rate: 2 in 00:00:22:585       |                        |         | Un: 0 (0%)       |
|                                     |                        |         | Ti: 0 (0%)       |
+-------------------------------------+------------------------+---------+------------------+
| HadoopProtocolSubmitJobTask(@t3)    | min: 00:00:00:358      | min: 1  | Total: 2         |
|                                     | avg: 00:00:02:181      | avg: 1  |                  |
| Oldest: 09/06/16, 16:01:32          | max: 00:00:04:005      | max: 1  | St: 0 (0%)       |
| Latest: 09/06/16, 16:01:53          |                        |         | Fi: 2 (100%)     |
|                                     |                        |         | Fa: 0 (0%)       |
| Exec. Rate: 2 in 00:00:21:024       |                        |         | Un: 0 (0%)       |
|                                     |                        |         | Ti: 0 (0%)       |
+-------------------------------------+------------------------+---------+------------------+
```

Figure 5.11

In figure 5.11, we can see the different statistics for different task executions. Total execution task is 39 with average 12 seconds.

Now that we have got the basics let's write more complex Pig script. Here we are going to use another dataset, *movies_data.csv*. The sample dataset is as follows:

```
1,The Nightmare Before Christmas,1993,3.9,4568
2,The Mummy,1932,3.5,4388
3,Orphans of the Storm,1921,3.2,9062
4,The Object of Beauty,1991,2.8,6150
5,Night Tide,1963,2.8,5126
6,One Magic Christmas,1985,3.8,5333
7,Muriel's Wedding,1994,3.5,6323
8,Mother's Boys,1994,3.4,5733
9,Nosferatu: Original Version,1929,3.5,5651
10,Nick of Time,1995,3.4,5333
```

Where the 2nd column is the name of the move, next column is the movie release year and the 4th column will be the overall rating of the certain movies. Let's upload the movies_data.csv file into Hadoop HDFS.

Step 1:

Upload movies_data.csv file into the HDFS.

```
bin/hdfs dfs -put /YOUR_PATH_TO_THE_FILE/movies_data.csv/wc-input
```

Step 2:

Execute the following pig statement to load the file from the HDFS.

```
movies = LOAD '/wc-input/hadoop/movies_data.csv' USING PigStorage(',') as (id:int,name:cha\
rarray,year:int,rating:double,duration:int);
```

Step 3:

Let's make a search of movies with the rating greater than four.

```
movies_rating_greater_than_four = FILTER movies BY (float) rating>4.0;
```

Step 4:

Dump the result into the console.

```
DUMP movies_rating_greater_than_four;
```

The output should be huge.

Step 5:

Search for the movie with the name Mummy;

```
movie_mummy = FILTER movies by (name matches '.*Mummy.*');
```

The output should be the same as shown below:

Figure 5.12

You can group movies by year or even count movies by year. The full source code of the Pig script is as follows:

```
movies = LOAD '/input/hadoop/movies_data.csv' USING PigStorage(',') as (id:int,name:charar\
ray,year:int,rating:double,duration:int);
movies_rating_greater_than_four = FILTER movies BY (float)rating > 4.0;
DUMP movies_rating_greater_than_four;
movie_mummy = FILTER movies by (name matches '.*Mummy.*');
grouped_by_year = group movies by year;
count_by_year = FOREACH grouped_by_year GENERATE group, COUNT(movies);
group_all = GROUP count_by_year ALL;
sum_all = FOREACH group_all GENERATE SUM(count_by_year.$1);
DUMP sum_all;
```

The dump command is only used to display the information on the standard output. If you need to store the result to a file, you can use the pig Store command as follows:

```
store sum_all into '/user/hadoop/sum_all_result;
```

In this section, we got a good feel of Apache Pig. We installed Apache Pig from scratch, loaded some data and executed some basic commands to query by in-memory Map/Reduce of Ignite. The next section will cover Apache Hive to analyze Big Data by Ignite in-memory Map/Reduce.

Near real-time data analysis with Hive

Apache Hive is a data warehouse framework for querying and analyzing data that is stored in Hadoop HDFS. Unlike Apache Pig, Hive provides SQL-like declarative language, called HiveQL, which is used for expressing queries. The Apache Hive was designed to appeal to a community comfortable with SQL. Its philosophy was that we don't need another scripting language. Usually, Hive engine compiles the HiveQL quires into Hadoop Map/Reduce jobs to be executed on Hadoop. In addition, custom Map/Reduce scripts can also be plugged into queries.

Hive operates on data stored in tables which consist of primitive data types and collection data types like arrays and maps. Hive query language is similar to SQL, where it supports subqueries. With Hive query language, it is possible to take a MapReduce joins across Hive tables. It has support for simple SQL-like functions- CONCAT, SUBSTR, ROUND, etc., and aggregation functions like SUM, COUNT, MAX, etc. It also supports GROUP BY and SORT BY clauses. It is also possible to write user defined functions in Hive query language.

Apache Ignite transparently supports Apache Hive for data analysis from the HDFS through in-memory Map/Reduce. No additional configurations to Ignite or the Hadoop cluster are necessary. Hive engines compile the HiveQL quires into Hadoop Map/Reduce jobs, which will be delegated into Ignite in-memory Map/Reduce jobs. Accordingly, the execution of the HiveQL quires is much faster than usual. Let's have a quick look at the features of Apache Hive. Hive provides the following features:

- It stores schema in a database such as derby and the processed data is stored in HDFS.

- It provides SQL-type language for scripting called HiveQL or HQL.
- It is fast, scalable and extensible.

Hive makes daily jobs easy when performing operations like:

- Ad-hoc quires.
- Analysis of huge datasets.
- Data encapsulation.

Unlike Apache Pig, Hive has a few important characteristics as follows:

1. In Hive, tables and databases are created first and then data is loaded into these tables.
2. The Apache Hive was designed for managing and querying only **structured** data that is stored in tables.
3. An important component of Hive i.e. Metastore used for storing schema information. This Metastore typically resides in a relational database.
4. For single user metadata storage, Hive uses derby database and for multiple users Metadata or shared Metadata case, Hive uses MYSQL.
5. Hive supports partition and buckets concepts for easy retrieval of data when the client executes the query.

For demonstration purpose, we are going to run wordcount example through HiveQL in the file Shakespeare all works. As we discussed before, we are not going to make any change to our Ignite or Hadoop cluster. In this section, we will explain how to properly configure and start Hive to execute HiveQL over Ignite Map/Reduce engine. Let's have a look at our sandbox configuration:

VM	VMWare
OS	RedHat enterprise Linux
CPU	2
RAM	2 Gb
JVM version	1.7_60
Ignite version	1.6, single node cluster
Hadoop version	2.7.2, pseudo cluster
Hive version	2.1.0

We are going to use Hive 2.1.0 version in our sandbox. You can download it by visiting the following link[40]. Let's assume that it gets downloaded into any of your local directory of the sandbox.

Step 1:

---
[40] http://apache-mirror.rbc.ru/pub/apache/hive/hive-2.1.0/

To install Hive, do the following:

```
tar zxvf apache-hive-2.1.0-bin.tar.gz
```

The above command will extract the archive into the directory called `hive-2.1.0-bin`. This directory will be your Hive home directory.

Step 2:

Let's create a new directory under `HADOOP_HOME/etc` with the following command and copy all the files from the hadoop directory. Execute the following command from the HADOOP_HOME/etc directory.

```
$ cd $HADOOP_HOME/etc
$ mkdir hadoop-hive
$ cp ./hadoop/*.* ./hadoop-hive
```

This `hadoop-hive` directory will be our `HIVE_CONF_DIRECTORY`.

Step 3:

Create a new file named `hive-site.xml` in the *hadoop-hive* directory with the following contents.

```xml
<?xml version="1.0"?>
<?xml-stylesheet type="text/xsl" href="configuration.xsl"?>
<configuration>
    <!--
        Ignite requires query plan to be passed not using local resource.
    -->
    <property>
        <name>hive.rpc.query.plan</name>
        <value>true</value>
    </property>
</configuration>
```

Step 4:

Here, we will create a simple bash script, which will properly set all required variables and run Hive like this:

```bash
#!/usr/bin/env bash
# Specify Hive home directory:
export HIVE_HOME=<Hive installation directory>

# If you did not set hadoop executable in PATH, specify Hadoop home explicitly:
export HADOOP_HOME=<Hadoop installation folder>

# Specify configuration files location:
export HIVE_CONF_DIR=$HADOOP_HOME/etc/hadoop-hive

# Avoid problem with different 'jline' library in Hadoop:
export HADOOP_USER_CLASSPATH_FIRST=true

${HIVE_HOME}/bin/hive "${@}"
```

Place the bash script into the $HIVE_HOME/bin directory with name hive-ig.sh. Make the file runnable with the following command:

```
chmod +x ./hive-ig.sh
```

Step 5:

By default, Hive stores metadata information into Derby database. Before running Hive interactive console, run the following command to initialize Derby database.

```
schematool -initSchema -dbType derby
```

The above command will create a directory called metastore-db.

Warning:
If you have any existing directory called metastore-db, you have to delete it before you initialize the derby database.

Step 6:

Start your Hive interactive console with the following command:

```
hive-ig.sh
```

It will take a few moments to run the console. If everything goes fine, you should have the following screen into your console.

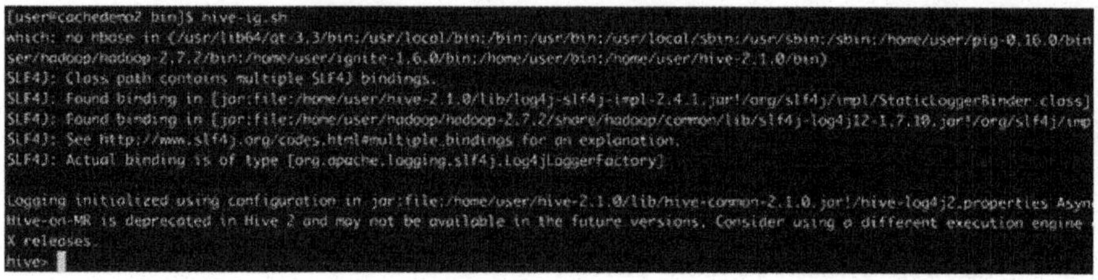

Chapter five: Accelerating Big Data computing

Figure 5.13

Step 7:

Now, you can run HiveQL into the console. Let's create a table in Hive and load the file t8.shakespeare.txt, then run the SQL query to count the words from the file.

```
CREATE TABLE input (line STRING);
```

Check the table by the following command.

```
hive> show tables;
OK
input
Time taken: 0.028 seconds, Fetched: 1 row(s)
```

Now, we can load the data from the host file system by Hive load command.

```
LOAD DATA LOCAL INPATH '/home/user/hadoop/t8.shakespeare.txt' OVERWRITE INTO TABLE input;
```

Note that, you have to change the INPATH of the file according to your local path. The above command loads the whole file into the column line in table input. Here, we are ready to execute any HiveQL quires against our data. Let's run the query to count the words from the table called input.

```
SELECT word, COUNT(*) FROM input LATERAL VIEW explode(split(line, ' ')) lTable as word GRO\
UP BY word;
```

After running the above query, you should have the following information into your console.

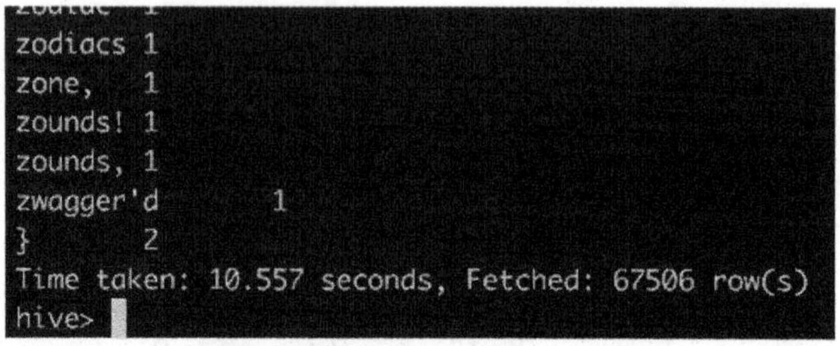

Figure 5.14

Chapter five: Accelerating Big Data computing

If you switch to the Ignite console, you should have a huge amount of logs into the console as follows:

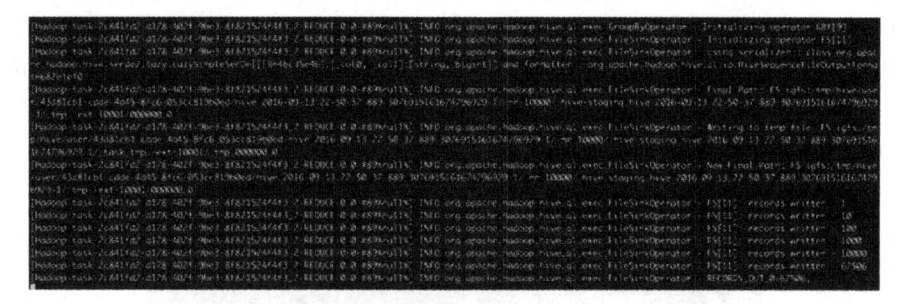

Figure 5.15

You can also use Limit keyword to restrict the maximum number of rows for the result set. With `Limit` clause, the above statement will look as follows:

```
SELECT word, COUNT(*) FROM input LATERAL VIEW explode(split(line, ' ')) lTable as word GRO\
UP BY word limit 5;
```

Now, let's try one more advanced example. We will use the dump of movies from the previous section to create a table into Hive and execute some HiveQL quires.

Step 8:

Create a new table into Hive with the following commands:

```
CREATE TABLE IF NOT EXISTS movies
 (id STRING,
 title STRING,
 releasedate STRING,
 rating INT,
 Publisher STRING)
 ROW FORMAT DELIMITED
 FIELDS TERMINATED BY ','
 STORED AS TEXTFILE;
```

Load some data from local directory as follows:

```
LOAD DATA local INPATH '/home/user/hadoop/hadoop-2.7.2/etc/hadoop/movies_data.csv' OVERWRI\
TE INTO TABLE movies;
```

You can get the *movies_data.csv* CSV data file from the GitHub project /chapter-bigdata/src/main/input.

Tip:

You can also load the data from the HDFS and IGFS file system. If you wish to load the data from the IGFS, you should configure the IGFS file system along with HDFS. In the next chapter, we will describe the complete process of deployment of the IGFS file system and run some Hive query.

Chapter five: Accelerating Big Data computing

Step 9:

Now that we have the data ready, let's do something interesting with it. The simple example is to see how many movies were released per year. We'll start with that, then see if we can do a bit more.

```
Select releasedate, count(releasedate) from movies m group by m.releasedate;
```

The above query should return the following output.

```
2005    1937
2006    2416
2007    2892
2008    3358
2009    4451
2010    5107
2011    5511
2012    4339
2013    981
2014    1
Time taken: 9.045 seconds, Fetched: 101 row(s)
```

Figure 5.16

You can see the listing of years, along with the number of films released by that year. There's a lot more data in the set beyond years and films counts. Let's finding the films with the rating more than 3 per year. In Hive, this can be accomplished by the following query.

```
Select releasedate, count(releasedate) from movies m where rating >3  group by m.releaseda\
te;
```

The execution time of all the queries in Hive is very impressive. Execution time is around 9 second for the last query. It's very hard to compare the executions time between the Hive and Pig because of the data processing paradigm is different.

This ends the Hive section . In this section, we described how to install and configure Hive for use with Ignite in-memory Map/Reduce. We also loaded a few samples data sets and executed HiveQL quires.

Anyway, we can improve the query performance by using IGFS file system instead of HDFS. In the next section, we will briefly discuss the benefits of IGFS and how to use it.

Replace HDFS by Ignite In-memory File System (IGFS)

Apache Ignite provides a vanilla distributed in-memory file system called Ignite File System (IGFS) with similar functionality to Hadoop HDFS. This is one of the unique features of Apache Ignite to accelerate big data computing. IGFS implements Hadoop file system API and is designed to support Hadoop v1 and Yarn Hadoop v2. ignite IGFS can transparently plug into Hadoop or Spark deployment.

One of the greatest benefits of the IGFS is that it does away with Hadoop NamedNode in the Hadoop deployment, it seamlessly utilizes Ignite's in-memory database under the hood to provide completely automatic scaling and failover without any additional shared storage. IGFS uses memory instead of disk to produce a distributed, fault-tolerant and high throughput file system. Removing NamedNode from the architecture enabled which leads to a dramatically better performance of I/O operations. Furthermore, IGFS provides native file system API to working with directories and files in the in-memory file system.

IgniteFileSystem or IGFS interface provides methods for regular file system operations such as create, update, delete, mkdirs etc., as well as Map/Reduce task executions. Another interesting feature of IGFS is its amazing smart usages of the file level caching and eviction design. IGFS utilizes file level caching to ensure corruption free storage.

Note that, IGFS is not an alternative like RAM disk, it's a full compliant in-memory file system like HDFS. A high-level architecture of the IGFS is shown below in figure 5.17.

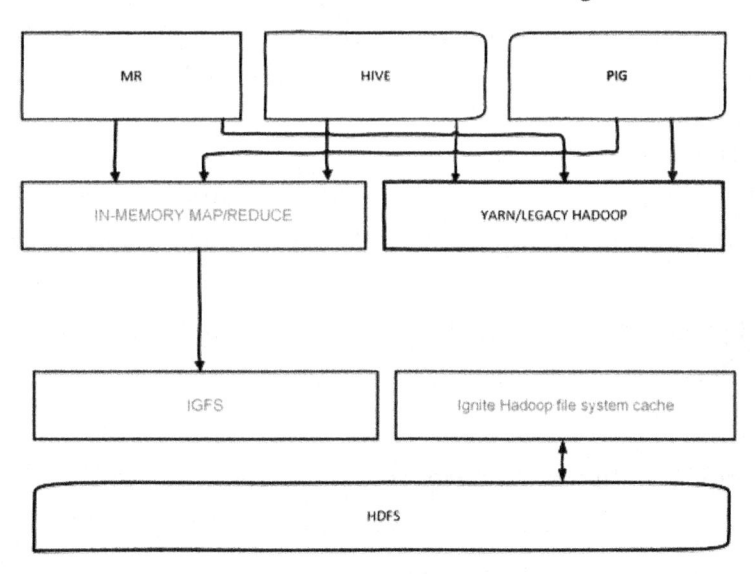

Figure 5.17

In this chapter, we are going to cover basic operations of the IGFS and deploy the IGFS in standalone mode to store files into IGFS and performs a few Map/Reduce tasks on top of it.

> **Note:**
> We are not going to replace the HDFS completely, otherwise, we will not be able to start the Hadoop datanode anymore. We are going to use both IGFS and HDFS simultaneously.

Chapter five: Accelerating Big Data computing 211

From the bird's eyes view, running Map/Reduce in IGFS on top of HDFS looks like as follows:

- Configure the IGFS for the Ignite nodes.
- Put files into IGFS.
- Configure the Hadoop.
- Run Map/Reduce.

There are a several ways to configure the IGFS on the Ignite cluster. Later in this section, we will explore the different approach for configuring and running the Ignite node with IGFS.

Unfortunately, Apache Ignite doesn't provide any comprehensive GUI-based management tools nor command line interface for maintaining Hadoop accelerator. However, GridGain Visor (Ignite commercial version) as a management tool provides IGFS monitoring and file management between HDFS, local and IGFS file systems. To demonstrate, how to use IGFS, we will perform the following steps:

1. Configure the IGFS file system in the Ignite cluster (default-config.xml).
2. Run a standalone Java application to ingest a file into IGFS. In our case, the file will be the t8.shakespeare.txt.
3. Configure the Hadoop.
4. Run Map/Reduce *wordcount* job to compute the count of the words from the IGFS file.
5. Run a standalone Java application to check the result of the Map/Reduce job.

Now that, we have dipped our toe into the IGFS, let's configure the standalone IGFS and run some Map/Reduce jobs on it.

Step 1:

Add the following springs configuration beans into the `default-config.xml` file of the Ignite node as follows:

```xml
<bean id="igfsCfgBase" class="org.apache.ignite.configuration.FileSystemConfiguration" abs\
tract="true">
        <property name="blockSize" value="#{128 * 1024}"/>
        <property name="perNodeBatchSize" value="512"/>
        <property name="perNodeParallelBatchCount" value="16"/>
        <property name="prefetchBlocks" value="32"/>
    </bean>
    <bean id="dataCacheCfgBase" class="org.apache.ignite.configuration.CacheConfiguration" a\
bstract="true">
        <property name="cacheMode" value="PARTITIONED"/>
        <property name="atomicityMode" value="TRANSACTIONAL"/>
        <property name="writeSynchronizationMode" value="FULL_SYNC"/>
```

```xml
        <property name="backups" value="0"/>
        <property name="affinityMapper">
            <bean class="org.apache.ignite.igfs.IgfsGroupDataBlocksKeyMapper">
                <constructor-arg value="512"/>
            </bean>
        </property>
    </bean>
    <bean id="metaCacheCfgBase" class="org.apache.ignite.configuration.CacheConfiguration" a\
bstract="true">
        <property name="cacheMode" value="REPLICATED"/>
        <property name="atomicityMode" value="TRANSACTIONAL"/>
        <property name="writeSynchronizationMode" value="FULL_SYNC"/>
    </bean>
    <bean id="ignite.cfg" class="org.apache.ignite.configuration.IgniteConfiguration">
        <property name="discoverySpi">
            <bean class="org.apache.ignite.spi.discovery.tcp.TcpDiscoverySpi">
                <property name="ipFinder">
                    <bean class="org.apache.ignite.spi.discovery.tcp.ipfinder.vm.TcpDiscover\
yVmIpFinder">
                        <property name="addresses">
                            <list>
                                <value>127.0.0.1:47500..47509</value>
                            </list>
                        </property>
                    </bean>
                </property>
            </bean>
        </property>
        <property name="fileSystemConfiguration">
            <list>
                <bean class="org.apache.ignite.configuration.FileSystemConfiguration" parent\
="igfsCfgBase">
                    <property name="name" value="igfs"/>
                    <property name="metaCacheName" value="igfs-meta"/>
                    <property name="dataCacheName" value="igfs-data"/>
                    <property name="blockSize" value="1024"/>
                    <property name="streamBufferSize" value="1024"/>
                    <property name="ipcEndpointConfiguration">
                        <bean class="org.apache.ignite.igfs.IgfsIpcEndpointConfiguration">
                            <property name="type" value="SHMEM"/>
                            <property name="host" value="127.0.0.1"/>
                            <property name="port" value="10500"/>
                        </bean>
                    </property>
                </bean>
```

Chapter five: Accelerating Big Data computing 213

```
            </list>
        </property>
        <property name="cacheConfiguration">
            <list>
                <bean class="org.apache.ignite.configuration.CacheConfiguration" parent="met\
aCacheCfgBase">
                    <property name="name" value="igfs-meta"/>
                </bean>
                <bean class="org.apache.ignite.configuration.CacheConfiguration" parent="dat\
aCacheCfgBase">
                    <property name="name" value="igfs-data"/>
                </bean>
                <bean class="org.apache.ignite.configuration.CacheConfiguration">
                    <property name="name" value="TokenManager"/>
                    <property name="cacheMode" value="REPLICATED"/>
                    <property name="atomicityMode" value="TRANSACTIONAL"/>
                </bean>
                <bean class="org.apache.ignite.configuration.CacheConfiguration">
                    <property name="name" value="ConfigurationRegistry.AliasCache"/>
                    <property name="cacheMode" value="REPLICATED"/>
                    <property name="atomicityMode" value="ATOMIC"/>
                </bean>
            </list>
        </property>
</bean>
```

If you are curious about the full listing of the `default-config.xml` file, it's available in the project `chapter-bigdata/src/main/resources` folder. Let's have a detailed look at the previous listing and go through every spring bean.

First of all, we have declared IGFS base configuration called *igfsCfgBase*, which will be our base configuration for the IGFS file configuration. We have configured the following properties as shown below:

Name	Description
blockSize	Files data block size.
perNodeBatchSize	The number of file block collected on a local node before sending to the remote node. In our case, the value is 512.
perNodeParallelBatchCount	The number of the parallel batch count of each node. In our case, the value is 16.
prefetchBlocks	The number of pre-fetched blocks.

Next, we have configured base cache configuration called *dataCacheCfgBase*, which will be the parent of the IGFS data cache. Most of the properties of this configuration we have already discussed in chapter three and four. Note that, for demonstration purpose, we have set the backup value to 0.

In a production environment, you should properly set the backup value. In our case, the cache will be transactional and partitioned, if data consistency and performance is your not main goal, you can use atomic mode instead of transactional.

Our subsequent configuration is the base configuration for the meta-data cache called *metaCacheCfgBase*. Probably it is the most unfamiliar part of this configuration. IGFS contains metadata for all files ingested into the in-memory file system. The configuration of this property is very similar to the previous base cache configuration.

Next, we are going to configure the IGFS file system, it is the main part of the Ignite configuration. We set the name of the IGFS file system to igfs. The block size and the stream buffer size of the IGFS file system will be 1024. To let IGFS accept requests from Hadoop, an endpoint should be configured. Ignite offers two endpoint types:

- **shmem** - working over shared memory (not available on Windows);
- **tcp** - working over standard socket API.

Shared memory endpoint is the recommended approach when the code executing file system (Hadoop node) is on the same machine as Ignite node. TCP endpoint should be used when Ignite node is either located on another machine, or shared memory is not available. In our configuration, we used a shared memory (shmem) endpoint with default port 10500. If *ipcEndpointConfiguration* is not set, then shared memory endpoint with default port will be used for Linux systems, and TCP endpoint with default port will be used for the Windows operating system.

Step 2:

When each Ignite node is configured (default-config.xml), start every node with the following commands:

```
$ignite.sh
```

Step 3:

In this step, we are going to ingest our t8.shakespeare.txt file into the IGFS file system. As we described before, we will use a Java application to ingest the file into IGFS. The Application is very simple, it ingests *t8.shakespeare.txt* file once every time the application is launched. The application will take the name of the directory and the filename as an input parameter to put the files into IGFS. Open the pom.xml file and add the following code in the <dependency> section.

Chapter five: Accelerating Big Data computing 215

```xml
<dependency>
    <groupId>org.apache.ignite</groupId>
    <artifactId>ignite-core</artifactId>
</dependency>
<dependency>
    <groupId>org.apache.ignite</groupId>
    <artifactId>ignite-spring</artifactId>
</dependency>
<dependency>
    <groupId>org.apache.ignite</groupId>
    <artifactId>ignite-hadoop</artifactId>
    <version>1.6.0</version>
</dependency>
<dependency>
    <groupId>com.google.guava</groupId>
    <artifactId>guava</artifactId>
    <version>19.0</version>
</dependency>
```

Now, add a new Java class with the name `IngestFileInIGFS`. The full listing of the Java class is shown below:

```java
public class IngestFileInIGFS {
    private final static Logger LOGGER = LoggerFactory.getLogger(IngestFileInIGFS.class);
    private final static String IGFS_FS_NAME= "igfs";

    public static void main(String... args) {
        if(args.length < 2){
            LOGGER.error("Usages [java -jar chapter-bigdata-1.0-SNAPSHOT.jar DIRECTORY_NAM\
E FILE NAME, for example java -jar chapter-bigdata-1.0-SNAPSHOT.jar myDir myFile]");
            System.exit(0);
        }
        Ignite ignite = Ignition.start("default-config.xml");
        Ignition.setClientMode(true);
        Collection<IgniteFileSystem> fs = ignite.fileSystems();
        for (Iterator ite = fs.iterator();ite.hasNext();){
            IgniteFileSystem igniteFileSystem = (IgniteFileSystem) ite.next();
            LOGGER.info("IGFS File System name:" + igniteFileSystem.name());
        }
        IgniteFileSystem igfs = ignite.fileSystem(IGFS_FS_NAME);
        // Create directory.
        IgfsPath dir = new IgfsPath("/" + args[0]);
        igfs.mkdirs(dir);
        // Create file and write some data to it.
        IgfsPath file = new IgfsPath(dir, args[1]);
```

```
        // Read the File Shakespeare
        InputStream inputStream = IngestFileInIGFS.class.getClassLoader().getResourceAsStr\
eam("t8.shakespeare.txt");
        byte[] filesToByte;
        try {
            filesToByte = ByteStreams.toByteArray(inputStream);
            OutputStream out = igfs.create(file, true);
            out.write(filesToByte);
            out.close();
        } catch (IOException e) {
            LOGGER.error(e.getMessage());
        } finally {
            try {
                inputStream.close();
            } catch (IOException e) {
                LOGGER.error(e.getMessage());
            }
        }
        LOGGER.info("Created file path:" + file.toString());
    }
}
```

Let's go line by line through the above listing. First of all, we make sure the input parameter of the applicationThis . Next, we initialized the Ignite instance with the `default-config.xml` file, which is located in our classpath. In the next few lines, we print out existing IGFS file systems directories. In the preceding line of code, we obtain an instance of IGFS named *igfs*. Later in the above pseudo code, we created a directory and file with the input parameter, also we read the file *t8.shakespeare.txt* from the classpath and stored it into IGFS. Very simple!

To compile and run the application, execute the following command:

```
mvn clean install
java -jar ./ IngestFileInIGFS.jar myDir myFile
```

After successfully compiling the maven project, there will be a java executable jar files in the *target* folder. *IngestFileInIGFS.jar* file is for ingesting file into IGFS. The next command will execute IngestFileInIGFS.jar, which will read the file *t8.shakespeare.txt* from the classpath and put the file into the IGFS with the following path `/myDir/myFile`. The next screenshot will show the execution in action.

Chapter five: Accelerating Big Data computing

```
2016-09-12 14:58:19 INFO  IgniteKernal:475 - To start Console Management & Monitoring run ignitevisorcmd.{sh|bat}
2016-09-12 14:58:19 INFO  IgniteKernal:475 -
2016-09-12 14:58:19 INFO  IgniteKernal:475 -
>>> +----------------------------------------------------------------+
>>> Ignite ver. 1.6.0#20160518-sha1:0b22c45bb9b97692208fd0705ddf8045ff34a031
>>> +----------------------------------------------------------------+
>>> OS name: Linux 2.6.32-573.el6.x86_64 amd64
>>> CPU(s): 2
>>> Heap: 0.41GB
>>> VM name: 57561@cachedemo2
>>> Local node [ID=CED1178B-78AA-45EA-AB46-5394BA8AB096, order=1, clientMode=false]
>>> Local node addresses: [cachedemo2.vps.at-consulting.ru/0:0:0:0:0:0:0:1%1, /127.0.0.1, /192.168.15.150]
>>> Local ports: TCP:10500 TCP:11211 TCP:11400 TCP:47100 TCP:47500 TCP:48100

2016-09-12 14:58:19 INFO  GridDiscoveryManager:475 - Topology snapshot [ver=1, servers=1, clients=0, CPUs=2, heap=0.41GB]
2016-09-12 14:58:19 INFO  IngestFileInIGFS:39 - IGFS File System name:igfs
2016-09-12 14:58:21 INFO  IngestFileInIGFS:70 - Created file path:/myDir/myFile
[14:58:28] New version is available at ignite.apache.org: 1.7.0
2016-09-12 14:58:28 WARN  GridUpdateNotifier:480 - New version is available at ignite.apache.org: 1.7.0
```

Figure 5.18

Step 4:

It's time for configuring Hadoop, IGFS file system must be configured in Hadoop.

> **Note:**
>
> All the configurations of Hadoop from the previous section will be unchanged here. We will create individual configurations for IGFS in a separate folder and pass these configurations into the Hadoop jobs.

This way you leave the Hadoop core configurations unchanged for existing jobs. This approach is considered as the best practice for applying the new configurations in Hadoop jobs. Let's create a new directory under *HADOOP_HOME/etc* with the following command and copy all the files from the Hadoop directory.

Execute the following command from the $HADOOP_HOME/etc directory.

```
cd $HADOOP_HOME/etc
$ mkdir hadoop-ignite
$ cp ./hadoop/*.* ./hadoop-ignite
```

Remove all the properties from the $HADOOP_HOME/etc/hadoop-ignite/core-site.xml and add the following properties as follows:

```
<configuration>
  <property>
        <name>fs.defaultFS</name>
        <value>igfs:///igfs@127.0.0.1:10500/</value>
  </property>
  <property>
        <name>fs.igfs.impl</name>
        <value>org.apache.ignite.hadoop.fs.v1.IgniteHadoopFileSystem</value>
  </property>
</configuration>
```

The full qualified file system class name `org.apache.ignite.hadoop.fs.v1.IgniteHadoopFileSystem` is sufficient for configuring the IGFS for Hadoop.

> **Note:**
>
> *v1* or *v2* doesn't stand for Hadoop 1.x and Hadoop 2.x. Instead, this is about either old *FileSystem* API or new *AbstractFileSystem* API.

Also, we set IGFS as default file system for our environment by the property `fs.defaultFS`. There are a several ways to set the file system URI for IGFS. IGFS file system URI has the following structure:

`igfs://[igfs_name@][host]:[port]/`

where,

- **igfs_name** - optional name of IGFS to connect to (as specified in the default-config.xml file). Must always end with @ character. Defaults to null if omitted.
- **host** - optional IGFS endpoint host (IgfsIpcEndpointConfiguration.host). Defaults to 127.0.0.1.
- **port** - optional IGFS endpoint port (IgfsIpcEndpointConfiguration.port). Defaults to 10500.

`hdfs-site.xml` and `mapred-site.xml` will remain unchanged as we discussed before.

However, Both of them are shown below:

hdfs-site.xml

Chapter five: Accelerating Big Data computing

```xml
<configuration>
    <property>
        <name>dfs.replication</name>
        <value>1</value>
    </property>
</configuration>
```

mapred-site.xml

```xml
<configuration>
    <property>
        <name>mapreduce.framework.name</name>
        <value>ignite</value>
    </property>
    <property>
        <name>mapreduce.jobtracker.address</name>
        <value>localhost:11211</value>
    </property>
</configuration>
```

Note that, we are using Ignite in-memory Map/Reduce framework as the runtime framework for executing Map/Reduce jobs. At this moment Hadoop configuration has been completed, and we are ready to execute Map/Reduce jobs.

Step 6:

There are a several ways to execute Map/Reduce jobs with Hadoop configuration. One of the easiest way is to pass the Hadoop config directory as an input parameter to the job as follows:

```
hadoop --config [path_to_config] [arguments]
```

Let's run our wordcount Map/Reduce job with the file from the IGFS with the following command.

```
time hadoop --config /home/user/hadoop/hadoop-2.7.2/etc/hadoop-ignite jar $HADOOP_HOME/sha\
re/hadoop/mapreduce/hadoop-mapreduce-examples-2.7.2.jar wordcount /myDir/myFile /myDir/out
```

where,

- /myDir/myFile – is the path of the **t8.shakespeare.txt** file.
- /myDir/out – is the output directory of the Map/Reduce results.

After running the above statement, you should get the similar output in your terminal as shown below.

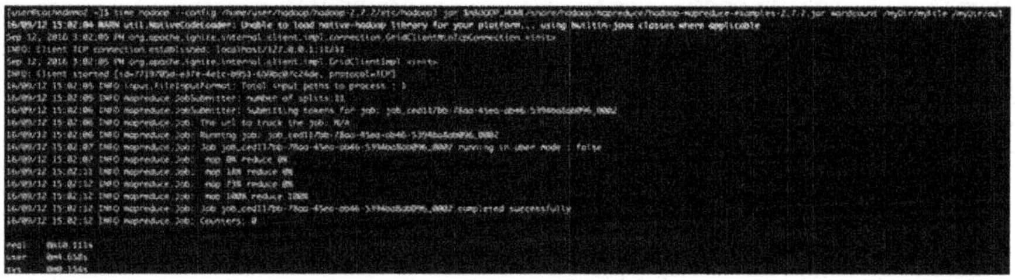

Figure 5.19

Note that, you have to change the name of the output directory every time you run the Map/Reduce job.

Next, we will develop a simple Java application, which will read the output results of the Map/Reduce from the IGFS.

Step 7:

Add a new Java class named *MapReduceResultReader* into your maven project and copy the following content into the class.

```java
public class MapReduceResultReader {
    private final static Logger LOGGER = LoggerFactory.getLogger(MapReduceResultReader.cla\
ss);
    private final static String IGFS_FS_NAME= "igfs";
    public static void main(String... args) {
        if(args.length < 1){
            LOGGER.error("Usages [java -jar chapter-bigdata-1.0-SNAPSHOT.jar MAP_REDUCE_OU\
TPUT_DIRECTORY_NAME] for example java -jar chapter-bigdata-1.0-SNAPSHOT.jar /myDir/out");
            System.exit(0);
        }
        // Initialize Ignite with default-config.xml from the classpath
        Ignite ignite = Ignition.start("default-config.xml");
        Ignition.setClientMode(true);
        Collection<IgniteFileSystem> fs = ignite.fileSystems();
        // look for any  existing IGFS file system
        for(Iterator ite = fs.iterator(); ite.hasNext();){
            IgniteFileSystem igniteFileSystem = (IgniteFileSystem) ite.next();
            LOGGER.info("IGFS File System name:" + igniteFileSystem.name());
        }
        IgniteFileSystem igfs = ignite.fileSystem(IGFS_FS_NAME);
        // Read from file.
        IgfsPath outputDir = new IgfsPath(args[0]);
        if(!igfs.exists(outputDir)){
            LOGGER.error("Output directory "+ args[0] +" doesn't exists!");
```

```java
                System.exit(0);
            }
            Collection<IgfsFile> files = igfs.listFiles(outputDir);
            for(Iterator ite = files.iterator() ; ite.hasNext();){
                IgfsFile maprFile = (IgfsFile) ite.next();
                LOGGER.info("Output file:"+ maprFile);
                // Read only the file part part-r-00000 if exists
                if(maprFile.isFile() && maprFile.path().name().endsWith("part-r-00000")){
                    String line="";
                    IgfsPath outputFilePart0 = new IgfsPath(args[0]+"/part-r-00000");
                    InputStream inFp0 = igfs.open(outputFilePart0);

                    BufferedReader reader = new BufferedReader(new InputStreamReader(inFp0));
                    try{
                        while ((line = reader.readLine())!= null ){
                            LOGGER.info(line);
                        }
                    } catch(IOException e){
                        LOGGER.error(e.getMessage());
                    } finally {
                        try {
                            inFp0.close();
                        } catch (IOException e) {
                            LOGGER.error(e.getMessage());
                        }
                    }
                }
            }
        }
    }
}
```

The business logic of the above application is straight forward. The application accepts the directory path of the output directory of the Map/Reduce job and retrieves the first portion of the result (part-r-00000). If the directory path doesn't exist, the application exists with an error log. Compile the application with the following command.

```
$ mvn clean install
```

The above command will create `MapReduceResultReader.jar` executable jar into the target directory. Use the following command to run the application:

```
$ java -jar ./MapReduceResultReader.jar /myDir/out
```

Chapter five: Accelerating Big Data computing 222

As it runs, the application will display startup information. Then it starts displaying lines similar to the following.

Figure 5.20

By looking at the logging, emitted by the Map/Reduce job, we can see that word *worshipful* count 5 times. I have executed the Map/Reduce job for three times to get the statistics of the execution time. Let's compare the result with the previous benchmark.

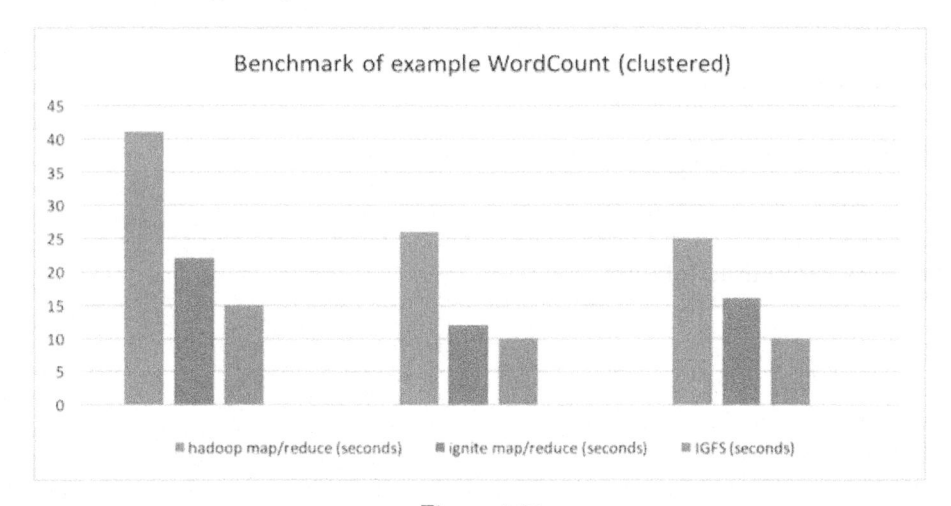

Figure 5.21

Three tests were run with the same datasets, and Map/Reduce with IGFS as a primary file system demonstrate a better performance as shown in figure 5.21. The average execution times for the Map/Reduce with IGFS as a file system are **11** seconds.

We can also use the Hive to query data from IGFS. First, we have to create a table to store data and load the data from Ignite IGFS. Let's run the `IngestFileInIGFS.jar` again to load the *t8.shakespeare.txt* file into IGFS as follows:

Chapter five: Accelerating Big Data computing 223

```
java -jar ./IngestFileInIGFS.jar myDir myFile
```

The above command will run the Ignite node and store the `t8.shakespeare.txt` file into IGFS (path should be /myDir/myFile). Now, we can run `hive-ig.sh` to start the hive interactive console. For details please refer to the previous section.

```
hive-ig.sh
```

Create a new table *igfsinput* and load the file from the IGFS.

```
CREATE TABLE igfsinput (line STRING);
LOAD DATA INPATH '/myDir/myFile' OVERWRITE INTO TABLE igfsinput;
```

Note that, we left the keyword `local` in the above command.

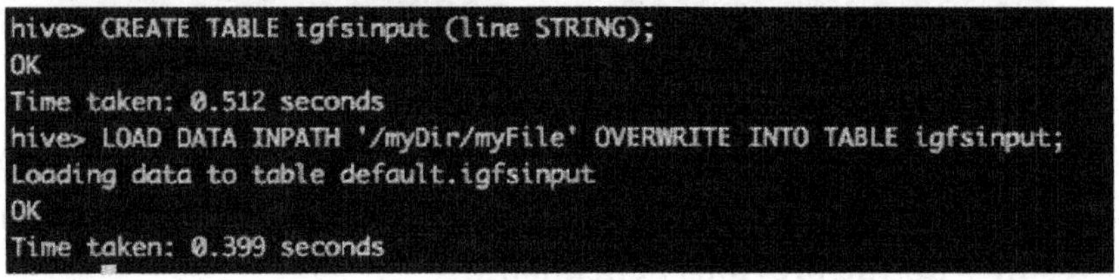

```
hive> CREATE TABLE igfsinput (line STRING);
OK
Time taken: 0.512 seconds
hive> LOAD DATA INPATH '/myDir/myFile' OVERWRITE INTO TABLE igfsinput;
Loading data to table default.igfsinput
OK
Time taken: 0.399 seconds
```

Figure 5.22

Let's run the *wordcount* query.

```
SELECT word, COUNT(*) FROM igfsinput LATERAL VIEW explode(split(line, ' ')) lTable as word\
 GROUP BY word;
```

The output should be similar as follows.

```
zodiac          1
zodiacs     1
zone,           1
zounds!     1
zounds,     1
zwagger'd       1

Time taken: 10.384 seconds, Fetched: 67498 row(s)
```

Execution time is very close to the Java Hadoop Map/Reduce. The execution can vary with the configuration of the Ignite node. In my sandbox, I have only 128Mb heap memory allocated for Ignite. For better performance, you should increase the Heap size for Ignite node in the cluster.

This is the end of the current section of this chapter. In the next section, we are going to take a closer look at the second approach of using IGFS, a second level cache for HDFS file system.

Hadoop file system cache

However, while we saw significant performance gain using IGFS over HDFS from the previous section, sometimes IGFS alone is not enough for many companies to increase the performance of their Map/Reduce execution. For lack of expertise, many companies can refuse to use IGFS. One of the major limitation of IGFS is that you have to ingest all the existing files from the HDFS to IGFS manually. To overcome this limitation, Ignite provides an intelligent secondary in-memory distributed cache over the primary disk-based HDFS file system. This mode is called Hadoop file system cache, sometimes called 2nd level cache for HDFS.

In this mode, IGFS supports both synchronous, asynchronous read-through and write-through to and from HDFS. In this approach, IGFS uses block-level caching and eviction of cache entries. This enables a dramatically better memory utilization since IGFS can store only the most frequently used file blocks in memory – and not entire files which can easily measure in tons of gigabyte in Hadoop.

To cache input data, the application simply wraps its HDFS input format with a special *dataset input format* that saves key/value pairs in memory as they flow to the mappers during program execution. On subsequent runs, the cache serves these key/value pairs from the IGFS cache instead of HDFS. It also automatically handles cache invalidation, if the HDFS file changes. For getting better performance, HDFS datasets should fit within the memory of the in-memory grid. High-level architecture of the Hadoop file system cache is shown in the figure 5.23.

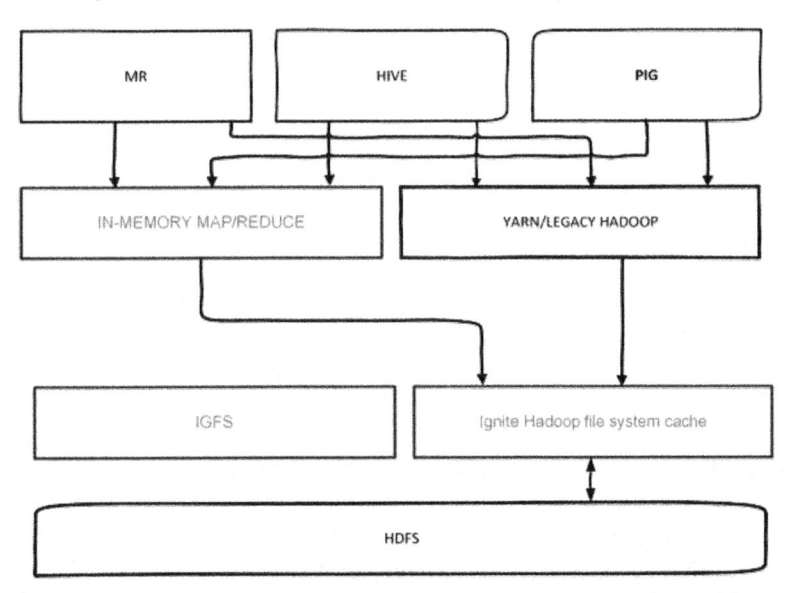

Figure 5.23

Apache Ignite provides implementations of the Hadoop secondary file system named IgniteHadoop-IgfsSecondaryFileSystem, which delegates call to a Hadoop file system. The configuration of the secondary file system or Hadoop cache is very simple. To use the secondary file system, you have to specify it in the IGFS configuration in spring or in Java code.

In this section, we will enable the Hadoop file system cache in the Ignite node and run some

Map/Reduce jobs to ensure the performance boost.

Step 1:

Add the secondaryFileSystem property into the IGFS `fileSystemConfiguration` properties block of the default-config.xml as follows (see *secondaryFileSystem* section of the listing below):

```xml
<property name="fileSystemConfiguration">
    <list>
        <bean class="org.apache.ignite.configuration.FileSystemConfiguration" parent="igfs\
CfgBase">
            <property name="name" value="igfs"/>
            <property name="metaCacheName" value="igfs-meta"/>
            <property name="dataCacheName" value="igfs-data"/>
            <property name="blockSize" value="1024"/>
            <property name="streamBufferSize" value="1024"/>
            <!--Hadoop file system properties goes here-->
            <property name="secondaryFileSystem">
                <bean class="org.apache.ignite.hadoop.fs.IgniteHadoopIgfsSecondaryFileSyst\
em">
                    <property name="fileSystemFactory">
                        <bean class="org.apache.ignite.hadoop.fs.CachingHadoopFileSystemFa\
ctory">
                            <property name="uri" value="hdfs://localhost:9000"/>
                            <property name="configPaths">
                                <list>
                                    <value>/home/user/hadoop/hadoop-2.7.2/etc/hadoop/core-\
site.xml</value>
                                </list>
                            </property>
                        </bean>
                    </property>
                </bean>
            </property>
            <property name="ipcEndpointConfiguration">
                <bean class="org.apache.ignite.igfs.IgfsIpcEndpointConfiguration">
                    <property name="type" value="SHMEM"/>
                    <property name="host" value="127.0.0.1"/>
                    <property name="port" value="10500"/>
                </bean>
            </property>
        </bean>
    </list>
</property>
```

FileSystemFactory method has two optional parameters, URI, and the configPaths, where,

Chapter five: Accelerating Big Data computing

- URI – URI of the Hadoop HDFS.
- configPaths – additional path to Hadoop configuration.

Rest of the configurations of IGFS from the previous section will remain unchanged. Note that, the following spring bean configuration is deprecated since Ignite 1.6 version.

```xml
<bean class="org.apache.ignite.configuration.FileSystemConfiguration">
   ...
  <property name="secondaryFileSystem">
    <bean class="org.apache.ignite.hadoop.fs.IgniteHadoopIgfsSecondaryFileSystem">
      <constructor-arg value="hdfs://localhost:9000"/>
    </bean>
  </property>
</bean>
```

At this stage, restart of the Ignite node is required.

Step 2:

Restart or start the each Ignite node.

```
$ ignite.sh
```

Step 3:

At this moment, we are ready to execute Hadoop Map/Reduce jobs in standard fashion. Assuming that we have already put our `t8.shakespeare.txt` file in /wc-input directory of HDFS (please refer to the section In-memory Map/Reduce to know how to add files in HDFS). For running Hadoop standard Map/Reduce jobs, execute the following command in your console.

```
time hadoop jar $HADOOP_HOME/share/hadoop/mapreduce/hadoop-mapreduce-examples-2.7.2.jar wo\
rdcount /wc-input/ output
```

If everything goes fine, you should get the following output on your terminal.

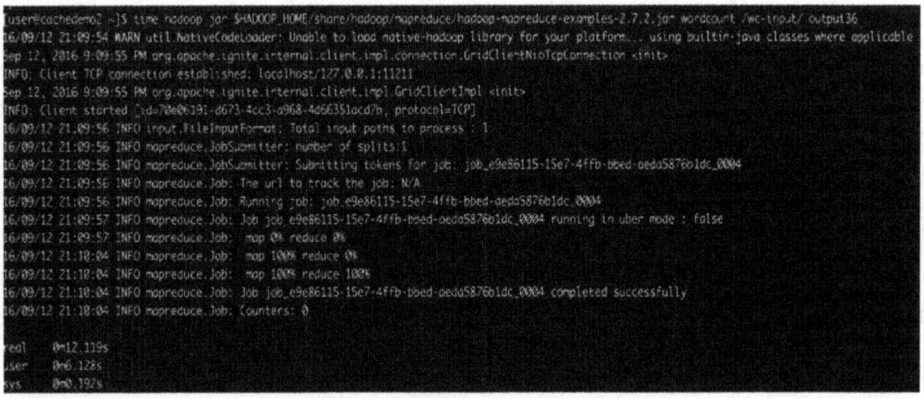

Figure 5.24

Chapter five: Accelerating Big Data computing 227

Let's execute the wordcount job for a few times.

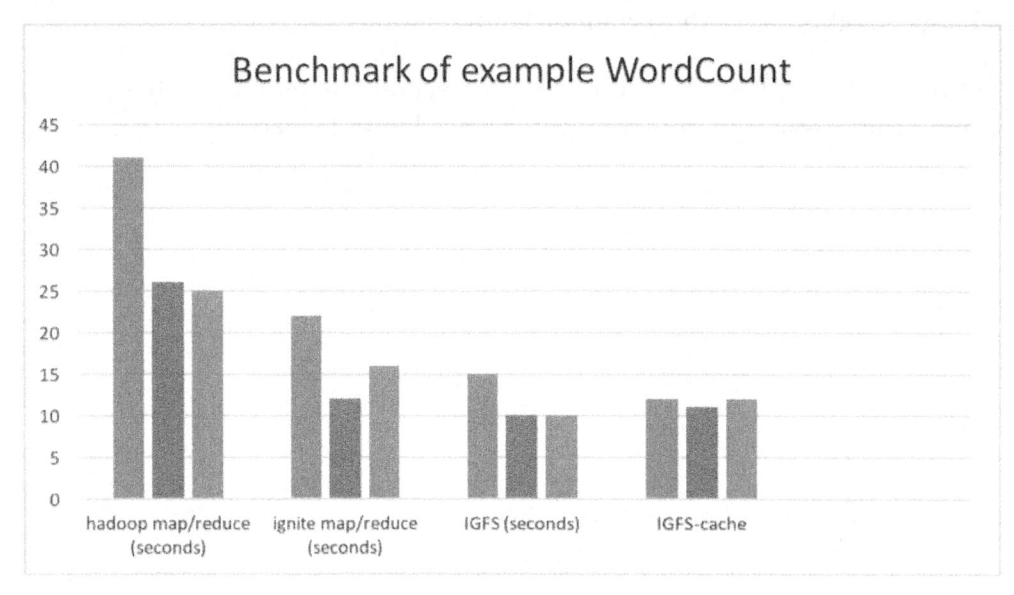

Figure 5.25

We have executed three Map/Reduce jobs with the same dataset. From the figure 5.25, we can see that average execution time of Map/Reduce with IGFS as a secondary cache is very close to the execution time of Map/Reduce to and from IGFS. It indicates that IGFS as a secondary cache for the HDFS files is also very useful to boost Hadoop Map/Reduce jobs performance.

In the next section, we will explore the concept of in-memory RDD to increase the performance of the Spark applications.

Ignite for Apache Spark

Apache Ignite offers several ways to improve the Spark job's performance: **Ignite RDD**, which represents Ignite cache as Spark RDD abstraction and Ignite IGFS (in-memory file system), which can be transparently plugged into the Spark deployments. Ignite RDD allows sharing states easily in-memory between different Spark jobs or applications. On the other hand, IGFS delivers similar functionality to Hadoop HDFS, but only in-memory, it can replace Hadoop HDFS or can be deployed on top of HDFS, in which case it becomes a transparent caching layer for files stored in HDFS. In the previous section, we had a detailed look at the IGFS and installed it over Hadoop HDFS, the process is same for the Spark also.

In this section, we are going to walk through the steps on how to use Ignite RDD to share states between Spark jobs. A high-level view of using Ignite RDD is shown below in figure 5.26.

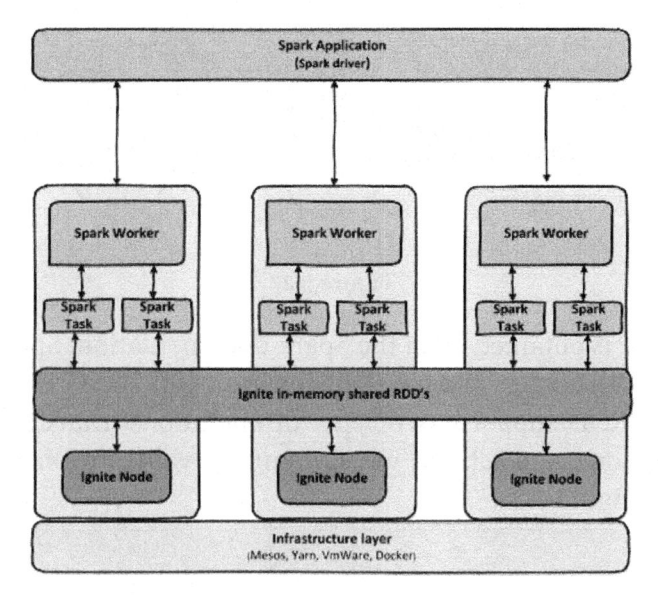

Chapter five: Accelerating Big Data computing 228

Figure 5.26

With Ignite in-memory shared RDD's, any Spark job can put some data into Ignite cache which will be accessible by another Spark jobs later. Ignite RDD is implemented as a view over Ignite distributed cache, which may be deployed either within the Spark job execution process or on a Spark worker. Before we move one to more advanced topics, let's have a look at the history of the Spark and which problems can solve by the Ignite RDD's.

Apache Spark – an introduction

Apache spark was invented by AMPLab for fast computation, built on top of the Hadoop Map/Reduce and it extends the Map/Reduce model to efficiently use more type of operations such as Interactive queries and Stream processing.

The Main difference between Spark and Hadoop Map/Reduce is that during execution, Spark tries to keep data into memory, whereas Hadoop Map/Reduce shuffling data in and out of disk. For Hadoop Map/Reduce it takes a significant time to write intermediate data to disk and read them back. The elimination of this redundant disk operations makes Spark magnitudes faster. Spark can store data (intermediately) into memory without any I/O, so you can keep operation on the same data very quickly.

In order to store data into memory, Spark provides special dataset named Spark RDD. Spark RDD stands for Spark Resilient Distributed Dataset. Spark RDD are fundamental components of the Apache Spark large scale data processing framework. The following illustration shows the iterative operations on Spark RDD.

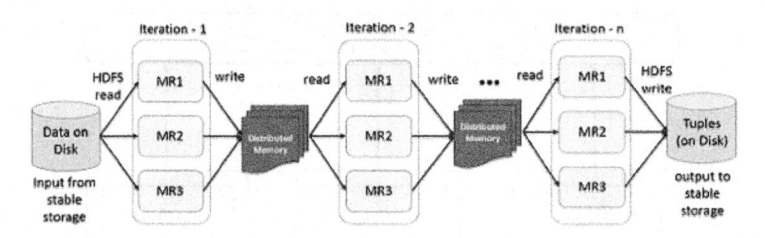

Chapter five: Accelerating Big Data computing 229

Figure 5.27

Note that, the above figure is obtained from the Spark documentation. Spark RDD is an immutable, fault-tolerant distributed collection of data elements, you can imagine Spark RDD as a Hadoop HDFS in memory. Spark RDD supports two types of operations: transformation, which creates a new dataset from existing one, and actions, which returns a value by performing a computation on the RDD as shown in the figure 5.28.

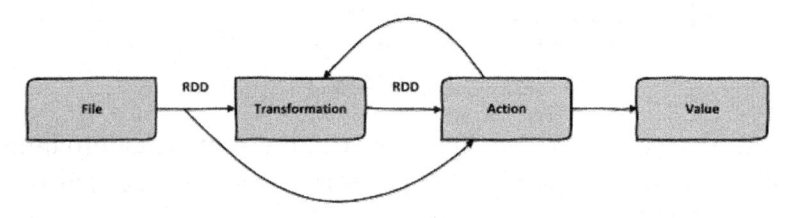

Figure 5.28

Spark RDD is created through the use of Spark transformation functions. Spark transformation functions can create Spark RDD from various sources, such as text file. In addition to creating Spark RDD from the text files, Spark RDD may be created from external storage such as RDBMS, HBase, Cassandra or any other data source compatible with Hadoop input format.

Most of the times Spark RDD are transformed from one to another new Spark RDD in order to prepare the dataset for future processing. Let's consider the following data transformations steps in Spark:

1. Load a text file with airlines names and it's arrival times for any airport into RDD1.
2. Load a text file with airlines names and its flight delay information for any airport into RDD2.
3. Join RDD1 and RDD2 by airlines name to get RDD3.
4. Map on RDD3 to get a nice report for each airline as RDD4.
5. Save the RDD4 to file.
6. Map RDD2 to extract the information of flight delay for certain airlines to get RDD5.
7. Aggregate the RDD5 to get a count of how many flights are delayed for each airline as RDD6.
8. Save the RDD6 into HDFS.

So, Spark RDD are utilized to perform computations on an RDD dataset through Spark Actions such as count or reduce. But there is a single problem with the Spark RDD, Spark RDD can't share between Spark Jobs or SparkContext. Because Spark RDD is bound to a Spark application. With native Spark distribution, the only way to share RDD's between different Spark jobs is to write the dataset into HDFS or somewhere in the file system and then pull the RDD's within the other jobs. However, the same functionality can be achieved by using:

1. Alluxio (formerly Tachyon)
2. Apache Ignite.

Apache Ignite memory-centric architecture enables RDD sharing in a very efficient and effective way. Apache Ignite provides `IgniteContext` and `IgniteRDD` to share RDD between Spark applications.

IgniteContext

IgniteContext is the main entry point to the Spark-Ignite integration. To create an instance of an Ignite context, a user must provide an instance of SparkContext and a closure creating IgniteConfiguration (configuration factory). Ignite context will make sure that server or client Ignite nodes exist in all involved job instances. Alternatively, a path to an XML configuration file can be passed to IgniteContext constructor which will be used to nodes being started.

Once IgniteContext is created, instances of IgniteRDD may be obtained using *fromCache* methods. It is not required that requested cache exists in the Ignite cluster when RDD is created. If the cache with the given name does not exist, it will be created using provided configuration or template configuration.

IgniteRDD

IgniteRDD is an implementation of Spark RDD abstraction representing a live view of Ignite cache. IgniteRDD is not immutable, all changes in Ignite cache (regardless whether they were caused by another RDD or external changes in cache) will be visible to RDD users immediately.

IgniteRDD utilizes partitioned nature of Ignite caches and provides partitioning information to Spark executor. A number of partitions in IgniteRDD equals to the number of partitions in underlying Ignite cache. IgniteRDD also provides affinity information to Spark via *getPrefferredLocations* method so that RDD computations use data locality.

Next, we are going to install Apache Spark and do the following:

1. Run the *wordcount* example to verify the Spark installation.
2. Configure Apache Ignite to share RDD between Spark applications.
3. Run Spark applications through Spark Shell to use Ignite RDD.
4. Develop a Scala Spark application to put some Ignite RDD into the Ignite cluster and pull them from another Scala Spark application.

Chapter five: Accelerating Big Data computing

Download and installation

Apache Ignite allows three different deployments of Apache Ignite with Spark cluster.

Shared deployment.

Shared deployment implies that Apache Ignite nodes are running independently from Apache Spark applications and store state even after Apache Spark jobs die.

Standalone deployment.

In Standalone deployment mode, Ignite nodes should be deployed together with Spark Worker nodes. After you install Ignite on all worker nodes, start a node on each Spark worker with your config using `ignite.sh` script.

Embedded deployment.

Embedded deployment means that Apache Ignite nodes are started inside Apache Spark job processes and are stopped when job dies. There is no need for additional deployment steps in this case. Apache Ignite code will be distributed to the worker machines using Apache Spark deployment mechanism and nodes will be started on all workers as a part of IgniteContext initialization.

Preparing the sandbox

The easiest way to get started with Apache Ignite and Apache Spark is to use the standalone deployment. We need at least one Spark master node and a worker node running on a single host. I will have the following versions of Apache Ignite and Spark in my sandbox.

Name	Version
Apache Ignite	1.6.0 or above
Apache Spark	1.6.0 with Hadoop 2.6
JDK	1.8.0

Download the Spark pre-build binary from the following link[41] and extracts the archive in some location. Let's us call this directory *SPARK_HOME*. Add the SPARK_HOME directory to your PATH environmental variable as follows:

```
export SPARK_HOME=/PATH_TO_SPARK_HOME/spark-1.6.0-bin-hadoop2.6
export PATH=$IGNITE_HOME/bin:$SPARK_HOME/sbin:$PATH
```

Start Spark master node

Run the following command into your console.

---

[41] http://spark.apache.org/downloads.html

Chapter five: Accelerating Big Data computing   232

```
$ start-master.sh
```

It should give a logging file info saying *starting org.apache.spark.deploy.master.Master, logging to /spark-1.6.0-h2/spark-1.6.0-bin-hadoop2.6/logs/spark-shamim-org.apache.spark.deploy.master.Master-1-shamim.local.out.* Print the log file with linux command *cat* as follows:

```
$cat /spark-1.6.0-h2/spark-1.6.0-bin-hadoop2.6/logs/spark-shamim-org.apache.spark.deploy.m\
aster.Master-1-shamim.local.out
```

The log file should print you the **master URL** and the **port** as shown below in figure 5.29.

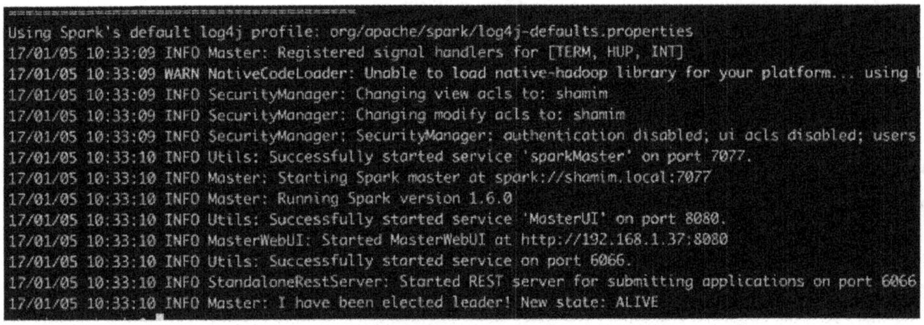

Figure 5.29

Start Spark worker node

Run the following command to start the Spark worker node.

```
$SPARK_HOME/bin/spark-class org.apache.spark.deploy.worker.Worker spark://YOUR_HOST:7077
```

This above command will start the Spark worker node and connect to the Spark master node as shown below.

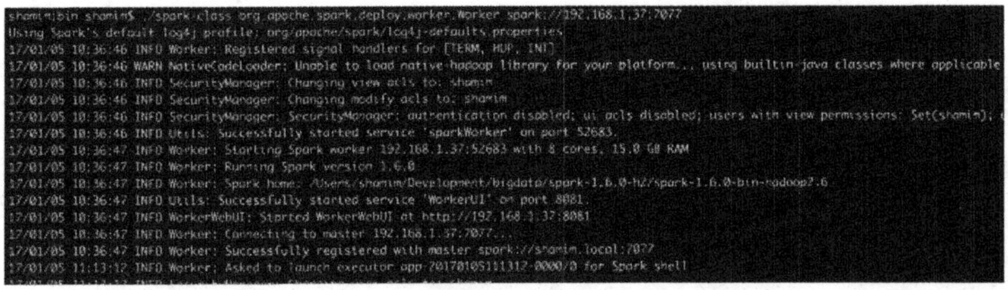

Figure 5.30

At this moment, you can open Spark *MasterWebUI* in the browser. Open your favorite browser and open the following URL.

Chapter five: Accelerating Big Data computing

```
http://localhost:8080
```

You should see the following Spark master web page (WebUI) as follows:

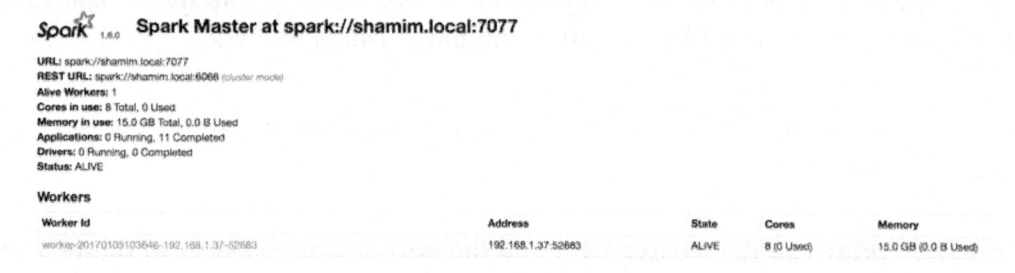

Figure 5.31

From the above web page, we can notice that our Spark master and one worker is alive and running. You can start a few more worker on a single host.

Once we have Spark cluster up and running, let's do some sanity test. Let's run a *wordcount* Spark application to count words from a text file.

Switch to the code sample project *chapter-bigdata-spark* or download it from the Github repository[42]. Compile the project *wordcount* with maven command as follows:

```
mvn clean install
```

It will create a snapshot library in the target folder of the project. Next, open a new command shell and submit a job into the Spark.

```
./spark-submit --class com.blu.imdg.JavaWordCount --master spark://localhost:7077 ~/PATH_T\
O_CODE_SAMPLE/ignite-book-code-samples/chapters/chapter-bigdata-spark/wordcount/target/wor\
dcount-1.0-SNAPSHOT.jar ~/Downloads/CHANGES.txt
```

> **Note:**
> You should properly pass the spark master URL and the file for count words. In my case, SPARK master URL is **spark://localhost:7077** and the file I passed for count words are **CHANGES.txt**.

After hit the enter button, you should be followed by the following text in your command shell.

---
[42] https://github.com/srecon/ignite-book-code-samples/tree/master/chapters/chapter-bigdata-spark/wordcount

Chapter five: Accelerating Big Data computing

Figure 5.32

From the above screenshot, we noticed that *ml.LogisticRegression* word has been found 2 times and so on. Let's start the Ignite node and configure Ignite for using Ignite RDD.

Start Ignite node.

To start an Ignite grid node with the default configuration, open the command shell and type the following (assume that, you already have configured the IGNITE_HOME):

```
$/ignite.sh
```

Spark-shell to run Spark jobs

Spark application deployment model allows dynamic jar distribution during application start. This model, however, has some drawbacks:

- Spark dynamic class loader does not implement `getResource` methods, so you will not be able to access resources located in jar files.
- Java logger uses application class loader (not the context class loader) to load log handlers, which results in `ClassNotFoundException` when using Java logging in Ignite.

There is a way to alter default Spark classpath for each launched application (this should be done on each machine of the Spark cluster, including a master, worker and driver nodes).

Locate the `$SPARK_HOME/conf/spark-env.sh file`. If this file does not exist, create it from template using `$SPARK_HOMR/conf/spark-env.sh.template`. Add the following lines to the end of the spark-env.sh file (uncomment the line setting IGNITE_HOME in case if you do not have it globally set):

Chapter five: Accelerating Big Data computing

```
# Optionally set IGNITE_HOME here.
# IGNITE_HOME=/path/to/ignite
IGNITE_LIBS="${IGNITE_HOME}/libs/*"
for file in ${IGNITE_HOME}/libs/*
do
if [ -d ${file} ] && [ "${file}" != "${IGNITE_HOME}"/libs/optional ]; then
IGNITE_LIBS=${IGNITE_LIBS}:${file}/*
fi
done
export SPARK_CLASSPATH=$IGNITE_LIBS
```

Let's verify the Ignite installation by changing the classpath of the Spark. Open the spark shell by the following command:

```
$SPARK_HOME/bin/spark-shell
```

Next, type the simple import statement.

```
scala> import org.apache.ignite.configuration._
```

It should return you the following message into the console.

```
import org.apache.ignite.configuration._
```

So far, so good. Now let's create an instance of Ignite context with default configuration through spark-shell.

```
scala> import org.apache.ignite.spark._
import org.apache.ignite.configuration._
val ic = new IgniteContext[Int, String](sc, () => new IgniteConfiguration())
```

You should have something like

```
ic: org.apache.ignite.spark.IgniteContext[Int,String] = org.apache.ignite.spark.IgniteCont\
ext@3631667d
```

Now, let's creates an instance of IgniteRDD

```
val igniteRdd = ic.fromCache("SparkIgniteRDD")
```

Note that creation of RDD is a local operation and will not create a cache in Ignite cluster.

Let's do something with the IgniteRDD. Add a list of publication names with a parallal operation of 2 as follows:

```
val RDDa = sc.parallelize(List("packt", "leanpub", "oreally", "wiston", "neahua"), 2)
```

Next, transform the RDDa into a map and make a tuple with key and a value. The key will be the length of the array elements. In the last step save the RDDb into the Ignite cache.

```
val RDDb = RDDa.map(x => (x.length, x))
igniteRdd.savePairs(RDDb)
```

After running the above command a new cache with name SparkIgniteRDD will be created in the Ignite node. Let's check the cache with the command-line *ignitevisior* as follows:

```
$cache -scan
```

It should return you the entries of the cache SparkIgniteRDD as shown in figure 5.33.

```
Entries in cache: SparkIgniteRDD
+===================================================================+
|     Key Class      | Key |     Value Class     |  Value  |
+===================================================================+
| java.lang.Integer  |  5  |  java.lang.String   |  packt  |
| java.lang.Integer  |  6  |  java.lang.String   |  wiston |
| java.lang.Integer  |  7  |  java.lang.String   | oreally |
+-------------------------------------------------------------------+
```

Figure 5.33

Now let's retrieve the IgniteRDD in a different Spark context and do some processing with the RDD. Shut down the Spark shell and run the following scripts in the Spark shell.

```
import org.apache.ignite.spark._
import org.apache.ignite.configuration._
val ic = new IgniteContext[Int, String](sc, () => new IgniteConfiguration())
val igniteRdd = ic.fromCache("SparkIgniteRDD")
val res = igniteRdd.foldByKey("")(_ + _).collect
```

In the above fragment codes, we first initialized the Ignite context and created an IgniteRDD from the cache SparkIgniteRDD. Next, we print the array elements by the foldByKey() function. The above code should return the following result.

```
res: Array[(Int, String)] = Array((5,packt), (7,leanpub), (7,oreally), (6,wiston), (6,neah\
ua))
```

Chapter five: Accelerating Big Data computing 237

If you switch back to the Spark WebUI, you should perceive all of the stages executed by the spark shell.

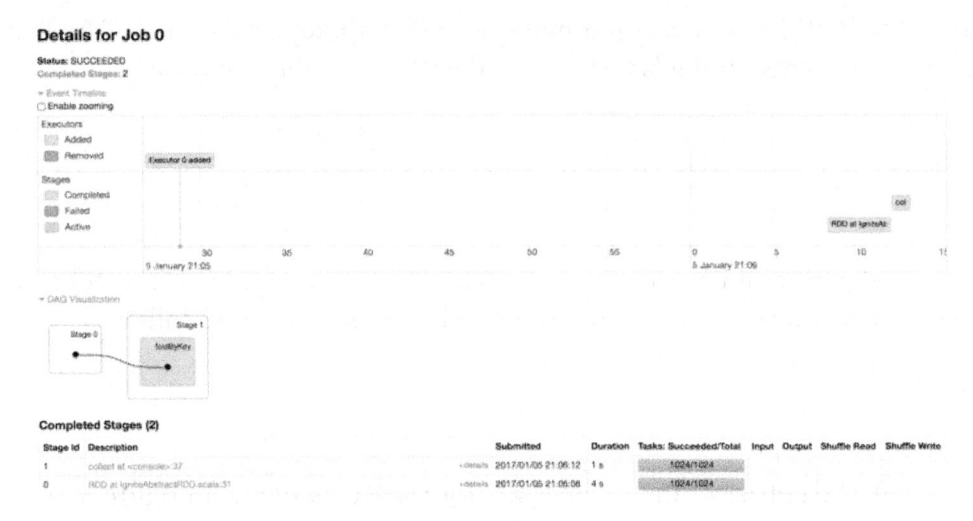

Figure 5.34

This way you can share SparkRdd between two different Spark applications. All the above scripts are available at Github repository[43]. Next, we are going to develop a Scala application to share state between different spark applications.

Spark application example in Scala to share states

In this last part of this chapter, we are going to develop a very simple Scala application, which will cache IgniteRDD with 1000 elements and another Spark application will retrieve and filter the element. The application is very much similar from the documentation, but we develop it as a Scala application through **maven**. In future, you can use this Scala application for developing your own application with IgniteRDD. Note that, in this sample application, we only use pure Scala and **maven plugin** to build the application.

Download the project **ignite-spark-scala** from the Github repository[44], if you didn't do it before. Compile the project with the following command.

```
mvn clean install
```

It will take a few minutes to build the application. During this time let's check the code snippet.

---

[43] https://github.com/srecon/ignite-book-code-samples/tree/master/chapters/chapter-bigdata-spark/spark-shell-srcipts
[44] https://github.com/srecon/ignite-book-code-samples/tree/master/chapters/chapter-bigdata-spark/ignite-spark-scala

Chapter five: Accelerating Big Data computing   238

```scala
package com.blu.imdg

import org.apache.ignite.configuration._
import org.apache.ignite.spark.{IgniteContext, IgniteRDD}
import org.apache.spark.{SparkConf, SparkContext}

object RDDProducer extends App {
  val conf = new SparkConf().setAppName("SparkIgniteProducer")
  val sc = new SparkContext(conf)
  val ic = new IgniteContext[Int, Int](sc, () => new IgniteConfiguration())
  val sharedRDD: IgniteRDD[Int, Int] = ic.fromCache("IgniteRDD")
  sharedRDD.savePairs(sc.parallelize(1 to 1000, 10).map(i => (i, i)))
}

object RDDConsumer extends App {
  val conf = new SparkConf().setAppName("SparkIgniteConsume")
  val sc = new SparkContext(conf)
  val ic = new IgniteContext[Int, Int](sc, () => new IgniteConfiguration())
  val sharedRDD = ic.fromCache("IgniteRDD")
  val lessThanTwenty = sharedRDD.filter(_._2 < 20)
  println("The count is::::::::::: "+lessThanTwenty.count())
}
```

In the above code, we have two Scala applications: RDDProducer and RDDConsumer. Let's go through it line by line. In the RDDProducer application, we created the IgniteContext by supplying the Spark configuration. After we successfully created the IgniteContext, sharedRDD (Ignite RDD) is created by invoking the method fromCache("IgniteRDD"). The last line of the RDDproducer application saves the Spark RDD into the Ignite cache.

The application RDDConsumer retrieves the RDD's from the cache by cache name and applies the transformation filter for the pair having values less than twenty and prints it.

Submit the applications

After successful compilation of the project, a java library will be created with name ignite-spark-scala-1.0-SNAPSHOT.jar. We can submit this application through spark shell. We will deploy this application **two times** with different Scala application. First, we will submit the **RDDProducer** as follows:

```
$./bin/spark-submit --class "com.blu.imdg.RDDProducer"  --master spark://192.168.1.37:7077\
 "/PATH_TO_THE_FILE/ignite-book-code-samples/chapters/chapter-bigdata-spark/ignite-spark-s\
cala/target/ignite-spark-scala-1.0-SNAPSHOT.jar"
```

This command will generate a lot of logs into the console as shown below.

Chapter five: Accelerating Big Data computing 239

Figure 5.35

You can also start the command-line tool **ignitevisor** and confirmed that IgniteRDD cache has been created. In the IgniteRDD cache, there should be **1000** cache entries.

Figure 5.36

Let's submit the RDDConsumer application and see what will happen.

Figure 5.37

RDDConsuler Spark application retrieves the RDD from the cache and filter for the pair having values less than twenty and prints it. The result is 10 instead of 20 because our cache is partitioned and half of the entries resides in another node. From here you can develop your own Scala application to share RDD's betweens Spark jobs.

Conclusion

In this chapter, we have covered Ignite Hadoop accelerator in details to get performance improvements with an existing Hadoop cluster. We configured Ignite in-memory Map/Reduce and executed a few examples. We also discover how to use Apache Pig and Hive for data analysis instead of Java Mp/Reduce application. We had a detailed view of the Ignite unique feature called IGFS to replace the Hadoop HDFS which can improve the performance of the Hadoop Map/Reduce jobs. At the end of the chapter, we described the use of 2nd level cache for the Hadoop file system. During the chapter, we did a few benchmarks, which indicates the performance boost of our application by using Ignite Hadoop accelerator. Also, we described how Ignite RDD could be shared between Spark applications. We installed Spark standalone cluster and configured Ignite to run some Scala applications to create Ignite context and Ignite RDD.

What's next

In the next chapter, we will describe the use of Data streaming and Complex event processing in Apache Ignite.

Chapter six: Streaming and complex event processing

There is no broad or highly accepted definition of the term Complex Event Processing or CEP. What Complex Event Processing is may be briefly described as the following quote from the Wikipedia:

Complex Event Processing, or CEP, is primarily an event processing concept that deals with the task of processing multiple events with the goal of identifying the meaningful events within the event cloud. CEP employs techniques such as detection of complex patterns of many events, event correlation and abstraction, event hierarchies, and relationships between events such as causality, membership, and timing, and event-driven processes.

For simplicity, Complex Event Processing (CEP) is a technology for low-latency filtering, aggregating and computing on real-world never ending or streaming event data. The quantity and speed of both raw infrastructure and business events are exponentially growing in IT environments. In addition, the explosion of mobile devices and the ubiquity of high-speed connectivity add to the explosion of mobile data. At the same time, demand for business process agility and execution has also grown. These two trends have put pressure on organizations to increase their capability to support event-driven architecture patterns of implementation. Real-time event processing requires both the infrastructure and the application development environment to execute on event processing requirements. These requirements often include the need to scale from everyday use cases to extremely high velocities or varieties of data and event throughput, potentially with latencies measured in microseconds rather than seconds of response time.

Apache Ignite allows processing continuous never-ending streams of data in a scalable and fault-tolerant fashion in-memory, rather than analyzing data after it has reached the database. Not only does this enable you to correlate relationships and detect meaningful patterns from significantly more data that you can process it faster and much more efficiently. Event history can live in-memory for any length of time (critical for long-running event sequences) or be recorded as transactions in a stored database.

Apache Ignite CEP can be used in a wealth of industries area; the following are some first class use cases:

1. **Financial services:** the ability to perform real-time risk analysis, monitoring and reporting of financial trading and fraud detection.
2. **Telecommunication:** the ability to perform real-time call detail record, SMS monitoring and DDoS attack.

3. **IT systems and infrastructure**: the ability to detect failed or unavailable applications or servers in real-time.
4. **Logistics**: the ability to track shipments and order processing in real-time and reports on potential delays on arrival.

There are a few more industrials or functional areas, where you can use Apache Ignite to process streams event data such as Insurance, transportation and Public sector. Complex event processing or CEP contains three main parts of its process:

1. Event capture or data ingesting.
2. Compute or calculation of these data.
3. Response or action.

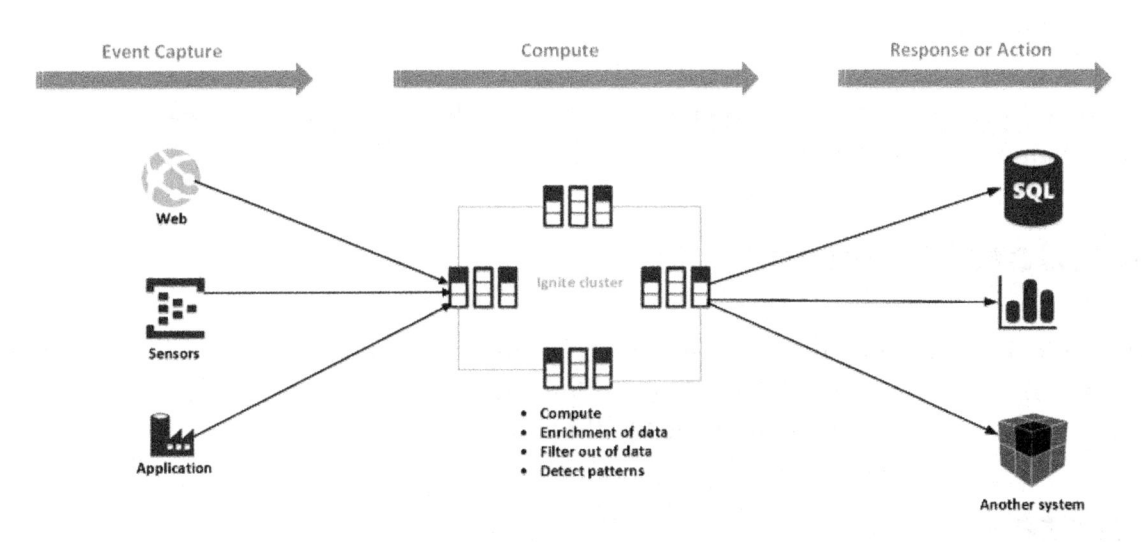

Figure 6.1

As shown in figure 6.1, data are ingesting from difference sources. Sources can be any sensors (IoT), web applications or industry applications. Stream data can be concurrently processed directly on the Ignite cluster in a distributed fashion. In addition, data can be enriched from other sources or filtered out. After processing the data, computed or aggregated data can be exported to other systems for visualizing or for taking action.

Introducing data streamer

Apache Ignite provides native data streamers for streaming large amounts of data into Ignite cluster. Data streamers are defined by *IgniteDataStreamer* API and are built to inject large amounts of never-ending stream data into Ignite caches. *IgniteDataStreamer* can ingest data from various sources such as files, FTP, queues, etc., but the adapter for connecting to sources must be developed by the users,

Chapter six: Streaming and complex event processing

sometimes it could be non-trivial and error prone. In addition, Ignite provides a bunch of built-in modern data streamers to collect and ingest data from multiple sources. *JMS Streamer*, *Camel Streamer* or *Kafka Streamer* is the most popular built-in Ignite streamer. At the time of writing this book, Ignite provides the following data streamers for streaming a large amount of data into Ignite cluster:

- IgniteDataStreamer.
- JMS Streamer.
- Flume sink.
- MQTT Streamer.
- Camel Streamer.
- Kafka Streamer.
- Storm Streamer.
- Flink Streamer.

In the rest of the chapter, we will briefly introduce most of the popular data streamers and real-world running examples for each streamer.

IgniteDataStreamer

Apache Ignite Data streamer is responsible for streaming external data into the cache. *IgniteDataStreamer* streams data concurrently by using multiple internal threads, so the data may get to remote nodes in a different order than it was added to the streamer.

> **Note:**
> *IgniteDataStreamer* is highly coupled with Ignite cache. So, to use Ignite data streamer, you must have a cache for this streamer.

The high loading speed in IgniteDataStreamer is achieved with the following techniques:

1. Entries that are mapped to the same cluster member (node) will be batched together in a buffer.
2. Multiple buffers can coexist at the same time.
3. To avoid running out of memory, a data streamer has a maximum number of buffers it can process concurrently.

To add data to the data streamer, you should call *IgniteDataStreamer.addData(...)* method. By default, the data streamer will not overwrite the existing data, which means that if it encounters an entry already in cache, it will skip the entry. This is the most efficient and performant mode, as the data streamer does not have to worry about data versioning in the background. If you anticipate that the data may already be in the streaming cache and you need to overwrite it, you should set *IgniteDataStreamer.allowOverwrite(true)* parameter.

Note that, IgniteDataStreamer is not the only way to add entries in caches, you can also use cache put() and putall() method as well, but they most likely will not perform as well as the class for adding data.

IgniteDataStreamer supports the following configuration properties:

- *perNodeBufferSize(int)* - this setting controls the size of the internal per-node buffer before buffered data is sent to the remote node. Default is defined by *DFLT_PER_NODE_BUFFER_-SIZE* value.
- *perNodeParallelOperations(int)* - sometimes data may be added to the data streamer via addData(Object, Object) method faster than it can be put in cache. In this case, new buffered stream messages are sent to remote nodes before responses from previous ones are received. This could cause unlimited heap memory utilization growth on local and remote nodes. To control memory utilization, this setting limits the maximum allowed number of parallel buffered stream messages that are being processed on remote nodes. If this number is exceeded, then addData(Object, Object) method will block to control memory utilization. The default is defined by **DFLT_MAX_PARALLEL_OPS** value.
- *autoFlushFrequency(long)* - automatic flush frequency in milliseconds.
- *allowOverwrite(boolean)* - Sets flag enabling overwriting existing values in cache. Data streamer will perform better if this flag is disabled, which is the default setting.

Now we have got the basics, let's build something useful and study how the IgniteDataStreamer works. We are going to develop an application that allows us to generate some application health data and stream it into Ignite cache. Therefore, we will execute some analytical query to analyze the data. The use case is very simple, let's assume we have a few public services, which we have to monitor for availability. If any of them is out of order, we have to send notifications to the service provider. There are three moving parts of this current process:

1. Data streamer.
2. Process queries to analyze the data.
3. Ignite cluster itself.

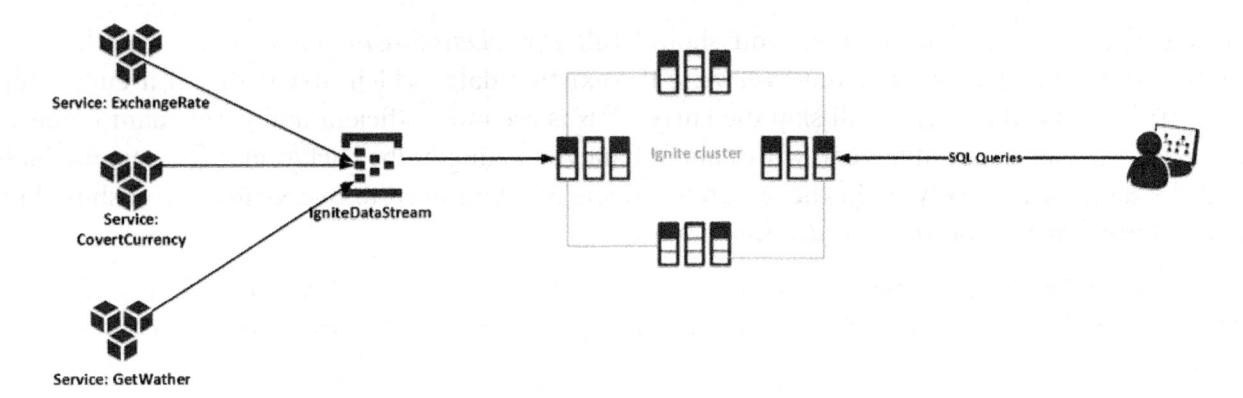

Chapter six: Streaming and complex event processing   245

Figure 6.2

We will query for that service, which is not available or return 404 http error. To keep things simple, we will roughly generate the health check data for the services. You can find the full source code in `chapter-cep` module at the GitHub[45] repository.

To run the Ignite node, execute the following command:

```
java -jar ./target/node-runner-runnable.jar
```

The next command will run the simple data streamer:

```
java -jar ./target/streamer-runnable.jar
```

which will randomly generate service health data for seven services. To execute the queries on the data, run the following command:

```
java -jar ./target/query-runnable.jar
```

As a result, you should have the following logs in the console.

```
[16:43:20] Topology snapshot [ver=3, servers=1, clients=2, CPUs=8, heap=11.0GB]
Service Health check status
(GETEXCHANGERATE,404)
Service Health check status
(CONVERTCURRENCY,404)
(GETEXCHANGERATE,404)
```

Figure 6.3

Let's have a detailed look at the application.

Step 1:

Add the following maven dependencies in the maven project.

---
[45] https://github.com/srecon/ignite-book-code-samples

```xml
<dependency>
  <groupId>org.apache.ignite</groupId>
  <artifactId>ignite-indexing</artifactId>
  <version>${ignite.version}</version>
</dependency>
<dependency>
  <groupId>org.apache.ignite</groupId>
  <artifactId>ignite-log4j</artifactId>
  <version>1.6.0</version>
</dependency>
<dependency>
  <groupId>com.h2database</groupId>
  <artifactId>h2</artifactId>
  <version>1.3.175</version>
</dependency>
```

Note that, at the moment of writing the book, Ignite only support *1.3.175* version of h2 database.

We uses *ignite-indexing* library to index the entity for querying.

Step 2:

We have a simple Java class *ServiceStatus*, which represents the current status of public services.

```java
public class ServiceStatus implements Serializable{
    @QuerySqlField(index = true)
    private String serviceName;
    @QuerySqlField(index = true)
    private int statusCode;
    @QuerySqlField(index = true)
    private long responseTime;
    @QuerySqlField(index = true)
    private long unavailableCnt;
    @QuerySqlField(index = true)
    private long healthCheckCnt;

    public ServiceStatus(String name, int statusCode){
        this.serviceName = name;
        this.statusCode =statusCode;
    }
    // setter and getter.
}
```

Probably the most unfamiliar part of this preceding code is the @QuerySqlField annotation. Given annotation enables the field to be part of the sql query (See chapter four for more details). Next, we will configure the stream to ingest data.

Chapter six: Streaming and complex event processing 247

Step 3:

In this step, we will create a cache configuration with name *Healthcheck* and set the index type to our `ServiceStatus` class. Next, we will create a cache based on this configuration and a data streamer.

```java
public class HealthCheckStreamer {
    private static final Random RAND = new Random();
    private static final String[] SERVICE_NAME = new String[] {"GETINN", "GETWEATHER", "GE\
TEXCHANGERATE", "CONVERTCURRENCY", "GETPUBLICSERVICELIST", "SEARCHBRANCHES", "GETNEWSBYTOP\
ICS"};
    private static final int[] STATUS_CODE = new int[] {200, 404, 504};

    public static void main(String[] args) throws Exception{
        System.out.println("Streamer for service health check!!");
        // Mark this cluster member as client.
        Ignition.setClientMode(true);
        try(Ignite ignite = Ignition.start("example-ignite.xml")){
            if(!ExamplesUtils.hasServerNodes(ignite))
                return;
            // healthcheck cache configuration
            CacheConfiguration<String, ServiceStatus> healthcheck_cfg = new CacheConfigura\
tion<>("healthchecks");
            // set index
            healthcheck_cfg.setIndexedTypes(String.class, ServiceStatus.class);

            IgniteCache<String, ServiceStatus> healthCheckCache = ignite.getOrCreateCache(\
healthcheck_cfg);

            try(IgniteDataStreamer<String, ServiceStatus> healthCheckStreamer = ignite.dat\
aStreamer(healthCheckCache.getName())){
                healthCheckStreamer.allowOverwrite(true);
                while(true ){
                    int idx_service_name = RAND.nextInt(SERVICE_NAME.length);
                    int idx_code = RAND.nextInt(STATUS_CODE.length);
                    ServiceStatus serviceStatus = new ServiceStatus(SERVICE_NAME[idx_servi\
ce_name], STATUS_CODE[idx_code]);
                    healthCheckStreamer.addData(SERVICE_NAME[idx_service_name], serviceSta\
tus);
                }
            }
        }
    }
}
```

Note that, we also allow data streamer to overwrite entries. The above preceding code is very straight forward, after creating the data streamer, we randomly generates a service status. Service status can be *200, 404* or *504.*

Step 4:

Here, we defined a *QueryStatus* class, which will periodically query the cache to get the status of the services. Here we are using standard *ANSI SQL* query. Ignite SQL treats Java classes as SQL tables, properties of the classes remain as table columns.

```
public class QueryStatus {
    private static final String QUERY_404="SELECT serviceName, statusCode from ServiceStat\
us where statusCode = 404";
    private static final String QUERY_CNT= "select count(*) from ServiceStatus where statu\
sCode = 404";
    public static void main(String[] args) throws Exception {
        // Mark this cluster member as client.
        Ignition.setClientMode(true);

        try (Ignite ignite = Ignition.start("example-ignite.xml")) {
            if (!ExamplesUtils.hasServerNodes(ignite))
                return;
            // query code goes here.
            CacheConfiguration<String, ServiceStatus> healthchecksCfg = new CacheConfigura\
tion<>("healthchecks");
            IgniteCache<String, ServiceStatus> instCache = ignite.getOrCreateCache(healthc\
hecksCfg);
            SqlFieldsQuery query = new SqlFieldsQuery(QUERY_404);
            while(true){
                // Execute queries.
                List<List<?>> res = instCache.query(query).getAll();
                System.out.println("Service Health check status");
                ExamplesUtils.printQueryResults(res);
                Thread.sleep(1000);
            }
        }
    }
}
```

Let's go through line by line. First, we have configured our cache with the same Index types. Create SqlFieldsQuery with the SQL query `SELECT serviceName, statusCode from ServiceStatus where statusCode = 404`. We are retrieving only those services; which status is 404 with an interval of one second.

In order to run the example, see the instructions from the beginning of this section. If you run the example again, you should get the information log into the console as shown in figure 6.3.

Chapter six: Streaming and complex event processing 249

So far in this chapter, we have looked at a minimal ability of IgniteDataStreamer. Before we move on to a more advanced topic, let's have a look at the other opportunities of IgniteDataStreamer such as StreamReceiver.

StreamReceiver

Ignite `StreamReceiver` allow us to execute some custom logics during data streaming. There are two different flavors of StreamReceiver in Apache Ignite: *StreamTransformer* and *StreamVisitor*. StreamTransformer is the simplest implementation of StreamReceiver, which updates data in the stream cache based on its previous value. I didn't find any real technical value of using this StreamReceiver and going to skip this functionality. If you really want to manipulate entries over a data stream, you have to use StreamVisitor, which visits every key-value tuple in streams and gives you the ability to change the value of the cache. Tuples, an ordered list of elements, for example, 3 `tuples` might be (1,7,5).

StreamVisitor

A convenience adapter of stream data, which can perform the update in cache entries.

> **Note:**
> The visitor doesn't update the cache itself. If the tuple needs to be stored in the cache, an explicitly `cache.put()` or `cache.putall()` method should be called.

To see the visitor in action, we will modify our previous example slightly. In the following example, we are going to use two caches: *healthcheck* and *alerts* and one data streamer. Healthcheck cache will be configured with the data streamer, and whenever any service status arrives in the data stream, we will check its status code. If the status code is *404*, we will add a new entry with Alert level *RED*. Note that, we do not update the healthcheck cache entries, healthcheck cache will always remain empty in the Ignite cluster.

```
public class HealthCheckStreamVisitor {
    private static final Random RAND = new Random();
    private static final String[] SERVICE_NAME = new String[] {"GETINN", "GETWEATHER", "GE\
TEXCHANGERATE", "CONVERTCURRENCY", "GETPUBLICSERVICELIST", "SEARCHBRANCHES", "GETNEWSBYTOP\
ICS"};
    private static final int[] STATUS_CODE = new int[] {200, 404, 504};

    public static void main(String[] args) throws Exception{
        System.out.println("Streamer for service health check!!");
```

```java
        // Mark this cluster member as client.
    Ignition.setClientMode(true);
    try(Ignite ignite = Ignition.start("example-ignite.xml")){
        if(!ExamplesUtils.hasServerNodes(ignite))
            return;
        // healthcheck cache configuration
        CacheConfiguration<String, ServiceStatus> healthcheck_cfg = new CacheConfigura\
tion<>("healthchecks");
        CacheConfiguration<String, Alert> alert_cfg = new CacheConfiguration<>("alerts\
");
        alert_cfg.setIndexedTypes(String.class, Alert.class);
        // create cache
        IgniteCache<String, ServiceStatus> healthCheckCache = ignite.getOrCreateCache(\
healthcheck_cfg);
        IgniteCache<String, Alert> alertCache = ignite.getOrCreateCache(alert_cfg);

        try(IgniteDataStreamer<String, ServiceStatus> healthCheckStreamer = ignite.dat\
aStreamer(healthCheckCache.getName())){
            healthCheckStreamer.allowOverwrite(true);
            healthCheckStreamer.receiver(StreamVisitor.from((cache, e) ->{
                String serviceName = e.getKey();
                ServiceStatus serviceStatus = e.getValue();
                // get Alert by key
                Alert alert = alertCache.get(serviceName);
                if (alert == null)
                    alert = new Alert(serviceName, Level.GREEN);
                if (serviceStatus != null && serviceStatus.getStatusCode() == 404){
                    alert.setAlertLevel(Level.RED);
                } else if (serviceStatus != null && serviceStatus.getStatusCode() == 2\
00){
                    alert.setAlertLevel(Level.GREEN);
                } else {
                    alert.setAlertLevel(Level.YELLOW);
                }
                alertCache.put(serviceName, alert);
            }));
            while(true){
                int idx_service_name = RAND.nextInt(SERVICE_NAME.length);
                int idx_code = RAND.nextInt(STATUS_CODE.length);
                ServiceStatus serviceStatus = new ServiceStatus(SERVICE_NAME[idx_servi\
ce_name], STATUS_CODE[idx_code]);
                healthCheckStreamer.addData(SERVICE_NAME[idx_service_name], serviceSta\
tus);
            }
        }
```

Chapter six: Streaming and complex event processing   251

```
        }
    }
}
```

In the preceding section of the code, we are getting the current entries from the data stream. Next, we retrieved the current entries from the cache by the current key from the stream. The next few instructions performs an update on entries of *alertLevel* and stored the entry into the cache *Alert*. In order to run the example, you have to start the Ignite node first as before, and execute the following command:

```
java -jar ./target/streamer-visitor-runnable.jar
java -jar ./target/query-alert-runnable.jar
```

You should get the following logs into the console.

```
[21:52:23] Topology snapshot [ver=3, servers=1, clients=2, CPUs=8, heap=11.0GB]
Service Health Monitoring
(GREEN,1)
Service Health Monitoring
(GREEN,2)
(YELLOW,1)
(RED,1)
```

Figure 6.4

If we study the Ignite cache through *Ignite visor*, we should find that *healthcheck* cache is empty.

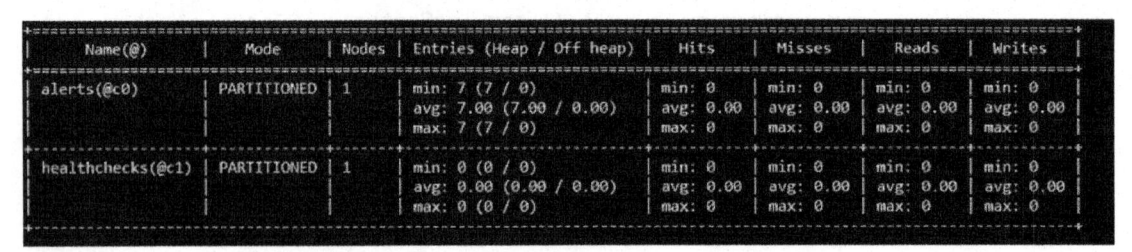

```
+===================================================================================================================+
|    Name(@)       |    Mode       | Nodes | Entries (Heap / Off heap) |     Hits     |    Misses    |    Reads     |    Writes    |
+===================================================================================================================+
| alerts(@c0)      | PARTITIONED   |   1   | min: 7 (7 / 0)            | min: 0       | min: 0       | min: 0       | min: 0       |
|                  |               |       | avg: 7.00 (7.00 / 0.00)   | avg: 0.00    | avg: 0.00    | avg: 0.00    | avg: 0.00    |
|                  |               |       | max: 7 (7 / 0)            | max: 0       | max: 0       | max: 0       | max: 0       |
| healthchecks(@c1)| PARTITIONED   |   1   | min: 0 (0 / 0)            | min: 0       | min: 0       | min: 0       | min: 0       |
|                  |               |       | avg: 0.00 (0.00 / 0.00)   | avg: 0.00    | avg: 0.00    | avg: 0.00    | avg: 0.00    |
|                  |               |       | max: 0 (0 / 0)            | max: 0       | max: 0       | max: 0       | max: 0       |
+===================================================================================================================+
```

Figure 6.5

Because, we didn't store the data stream into the cache *healthcheck*, rather we manipulated with the Alerts cache. Let's check, how the entries look like into the cache alerts.

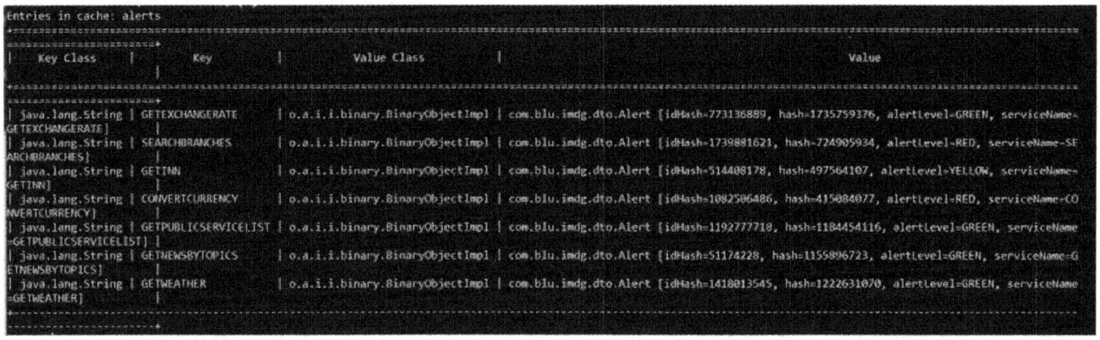

Chapter six: Streaming and complex event processing 252

Figure 6.6

As we can see, Alert entries are stored in deserialized mode. To getting the alert continuously, we can also use Ignite continuous query feature. Continuous queries are good for cases when you want to execute a query and then continue to get notified about the data changes that fall into your query filter.

I strongly guess that the Ignite StreamData concept is now clear to you. This is the end of the section of Ignite native data streamer. Next, we will cover Camel, Flume and Storm streamers.

Camel data streamer

Integration and data exchange between several systems are one of the most challenging tasks for any industry. Different systems use different interfaces, protocols to interact with each other, which dramatically increase the complexities of communications with other systems. Traditional system integrations, in the way that we built them in the past decades, require a lot of code to be created that has absolutely nothing to do with the higher level integration problem. The majority of this is boilerplate code, dealing with common, repetitive tasks of setting up and tearing down libraries for the messaging transports, connecting to the database, etc. Writing such boilerplate code for integration systems prevents developers to focus on business logic.

After publishing the book **Enterprise Integration Patterns: Designing, Building and deploying Messaging solution**, EIP became the industry standard for describing, documenting and implementing integration problems.

Apache camel is a powerful open source integration framework based on known Enterprise integration patterns.

Apache camel framework hides all the complexity of integrations, so you can focus only on implementing your business logics. Apache Camel is also known as a routing, and mediation engine as it effectively routes data between endpoints, while taking a heavy load of data transformation, endpoint connectivity and much more.

Apache Ignite provides camel streamer, which they described as a universal streamer because it allows consuming data from a verity of sources into Ignite cache. At the moment of writing the

Chapter six: Streaming and complex event processing   253

book, there are more than 200+ adapters and components available for Camel, which gives the ability to consumes any type of data through the various protocol such as JMS, SOAP, SFTP, SMTP, POP3, etc. and provides opportunities to integrate with any kind of information system.

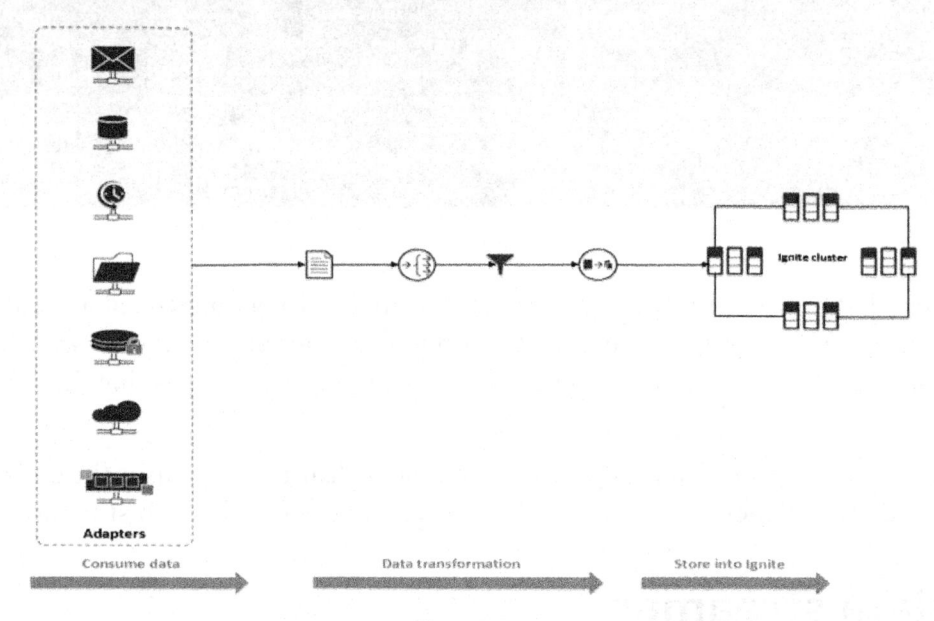

Figure 6.7

Apache Camel not only provides the opportunities to consumes data but also, through camel you can route data from one end point to another, enrich data or transform data from one format to another. In Camel, you can also execute any custom logic into the data stream.

There are two different components for Camel to work with Apache Ignite.

1. Camel-Ignite component.
2. and Ignite-camel streamer.

The `Camel-Ignite` library or component offers seamless integration of Camel with Ignite. If you already have any application developed on Camel, you can use these components to integrate with Ignite. The Camel-ignite component can help you to consume entries from cache or store any entries into the Ignite cache. This component offers several endpoints to cover most of the Ignite's functionality.

№	Endpoint Name	Description
1	Ignite Cache	Allows you to interact with Ignite Cache.
2	Ignite Compute	Allows you to run compute operations on Ignite cluster, this endpoint only supports producer.
3	Ignite Messaging	Allows you to send and consume messages to and from Ignite topics.
4	Ignite Events	Allows you to consume events from Ignite cluster, this endpoint only works as consumers.
5	Ignite Sets	Allows you to manipulate with Ignite Set data structures.

№	Endpoint Name	Description
6	Ignite Queues	Allows you to manipulate with Ignite Queue data structures.
7	Ignite Id Generator	Allows you to invoke the Ignite Id Generator.

This component lacks one functionality; it can't help you to work with the stream data. For working with streaming data, you have to use Ignite camel streamer.

Ignite camel stream library can stream data with two different flavors.

1. Direct Ingestion.
2. Mediated Ingestion.

Direct Ingestion

In direct ingestion, you consume data from any source through camel endpoint and ingest the data directly into Ignite Cache. In other words, you can use this approach when you do not need to alter the incoming messages before storing them into Ignite cache. In this case, no data transformation or custom logic to compute with the data. However, you have to extract the tuples and create the key and the values from tuples manually. Ignite provides two types of tuple extractor: **StreamSingleTupleExtractor** and **StreamMultipleTupleExtractor**.

- *StreamSingleTupleExtractor*, which extracts either no or one tuple out of the message and send them to Ignite to store.
- *StreamMultipleTupleExtractor*, which is capable of extracting multiple tuples out of a single message.

Next, we will develop an example of direct ingestion of streaming data into the Ignite cache. To keep things simple, we will use the basic features of the Camel in our examples. To demonstrate the power of the Camel and the direct ingestion mechanism of Ignite, we will do the following:

1. Consume messages from the file system (directory input in maven project) in JSON format.
2. Convert the JSON data into Java objects.
3. Directly store the Java object into Ignite Cache.

Now, let's start building the application.

Step 1:

Let's add the following maven dependencies to work with the Ignite-camel streamer.

Chapter six: Streaming and complex event processing

```xml
<dependency>
    <groupId>org.apache.ignite</groupId>
    <artifactId>ignite-spring</artifactId>
    <version>1.6.0</version>
</dependency>
<dependency>
    <groupId>org.apache.ignite</groupId>
    <artifactId>ignite-log4j</artifactId>
    <version>1.6.0</version>
</dependency>
<dependency>
    <groupId>org.apache.ignite</groupId>
    <artifactId>ignite-camel</artifactId>
    <version>1.6.0</version>
</dependency>
<dependency>
    <groupId>org.slf4j</groupId>
    <artifactId>slf4j-simple</artifactId>
    <version>1.6.6</version>
</dependency>
<dependency>
    <groupId>org.apache.camel</groupId>
    <artifactId>camel-jackson</artifactId>
    <version>2.16.0</version>
</dependency>
<dependency>
    <groupId>com.fasterxml.jackson.core</groupId>
    <artifactId>jackson-databind</artifactId>
    <version>2.6.3</version>
</dependency>
```

The following library are **mandatory** for using Ignite-camel streamer.

```xml
<dependency>
    <groupId>org.apache.ignite</groupId>
    <artifactId>ignite-spring</artifactId>
    <version>1.6.0</version>
</dependency>
```

Step 2:

Create a plain java object as follows:

```java
public class MnpRouting {
    @QuerySqlField(index = true)
    private String telephone;
    @QuerySqlField(index = true)
    private long    credit;
    @QuerySqlField(index = true)
    private String routeTo;
 // setter and getter goes here.
  @Override
    public String toString() {
        return "Routing {" +
                "telephone='" + telephone + '\'' +
                ", credit=" + credit +
                ", routeTo='" + routeTo + '\'' +
                '}';
    }
}
```

Class *MnpRounting* has three properties: telephone, credit, and the routeTo, where the *telephone* number is the client telephone number and the *routeTo* properties is the telephone operator, where the call should be routed.

Step 3:

Create a text file in the input directory with the following text.

```
{"telephone" : "89096860917", "credit" : "129", "routeTo" : "MTS"}
```

This file will be our source of data. Camel file adapter will consume this file periodically and sends to the Camel Ignite streamer.

Step 4:

Now, it's the time to add our main functionality, add the following class to the maven project.

```java
public class CamelStreamerDirectIngestion {
    private static final String FILE_PROPERTIES= "camel.properties";
    public static void main(String[] args) {
        Ignition.setClientMode(true);
        Ignite ignite = Ignition.start("example-ignite.xml");
        if (!ExamplesUtils.hasServerNodes(ignite))
           return;
        if(getFileLocation() == null || getFileLocation().isEmpty()){
            System.out.println("Properties file is empty or null!");
            return;
        }
```

Chapter six: Streaming and complex event processing

```java
        // camel_cache cache configuration
        CacheConfiguration<String, MnpRouting> camel_cache_cfg = new CacheConfiguration<>(\
"camel-direct");
        camel_cache_cfg.setIndexedTypes(String.class, MnpRouting.class);
        IgniteCache<String, MnpRouting> camel_cache = ignite.getOrCreateCache(camel_cache_\
cfg);
        // Create an streamer pipe which ingests into the 'camel_cache' cache.
        IgniteDataStreamer<String, MnpRouting> pipe = ignite.dataStreamer(camel_cache.getN\
ame());
        pipe.autoFlushFrequency(11);
        pipe.allowOverwrite(true);
        // Create a Camel streamer and connect it.
        CamelStreamer<String, MnpRouting> streamer = new CamelStreamer<>();
        streamer.setIgnite(ignite);
        streamer.setStreamer(pipe);
        streamer.setEndpointUri("file://"+getFileLocation());
        streamer.setSingleTupleExtractor(new StreamSingleTupleExtractor<Exchange, String, \
MnpRouting>() {
            @Override
            public Map.Entry<String, MnpRouting> extract(Exchange exchange) {
                ObjectMapper mapper = new ObjectMapper();
                String msgBody = exchange.getIn().getBody(String.class);
                MnpRouting obj = null;
                try {
                    obj = mapper.readValue(msgBody, MnpRouting.class);
                } catch (IOException e) {
                    e.printStackTrace();
                }
                if (obj != null){
                    return new GridMapEntry<String, MnpRouting>(obj.getTelephone(), obj);
                }
                return new GridMapEntry<String, MnpRouting>(null, null);
            }
        });
        streamer.start();
    }
}
```

Let's have a deeper look at the class and go through line by line. First of all, we declared this Ignite node as a client node by the statement of *Ignition.setClientMode(true)*. In the next few lines, we started the Ignite node and read the *camel.properties* file from the classpath. Next, we declared the Cache configuration with name *came-direct* and set the Index type for executing SQL queries on Cache. In the next few lines of code we created an Ignite cache from the cache configuration and one Ignite data streamer with name *pipe*. Note the next statement.

```
pipe.autoFlushFrequency(11)
```

> **Note:**
> It indicates the auto flash interval for the data stream. By default, auto flash is disabled for data streamer. If you want to store the entries immediately, set the value near 1 milliseconds.

Next, we created the camel streamer and set the Ignite-streamer pipe on it. Also, we point the endpoint properties to our input directory for the camel streamer. JSON files will be consumed from the input directory. We also added single tuple extractor to the camel streamer and implemented the method extract. In the extract function, we retrieved message payload from the camel exchange object and converted the JSON text to *MnpRouting* java object. Next, we filled the Map with the telephone number as the key and the MnpObject as the value of the cache entry. The preceding code is very straight forward, if you are curious about the complete code, please check the maven project *chapter-cep/camel* in GitHub repository[46].

Step 5:

Compile and build the project with maven by executing the following command:

```
maven clean install
```

The above command will create *camel-direct-ingestion-runnable.jar* executable jar in the target directory.

Step 6:

To run the example application, follow this step:

1. Run the `node-runner-runnable.jar` executable jar to run Ignite node from the directory *chapter-cep/camel*: `java -jar ./target/node-runner-runnable.jar`
2. Put a JSON file into the input directory as described earlier.
3. Run the `camel-direct-ingestion-runnable.jar` executable jar from the folder *chapter-cep/camel* to run the camel Ignite streamer as follows: `java -jar ./target/camel-direct-ingestion-runnable.jar`

The following screenshot shows an example of running Camel streamer.

---

[46] https://github.com/srecon/ignite-book-code-samples

Chapter six: Streaming and complex event processing 259

Figure 6.8

Whenever you put a new file in the *input* directory, Camel file adapter consumes the JSON file from the directory and dispatch into the Ignite cache. Now, we can scan the Ignite cache `camel-direct` by using the Ignite Visior commandline tool to verify the cache entry.

Figure 6.9

For simplicity, in this example, we used only one JSON object to store into the cache. However, you can modify the application to consume multiple JSON objects from one source file by using *StreamMultipleTupleExtractor* extractor.

In the next section, we will go through the mediated ingestion approach of the Ignite-camel streamer to streaming data into the Ignite cache.

Mediated Ingestion

In real life, often you need to do some complex computing or executing a few business logics on to streaming data rather than directly store them into the cache, where the Ignite mediated ingestion approach fits well. The complex computing could be validating, splitting, routing or aggregating the incoming messages and ingest only the result of the computed value into the Ignite cache. There are a several basic patterns or components for message mediation, a more complex pattern can be built by combining the simple patterns. The basic mediation patterns are:

- Protocol switch
- Transform
- Enrich
- Aggregate
- Distribute
- Correlate.

Chapter six: Streaming and complex event processing

All of these above patterns can be combined in one Camel route or use separately whenever necessary. These patterns operate on one-way operations rather than on request-response pairs.

So far in this section, we have looked at minimal possibilities of Camel framework. In this section, we will modify our application for executing a few business logics on incoming data. We are going to validate the telephone number and the credit properties from the JSON objects and finally store only those objects that passed the validation process. To achieve this functionality, we are going to use Camel Route with a custom bean processor. Note that, validated objects will be dispatched to the *direct:ignite.ingest* endpoint, where the streamer is consuming from. Now that we have discussed all the basics, let's start building our application.

Step 1:

Create a new Java class with name *RouteProcessor* and implements the Camel *Processor* interface as shown below.

```java
public class RouteProcessor implements Processor {
    private static final long CREDIT_LIMIT = 1001;
    @Override
    public void process(Exchange exchange) throws Exception {
        MnpRouting mnpRouting = (MnpRouting) exchange.getIn().getBody();
        if(mnpRouting != null){
            // validate phone numbers of format "1234567890"
            if (!mnpRouting.getTelephone().matches("\\d{11}") || mnpRouting.getCredit() < \
CREDIT_LIMIT){
                exchange.getOut().setBody("Message doesn't pass validation");
                exchange.getOut().setHeader("key", mnpRouting.getTelephone());
            } else{
                exchange.getOut().setBody(mnpRouting.toString());
                exchange.getOut().setHeader("key", mnpRouting.getTelephone());
            }
        }
    }
}
```

In the above preceding code, business logic is pretty simple. We validate the MnpRouting objects if the telephone number is ambiguous or the credit is less than 100, then we pass the object and write an alert into the cache. Next, we will create an another Java class for streaming data into the cache.

Step 2:

Create an another Java class *CamelStreamerMediationIngestion* or you can modify the previous one, which we used for direct ingestion before.

Chapter six: Streaming and complex event processing

```java
public class CamelStreamerMediationIngestion {
    private static final String FILE_PROPERTIES= "camel.properties";
    public static void main(String[] args) throws Exception {
        System.out.println("Camel Streamer Mediation ingestion!");
        Ignition.setClientMode(true);
        Ignite ignite = Ignition.start("example-ignite.xml");
        if (!ExamplesUtils.hasServerNodes(ignite))
            return;
        if (getFileLocation() == null || getFileLocation().isEmpty()){
            System.out.println("properties file is empty or null!");
            return;
        }
        // camel_cache cache configuration
        CacheConfiguration<String, String> camel_cache_cfg = new CacheConfiguration<>("cam\
el-direct");
        camel_cache_cfg.setIndexedTypes(String.class, String.class);
        IgniteCache<String, String> camel_cache = ignite.getOrCreateCache(camel_cache_cfg);
        // Create a streamer pipe which ingests into the 'camel_cache' cache.
        IgniteDataStreamer<String, String> pipe = ignite.dataStreamer(camel_cache.getName(\
));

        pipe.autoFlushFrequency(11);
        pipe.allowOverwrite(true);

        CamelStreamer<String, String> streamer = new CamelStreamer<>();
        streamer.setIgnite(ignite);
        streamer.setStreamer(pipe);
        streamer.setEndpointUri("direct:ignite.ingest");
        CamelContext context = new DefaultCamelContext();
        context.addRoutes(new RouteBuilder() {
            @Override
            public void configure() throws Exception {
                from("file://"+getFileLocation())
                    .unmarshal().json(JsonLibrary.Jackson, MnpRouting.class)
                    .bean(new RouteProcessor(), "process")
                    .to("direct:ignite.ingest");
            }
        });
        streamer.setCamelContext(context);
        streamer.setSingleTupleExtractor(new StreamSingleTupleExtractor<Exchange, String, \
String>() {
            @Override
            public Map.Entry<String, String> extract(Exchange exchange) {
                String key = exchange.getIn().getHeader("key", String.class);
                String routeMsg = exchange.getIn().getBody(String.class);
```

```
                return new GridMapEntry<>(key, routeMsg);
            }
        });
        streamer.start();
    }
}
```

Most of the part of this above Java class has not changed, let us go through the most important part of this Java class. Here, we are using a new endpoint for the Ignite streamer `direct:ignite.ingest`. Ignite streamer is now consuming data from the direct endpoint above. Next, we use the default Camel context and add one route on it. For the ultimate clean and quick code, we are using camel Java *DSL* here.

```
context.addRoutes(new RouteBuilder() {
    @Override
    public void configure() throws Exception {
        from("file://"+getFileLocation())
            .unmarshal().json(JsonLibrary.Jackson, MnpRouting.class)
            .bean(new RouteProcessor(), "process")
            .to("direct:ignite.ingest");
    }
});
```

First, we consume the file from the input directory. Next, we unmarshal the JSON objects to Java objects and route to our RouteProcessor for validating the object. Note that, we are using `bean(new RouteProcessor(), "process")` bean binding approach, there are a few more ways to binding bean into the camel route. If you are curious about the Camel bean binding, please visit the Camel site for more information. After validating the objects, we dispatch it to Ignite streamer for storing into the cache.

Step 3:

Let's compile and run the application to see it in action:

1. Build the project with `maven clean install` command.
2. Run the `node-runner-runnable.jar` executable jar to run Ignite node from the directory *chapter-cep/camel*: `java -jar ./target/node-runner-runnable.jar`
3. Put a few JSON files into the input directory as described before.
4. Run the `camel-mediation-ingestion-runnable.jar` executable jar from the directory *chapter-cep/camel* to run the camel Ignite streamer as follows: `java -jar ./target/camel-mediation-ingestion-runnable.jar`

Chapter six: Streaming and complex event processing 263

Figure 6.10

We have added two JSON files into the input directory with differents credit information and telephone numbers. Camel file adapter starts consuming the files and our custom Processor validates the objects. Let's verify the Ignite cache using *ignitevisior*..

Figure 6.11

We got, what we have expected, whenever the telephone number is not valid or the credit is less than 100, we get an alert message into the cache *camel-direct*.

That's it, we have just completed our Camel Ignite streamer section, in the next section, we will deep dive into the Apache Flume: another framework to load a massive amount of data into the Ignite cache.

Flume streamer

Apache Flume is a data ingestion mechanism for collecting, filtering, aggregating and transporting large amounts of streaming data such as log files, event's from various sources to a centralized data store, data store might be HDFS, RDBMS or in-memory data store. In plain English, words **flume** means channel. This tool is designed to manage the flow of the data, collected from different sources and send them to a centralized repository.

Advantages:

- It is reliable, meaning if an event is introduced into Flume event processing framework, it is guaranteed not to be lost.
- Flume supports any kind of centralized data store, HDFS, RDBMS or In-memory data store. With customizing Flume sink, you can store data into any persistence store.
- It is scalable; by adding more number of processing agents, known as Flume agents, we can have scalability as far as processing is concerned. Thus, we can process more if more agents are added.
- Flume provides the feature of contextual routing.
- When the rate of incoming data exceeds the rate at which data can be written to the destination, Flume acts as a mediator between data producers and the centralized stores and provides a steady flow of data between them.

Chapter six: Streaming and complex event processing 264

- Finally, it is feature rich and fully extensible; so we can extend the Flume framework to our needs.

Thus, Flume is a framework that is useful for moving data. What Flume lets us do is move data from point A to point B, and while moving the data, it lets us also to transform the data. So in that sense, it is more like an *ETL (Extract Transform Load)* tool.

High level architecture:

Let's describe the architecture of the Flume with the definitions of the basic concepts.

1. Event: A unit of data transmitted from place A to place B. An event has a byte payload and an optional set of string attributes.
2. Flow: The path of the movement of an event from place A to place B.
3. Client: Any application or source that ships the event to the Flume agent.
4. Agent: An independent Java process that hosts components such as sources, channels, and sinks; storing events and ship event's to the next node.
5. Source: It's an interface, which can receive events from various sources through different protocols.
6. Channel: Temporary storage for events, the event is in the channel until it is taken by the sink.
7. Sink: Implementation of the interface, which takes events from the channel and transmits it to the destination. A Sink that conveys the event in the target store is called final sink. Examples of the final sink could be HDFS, Hive database or search server Solr.

Before we move on to a more advanced topic, let's have a look at the high-level architecture of the Flume.

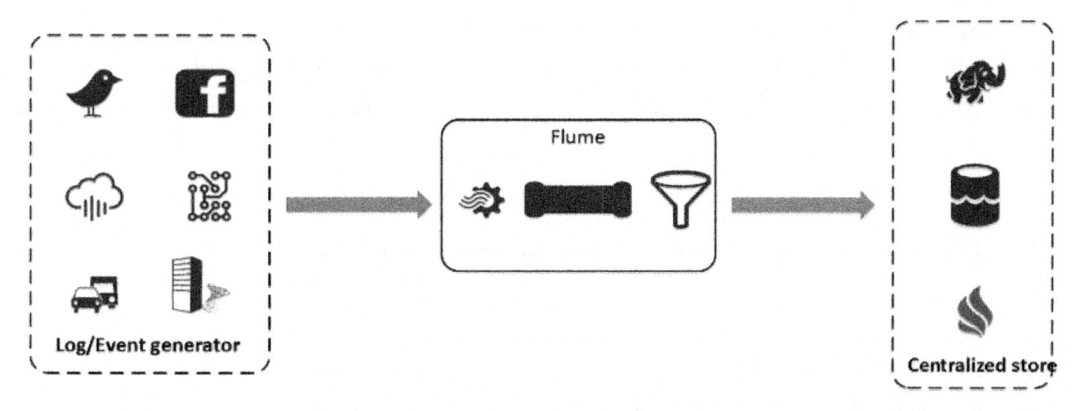

Figure 6.12

Historically, Flume is used for ingesting high volume of logs from various sources like Nginx web servers or Application servers to Hadoop file system, and it is more tightly integrated with the Hadoop ecosystems. So, it's common use case is to act as a data pipeline to ingest massive volume of data into the Hadoop file system. However, you can use Flume for ingesting any type of event data

Chapter six: Streaming and complex event processing 265

into any centralized store. As for example, you can use Flume for ingesting transaction data from a credit card processing system like way4 and store them into Apache Ignite for real-time analysis. Also, you can use Flume interceptor to do a variety of processing against incoming event as they pass through the Flume pipeline. For instance, you can calculate a basic *Travel score* or anti-fraud system to attempt to identify whether a bank customer is traveling while they are using their debit or credit card. The above use case is quite fabricated, but Flume architecture can be used to apply virtually any online model or scoring while returning results in sub-seconds times.

Apache Ignite provides *IgniteSink* that extracts events from a flume channel and ingests into Ignite cache. At the time of writing of this book, IgniteSink support Flume-1.6.0 version.

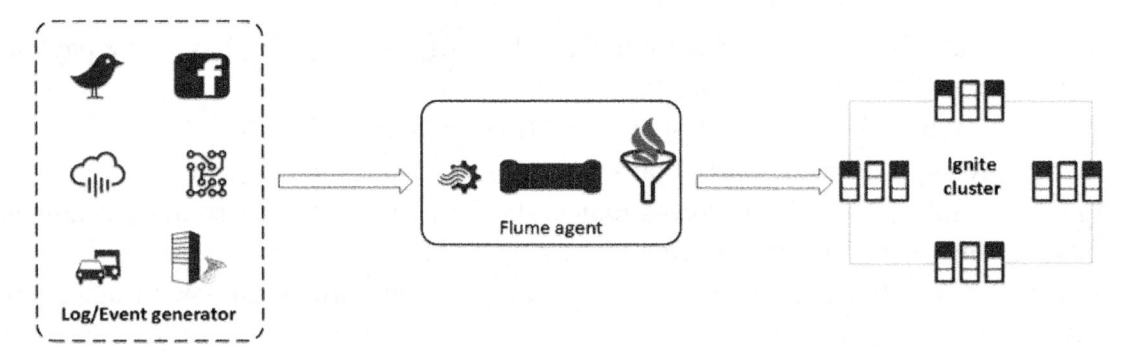

Figure 6.13

An *IgniteSink* is associated with exactly one channel as configured in the Flume configuration file. Also, there is one *SinkRunner* instance correlated with every configured sink, and when the Flume framework call *SinkRunner.start()* a new thread is created to run the IgniteSink. Now that we have dipped our toes into Flume, let's build a (nearly) minimal example of IgniteSink to demonstrate the core functionality of the IgniteSink. To keep things simple, we are going to use two sources of events in our example: Linux Netcat utility and a custom RPC event generator. We will simulate ingesting transaction events into Ignite cache. Through Netcat utility or RPC generator, we will generate transaction events in the format *string:string* for Flume source and the flume agent will ship this event through a channel to IgniteSink. IgniteSink will convert the list of events into cache entries.

Step 1:

Add the following IgniteSink maven dependency into your project.

```
<dependency>
    <groupId>org.apache.ignite</groupId>
    <artifactId>ignite-flume</artifactId>
    <version>1.6.0</version>
</dependency>
```

Step 2:

First of all, we have to develop our own custom *EventTransformer* class by implementing the EventTransformer interface provided by IgniteSink. The main purpose of this class is to convert a list of Flume events to Ignite cache entries.

> **Note:**
>
> Before implementing the interface *EventTransformer*, we have to specify the format and the type of the event. In our case, event type will be String and the format will be *String:String*.

```
public class FlumeEventTransformer implements EventTransformer <Event, String, Integer> {
    @Nullable
    @Override
    public Map<String, Integer> transform(List<Event> list) {
        final Map<String, Integer> map = new HashMap<>(list.size());
        for (Event event : list){
            map.putAll(transform(event));
        }
        return map;
    }
    /**
     * Event format - String:String
     * example - transactionId:amount [56102:232], where transactionId is the key and amou\
nt is the value
     * */
    private Map<String, Integer> transform(Event event){
        final Map<String, Integer> map = new HashMap<>();
        String eventBody = new String(event.getBody());
        if(!eventBody.isEmpty()){
            // parse the string by the delimiter ":"
            String[] tokens = eventBody.split(":");
            map.put(tokens[0].trim(), Integer.valueOf(tokens[1].trim()));
        }
        return map;
    }
}
```

The above class is very straight forward. However, let's have a detailed look at the above fragment of the code. First, we implemented the interface *EventTransformer* and overrode the method transform. We also overload the method transform with a single Event. In the overloaded method, we extract the event body as String and split the body by the delimiter ":". The first part of the decoupled string will be our cache key and the rest of the part will be the value of the cache entry.

Chapter six: Streaming and complex event processing

Step 3:

Build the project with the following command:

```
mvn clean package
```

It will create a jar named *chapter-cep/flume/target/flume-1.0-SNAPSHOT.jar*.

Step 4:

Download the Apache Flume distributive from the following page[47]. Apache Flume is distributed in several formats for your convenience. You can pick a ready-made binary distribution or a source archive if you intend to build Apache Flume yourself. In order to guard against corrupted downloads/installations, it is highly recommended to verify the signature of the release bundles against the public KEYS used by the Apache Flume developers. At the time of writing this book, Apache Flume 1.6 version is the current stable version.

Step 5:

Ensure JAVA_HOME environment variable is set and points to your JDK installation. In our case, we are using JVM 1.8. Extract the distribution archive into any directory.

```
tar xzvf apache-flume-1.6.0-bin.tar.gz
```

Move the content of the `apache-flume-1.6.0-bin.tar.gz` file to the directory */home/user/apache-flume-1.6.0-bin* as follows:

```
mv apache-flume-1.6.0-bin/* /home/user/apache-flume-1.6.0-bin
```

Step 6:

Verify the installation of Apache Flume by browsing through the bin folder of the Flume home directory and typing the following command.

```
./flume-ng version
```

If you have successfully installed Flume, you will get the following information in your console as shown below:

---

[47] https://flume.apache.org/download.html

```
Flume 1.6.0
Source code repository: https://git-wip-us.apache.org/repos/asf/flume.git
Revision: 2561a23240a71ba20bf288c7c2cda88f443c2080
Compiled by hshreedharan on Mon May 11 11:15:44 PDT 2015
From source with checksum b29e416802ce9ece3269d34233baf43f
```

Step 7:

Create a directory *plugins.d* inside the Flume home directory. In our case it should be */home/user/apache-flume-1.6.0-bin/plugins.d*. Create *ignite-sink* directory under `plugins.d` directory. Create two more directories under *ignite-sink* directory:

- lib
- libext

Copy the previously build file *flume-1.0-SNAPSHOT.jar* to `${FLUME_HOME}/plugins.d/ignite-sink/lib`.

Copy other *Ignite-related* jar files from the Apache Ignite distribution to `${FLUME_HOME}/plugins.d/ignite-sink/libext` folder as shown below.

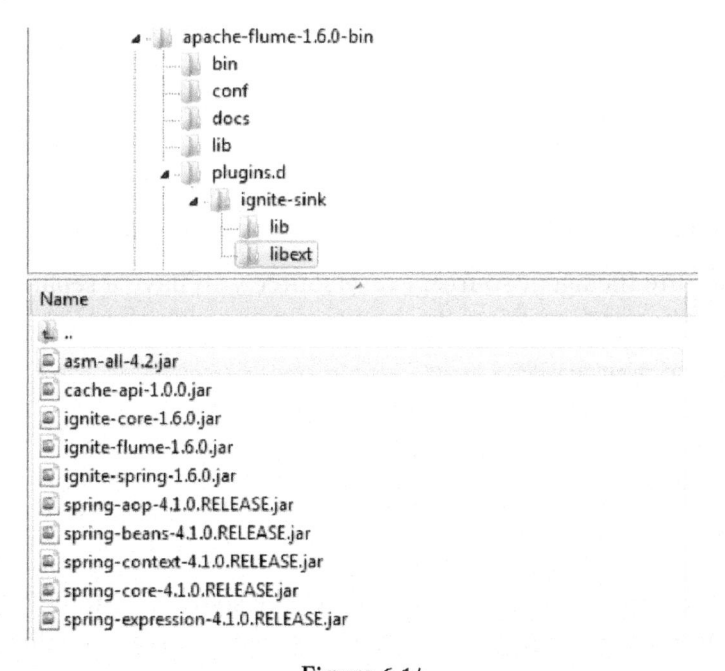

Figure 6.14

Note that, the `asm-all-*.*.jar` library is also needed to run the Ignite sink with Flume agent.

Step 8:

Copy the file *example-ignite.xml* and *demo.properties* from */chapters/chapter-cep/flume/src/main/java/com/blu/imdg/flume/config* to `${FLUME_HOME}/conf` directory. Note that, in the example-ignite.xml file you have to specify the Ignite cache name, which will be the same as the cache name from the file demo.properties. In our case, the cache name is the *testCache*. Now, we have to configure the Flume agent properties into the file demo.properties, which is a java property file having key-value pairs. In the Flume configuration file, we need to configure the following components:

- Name of the components for the current agent.
- Configure the source.
- Configure the channel.
- Configure the sink.
- Bind the source and the sink to the channel.

Generally, we can have multiple agents in Flume. We can differentiate each agent by the unique name. And using this unique name we can configure each agent. Let's have a detailed look at the file *demo.properties*.

First of all, you have to give a name to the components such as sources, sinks, and the channels of the agent, as shown below.

```
# Name the components for this agent
a1.sources = r1
a1.sinks = k1
a1.channels = c1
```

Where, *a1* is the name of the agent, *r1* is the name of the source and so on.

Next, we have to configure the agent source; every source will have a separate list of properties.

```
# Describe/configure the source
#a1.sources.r1.type = netcat
a1.sources.r1.type = avro
a1.sources.r1.bind = localhost
a1.sources.r1.port = 44444
```

Property *type* is one of the most common properties of the source: it can be Netcat, Avro or Twitter. Also, the source should bind to a Host and with a Port. We are using localhost with port **44444**. In our example, we will use the source Netcat and Avro to generate events.

Flume out of the box provides a bunch of different channels to transfer data between sources and sinks. To describe the channel, you have to set the required properties, as follows.

```
# Use a channel which buffers events in memory
a1.channels.c1.type = memory
a1.channels.c1.capacity = 1000
a1.channels.c1.transactionCapacity = 100
```

Here, the maximum channel capacity of events is 1000 entries, and the maximum number of events stored in the channel per transaction is 100. Like source, sink must be configured in a separate list. The property named type is common to every sink, and it is used to specify the type of the sink we are using. Along with the property type, it also needs to provide the values of all the required properties of a particular sink as shown below.

```
# ignite sink
a1.sinks.k1.type = org.apache.ignite.stream.flume.IgniteSink
a1.sinks.k1.igniteCfg = /home/user/apache-flume-1.6.0-bin/conf/example-ignite.xml
a1.sinks.k1.cacheName = testCache
a1.sinks.k1.eventTransformer = com.blu.imdg.flume.Transformer.FlumeEventTransformer
a1.sinks.k1.batchSize = 100
```

Here, the type of the sink is *org.apache.ignite.stream.flume.IgniteSink*. The configuration of the Ignite sink is located in $FLUME_HOME/conf directory. Name of the cache for ingesting events is *testCache* and the event transformer class is our custom *FlumeEventTransformer* class.

So far, we configured the source, channel, and the sink. The Flume sink channel connects the source and the sink together; it is required to bind both of them to channel as follows.

```
# Bind the source and sink to the channel
a1.sources.r1.channels = c1
a1.sinks.k1.channel = c1
```

Step 9:

Now that we have configured all the necessary configuration and we are ready to run the Flume agent. First, we will have to start an Ignite node and then start the flume agent by executing the following command:

```
./flume-ng agent --conf conf --conf-file /home/user/apache-flume-1.6.0-bin/conf/ demo.prop\
erties --name a1
```

If everything goes fine, you should get a similar output in the console as shown below.

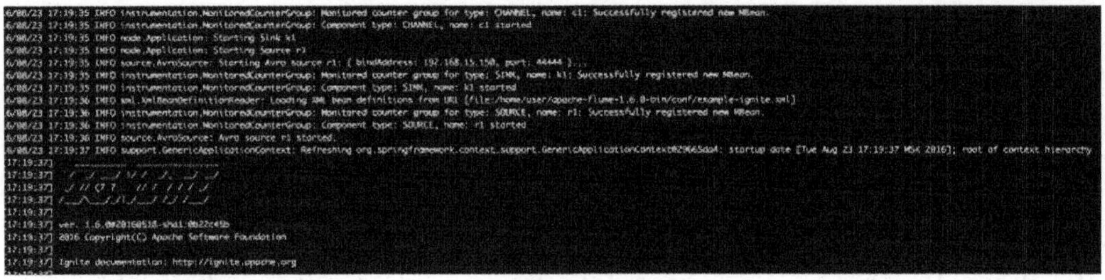

Chapter six: Streaming and complex event processing

Figure 6.15

Now, we can run our Avro event generator class to generate events. Run the *RunClient* java class, and it will generate 99 events to the Flume agent source. The format of the event is **transactionId:amount** as described earlier of this section.

If we will start *ignitevisor* and scan the cache *testCache*, we will discover generated 99 elements into the cache.

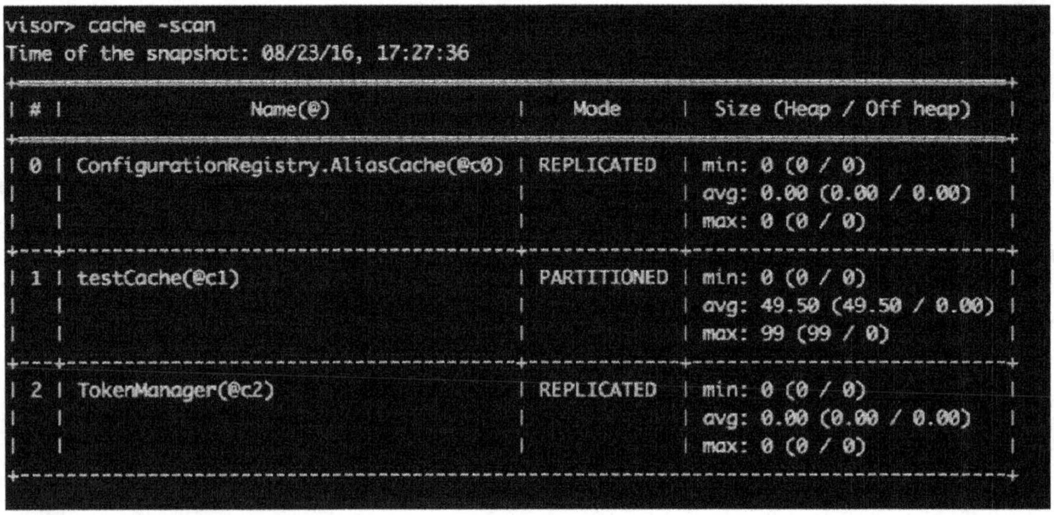

Figure 6.16

Next, we are going to reconfigure the Flume agent source to use Linux Netcat tool and will try to make it generate some events by using nc tool for ingesting events into the Ignite cache. To keep things simple, we will edit the agent source section into our *demo.properties* file as shown below.

```
# Describe/configure the source
a1.sources.r1.type = netcat
#a1.sources.r1.type = avro
a1.sources.r1.bind = localhost
a1.sources.r1.port = 44444
```

That's it! We have disabled avro source section in the properties file and enable the source Netcat. Netcat is a simple Unix tool that reads and writes data across a network connection, widely used as a debugging and exploration tool. The rest of the configurations int the file will be untouched. Let's re-execute the Flume agent as follows.

Chapter six: Streaming and complex event processing

```
./flume-ng agent --conf conf --conf-file /home/user/apache-flume-1.6.0-bin/conf/demo.prope\
rties --name a1 -Dflume.root.logger=INFO,console
```

You should notice that a `Netcat` source has been started on the specified host and ports in the console as shown in the figure 6.17.

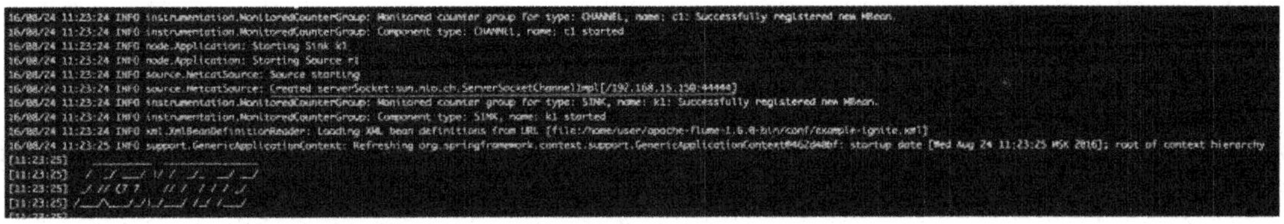

Figure 6.17

Let's start a new terminal and execute the following command.

```
nc YOUR_HOST 44444
```

Now you can send any command by entering key *enter*. Let's type `transaction1:101` and enter. Now, have a look into the cache *testCache* by ignitevisior to make sure that, our event has been ingested into the Ignite cache.

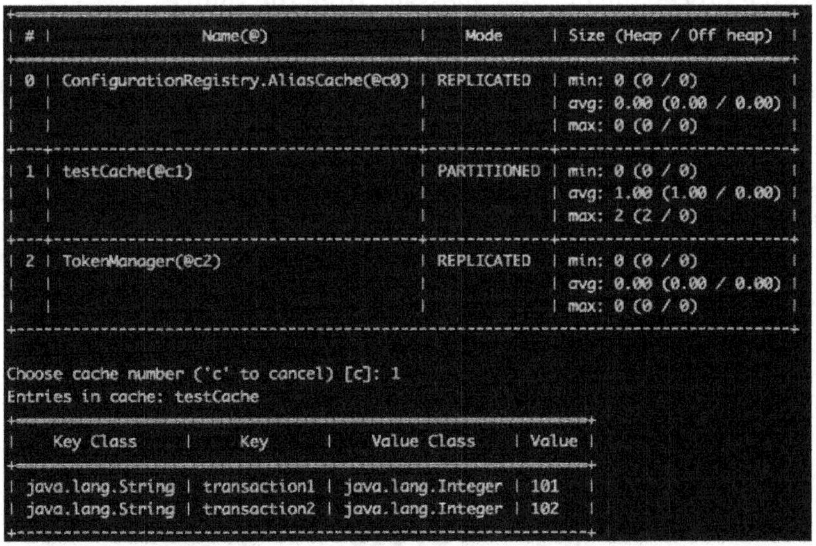

Figure 6.18

In the *ignitevisior* console, we can confirm our transaction event in the cache. The Netcat tool is very useful to debug event processing or ingestion data processing into the Ignite cache.

In the next section, we are going to describe the Strom data streamer to streaming data into the Ignite cache.

Storm data streamer

Apache storm is a distributed fault-tolerant real-time computing system. In the era of *IoT (Internet Of Things - the next big thing)*, many companies regularly generate terabytes of data in their daily operations. The sources include everything from data captured from network sensors, vehicles, physical devices, the web, social data, transactional business data. With the volume of data being generated, real-time computing has become a major challenge for most of the organization. In a short time, Apache Storm became a standard for distributed real-time processing system that allows you to process a large amount of data. Apache Storm project is open source and written in Java and Clojure. It became a first choose for real-time analytics. Apache Ignite Storm streamer module provides a convenience way to streaming data via Storm to Ignite cache.

Although Hadoop and Storm frameworks are used for analyzing and processing big data, both of them complement each other and differs in a few aspects. Like Hadoop, Storm can process a huge amount of data but does it in real-time with guaranteed reliability, meaning every message will be processed. It has these advantages as well:

1. Simple scalability, to scale horizontally, you simply add machines and change parallelism settings of the topology.
2. Stateless message processing.
3. It guarantees the processing of every message from the source.
4. It has fault tolerance.
5. The topology of Storm can be written in any languages, although mostly Java is used.

Key concepts:

Apache Storm reads raw streams of data from the one end and passes it through a sequence of small processing units and output the processed information at the other end. Let's have a detailed look at the main components of Apache Storm –

Tuples – It is the main data structure of Storm. It's an ordered list of elements. Generally, tuple supports all primitives data types.

TUPLES

ordered list of elements
("bion@at-consulting.ru","ignite-demo@ignite.com")

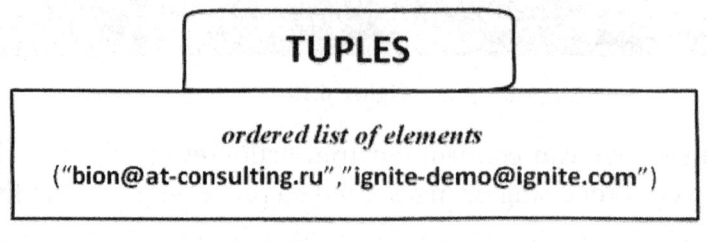

Figure 6.19

Streams – It's an unbound and unordered sequence of tuples.

Chapter six: Streaming and complex event processing 274

STREAMS
unbound and un ordered sequence of tuples
tuples | tuples | tuples | tuples | tuples

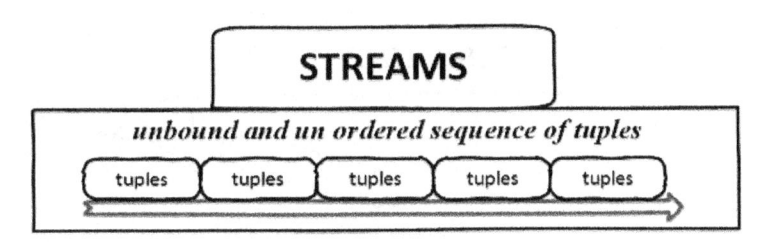

Figure 6.20

Spouts - Source of the streams, in simple terms, a spout reads the data from a source for use in the topology. A spout can be reliable or unreliable. A spout can talk with Queues, Weblogs, event data, etc.

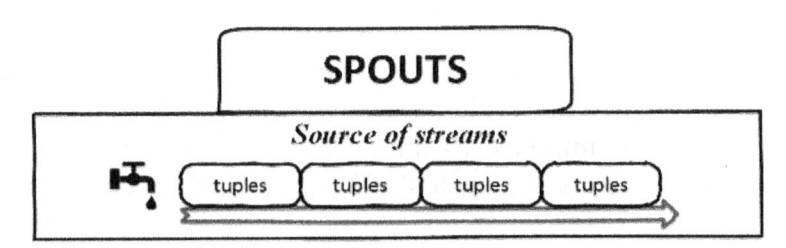

SPOUTS
Source of streams
tuples | tuples | tuples | tuples

Figure 6.21

Bolts - Bolts are logical processing units, it is responsible for processing data and creating new streams. Bolts can perform the operations of filtering, aggregation, joining and interacting with files/database and so on. Bolts receive data from the spout and emit to one or more bolts.

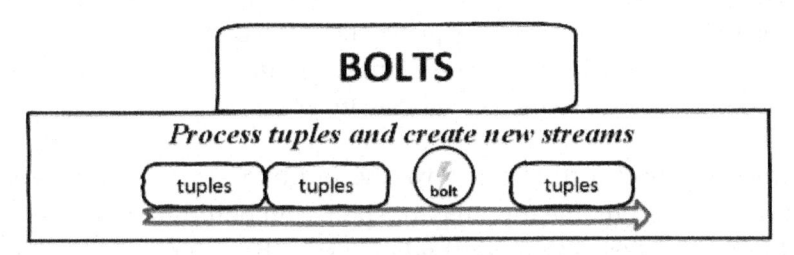

BOLTS
Process tuples and create new streams
tuples | tuples | bolt | tuples

Figure 6.22

Topology – A topology is a directed graph of Spouts and Bolts, each node of this graph contains the data processing logic (bolts) while connecting edges define the flow of the data (streams).

Unlike Hadoop, Storm keeps the topology running forever until you kill it. A simple topology starts with spouts, emit stream from the sources to bolt for processing data. Apache Storms' main job is to run any topology at a given time.

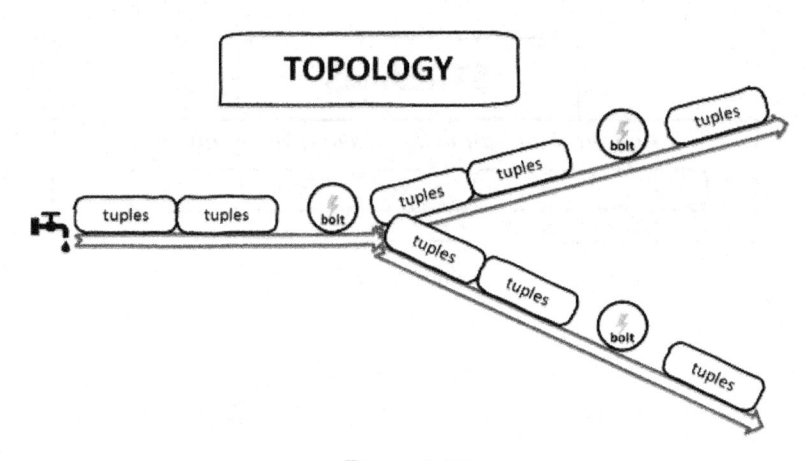

Chapter six: Streaming and complex event processing 275

Figure 6.23

Ignite out of the box provides an implementation of Storm Bolt (StormStreamer) to streaming the computed data into the Ignite cache. On the other hand, you can write your custom Strom Bolt to ingest stream data into Ignite. To develop a custom Storm Bolt, you just have to implement *BaseBasicBolt* or *IRichBolt* Storm interface. However, if you decide to use StormStreamer, you have to configure a few properties to work the Ignite Bolt correctly. All mandatory properties are shown below:

№	Property Name	Description
1	CacheName	Cache name of the Ignite cache, in which the data will be stored.
2	IgniteTupleField	Names of the Ignite Tuple field, by which tuple data is obtained in topology. By default the value is *ignite*.
3	IgniteConfigFile	This property will set the Ignite spring configuration file. This allows you to send and consume message to and from Ignite topics.
4	AllowOverwrite	It will enable overwriting existing values in the cache; default value is false.
5	AutoFlushFrequency	Automatic flush frequency in milliseconds. Essentially, this is the time after which the streamer will make an attempt to submit all data added to remote nodes. The default value is 10 sec.

Now, let's build something useful to check how the Ignite *StormStreamer* works. The basic idea behind the application is to design one topology of spout and bolt that can process a huge amount of data from a traffic log files and trigger an alert when a specific value crosses a predefined threshold. Using a topology, the log file will be consumed line by line and the topology is designed to monitor the incoming data. In our case, the log file will contain data, such as vehicle registration number, speed and the highway name from highway traffic camera. If the vehicle crosses the speed limit (for example 120km/h), Storm topology will send the data to Ignite cache.

Next listing will show a CSV file of the type we are going to use in our example, which contain vehicle data information such as vehicle registration number, the speed at which the vehicle is traveling and the location of the highway.

Chapter six: Streaming and complex event processing   276

```
AB 123, 160, North city
BC 123, 170, South city
CD 234, 40, South city
DE 123, 40, East city
EF 123, 190, South city
GH 123, 150, West city
XY 123, 110, North city
GF 123, 100, South city
PO 234, 140, South city
XX 123, 110, East city
YY 123, 120, South city
ZQ 123, 100, West city
```

The idea of the above example is taken from the *Dr. Dobbs* journal. Since this book is not for studying Apache Storm, I am going to keep the example as simple as possible. Also, I have added the famous word count example of Storm, which ingests the word count value into Ignite cache through StormStreamer module. If you are curious about the code, it's available at **chapter-cep/storm**. The above CSV file will be the source for the Storm topology.

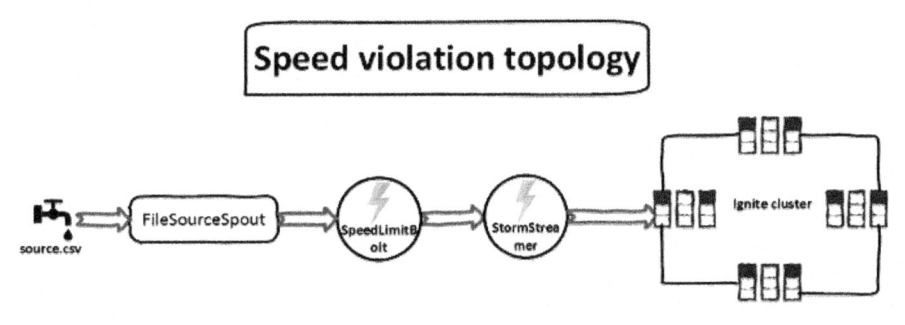

Figure 6.24

As shown in figure 6.24, the *FileSourceSpout* accepts the input CSV log file, reads the data line by line and emits the data to the `SpeedLimitBolt` for further threshold processing. Once the processing is done and found any car with exceeding the speed limit, the data is emitted to the Ignite StormStreamer bolt, where it is ingested into the cache. Let's dive into the detailed explanation of our Storm topology.

Step 1:

Because this is a Storm topology, you must add the Storm and the Ignite *StormStreamer* dependency in the maven project.

Chapter six: Streaming and complex event processing

```xml
<dependency>
    <groupId>org.apache.ignite</groupId>
    <artifactId>ignite-storm</artifactId>
    <version>1.6.0</version>
</dependency>
<dependency>
    <groupId>org.apache.ignite</groupId>
    <artifactId>ignite-core</artifactId>
    <version>1.6.0</version>
</dependency>
<dependency>
    <groupId>org.apache.ignite</groupId>
    <artifactId>ignite-spring</artifactId>
    <version>1.6.0</version>
</dependency>
<dependency>
    <groupId>org.apache.storm</groupId>
    <artifactId>storm-core</artifactId>
    <version>0.10.0</version>
    <exclusions>
        <exclusion>
            <groupId>log4j</groupId>
            <artifactId>log4j</artifactId>
        </exclusion>
        <exclusion>
            <groupId>org.slf4j</groupId>
            <artifactId>slf4j-log4j12</artifactId>
        </exclusion>
        <exclusion>
            <groupId>commons-logging</groupId>
            <artifactId>commons-logging</artifactId>
        </exclusion>
        <exclusion>
            <groupId>org.slf4j</groupId>
            <artifactId>slf4j-simple</artifactId>
        </exclusion>
        <exclusion>
            <groupId>org.slf4j</groupId>
            <artifactId>log4j-over-slf4j</artifactId>
        </exclusion>
        <exclusion>
            <groupId>org.apache.zookeeper</groupId>
            <artifactId>zookeeper</artifactId>
        </exclusion>
    </exclusions>
```

Chapter six: Streaming and complex event processing 278

```
</dependency>
```

At the time of writing this book, Apache Storm version 0.10.0 is the only supported version.

> **Note:**
> You do not need any **Kafka** module to run or execute this example.

Step 2:

Create an Ignite configuration file (see example-ignite.xml file in /chapter-cep/storm/src/resources/example ignite.xml) and make sure that it is available from the classpath. The content of the Ignite configuration is identical from the previous section of this chapter.

```xml
<beans xmlns="http://www.springframework.org/schema/beans"
       xmlns:xsi="http://www.w3.org/2001/XMLSchema-instance"
       xmlns:util="http://www.springframework.org/schema/util"
       xsi:schemaLocation="
        http://www.springframework.org/schema/beans
        http://www.springframework.org/schema/beans/spring-beans.xsd
        http://www.springframework.org/schema/util
        http://www.springframework.org/schema/util/spring-util.xsd">
    <bean id="ignite.cfg" class="org.apache.ignite.configuration.IgniteConfiguration">
        <!-- Enable client mode. -->
        <property name="clientMode" value="true"/>
        <!-- Cache accessed from IgniteSink. -->
        <property name="cacheConfiguration">
            <list>
                <!-- Partitioned cache example configuration with configurations adjusted \
to server nodes'. -->
                <bean class="org.apache.ignite.configuration.CacheConfiguration">
                    <property name="atomicityMode" value="ATOMIC"/>

                    <property name="name" value="testCache"/>
                </bean>
            </list>
        </property>
        <!-- Enable cache events. -->
        <property name="includeEventTypes">
            <list>
                <!-- Cache events (only EVT_CACHE_OBJECT_PUT for tests). -->
                <util:constant static-field="org.apache.ignite.events.EventType.EVT_CACHE_\
OBJECT_PUT"/>
```

Chapter six: Streaming and complex event processing

```xml
                </list>
            </property>
            <!-- Explicitly configure TCP discovery SPI to provide list of initial nodes. -->
            <property name="discoverySpi">
                <bean class="org.apache.ignite.spi.discovery.tcp.TcpDiscoverySpi">
                    <property name="ipFinder">
                        <bean class="org.apache.ignite.spi.discovery.tcp.ipfinder.vm.TcpDiscov\
eryVmIpFinder">
                            <property name="addresses">
                                <list>
                                    <value>127.0.0.1:47500</value>
                                </list>
                            </property>
                        </bean>
                    </property>
                </bean>
            </property>
        </bean>
</beans>
```

Step 3:

Create an *ignite-storm.properties* file to add the cache name, tuple name and the name of the Ignite configuration file as shown below.

```
cache.name=testCache
tuple.name=ignite
ignite.spring.xml=example-ignite.xml
```

Step 4:

Next, create *FileSourceSpout* Java class as shown below,

```java
public class FileSourceSpout extends BaseRichSpout {
    private static final Logger LOGGER = LogManager.getLogger(FileSourceSpout.class);
    private SpoutOutputCollector outputCollector;
    @Override
    public void open(Map map, TopologyContext topologyContext, SpoutOutputCollector spoutO\
utputCollector) {
        this.outputCollector = spoutOutputCollector;
    }
    @Override
    public void nextTuple() {
        try {
            Path filePath = Paths.get(this.getClass().getClassLoader().getResource("source\
```

```
.csv").toURI());
            try(Stream<String> lines = Files.lines(filePath)){
                lines.forEach(line ->{
                    outputCollector.emit(new Values(line));
                });
            } catch(IOException e){
                LOGGER.error(e.getMessage());
            }
        } catch (URISyntaxException e) {
            LOGGER.error(e.getMessage());
        }
    }
    @Override
    public void declareOutputFields(OutputFieldsDeclarer outputFieldsDeclarer) {
        outputFieldsDeclarer.declare(new Fields("trafficLog"));
    }
}
```

The *FileSourceSpout* code has three important methods:

- **open()**: This method would get called at the start of the spout and will give you the context information.
- **nextTuple()**: This method would allow you to pass one tuple to Storm topology for processing at a time, in this method, I am reading the CSV file line by line and emitting the line as a tuple to the bolt.
- **declareOutputFields()**: This method declares the name of the output tuple. In our case, the name should be *trafficLog*.

Step 5:

Now create *SpeedLimitBolt.java* class which implements the *BaseBasicBolt* interface.

```
public class SpeedLimitBolt extends BaseBasicBolt {
    private static final String IGNITE_FIELD = "ignite";
    private static final int SPEED_THRESHOLD = 120;
    private static final Logger LOGGER = LogManager.getLogger(SpeedLimitBolt.class);
    @Override
    public void execute(Tuple tuple, BasicOutputCollector basicOutputCollector) {
        String line = (String)tuple.getValue(0);
        if(!line.isEmpty()){
            String[] elements = line.split(",");
            // we are interested in speed and the car registration number
            int speed = Integer.valueOf((elements[1]).trim());
            String car = elements[0];
```

Chapter six: Streaming and complex event processing

```
            if(speed > SPEED_THRESHOLD){
                TreeMap<String, Integer> carValue = new TreeMap<String, Integer>();
                carValue.put(car, speed);
                basicOutputCollector.emit(new Values(carValue));
                LOGGER.info("Speed violation found:"+ car + " speed:" + speed);
            }
        }
    }
    @Override
    public void declareOutputFields(OutputFieldsDeclarer outputFieldsDeclarer) {
        outputFieldsDeclarer.declare(new Fields(IGNITE_FIELD));
    }
}
```

Let's go through line by line again.

- *execute():* This is the method where you implement the business logic of your bolt. In this case, I am splitting the line by the comma (,) and check the speed limit of the car. If the speed limit of the given car is higher than the threshold, we are creating a new treemap data type from this tuple and emit the tuple to the next bolt. In our case the next bolt will be the StormStreamer.
- *declareOutputFields():* This method is similar to declareOutputFields() method in FileSourceSpout. It declares that it is going to return Ignite tuple for further processing.

> **Note:**
> The tuple name IGNITE is important here, the StormStreamer will only process the tuple with name ignite.

Note that, Bolts can do anything, for example, computation, persistence or talking to external components.

Step 6:

It's the time to create our topology to run our example. Topology ties the spouts and bolts together in a graph, which defines how the data flows between the components. It also provides parallelism hints that Storm uses when creating instances of the components within the cluster. To implement the topology, create a new file named *SpeedViolationTopology.java* in the src\main\java\com\blu\imdg\storm\topology directory. Use the following as the contents of the file:

```java
public class SpeedViolationTopology {
    private static final int STORM_EXECUTORS = 2;

    public static void main(String[] args) throws Exception {
        if (getProperties() == null || getProperties().isEmpty()) {
            System.out.println("Property file <ignite-storm.property> is not found or empt\
y");
            return;
        }
        // Ignite Stream Ibolt
        final StormStreamer<String, String> stormStreamer = new StormStreamer<>();

        stormStreamer.setAutoFlushFrequency(10L);
        stormStreamer.setAllowOverwrite(true);
        stormStreamer.setCacheName(getProperties().getProperty("cache.name"));

        stormStreamer.setIgniteTupleField(getProperties().getProperty("tuple.name"));
        stormStreamer.setIgniteConfigFile(getProperties().getProperty("ignite.spring.xml")\
);


        TopologyBuilder builder = new TopologyBuilder();

        builder.setSpout("spout", new FileSourceSpout(), 1);
        builder.setBolt("limit", new SpeedLimitBolt(), 1).fieldsGrouping("spout", new Fiel\
ds("trafficLog"));
        // set ignite bolt
        builder.setBolt("ignite-bolt", stormStreamer, STORM_EXECUTORS).shuffleGrouping("li\
mit");
        Config conf = new Config();
        conf.setDebug(false);
        conf.setMaxTaskParallelism(1);
        LocalCluster cluster = new LocalCluster();
        cluster.submitTopology("speed-violation", conf, builder.createTopology());
        Thread.sleep(10000);
        cluster.shutdown();
    }
    private static Properties getProperties() {
        Properties properties = new Properties();
        InputStream ins = SpeedViolationTopology.class.getClassLoader().getResourceAsStrea\
m("ignite-storm.properties");
        try {
            properties.load(ins);
        } catch (IOException e) {
            e.printStackTrace();
```

Chapter six: Streaming and complex event processing

```
            properties = null;
        }
        return properties;
    }
}
```

Let's go through the code line by line again. First, we read the *ignite-storm.properties* file to get all the necessary parameters to configure the StormStreamer bolt next. The storm topology is basically a Thrift structure. The *TopologyBuilder* class provides a simple and elegant way to build complex Storm topology. The TopologyBuilder class has methods to setSpout and setBolt. Next, we used the Topology builder to build the Storm topology and added the spout with name *spout* and parallelism hint of 1 executor. We also define the *SpeedLimitBolt* to the topology with parallelism hint of 1 executor. Next, we set the StormStreamer bolt with *shufflegrouping*, which subscribes to the bolt, and evenly distributes tuples (limit) across the instances of the StormStreamer bolt.

For demonstration purpose, we created a local cluster using *LocalCluster* instance and submitted the topology using the *submitTopology* method. Once the topology is submitted to the cluster, we will wait 10 seconds for the cluster to compute the submitted topology and then shut down the cluster using the *shutdown* method of *LocalCluster*.

Step 7:

Next, run a local node of Apache Ignite or cluster first. After building the maven project, use the following command to run the topology locally.

```
mvn compile exec:java -Dstorm.topology=com.blu.imdg.storm.topology.SpeedViolationTopology
```

The application will produce a lot of system logs as follows.

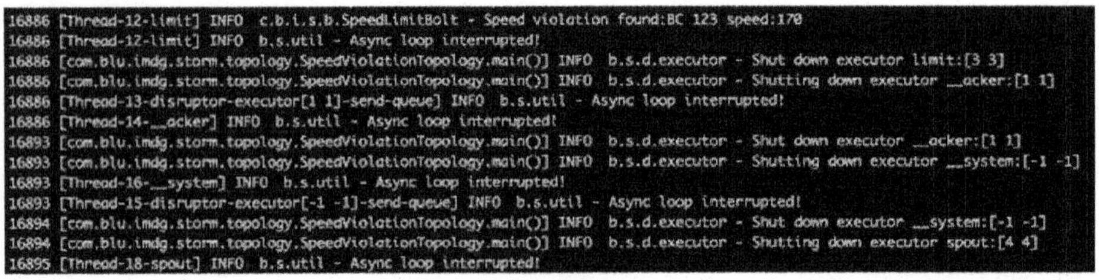

Figure 6.25

Now, if we verify the Ignite cache through *ignitevisor*, we should get the following output into the console.

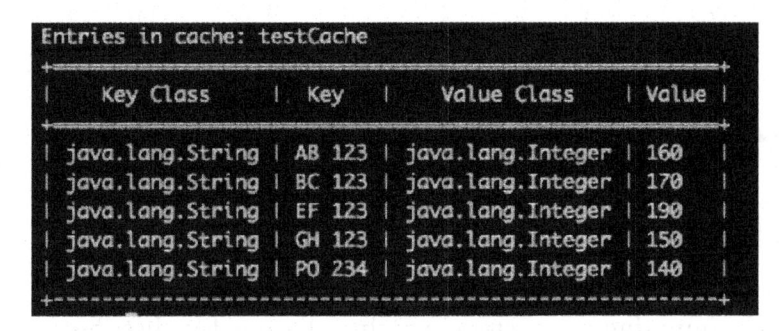

```
Entries in cache: testCache
+------------------------------------------------------------+
|   Key Class      |   Key   |    Value Class    | Value |
+------------------------------------------------------------+
| java.lang.String | AB 123  | java.lang.Integer |  160  |
| java.lang.String | BC 123  | java.lang.Integer |  170  |
| java.lang.String | EF 123  | java.lang.Integer |  190  |
| java.lang.String | GH 123  | java.lang.Integer |  150  |
| java.lang.String | PO 234  | java.lang.Integer |  140  |
+------------------------------------------------------------+
```

Figure 6.26

The output shows the result of what we expected. From our `source.csv` log file, only five vehicles exceed the speed limit of 120 km/h.

This is pretty much sums up the practical overview of the Ignite Storm Streamer.

Conclusion

In this chapter, we became familiar with the Real-time data streaming and complex event processing. We went through the theory and into practicing the following Ignite Data streamer components:

- Ignite DataStream.
- Camel Data Streamer.
- Flume Data Streamer.
- Storm Data Streamer.

For each section, we provided complete sample code and showed how to build real-time data processing application with these modules.

What's next

In the next and the final chapter of this book, we are going to get familiar with the Ignite compute grid, which provides a set of simple APIs that allow users to distribute computations and data processing across multiple Ignite nodes in the cluster.

Chapter seven: Distributed computing

Generally, distributed computing is a system, which is designed to distribute application tasks over a cluster of computers or nodes and coordinate their tasks in parallel. The main principle of the distributed computing is to split a task into multiple parts and execute them on different nodes of the cluster in a parallel fashion. Figure 7.1 shows a very high-level view of a typical distributed system, where each computer has its own local memory, and information can be exchanged only by passing messages from one node to another by using the available communication links.

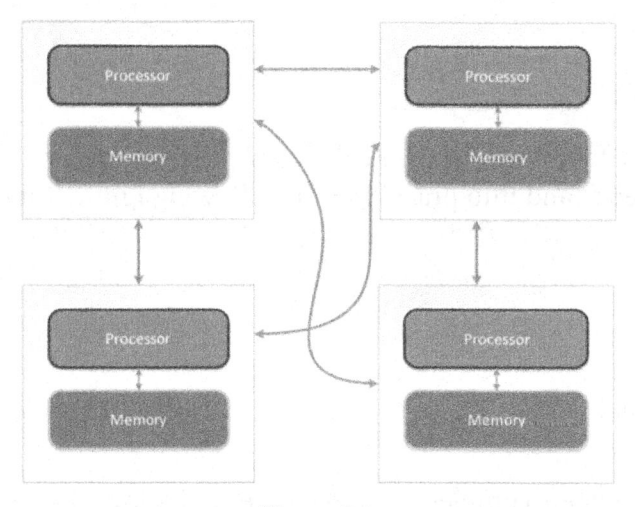

Figure 7.1

The main benefit here is that computations will be performed faster as it can now use resources from local node (local data) and also from all grid nodes in parallel. Apache Ignite is not only the distributed data storage but also a distributed compute grid. Apache Ignite offers a few advantages and differences over the classic approaches for creating distributed computing system. Some of these are:

- The classic approach requires resources to be manually allocated and tasks distributed across clusters.
- In a classic way, you have to develop a system for monitoring task progress and restart them in the case of errors.
- Very difficult to use data locality with **compute task**.

Apache Ignite provides a set of simple APIs that allows the user to distribute computation and data processing across multiple nodes in the cluster to gain high performance. The key features of Apache Ignite distributed computing include:

1. Data locality: tasks can be bound to local data.
2. Fork-join: there is a standard mechanism for the fork-join framework, which provides reliable data transfer between nodes and restarts task in case of failure.
3. Auto deployment: no need to install your application/task code on a server, just connect to the server and any new code is automatically taken into account. Users usually are able to simply execute a task from one grid node, and as task execution penetrates the grid, all classes and resources are also automatically deployed.
4. Checkpoint: a task can save their states in a checkpoint and recover from the checkpoint in case of failure. This feature is very useful for the long running task.
5. Failover and recovery: provide built-in failover and recovery for all task in the cluster.
6. Scalability: scalability up to an arbitrary number of processing nodes.
7. Asynchronous communication: API supports asynchronous communication model for high level of concurrency.
8. Load balancing: allows balancing load in the cluster properly. Provides a set of algorithms such as Round-robin, Random or Adaptive for load balancing over the cluster.
9. Task's session: through the session, separate job running in the same task can see and interact with each other.

Figure 7.2 is a schematic view of Apache Ignite distributive computing. The illustration has been taken from the Apache Ignite documentation.

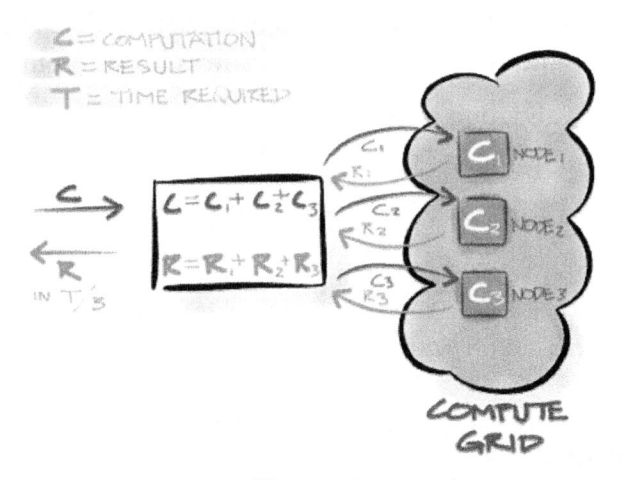

Figure 7.2

In a nutshell, Apache Ignite provides two different approaches to distributed computing: *Compute* task and *Service* task.

> **Note:**
>
> The main difference between them is that **Service task** is a long running process, continuously available independent of topology changes or crashes. Distributed service can also be accessible through service proxy remotely. In the other hand, **Compute task** can execute very short live tasks

> and return an immediate result of the tasks.

For example, calculating cash back for a client of the bank is the ideal example of a *compute* task. At every month, you execute compute tasks in the Ignite cluster to calculate cash back for a client of the internet bank. On the contrary, you can *deploy* a distributed service in the Ignite cluster to return the last 10 transactions to displayed on the client profile of the bank. Apache Ignite distributed services is very useful to develop and execute *microservice* like architecture. In the later of this chapter, we will briefly describe the possibilities of Apache Ignite distributed services.

Compute grid

So far in this chapter, we have learned that compute grid is used to split the task into multiple parts and runs on different nodes. However, Compute grid are useful even if you don't need to split your computation, they can help you improve overall scalability and fault-tolerance of your system by offloading your computations onto most available nodes. In this chapter, we are going to develop a step by step application with subsequent complication to study all the major features of the Ignite Compute grid. We will have the following use case:

Consider a system, where we have to validate XML messages with different XSD schemas depending on the message type and executes a few additional business logics on messages.

A sample XML message for validation is as follows:

```xml
<t:message xmlns:t="http://test.msg/">
    <t:headers>
        <t:header>
            <t:name>header1</t:name>
            <t:value>transaction</t:value>
        </t:header>
        <t:header>
            <t:name>header2</t:name>
            <t:value>atm</t:value>
        </t:header>
    </t:headers>
    <t:priority>1</t:priority>
    <t:body>transaction ID: 12dsbfe231df, overdraft</t:body>
</t:message>
```

Where, `header1` indicates the type of the header, such as transaction and the priority tag provides the priority of the message. Also, the body part contains the transaction details. The XML schema looks like bellow:

```xml
<?xml version="1.0" encoding="UTF-8"?>
<xs:schema targetNamespace="http://test.msg/" elementFormDefault="qualified"
        xmlns:xs="http://www.w3.org/2001/XMLSchema" xmlns:t="http://test.msg/">
    <xs:element name="message" type="t:messageType"/>
    <xs:complexType name="headersType">
        <xs:sequence>
            <xs:element type="t:headerType" name="header" maxOccurs="unbounded" minOccurs=\
"0"/>
        </xs:sequence>
    </xs:complexType>
    <xs:complexType name="messageType">
        <xs:sequence>
            <xs:element type="t:headersType" name="headers"/>
            <xs:element type="xs:int" name="priority"/>
            <xs:element type="xs:string" name="body"/>
        </xs:sequence>
    </xs:complexType>
    <xs:complexType name="headerType">
        <xs:sequence>
            <xs:element name="name">
                <xs:simpleType>
                    <xs:restriction base="xs:string">
                        <xs:enumeration value="header1"/>
                        <xs:enumeration value="header2"/>
                    </xs:restriction>
                </xs:simpleType>
            </xs:element>
            <xs:element type="xs:string" name="value"/>
        </xs:sequence>
    </xs:complexType>
</xs:schema>
```

Also, we have a simple validation script written in *JAVASCRIPT*. The next pseudo code shows the validation script.

```
xpath("//*[local-name()='message']/*[local-name()='body']").length >0 && xpath("//*[local-\
name()='message']/*[local-name()='priority']")==1
```

Validation script contains XPATH expression to check a simple business logic and delivered as JAVASCRIPT. The XPATH expression checks only the value of the priority tag, if the value does not equal 1 the validation should fail. So, we are validating high priority messages from the ATM. Next, we are going to study the Ignite's Compute grid very primitive feature: Distributive closure.

Distributed Closures

Distributive closures allow you to broadcast and execute business logic (computation) across cluster nodes, including plain Java runnable and callables. This is the simplest way to run computation on the remote cluster node. The main entry point of the compute grid API is the `IgniteCompute`. Interface IgniteCompute defines compute grid functionality for executing tasks and closures over nodes in the Ignite cluster or ClusterGroup. The given interface provides the following methods to execute different levels of jobs in the Ignite cluster or ClusterGroup.

Method name	Description
apply()	execute IgniteClosure jobs over nodes in the cluster or the cluster group.
call()	execute IgniteCallable jobs over nodes in the cluster or the cluster group.
run()	execute IgniteRunnable jobs over nodes in the cluster or the cluster group.
broadcast()	broadcast jobs to all nodes in the cluster or the cluster group.
affinityCall()	collocate jobs with nodes on which a specified key is cached.

> **Note:**
> If an attempt is made to execute a computation over an empty cluster group (i.e. cluster group that does not have any alive nodes), then Ignite will throw the org.apache.ignite.cluster.ClusterGroupEmptyException exception out of the result.

So far, we already have the XSD schema, JAVASCRIPT validation file, let's exccute the computation on Ignite cluster. All the sample code of this chapter is available on GitHub[48] for download. For this section, we are going to use the maven module **example1**.

Step 1:

Create a new maven project (see module chapte-dist-computing) and the following maven dependencies:

```
<dependency>
    <groupId>org.apache.ignite</groupId>
    <artifactId>ignite-core</artifactId>
    <version>1.6.0</version>
</dependency>
<dependency>
    <groupId>org.apache.ignite</groupId>
    <artifactId>ignite-spring</artifactId>
    <version>1.6.0</version>
</dependency>
```

---
[48] https://github.com/srecon/ignite-book-code-samples/tree/master/chapters/chapter-dist-computing

```
<dependency>
    <groupId>org.apache.ignite</groupId>
    <artifactId>ignite-indexing</artifactId>
    <version>1.6.0</version>
</dependency>
<dependency>
    <groupId>org.apache.ignite</groupId>
    <artifactId>ignite-schedule</artifactId>
    <version>1.0.0</version>
</dependency>
```

Step 2:

Create a new Java class named com.blu.imdg.example1.SimpleComputation with the following content:

```java
public class SimpleComputation {
    public static void main(String[] args) throws IOException {
        String sample1 = TestDataGenerator.getSample1();
        byte[] vaidateSchema = TestDataGenerator.getValidateSchema();
        String validateScript = TestDataGenerator.getValidateScript();

        try (Ignite ignite = Ignition.start(CLIENT_CONFIG)) {
            IgniteCompute compute = ignite.compute();

            Boolean result = compute.call(() -> {
                boolean validateXsdResult = XsdValidator.validate(sample1, vaidateSchema);
                boolean validateByJs = JSEvaluate.evaluateJs(sample1, validateScript);

                System.out.println("validateXsdResult=" + validateXsdResult);
                System.out.println("validateByJs=" + validateByJs);

                return validateXsdResult && validateByJs;
            });

            System.out.println("result=" + result);
        }
    }
}
```

Now, let's take a closer look at the above code. In the first three lines of code in the main method, we initialize our XML schema, validation script, and the XML message. Next, we initialize the IgniteCompute and creates a very simple Ignite callable job and call the job with the method IgniteCompute.call(). In the callable job, we validate the XML message itself against XML schema and validate the priority value of the message. After running the method, we return the result of

Chapter seven: Distributed computing 291

the computation and printout into the console. Note that, IgniteCompute.call serialized the object `IgniteCallable` and executed the object at any of the Ignite nodes in the cluster. The result will also be serialized and returned to the client.

Step 3:

Let's run the application. First, we have to compile and run the Ignite server. In my case, I am going to run two cluster node.

```
mvn clean install && mvn exec:java -Dexec.mainClass=com.blu.imdg.StartCacheNode
```

The above code will run Ignite node.

Step 4:

Run the Ignite computation on a cluster by the following command:

```
mvn exec:java -Dexec.mainClass=com.blu.imdg.example1.SimpleComputation
```

You should see the following output in the console.

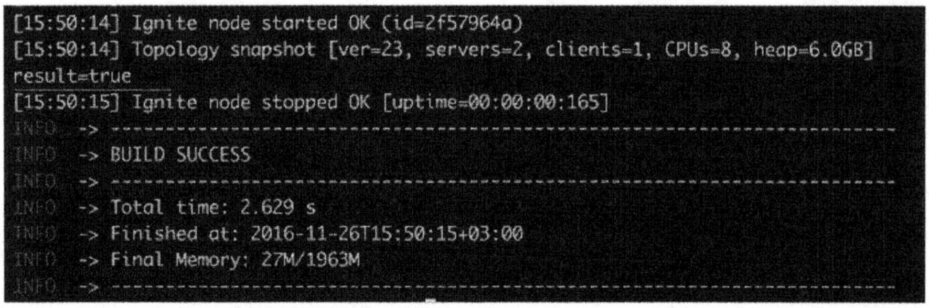

Figure 7.3

Let's see what has happened on the side of the Ignite cluster (I have two nodes Ignite Cluster).

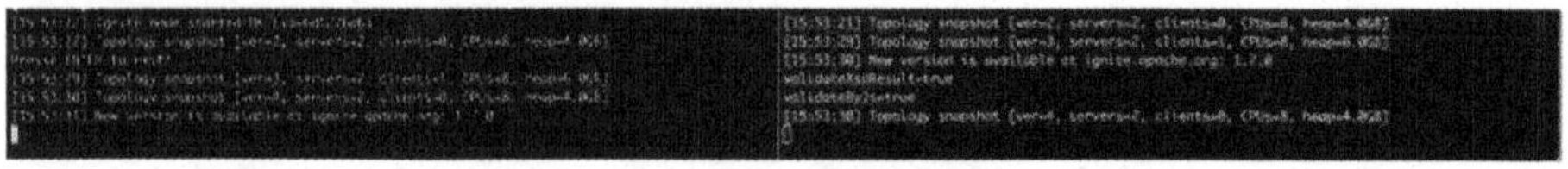

Figure 7.4

One of the nodes of the Ignite cluster executed the computation and returned back the result to the client. In all cases other than broadcast(...), Ignite must select a node for a computation to be executed. The node will be selected based on the underlying `LoadBalancingSpi`, which by default sequentially picks next available node from the underlying cluster group. Other load balancing policies, such as *random* or *adaptive*, can be configured as well.

Ignite also guarantees that as long as there is at least one grid node standing, every job will be executed. Jobs will automatically failover to another node if a remote node crashed or has rejected execution due to lack of resources. By default, in the case of failover, next load-balanced node will be picked for job execution. Also, jobs will never be re-routed to the nodes they have failed on. This behavior can be changed by configuring any of the existing or a custom FailoverSpi in a grid configuration.

You can also execute an IgniteClosure through an IgniteCompute.apply method in Ignite cluster. A closure is a block of code that encloses its body and any outside variables used inside of it as a function object. You can then pass such function object anywhere you can pass a variable and execute it. All apply(...) methods execute closures on the cluster. A new job is executed for every argument passed in the collection. The number of actual job executions will be equal to the size of the job arguments collection.

Step 5:

Create a new Java class SimpleComputationClosure in the /src/main/com/blu/imdg/example1 directory. Add the following content in to the Java class.

```java
public class SimpleComputationClosure {
    public static void main(String[] args) throws IOException {
        try (Ignite ignite = Ignition.start(CLIENT_CONFIG)) {
            IgniteCompute compute = ignite.compute();
            // Execute closure on all cluster nodes.
            Collection<Integer> res = compute.apply(
                new IgniteClosure<String, Integer>() {
                    @Override
                    public Integer apply(String word) {
                        // Return number of letters in the sentence.
                        return word.length();
                    }
                },
                Arrays.asList("Count characters using closure".split(" "))
            );
            int sum = 0;
            // Add up individual word lengths received from remote nodes
            for (int len : res)
                sum += len;
            System.out.println("Length of the sentence: "+ sum);
        }
    }
}
```

The above code will define IgniteClosure with apply function. As an argument of the function, we pass the words split by the " ". In return, we got the collection of word length, which we aggregate together and output into the console.

Step 6:

Run the application with the following command:

Chapter seven: Distributed computing

```
mvn exec:java -Dexec.mainClass=com.blu.imdg.example1.SimpleComputationClosure
```

Which should return the result of the sentence as follows.

```
[16:37:01]
[16:37:01] Ignite node started OK (id=efe602d7)
[16:37:01] Topology snapshot [ver=4, servers=1, clients=1, CPUs=8, heap=4.0GB]
Length of the sentence: 27
[16:37:01] Ignite node stopped OK [uptime=00:00:00:092]
INFO  -> -----------------------------------------------------------------
INFO  -> BUILD SUCCESS
```

Figure 7.5

In the above examples, there is a problem blocking the client thread. Client thread always waits for the result from the Ignite cluster. Since the computation can take a long time, it is always preferable to use an asynchronous call. Apache Ignite provides a simple and convenient way to call remote computing by `withAsync()` method.

Step 6:

Create an another Java class with name `AsyncComputation` in the /src/main/com/blu/imdg/example2. Add the following main method.

```java
public static void main(String[] args) throws IOException {
    String sample1 = TestDataGenerator.getSample1();
    byte[] vaidateSchema = TestDataGenerator.getValidateSchema();
    String validateScript = TestDataGenerator.getValidateScript();

    try (Ignite ignite = Ignition.start(CommonConstants.CLIENT_CONFIG)) {
        IgniteCompute compute = ignite.compute().withAsync();

        compute.call(() -> {
            boolean validateXsdResult = XsdValidator.validate(sample1, vaidateSchema);
            boolean validateByJs = JSEvaluate.evaluateJs(sample1, validateScript);

            System.out.println("validateXsdResult=" + validateXsdResult);
            System.out.println("validateByJs=" + validateByJs);

            return validateXsdResult && validateByJs;
        });

        compute.future().listen((result) -> {
            boolean res = (boolean) result.get();
            System.out.println("result=" + res);
        });
        System.out.println("Presse ENTER to exit!");
        System.in.read();
```

                }
        }

The above code is very similar to others we have written before. The main difference here is the `compute().withAsync()`, `compute.future()` methods. The `compute().withAsync()` method enable the Ignite asynchronous call to the Ignite cluster. Ignite compute.future() method allows to not wait for the result after invocation and gets the result asynchronously when any of the nodes returns the result. If you execute the application with the following command

```
mvn exec:java -Dexec.mainClass=com.blu.imdg.example2.AsyncComputation
```

you should get the same result but asynchronously.

MapReduce and Fork-join

In this section, we are going to complicate our validation process of XML messages. We have to validate a group of messages and get the final result for the entire group of a message. In such condition in-memory MapReduce approach is the best of all. Apache Ignite in-memory MapReduce implementation is very close to the Fork-join paradigm and considers as a light-weight MapReduce implementation.

Apache Ignite provides ComputeTask interface that simplified the in-memory MapReduce and defines a task that can be executed on the Ignite grid. ComputeTask is responsible for splitting business logic into multiple compute jobs, receiving results from individual compute jobs executing on remote nodes, and reducing (aggregating) received jobs results into final compute task result.

Ignite ComputeTask has three different phases as follows:

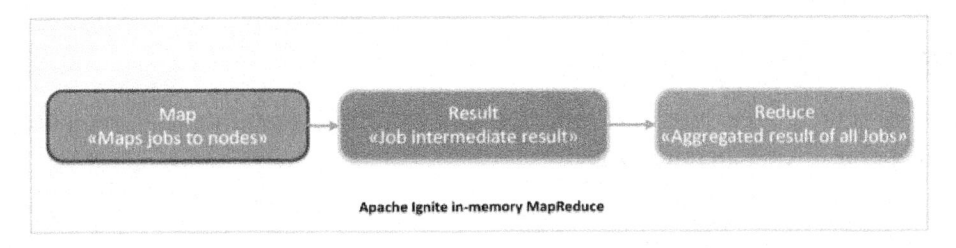

Figure 7.6

- Map: In this phase method `map(...)` instantiates the jobs and maps them to worker nodes. The method receives the collection of cluster nodes on which the task is run and the task argument. The method should return a map with jobs as keys and mapped worker nodes as values. The jobs are then sent to the mapped nodes and executed there.
- Result: It's an intermediate result of the completing job. Method `result(...)` is called each time a job completes on some cluster node. It receives the result returned by the completed job, as well as the list of all the job results received so far. The method should return a ComputeJobResultPolicy instance, indicating what to do next:

Chapter seven: Distributed computing

- WAIT - wait for all remaining jobs to complete (if any)
- REDUCE - immediately move to reduce step, discarding all the remaining jobs and unreceived results
- FAILOVER - failover the job to another node (see Fault Tolerance)
- Reduce: It is the aggregated result of all jobs. In this phase, method `reduce(...)` is called when all the jobs have completed (or REDUCE result policy was returned from the `result(...)` method). The method receives a list with all the completed results and should return a final result of the computation.

Figure 7.7 illustrates all the three execution phases in the Ignite grid.

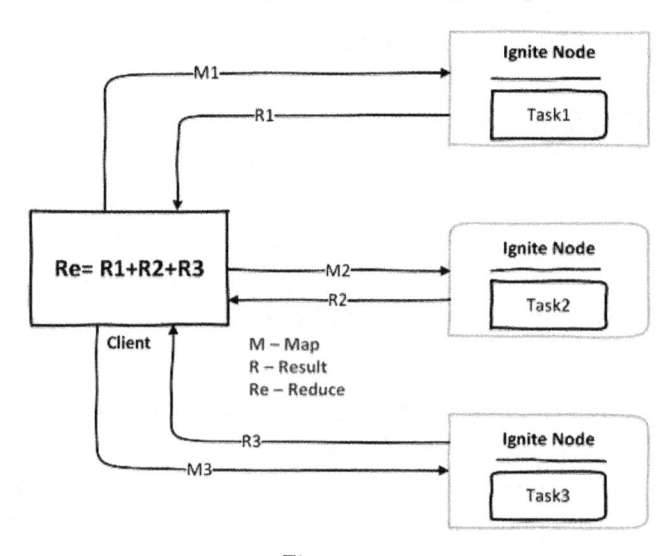

Figure 7.7

> **Note:**
> `ComputeTask` is preferable over Distributed closure when you need fine-grained control over job to node mapping or custom failover logic.

Let's implement the full version of the ComputeTask, and run some validation XML messages over Ignite cluster. The complete source code is available on GitHub[49] at project example3.

Step 1:

First, we have to add the structure of the message. Create a Java class with name ValidateMessage into directory `/src/main/java/com/blu/imdg/example3`. Add the following content into the Java class.

---
[49] https://github.com/srecon/ignite-book-code-samples/tree/master/chapters/chapter-dist-computing/src/main/java/com/blu/imdg/example3

```java
public class ValidateMessage {
    private String id;
    private String msg;
    private byte[] xsd ;
    private String js;
    public ValidateMessage(String id, String msg, byte[] xsd, String js) {
        this.id = id;
        this.msg = msg;
        this.xsd = xsd;
        this.js = js;
    }
    public String getMsg() {
        return msg;
    }
    public byte[] getXsd() {
        return xsd;
    }
    public String getJs() {
        return js;
    }
    public String getId() {
        return id;
    }
}
```

It's a plain Java class, which have the following fields:

- id: Message identifier.
- msg: the content of the message of type String.
- xsd: the content of the XSD schema of type byte array.
- js: the content of the JAVASCRIPT validation script of type String.

Step 2:

Add 3 XML messages into the src/main/resources/META-INF/org/book/examples directory with the following content.

Chapter seven: Distributed computing

```
/Users/shamim/Development/workshop/github/ignite-book-code-samples/chapters/chapter-dist-c\
omputing/<t:message xmlns:t="http://test.msg/">
    <t:headers>
        <t:header>
            <t:name>header1</t:name>
            <t:value>transaction</t:value>
        </t:header>
        <t:header>
            <t:name>header2</t:name>
            <t:value>atm</t:value>
        </t:header>
    </t:headers>
    <t:priority>1</t:priority>
    <t:body>transaction ID: 12dsbfe231df, overdraft</t:body>
</t:message>
```

In my case, I have renamed the XML document as sample1.xml, sample2.xml, sample3.xml. You can easily create the XML document from the XSD schema provide by the project. validate-schema.xsd file also placed in the same folder of this project.

Step 3:

Create or modify the Java class ForkJoinComputation in the `/src/main/java/com/blu/imdg/example3` directory. Add the following content to the Java class:

```java
public class ForkJoinComputation {

    public static void main(String[] args) throws IOException {

        try (Ignite ignite = Ignition.start(CommonConstants.CLIENT_CONFIG)) {

            IgniteCompute compute = ignite.compute();
            ValidateMessage[] validateMessages = TestDataGenerator.getValidateMessages();
            Boolean result = compute.execute(new ComputeTask<ValidateMessage[], Boolean>()\
 {
                @LoadBalancerResource
                private ComputeLoadBalancer balancer;
                @Nullable
                @Override
                public Map<? extends ComputeJob, ClusterNode> map(List<ClusterNode> list, \
@Nullable ValidateMessage[] validateMessages) throws IgniteException {
                    Map<ComputeJob, ClusterNode> result = Maps.newHashMap();
                    for (ValidateMessage msg : validateMessages) {
                        ComputeJobAdapter job = new ForkJoinJobAdapter(msg);
                        ClusterNode balancedNode = balancer.getBalancedNode(job, null);
                        result.put(job, balancedNode);
```

```
                    }
                    return result;
                }
                @Override
                public ComputeJobResultPolicy result(ComputeJobResult computeJobResult, Li\
st<ComputeJobResult> list) throws IgniteException {
                    IgniteException e = computeJobResult.getException();
                    if (e != null) {
                        if (!(e instanceof ComputeExecutionRejectedException) && !(e insta\
nceof ClusterTopologyException) && !e.hasCause(new Class[]{ComputeJobFailoverException.cla\
ss})) {
                            throw new IgniteException("Remote job threw user exception (ov\
erride or implement ComputeTask.result(..) method if you would like to have automatic fail\
over for this exception).", e);
                        } else {
                            return ComputeJobResultPolicy.FAILOVER;
                        }
                    } else {
                        return ComputeJobResultPolicy.WAIT;
                    }
                }
                @Nullable
                @Override
                public Boolean reduce(List<ComputeJobResult> list) throws IgniteException {
                    return list.stream().reduce(true, (acc, value) -> acc && (Boolean) val\
ue.getData(), (a, b) -> a && b);
                }
            }, validateMessages);
            System.out.println("result=" + result);
        }
    }
}
```

Let's go through the above code line by line. In line 8

`ValidateMessage[] validateMessages = TestDataGenerator.getValidateMessages();`

We have initialized and generate our sample XML documents. In the next line we have to define anonymous ComputeTask and implement the three main methods: Map, Result and Reduce.

- In the Map method: we used the original object computing Map<ComputeJob, ClusterNode>, create jobs for each XML message through ForJoinJobAdapter. Also we define the ComputeLoadBalancer interface that connects to the Ignite cluster and returns the next balanced node according to the underlying load balancing policy.

Chapter seven: Distributed computing

- In the Result method: we are analyzing the execution result ComputeJob. At first, we check for any error by calling the method computeJobResult.getException(), then returns ComputeJobResultPolicy.WAIT.
- In the Reduce method: gets all the result as a stream and process them.

Step 4:

Next, start a few Ignite nodes to run the ComputeTask. Run the following command from a few different command console to start a few Ignite node as follows:

```
mvn exec:java -Dexec.mainClass=com.blu.imdg.StartCacheNode
```

I have started three different Ignite node in one cluster.

Step 5:

Run the ForJoinComputation application from the command line through maven exec command.

```
mvn exec:java -Dexec.mainClass=com.blu.imdg.example3.ForkJoinComputation
```

If all your three XML messages are valid, you should notice the following output in the console.

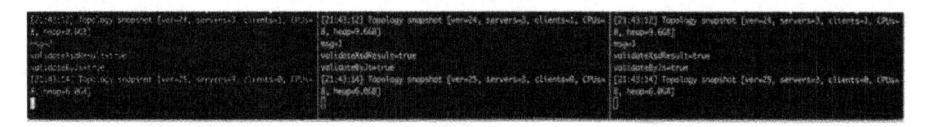

Figure 7.8

You can notice that, for every XML messages, one task is created in each Ignite node and all the XML messages are valid. Let's make a few changes in one of the XML messages as it will not be valid and re-execute the ComputeTask again. In my case, I have just changed the XML namespace in sample2.xml as follows:

```
<t:message xmlns:t="validate-schema.xsd">
```

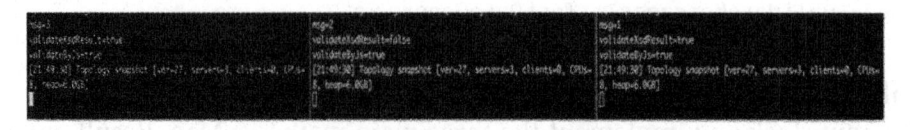

Figure 7.9

Now validation of the XML message of the sample2.xml not passed. If we check the entire result of the validation process, we should find the next result in the console.

Chapter seven: Distributed computing 300

```
[21:51:49] Ignite node started OK (id=1084985e)
[21:51:49] Topology snapshot [ver=28, servers=3, clients=1, CPUs=8, heap=8.0GB]
result=false
[21:51:49] Ignite node stopped OK [uptime=00:00:00:218]
```

Figure 7.10

The entire result is `false`, which is what we have expected. In this approach you can add thousand of XML messages to map over Ignite nodes and execute distributed computation.

Most often you donot need the full implementation of the ComputeTask. There is a number of helper classes that let you provide only a particular piece of your logic, leaving out all the rest to Ignite to handle automatically.

Compute job adapter.

A convenience adapter for ComputeJob implementations. All jobs that are generated by a task are implementations of the ComputeJob interface. The execute() method of this interface defines the job business logic and should return a job result. ComputeJobAdapter provides the default implementation of ComputeJob.cancel() method and ability to check whenever cancellation event occurred with isCancel() method. The adapter can get job arguments by method constructor or via setArguments(Object...) method. In our last example, we explicitly used the compute job adapter to execute our XML messages validation.

```
ComputeJobAdapter job = new ForkJoinJobAdapter(msg);
```

Where ForkJoinJobAdapter extends the ComputeJobAdapter and implements the following business logic.

```
@Override
public Boolean execute() throws IgniteException {
    boolean validateXsdResult = XsdValidator.validate(msg.getMsg(), msg.getXsd());
    boolean validateByJs = JSEvaluate.evaluateJs(msg.getMsg(), msg.getJs());
    System.out.println("msg=" + msg.getId());
    System.out.println("validateXsdResult=" + validateXsdResult);
    System.out.println("validateByJs=" + validateByJs);
    return validateXsdResult && validateByJs;
}
```

the method execute() executes the two validations of the XML messages, one for the XML schema and another for the XML messages contents validation.

Compute task adapter.

ComputeTaskAdapter is an implementation of *ComputeTask* interface and provides a default implementation of the *result()* method, which will wait for all jobs to complete before calling the reduce() method. If remote job threw an exception, a *FAILOVER* policy would be return. On the other hand, *WAIT* policy will be return, if jobs are waiting for finished.

Compute task split adapter.

This is the simplified adapter for `ComputeTask` interface. This adapter extends the `ComputeTaskAdapter` and adds the capability to assign jobs to nodes automatically. This adapter can be used when jobs can be randomly assigned to available grid nodes. This adapter is sufficient in most homogeneous environments where all nodes are equally suitable for executing grid job. It hides the `map()` method and adds a new `split()` method in which user only needs to provide a collection of the jobs to be executed. The split() method basically takes given an argument and splits it into a collection of ComputeJob using provided grid size as an indication of how many nodes are available.

> **Note:**
> If the number of jobs is greater than the number of grid nodes (i.e, grid size), the grid nodes will be reused and some jobs will end up on the same grid nodes.

Dependencies between the above classes and interfaces can be expressed by the UML Class diagram. Take a look at the class diagram below.

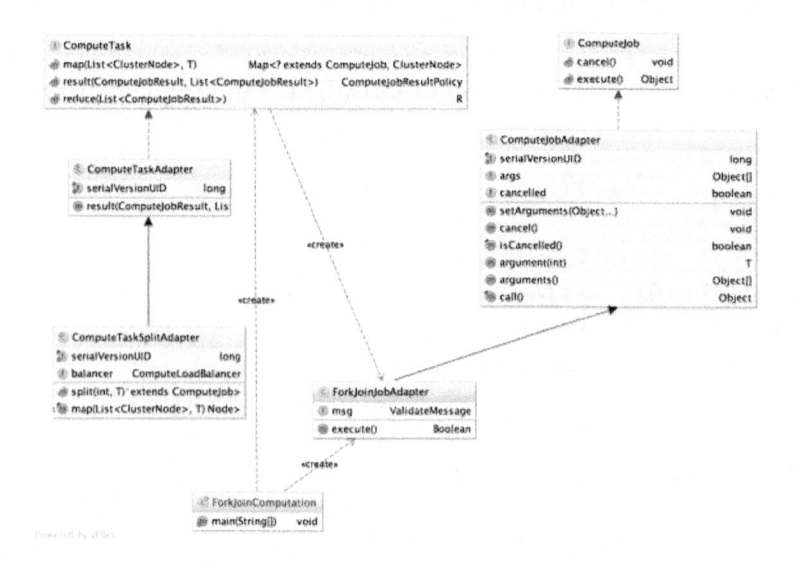

Figure 7.11

Where `ForJoinJobAdapter` class and the `ForkJoinComputation` is our user defined class. The `ComputeTask` interface and the `ComputeJob` interface is the two separate interfaces working with Tasks and Jobs.

In the next few section, we will extend our XML validation example by using Compute task split adapter and will explore a few new features of the Ignite compute grid.

Chapter seven: Distributed computing   302

Per-Node share state

Ignite provides access to special local data storage to each cluster node. This local data storage is available to all jobs running on this node. There is only one instance of local node storage per local node. the node local storage is based on `java.util.concurrent.ConcurrentMap` and safe for multi-threaded access. This local storage also provides the atomicity guarantees.

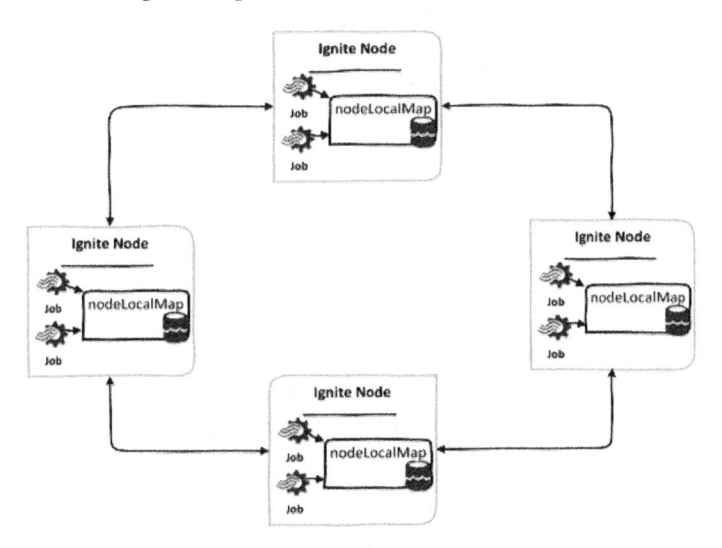

Figure 7.12

Node-local values are similar to thread locals in a way that, these values are not distributed and kept only on the *local node* (similar to thread local values are attached to the current thread only). Node-local values are used primarily by closures executed from the remote nodes to keep intermediate state on the local node between executions. This node local storage is useful to share a state between different compute jobs or different deployed services in a single node. For instance, we can create an HTTP connection pool per node in the local node storage for connecting to any third-party HTTP service. The process of establishing a connection from one host to another is quite complex and involves multiple packet exchanges between two endpoints, which can be quite time-consuming. The overhead of connection handshaking can be significant, especially for small HTTP messages. We can achieve a much higher data throughput if open connections can be re-used to execute multiple requests by using the local per-node HTTP connection pool.

Let's continue to modify our transactions validation application. This time, we want to organize the interaction of the message verification process with any external system, so we are going to send a few notifications of our validation result to an external HTTP server for audit. To effectively achieve this goal, we have to keep a pool of HTTP connection in each Ignite node. A high-level view of this process is shown below:

Chapter seven: Distributed computing

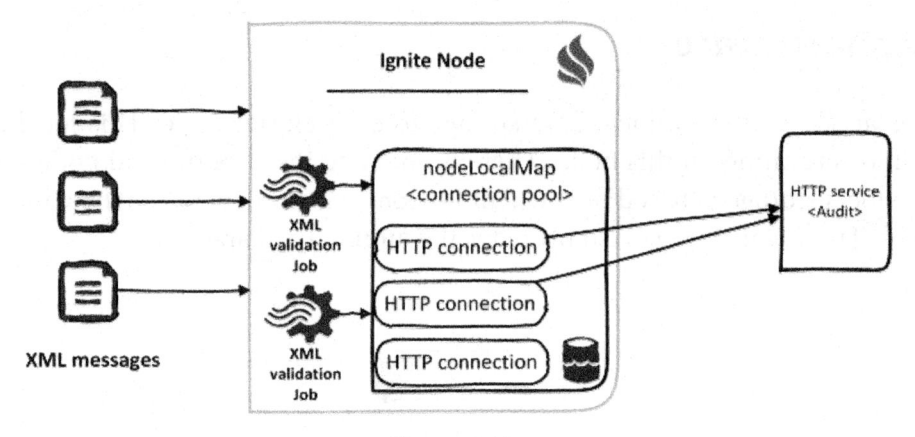

Figure 7.13

In the above scenario, we have three main components in our system.

- HTTP server: which can accept transaction validation result and act as a third-party service.
- HTTP connection pool: composed by the local node map and contain open connections. Whenever any job finished the XML validation and wants to send a notification to the HTTP server, it consumes a pre-created connection from the pool and sends the notification to the HTTP server rather than create an HTTP connection every time.
- XML validation job: an instance of a Compute task split adapter, the main purpose of this adapter is to validate incoming XML files and send the result of the validations to the HTTP server.

The full example is available at GitHub repositories[50]. You can execute the example by the following few commands. First, start the HTTP server emulator as follows:

```
mvn exec:java -Dexec.mainClass=com.blu.imdg.common.HttpAuditEmulator
```

Next, start an Ignite node with the following command:

```
mvn clean package exec:java -Dexec.mainClass=com.blu.imdg.StartCacheNode
```

Now, you can submit a job to Ignite node for validating XML files as follows:

```
mvn exec:java -Dexec.mainClass=com.blu.imdg.example4.ForkJoinComputationExt
```

You should see the validation result in the HTTP server console as shown below:

---

[50] https://github.com/srecon/ignite-book-code-samples/tree/master/chapters/chapter-dist-computing/src/main/java/com/blu/imdg/example4

Chapter seven: Distributed computing   304

```
INFO  ->
INFO  -> --- exec-maven-plugin:1.2.1:java (default-cli) @ chapter-dist-computing ---
log message validation result msgId=3 result=true
log message validation result msgId=1 result=true
log message validation result msgId=2 result=true
log message validation result msgId=2 result=true
log message validation result msgId=3 result=true
log message validation result msgId=1 result=true
```

Figure 7.14

Let's have a detailed look at the example of the chapter. Clone or download the chapter-dist-computing/example4 project from the GitHub repository. If you create your own maven project, add these dependencies to your pom.xml.

```xml
<dependency>
    <groupId>org.apache.ignite</groupId>
    <artifactId>ignite-core</artifactId>
    <version>1.6.0</version>
</dependency>
<dependency>
    <groupId>org.apache.ignite</groupId>
    <artifactId>ignite-spring</artifactId>
    <version>1.6.0</version>
</dependency>
<dependency>
    <groupId>org.apache.httpcomponents</groupId>
    <artifactId>httpclient</artifactId>
    <version>4.5.2</version>
</dependency>
```

The key dependencies are:

- Ignite-core: Ignite core module for working with Ignite compute grid. This maven dependency will pull all other required modules to work with the Ignite grid.
- Httpclient: is designed to work with any HTTP service on the web. It provides pluggable HTTP transport abstraction so you can use any low-level library such as java.net.HttpURLConnection.

Let's create the HTTP service emulator first. In our case, it will be a very simple HTTP REST service, which will accept the XML validation result by the following URL path /audit/log.

Step 1:

Add the following Java class with name HttpAuditEmulator in your project.

Chapter seven: Distributed computing

```java
@Path("/audit")
public class HttpAuditEmulator {
    @GET
    @Path("/log")
    @Produces(MediaType.TEXT_PLAIN)
    public String acceptResponse(
            @QueryParam("msgId") String msgId,
            @QueryParam("validationResult") boolean result
    ) {
        System.out.println("log message validation result msgId=" + msgId + " result=" + r\
esult);
        return "1";
    }

    public static void main(String[] args) {
        URI baseUri = UriBuilder.fromUri("http://localhost/").port(9998).build();
        ResourceConfig config = new ResourceConfig(HttpAuditEmulator.class);
        HttpServer server = JdkHttpServerFactory.createHttpServer(baseUri, config);
    }
}
```

We are using the very basic of the JAX-RS annotation for creating an HTTP service. HttpAuditEmulator has one method acceptResponse, which can accept HTTP GET request with the path /audit/log and can take query parameter msgID and validationResult. acceptResponse() method in response returns the HTTP result with value 1. Also, the HTTP server runs on the port 9998.

Step 2:

At this time, we have to add another Java class to create HTTP client factory.

```java
public class HttpAuditClient {

    public static Boolean sendResult(HttpClient client, Boolean result, String messageId) \
throws URISyntaxException, IOException {
        URI uri = new URIBuilder().setScheme("http").setHost("localhost").setPort(9998).se\
tPath("/audit/log")
                .setParameter("msgId", messageId)
                .setParameter("validationResult", result.toString())
                .build();
        HttpGet httpget = new HttpGet(uri);
        try (CloseableHttpResponse resp = (CloseableHttpResponse) client.execute(httpget))\
 {
            System.out.println("msg=" + messageId + " result=" + result);
            return result;
        }
    }
}
```

```
    public static HttpClient createHttpClient(ConcurrentMap<Object, Object> nodeLocalMap) {
        return (HttpClient) nodeLocalMap.computeIfAbsent("httpClient", new Function<Object\
, HttpClient>() {
            @Override
            public HttpClient apply(Object o) {
                return createHttpClient();
            }
        });
    }

    public static HttpClient createHttpClient() {
        PoolingHttpClientConnectionManager cm = new PoolingHttpClientConnectionManager();
        return HttpClients.custom()
                .setConnectionManager(cm)
                .build();
    }
}
```

The above code fragment illustrates the creation of HTTP clients with connection pooling ability. Let's have a detailed look at the Java class. First, we create a java method `createHttpClient` without any parameter. The given class uses `PoolingHttpClientConnectionManager`, a more complex implementation that manages a pool of client connections and is able to service connection requests from multiple execution threads. By default, this implementation will create no more than 2 concurrent connections per given route and no more than 20 connections in total. However, you can increase the total connections for the connection pool as follows:

```
cm.setMaxTotal(200);
```

This will increase the total connections of the connection pool to 200. Next, we have another override method `createHttpClient(ConcurrentMap<Object, Object> nodeLocalMap)` with parameter of Ignite `nodeLocalMap`. In this method, we used the `ConcurrentMap.computeIfAbsent()` method to create an instance of the HTTPClient with name `httpClient` whenever needed. Our final method of this class is sendResult. In a nutshell, this method constructs an HTTP Get request from the method parameters and send the request to the HTTP server.

Step 3:

This is the final part of our application. In this step, we will create a job adapter, and a compute task split adapter. Let's create the Job adapter first.

Chapter seven: Distributed computing

```java
public class ForkJoinJobAdapterExt extends ComputeJobAdapter {
    @IgniteInstanceResource
    private Ignite ignite;

    private ValidateMessage msg;

    public ForkJoinJobAdapterExt(ValidateMessage msg) {
        this.msg = msg;
    }

    @Override
    public Boolean execute() throws IgniteException {
        try {
            boolean validateXsdResult = XsdValidator.validate(msg.getMsg(), msg.getXsd());
            boolean validateByJs = JSEvaluate.evaluateJs(msg.getMsg(), msg.getJs());

            Boolean result = validateXsdResult && validateByJs;

            ConcurrentMap<Object, Object> nodeLocalMap = ignite.cluster().nodeLocalMap();

            HttpClient client = HttpAuditClient.createHttpClient(nodeLocalMap);

            return HttpAuditClient.sendResult(client, result, msg.getId());

        } catch (Exception err) {
            throw new IgniteException(err);
        }
    }
}
```

It is basically an instance of ComputeJobAdapter, which we have seen before. In this adapter, we implemented our validation process and peek an HTTP client from the local node storage to send the result to HTTP server for audit. Also, note that we used the annotation @IgniteInstanceResource to auto-inject the Ignite current instance to the compute adapter. Ignite instance can be injected into grid tasks and grid jobs. The next few instructions performed the main setup of the HTTP client into the local node map as follows:

```
ConcurrentMap<Object, Object> nodeLocalMap = ignite.cluster().nodeLocalMap();
HttpClient client = HttpAuditClient.createHttpClient(nodeLocalMap);
return HttpAuditClient.sendResult(client, result, msg.getId());
```

Instance of the per-node shared state we got by the method call ignite.cluster().nodeLocalMap() and construct the HTTP connection pool with default HTTP client. Later we invoke the HTTP get method by the method HttpAuditClient.sendResult(). Next, we are going to implements a Compute task split adapter, in which we only need to provide a collection of jobs to be executed.

```java
public class ForkJoinComputationExt extends ComputeTaskSplitAdapter<ValidateMessage[], Boo\
lean> {
    @Override
    protected Collection<? extends ComputeJob> split(int i, ValidateMessage[] messages) th\
rows IgniteException {
        return Arrays.stream(messages).map(ForkJoinJobAdapterExt::new).collect(Collectors.\
toList());
    }

    @Nullable
    @Override
    public Boolean reduce(List<ComputeJobResult> list) throws IgniteException {
        return list.stream().reduce(true, (acc, value) -> acc && (Boolean) value.getData()\
, (a, b) -> a && b);
    }

    public static void main(String[] args) throws IOException {

        try (Ignite ignite = Ignition.start(CLIENT_CONFIG)) {
            IgniteCompute compute = ignite.compute();

            ValidateMessage[] validateMessages = TestDataGenerator.getValidateMessages();
            Boolean result = compute.execute(new ForkJoinComputationExt(), validateMessage\
s);
            System.out.println("result=" + result);
        }
    }
}
```

We add a new split() method in which we provide our ForkJoinJobAdapterExt adapter to be executed in the cluster. The split() method basically takes given arguments and splits it into a collection of ComputeJob using provided grid size as an indication of how many nodes are available. Also, we override the reduce() method to compute the final result of the XML file validations. If any of the XML files doesn't pass the validation the entire result will be invalid. Finally, we have the main() method to initialize the Ignite client and deploy the job into the Ignite compute grid.

Step 4:

Rename the XML namespace of the sample3.xml file as follows:

```
<t:message xmlns:t="http://test.msg111/">
```

Now, the entire XML file is invalid against XSD schema. Run the application again.

```
mvn exec:java -Dexec.mainClass=com.blu.imdg.example4.ForkJoinComputationExt
```

You should notice the following log into the console.

```
log message validation result msgId=3 result=false
log message validation result msgId=1 result=true
log message validation result msgId=2 result=true
```

Figure 7.15

If you check the console of the `ForkJoinComputationExt` application, you should discover that the entire validation result is false.

Ignite per-node share state is a very powerful feature and you can use it to solve not only simple use cases but also very complex use cases to achieve a much higher data throughput such as HTTP connection pooling, database connection pooling and so on. In the next section, we will explore the Ignite distributed task session to share state between different jobs.

Distributed task session

Ignite provides a distributed session for particular task execution. Distributed task session is created for every task execution. It is defined by the ComputeTaskSession interface. Task session is distributed across the parent task and all grid jobs spawned by it, so attributes set on a task or on a job can be viewed on other jobs. Correspondingly attributes set on any of the jobs can also be viewed on a task. Task session also allows to receiving notifications when attributes are set or wait for an attribute to be set.

Distributed task session has 2 main features: attribute and checkpoint management. Both attributes and checkpoints can be used for the task itself and from the jobs belonging to this task. Session attributes and checkpoints can be set from any task or job methods. Session attribute and checkpoint consistency is fault tolerant and is preserved whenever a job gets failed over to another node for execution. Whenever task execution ends, all checkpoints saved within a session with ComputeTaskSessionScope scope will be removed from checkpoint storage. We will explore the Ignite checkpoint feature a little bit later.

The sequence in which session attributes are set is consistent across the task and all job siblings within it. There will never be a case when one job sees attribute A before attribute B, and another job sees attribute B before A. Attribute order is identical across all session participants. Attribute order is also fault tolerant and is preserved whenever a job gets failed over to another node.

With distributed task session, we can coordinate and synchronize all the jobs across the task. For example, assume that we are getting bundle of XML messages with more than 100 messages in one package. First, we have to validate all the messages from the package, if all of them are validate then we deligate all the message for content validation through JAVASCRIPT (see section Distributed closure for more details about the validation process). If any of the XML messages will fail to pass

Chapter seven: Distributed computing 310

the validation against XSD schema, we immediately stop the rest of the processing and send a notification for audit. To do that, in the grid environment, we could execute a few jobs which will start validating the XML messages against XSD schema one by one again.

If any of the XML messages will fail to pass the validation, we immediately stop the further validation process and send the result to the HTTP server for audit. Without session attribute, to coordinate this process would be much harder to solve.

We have to slightly modify our previous ComputeJobAdapter adapter to use the task session. Also, we are going to use the ComputeJobContext to get the job identifier.

> **Note:**
> Unlike ComputeTaskSession, which distributes all attributes to all jobs in the task including the task itself, job context attributes belong to a job and do not get sent over the network unless a job moves from one node to another.

The full example is available at the GitHub repositories[51]. Now that we have got the basics, let's start creating the necessary classes.

Step 1:

Create a new Java class with the name ForkJoinWithSessionJobAdapter and extends it from the *ComputeJobAdapter*. Add the following content into the class.

```java
public class ForkJoinWithSessionJobAdapter extends ComputeJobAdapter {
    @TaskSessionResource
    private ComputeTaskSession session;

    @JobContextResource
    private ComputeJobContext jobCtx;

    @IgniteInstanceResource
    private Ignite ignite;

    private ValidateMessage msg;

    public ForkJoinWithSessionJobAdapter(ValidateMessage msg) {
        this.msg = msg;
    }
    @Override
    public Boolean execute() throws IgniteException {
        try {
```

---

[51] https://github.com/srecon/ignite-book-code-samples/tree/master/chapters/chapter-dist-computing/src/main/java/com/blu/imdg/example5

```
            boolean validateXsdResult = XsdValidator.validate(msg.getMsg(), msg.getXsd());
            session.setAttribute(jobCtx.getJobId(), validateXsdResult);
            if (!validateXsdResult) {
                System.out.println("force return result false!");
                return sendResultAndReturn(false);
            }

            for (ComputeJobSibling sibling : session.getJobSiblings()) {
                Boolean siblingStep1Result = session.waitForAttribute(sibling.getJobId(), \
0);
                if(!siblingStep1Result) {
                    System.out.println("one sibling return false!");
                    return sendResultAndReturn(false);
                }
            }

            boolean validateByJs = JSEvaluate.evaluateJs(msg.getMsg(), msg.getJs());
            return sendResultAndReturn(validateByJs);

        } catch (Exception err) {
            throw new IgniteException(err);
        }
    }
    @NotNull
    private Boolean sendResultAndReturn(Boolean result) throws URISyntaxException, IOExcep\
tion {
        ConcurrentMap<Object, Object> nodeLocalMap = ignite.cluster().nodeLocalMap();
        HttpClient client = HttpAuditClient.createHttpClient(nodeLocalMap);
        return HttpAuditClient.sendResult(client, result, msg.getId());
    }
}
```

Let's go through the code line by line. First, we auto-inject the following resources into the adapter.

- ComputeTaskSession
- ComputeJobContext
- Ignite

Next, we override the execute() method with our custom logics. First, we used our XsdValidator to validate the XML message and set the session attribute. Session attribute name will be the job identifier, and the value will be the result of the XML file validation. In the next few lines, we check the validation result, if it is false, we immediately return the result. Otherwise, we go through all of the job siblings and waits for the attribute's value from other jobs. If any of the sibling jobs returns a negative result of validation, we stop further processing of the XML validation and send the result to the HTTP server. Once all the message passed the XSD validation process, we start doing message content validation through XPATH expression.

Rest of the parts of this example is same as before. In compute task split adapter, we split the task across the nodes in the grid. Let's run the application, first start the HTTP server as follows (if it is not already started)

```
mvn exec:java -Dexec.mainClass=com.blu.imdg.common.HttpAuditEmulator
```

Next, start the an Ignite node with the following command:

```
mvn clean package exec:java -Dexec.mainClass=com.blu.imdg.StartCacheNode
```

Now, run the application with the following command::

```
mvn exec:java -Dexec.mainClass=com.blu.imdg.example5.ForkJointWithSessionComputation
```

You should see the validation result in the Ignite server console as shown below.

```
Job id:5235db9e851-77256dad-379b-4dd9-85af-072f7863fc08
force return result false!
one sibling return false!
```

Figure 7.16

One of the XML validation has failed, and Ignite cancels rest of the processing and returns the result. In this case, the result is negative. This is very simple and straight-forward approach of Apache Ignite to synchronize the state between jobs. In the next sub-section, we are going to study the fault tolerance feature of the compute jobs.

Fault tolerance and checkpointing

In a large scale grid system, the probability of a job failure is much greater than the traditional parallel system. Therefore, fault tolerance has become a crucial area in grid computing. Ignite supports automatic job failover. In the case of a node crash, jobs are automatically transferred to other available nodes for re-execution. Designing of a fault tolerance system in a grid environment with optimized resource utilization and execution time is a critical and challenging task. A good fault tolerant job scheduling approach should be able to handle not only the complexity of the resources also various faults occurring during the job execution.

For a long-running computationally intensive application like compressing a very large file, parsing tons of messages, decoding may require hours or even days to carry out the execution which they are prone to various types of fails. Different types of faults, classified based on several factors are mentioned in the following:

Chapter seven: Distributed computing

- Physical server faults: fault in CPU/memory/disk
- Network faults: fault due to network partition, packet loss.
- Processor faults: Operating system faults.
- Lifecycle faults: Legacy or versioning faults.
- Process faults: software bug, resource shortage.

There are many conditions that may result in a failure within your application, and you can trigger a failover. Moreover, you have the ability to choose to which node a job should be failed over to, as it could be different for different applications or different computations within the same application. High-level view of the fault tolerance support in Ignite are shown below:

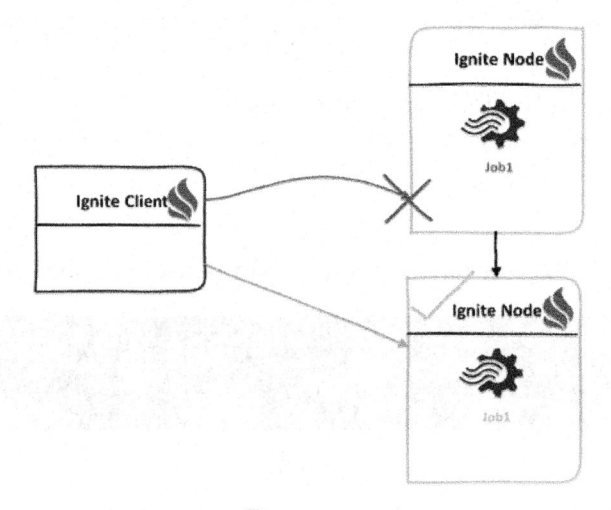

Figure 7.17

When designing fault tolerance system, a checkpoint is important to take into account. It's very crucial to recovering the job from the state, where it failed. Checkpointing is a technique which allows a process to preserve its state during an arbitrary time interval and resuming its normal operation to reduce faults during recovery process after failure. Note that, in Grid computing to improve the reliability and system availability a commonly used fault tolerance technique is checkpointing.

In Ignite, checkpointing is optional; the default checkpointing is disabled for performance reasons. Without checkpointing, Ignite will restart the job in another node from the beginning. Job fault tolerance in Ignite with checkpoint shown in figure 7.18.

Chapter seven: Distributed computing 314

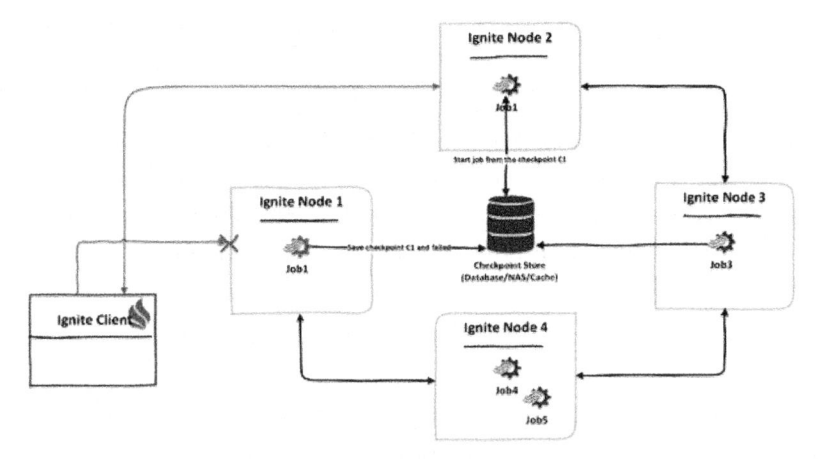

Figure 7.18

When a checkpoint is enabled, every job saves their state in checkpoint store such as Database, NAS or Ignite cache. When one of the jobs failed with an error, Apache Ignite restarts the same job in another node and retrieve the checkpoint from the store to start the job from the checkpoint. In the above figure, Job1 save the state C1 into the store and failed, Apache Ignite restarts the Job1 in the Node 2 and start processing from the previously saved state C1.

Apache Ignite provides `FailoverSpi`, which is responsible for handling the selection of a new node for the execution of a failed job. Moreover, FailoverSpi interface offers developers the possibility to supply custom logic for handling failed execution of a grid job. In all cases of failure, FailoverSpi takes failed job (as failover context) and the list of all grid nodes and provides another node on which the job execution will be retried. It is up to failover SPI to make sure that job is not mapped to the node it failed on. Failover is triggered when the method `ComputeTask.result(...)` returns the `ComputeJobResultPolicy.FAILOVER` policy. Ignite comes with the following built-in failover SPI implementations:

- *NeverFailoverSpi* – failover SPI implementation that never fails over.
- *AlwaysFailoverSpi* - failover SPI that always reroutes a failed job to another node. Ignite fail over default mode.
- *JobStealingCollisionSpi* - Collision SPI that supports job stealing from over-utilized nodes to under-utilized nodes. This SPI is especially useful if you have some jobs within task complete fast, and others sitting in the waiting queue on slower nodes. In such case, the waiting jobs will be stolen from the slower node and moved to the fast under-utilized node.
- *JobStealingFailoverSpi* - job stealing failover SPI needs always to be used in conjunction with JobStealingCollisionSpi SPI. When JobStealingCollisionSpi receives a steal request and rejects jobs so they can be routed to the appropriate node, it is the responsibility of this JobStealingFailoverSpi SPI to make sure that the job is indeed re-routed to the node that has sent the initial request to steal it.

Chapter seven: Distributed computing 315

> **Note:**
> **AlwaysFailoverSpi** is enabled by default. In this mode, an attempt will be made to reroute the failed job to a node that was not part of initial split for a better chance of success. If no such nodes are available, then an attempt will be made to reroute the failed job to the nodes in the initial split minus the node the job is failed on. If none of the above attempts succeeded, then the job will not be failed over and null will be returned.

Ignite guarantee that, as long as there is at least one node standing, no job will ever be lost. To set the maximum number of attempts to execute a failed task on another node, use the following setter method:

Method name	Interface name
setMaximumFailoverAttempts(int maxFailoverAttempts)	AlwaysFailoverSpi interface
setMaximumStealingAttempts(int maxStealingAttempts)	JobStealingCollisionSpi interface

Let's get back to the checkpoint feature again. Checkpoints are available through the following methods on `ComputeTaskSession` interface:

- **saveCheckpoint(String key, Object state)** - saves intermediate state of a job or task to a storage. This way whenever a job fails over to another node, it can load its previously saved state via loadCheckpoint(String) method and continue with execution. Parameters:
    1. key - Key to be used to load this checkpoint in future.
    2. state - Intermediate job state to save. This method defaults checkpoint scope to `ComputeTaskSessionScope.SESSION_SCOPE` and implementation will automatically remove the checkpoint at the end of the session.
- **saveCheckpoint(String key, Object state, ComputeTaskSessionScope scope, long timeout)** - Overloaded method of the saveCheckpoint().The life time of the checkpoint is determined by its timeout and scope. If `ComputeTaskSessionScope.GLOBAL_SCOPE` is used, the checkpoint will outlive its session, and can only be removed by calling `CheckpointSpi.removeCheckpoint` from Ignite or another task or job. Parameters:
    1. key - Key to be used to load this checkpoint in future.
    2. state - Intermediate job state to save.
    3. scope - Checkpoint scope. If equal to ComputeTaskSessionScope.SESSION_SCOPE, then state will automatically be removed at the end of task execution. Otherwise, if scope is ComputeTaskSessionScope.GLOBAL_SCOPE then state will outlive its session and can be removed by calling removeCheckpoint(String) from another task or whenever timeout expires.
    4. timeout - Maximum time this state should be kept by the underlying storage. Value 0 means that timeout will never expire.

- **saveCheckpoint(String key, Object state, ComputeTaskSessionScope scope, long timeout, boolean overwrite)** - the Overloaded method of the saveCheckpoint(). This method contains another extra parameter: overwrite, which determines, whether or not a checkpoint will be overwritten if it already exists.
- **loadCheckpoint(String key)** - Loads job's state previously saved via saveCheckpoint(...) method from an underlying storage for a given key. If the state was not previously saved, then null will be returned. Parameters:
    1. key - Key for intermediate job state to load.
- **removeCheckpoint(String key)** - Removes previously saved job's state for a given key from an underlying storage. Parameters:
    1. key - Key for intermediate job state to remove from the session.

> **Note:**
> There is a mistake on Apache Ignite documentation, Checkpoints are available on interface `ComputeTaskSession` rather than `GridTaskSession`.

1. **NoopCheckpointSpi** – it's the default implementation of the CheckpointSPI, if nothing is specified, no-op checkpoint SPI is used.
2. **CacheCheckpointSpi** – this is the cache-based implementation for checkpoint SPI.
3. **JdbcCheckpointSpi** – this is the RDBMS-based implementation for checkpoint SPI, this implementation uses a database to store checkpoints.
4. **SharedFsCheckpointSpi** – this provides the shared file system CheckpointSPI implementation for the checkpoint SPI. All checkpoints are stored on shared storage and available for all nodes in the grid. Note that every node must have access to the shared directory. The reason the directory needs to be shared is because a job state can be saved on one node and loaded on another. Shared storage would be NAS or SAN file shared system. For high-performance SAN is preferable.
5. **S3CheckpointSpi** – this is the amazon S3-based implementation for checkpoint SPI.

CheckpointSpi is provided in *IgniteConfiguration* class and passed into Ignition class at startup. Here is an example of uses *CacheCheckpointSPI* in Java on Ignite node startup with failover:

Chapter seven: Distributed computing   317

```
IgniteConfiguration cfg = new IgniteConfiguration();
//cache checkpointSPI implementation.
CacheCheckpointSpi cacheCheckpointSpi = new CacheCheckpointSpi();
cacheCheckpointSpi.setCacheName("checkpointCache");
// set the check point spi and failover spi in Ignite configuration
cfg.setCheckpointSpi(cacheCheckpointSpi).setFailoverSpi(new AlwaysFailoverSpi());
// Starts Ignite node.
Ignition.start(cfg);
```

Now that, we have got the basics, let's build something useful. We are going to extend our XML validation application to be failover across the Ignite cluster. Assume that, we have got the following non-functional requirements from the system analyst:

1. Every job must save their state (checkpoint) after completing the XSD validation phase into the Ignite cache.
2. If any of the jobs failed after completing the phase (XML validation), a new job will be executed in another Ignite node and load the state from the cache and continue execution.

Figure 7.19 illustrates the fail over process flow.

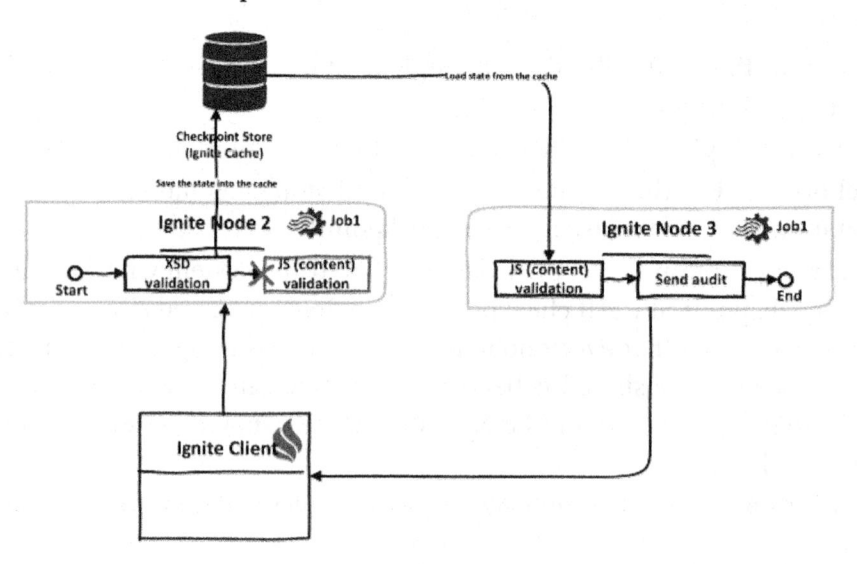

Figure 7.19

To implementation the fail-over through a checkpoint, we have to modify our validation application slightly. If you are curious about the code, it's available at GitHub repositories[52].

Here, we have two main class: ForkJoinWithCheckpointComputation and ForkJoinWithCheckpointJobAdapter. ForkJoinWithCheckpointComputation is very similar to the previous example. ForkJoinWithCheckpointComputation is a compute task split adapter and implements the split and

---
[52] https://github.com/srecon/ignite-book-code-samples/tree/master/chapters/chapter-dist-computing/src/main/java/com/blu/imdg/example6

reduce methods for task splitting and reduce the overall result. Although, we have configured the cache checkpoint SPI to store the checkpoint into the cache and also explicitly configured the AlwaysFailoverSpi as follows:

```java
try (Ignite ignite = Ignition.start(CLIENT_CONFIG)) {
    IgniteCompute compute = ignite.compute();
    CacheConfiguration cacheConfiguration = new CacheConfiguration("checkpoints");
    // explicitly uses of checkpoint
    CacheCheckpointSpi cacheCheckpointSpi = new CacheCheckpointSpi();
    cacheCheckpointSpi.setCacheName("checkpointCache");
    ignite.configuration().setCheckpointSpi(cacheCheckpointSpi)
                         .setFailoverSpi(new AlwaysFailoverSpi());
    // create or get cache
    ignite.getOrCreateCache(cacheConfiguration);
}
```

> **Note:**
> Checkpointing is disabled by default for performance reasons. To enable it attach *@Compute-TaskSessionFullSupport* annotation to the task class.

Let's have a look at the next class: ForkJoinWithCheckpointJobAdapter. Most of the part of this class is very much similar to what we have done so far in this chapter.

```java
public class ForkJoinWithCheckpointJobAdapter extends ComputeJobAdapter {
    @TaskSessionResource
    private ComputeTaskSession session;

    @JobContextResource
    private ComputeJobContext jobCtx;

    @IgniteInstanceResource
    private Ignite ignite;

    private ValidateMessage msg;

    public ForkJoinWithCheckpointJobAdapter(ValidateMessage msg) {
        this.msg = msg;
    }

    @Override
```

Chapter seven: Distributed computing 319

```java
        public Boolean execute() throws IgniteException {
            try {
                Boolean validateXsdResult = session.loadCheckpoint(msg.getId());

                Boolean checkpointValue = validateXsdResult;
                System.out.println("validateXsdResult=" + validateXsdResult + " msg=" + msg.ge\
tId());
                if (validateXsdResult == null) {
                    validateXsdResult = XsdValidator.validate(msg.getMsg(), msg.getXsd());
                    session.setAttribute(jobCtx.getJobId(), validateXsdResult);
                    session.saveCheckpoint(msg.getId(), true);
                }

                if (msg.getId().equals("1") && checkpointValue == null) {
                    //emulate error
                    System.out.println("throw err!!!");
                    throw new ComputeJobFailoverException("err!!");
                }

                System.out.println("real execute msg=" + msg.getId());

                if (!validateXsdResult) {
                    System.out.println("force return result false!");
                    return sendResultAndReturn(validateXsdResult);
                }

                for (ComputeJobSibling sibling : session.getJobSiblings()) {
                    Boolean siblingStep1Result = session.waitForAttribute(sibling.getJobId(), \
0);
                    if (!siblingStep1Result) {
                        System.out.println("one sibling return false!");
                        return sendResultAndReturn(false);
                    }
                }

                boolean validateByJs = JSEvaluate.evaluateJs(msg.getMsg(), msg.getJs());
                return sendResultAndReturn(validateByJs);

            } catch (Exception err) {
                throw new IgniteException(err);
            }
        }
    @NotNull
    private Boolean sendResultAndReturn(Boolean result) throws URISyntaxException, IOExcep\
tion {
```

```
            ConcurrentMap<Object, Object> nodeLocalMap = ignite.cluster().nodeLocalMap();
            HttpClient client = HttpAuditClient.createHttpClient(nodeLocalMap);
            return HttpAuditClient.sendResult(client, result, msg.getId());
    }
}
```

Let's go through the execute method of the above class line by line. With the next pseudo codes, we are trying to load the checkpoint by message id if available.

```
Boolean validateXsdResult = session.loadCheckpoint(msg.getId());
Boolean checkpointValue = validateXsdResult;
System.out.println("validateXsdResult=" + validateXsdResult + " msg=" + msg.getId());
if (validateXsdResult == null) {
        validateXsdResult = XsdValidator.validate(msg.getMsg(), msg.getXsd());
        session.setAttribute(jobCtx.getJobId(), validateXsdResult);
        session.saveCheckpoint(msg.getId(), true);
}
```

If the checkpoint (validateXsdResult) is null, we start executing the XSD validation and save the checkpoint with the message id. Also, note that we have set the job id and the result of the validation as a session attribute. Later, we will use this session attributes to check the entire job result. In the next few lines of code, we are trying to emulate the network error to interrupt the execution.

```
if (msg.getId().equals("1") && checkpointValue == null) {
//emulate error
System.out.println("throw err!!!");
throw new ComputeJobFailoverException("err!!");
}
```

The above code is very straight forward, for the message with id 1 and whenever there is no checkpoint available for this message, we throw compute job failover exception. This condition will execute only one time to emulate an error during job processing. The rest of the part of this method is as same as before. Let's run the application to ensure the fault tolerance of the application. First start the HTTP server as follows (if it is not already started).

```
mvn exec:java -Dexec.mainClass=com.blu.imdg.common.HttpAuditEmulator
```

Next, start the a few Ignite node with the following command (I am going to start 4 nodes):

```
mvn clean package exec:java -Dexec.mainClass=com.blu.imdg.StartCacheNode
```

Chapter seven: Distributed computing

> **Note:**
> You have to run more than one Ignite node for getting fault tolerance of Ignite job. Because, if you run only one Ignite node, and whenever one of the jobs fails, Ignite couldn't re-execute the job on another node. If you run the application on single Ignite node, probably, you would get the following exception in console `org.apache.ignite.cluster.ClusterTopologyException: Failed to failover a job to another node (failover SPI returned null)`.

Now, run the application with the following command:

```
mvn exec:java -Dexec.mainClass=com.blu.imdg.example6.ForkJoinWithCheckpointComputation
```

The entire result would be true as follows:

```
final result=true
```

Let's explain what's happend under the hood.

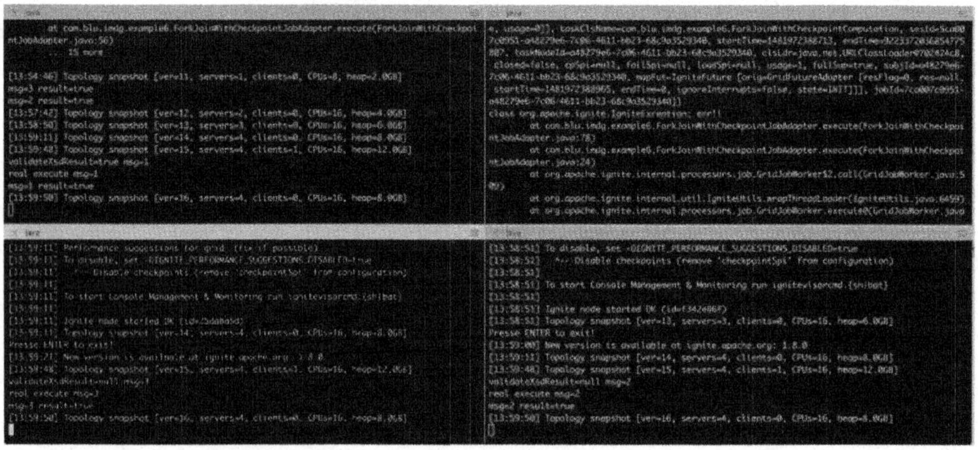

Figure 7.20

We have started 4 Ignite node for clarity. When we execute our application, it generated 3 jobs for each XML file. A job with the XML message of id 1 completed the XSD validation and failed, Ignite re-executed the job in the node four (upper right corner of figure 7.20) and completed the process.

One important use case for the checkpoint that is not readily apparent is to guard against failure of the **master** node - the node that started the original execution. When a master node fails, Ignite doesn't have where to send the results of job execution to, and thus the result will be discarded. To failover this scenario, one can store the final result of the job execution as a checkpoint and have the logic re-run the entire task in case of a "master" node failure. In such case, the task re-run will be much faster since all the jobs' can start from the saved checkpoints.

In the next section, we are going to study the compute grid affinity call (collocate the computation with the data).

Collocation of computation and data

Let's start with the definition of the collocation of data. The idea behind the data collocation is to keep all the related datasets in a single node. Datasets can be allocated into the different caches in the same node. With this approach, network roundtrip for the related data is decreasing, and the client application can retrieve the associated data from the single node. Composite columns of Cassandra is an example of the collocation data technics.

Apache Ignite provides `@AffinityKeyMapped` annotation for key-to-node affinity. Affinity key is a key which will be used to determine a node on which given cache key will be stored. This annotation allows marking a field or a method in the cache key object that will be used as an affinity key (instead of the entire cache key object that is used for affinity by default). Note that a class can have only one field or method annotated with @AffinityKeyMapped annotation.

For instance, in bank account-engine, we have followed by two entities: account and transactions. Account entity contains all the information about the client and the transaction entity holds all the transactions entries of the client. If these two entities are always accessed together, then for better performance and scalability it makes sense to collocate entity transactions with their account entity when storing them into the cache. To accomplished this, we can provide a common field of these two entities as an affinity key. Figure 7.21 illustrates the graphical view of the affinity key. Note that, we have some data duplication (account number) on each dataset.

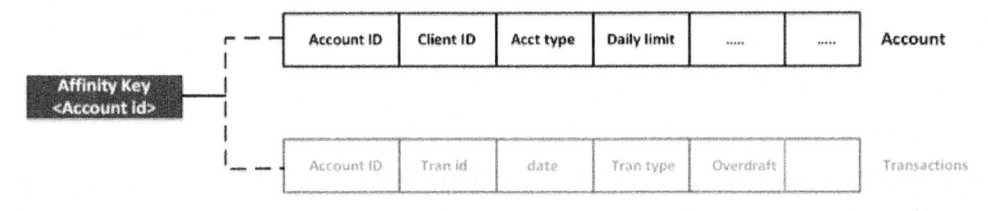

Figure 7.21

One of the main use cases for this @AffinityKeyMapped annotation is the routing of grid computations to the nodes where the data for this computation is cached. In Apache Ignite the concept is well known as Collocation of Computations and Data.

Apache Ignite provides two methods for executing a job on the node where data for provided affinity key is located: `affinityCall, affinityRun`. In other words, knowing a cache name and affinity key these methods will be able to find the node that is the primary for the given key and will execute a job there. The difference between the two methods is that affinityRun doesn't return any result. The two methods have the following signatures:

Chapter seven: Distributed computing

Method name	Description
cacheName	Name of the cache to use for affinity co-location.
affKey	Affinity key.
job	A job which will be co-located on the node with given affinity key.
Job result	Return value of the job, only affinityCall() function can return value.

Now that we have dipped our toes into theory, let's build a (nearly) minimal example of an affinity co-location. To keep things simple, we will use the account and transactions entity as described before. We are going to build an application to calculate the **Cashback** for given client. For each client, we will execute an affinity call function, which will return the cash back amount for the client based on his transactions history. Let's start building the application from the scratch. The full source code is available on GitHub[53].

Step 1:

Let's start with the *TransacionKey* class (this class is reside on package common at GitHub[54]) as follows:

```
public class TransactionKey implements AccountCacheKey, Serializable {
    @QuerySqlField(index = true)
    @AffinityKeyMapped
    private String account;
    private Date transactionDate;
    private String transactionId;
    public TransactionKey() {
    }
    ...
}
```

We annotate the field named account with the @AffinityKeyMapped annotation. This annotation specifies the affinity of the transaction entity with the account. Note that, we also use the *@QuerySqlField* to use this given field in SQL clause. Create another class with name AccountKey and add the following contents:

---

[53] https://github.com/srecon/ignite-book-code-samples/tree/master/chapters/chapter-dist-computing/src/main/java/com/blu/imdg/example8
[54] https://github.com/srecon/ignite-book-code-samples/tree/master/chapters/chapter-dist-computing/src/main/java/com/blu/imdg/common

Chapter seven: Distributed computing

```
public class AccountKey implements AccountCacheKey, Serializable {
    @AffinityKeyMapped
    private String account;
    public AccountKey(String account) {
        this.account = account;
    }

    public String getAccount() {
        return account;
    }
    ....
}
```

For the AccountKey class, field account also mapped as an affinity key.

Step 2:

Create a class for Transactions data as follows:

```
public class TransactionData implements AccountCacheData {
    private String fromAccount;
    private String toAccount;
    private BigDecimal sum;
    private String transactionType;

    public TransactionData() {
    }
    ....
}
```

We will use the above class to create transaction data objects and store into the cache. Appropriately, we have the class for storing account information as follows:

```
public class AccountData implements AccountCacheData {
    private String account;
    private String personId;
    private String accountType;
    private Date openedAt;

    private BigDecimal dailyLimit;
    private BigDecimal todayOperationSum;
    private LocalDate today;
    ....
}
```

Chapter seven: Distributed computing

Step 3:

We also need utility class to generate some data of accounts and transactions for the application. Create a new class BankDataGenerator and add the following static methods to generate some test data.

```java
public class BankDataGenerator {

    public static final String ACCOUNT_CACHE = "accountCache";
    public static final String SAVINGS_CACHE = "savingsDictionaryCache";
    public static final String TEST_ACCOUNT = "0000*1111";

    public static IgniteCache<AccountCacheKey, AccountCacheData> createBankCache(Ignite ig\
nite) {
        CacheConfiguration accountCacheCfg = new CacheConfiguration()
                .setName(ACCOUNT_CACHE)
                .setAtomicityMode(TRANSACTIONAL)
                .setIndexedTypes(
                        AccountKey.class, AccountData.class,
                        TransactionKey.class, TransactionData.class,
                        String.class, CashBackDictionaryData.class
                );

        IgniteCache<AccountCacheKey, AccountCacheData> result = ignite.getOrCreateCache(ac\
countCacheCfg);
        result.removeAll();
        return initData(result);
    }
    public static IgniteCache<String, CashBackDictionaryData> initSavigsCache(Ignite ignit\
e) {
        CacheConfiguration savingsCacheCfg = new CacheConfiguration().setName(SAVINGS_CACH\
E);
        IgniteCache<String, CashBackDictionaryData> result = ignite.getOrCreateCache(savin\
gsCacheCfg);
        result.removeAll();
        result.put("meal", new CashBackDictionaryData(new BigDecimal(0.01),"meal shopping"\
));;
        result.put("entertainment", new CashBackDictionaryData(new BigDecimal(0.02),"enter\
tainment"));;
        return result;
    }

    private static IgniteCache<AccountCacheKey, AccountCacheData> initData(IgniteCache<Acc\
ountCacheKey, AccountCacheData> result) {
        //init data
        result.put(new AccountKey(TEST_ACCOUNT), new AccountData(TEST_ACCOUNT, "John Doe",\
```

```
        "standard", new Date(), new BigDecimal(100)));
        result.put(new AccountKey(TEST_ACCOUNT), new AccountData(TEST_ACCOUNT, "Mr. Smith"\
, "premium", new Date(), new BigDecimal(200)));

        result.put(
                new TransactionKey(TEST_ACCOUNT, new Date(), UUID.randomUUID().toString()),
                new TransactionData(TEST_ACCOUNT,"1111*2222", new BigDecimal(100), "meal")
        );

        result.put(
                new TransactionKey(TEST_ACCOUNT, new Date(), UUID.randomUUID().toString()),
                new TransactionData(TEST_ACCOUNT,"3333*4444", new BigDecimal(100), "entert\
ainment")
        );

        return result;
    }
}
```

Static method createBankCache initialize the cache named *accountCache* and generate some test data for the account with transactions. Account number we are going to use for the test is 0000*1111. We have another static method named *initSavigsCache*, which initialize another cache with name savingsDictionaryCache and filled some data for cashback percent.

Step 4:

Now it is time to execute some affinityCall() function in the Ignite node. Create a class with a main method. In my case, the class name is TestAccountSavingsMain. Create the main method and add the following contents into the method:

```
public static void main(String[] args) {

    try (Ignite ignite = Ignition.start(CommonConstants.CLIENT_CONFIG)) {
        IgniteCompute compute = ignite.compute();

        IgniteCache<AccountCacheKey, AccountCacheData> cache = BankDataGenerator.createBan\
kCache(ignite);
        IgniteCache<String, CashBackDictionaryData> savingsCache = BankDataGenerator.initS\
avigsCache(ignite);

        SqlFieldsQuery sql = new SqlFieldsQuery("select * from TransactionData where accou\
nt = ?");

        BigDecimal result = compute.affinityCall(BankDataGenerator.ACCOUNT_CACHE, new Acco\
untKey(BankDataGenerator.TEST_ACCOUNT), () -> {
```

```
            List<List<?>> data = cache.query(sql.setArgs(BankDataGenerator.TEST_ACCOUNT)).\
getAll();
            BigDecimal cashBack = new BigDecimal(0);
            for (List row : data) {
                TransactionData tr = (TransactionData) row.get(1);
                CashBackDictionaryData cashBackDictionaryData = savingsCache.get(tr.getTra\
nsactionType());
                cashBack = cashBack.add(tr.getSum().multiply(cashBackDictionaryData.getCas\
hBackPercent()));
            }
            //System.out.println("savings="+cashBack);
            return cashBack;
        });

        System.out.println("CashBack="+result);
    }
}
```

Let's go through the codes line by line. First, we start our application as an Ignite client. In the next two lines of code, we initialized the caches and generated some data for the affinityCall function. We use a simple SQL query to retrieve all transactions for the account "0000*1111".

```
SqlFieldsQuery sql = new SqlFieldsQuery("select * from TransactionData where account = ?");
```

In the next line of code, we executed the affinityCall() function, where we provide the cache name as *accountCache*, affinity key as 0000*1111 (account number) and the job itself. In the execution block of the job, we executed the above SQL query to get all the transaction associated with the account 0000*1111. Next, we iterate over the transactions data and calculate the cash back for all the transaction of this account and returns the result. Let's run the application, start an Ignite node with the following command:

```
mvn clean package exec:java -Dexec.mainClass=com.blu.imdg.StartCacheNode
```

Next, run the application by the command as follows:

```
mvn exec:java -Dexec.mainClass=com.blu.imdg.example8.TestAccountSavingsMain
```

The application should return to you the following result on the console:

```
result=3.0
```

You can change the execution logic if you choose and can play with the affinityCall() function. From the version 1.8, Ignite provides consistency guaranty of affinityCall() function, which means, the partition, which the affinity key belongs to, will not be evicted from a node while a job, triggered by affinityCall(...) or affinityRun(...) is being executed there.

Chapter seven: Distributed computing 328

Job scheduling

In Ignite, jobs are submitted to a thread pool of the Ignite JVM and are executed in random order (see the figure 7-22). However, Ignite provides the ability to use the custom logic in determining how grid jobs should be executed on a destination grid node. Job scheduling can be achieved by the `CollisionSpi` interface.

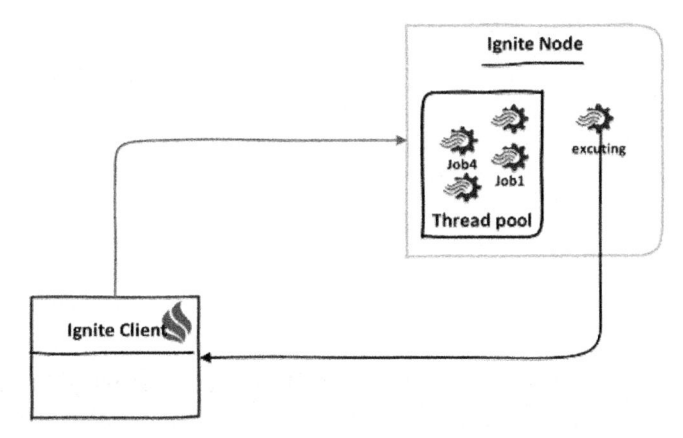

Figure 7.22

Collision SPI allows regulating how grid jobs get executed when they arrive on a destination node for execution. Its functionality is similar to tasks management via customizable GCD (Great Central Dispatch) on Mac OS X as it allows the developer to provide custom job dispatching on a single node. In general, a grid node will have multiple jobs arriving at it for execution and potentially multiple jobs that are already executing or waiting for execution on it. There are multiple possible strategies dealing with this situation, like all jobs can proceed in parallel, or jobs can be serialized, i.e., or only one job can execute at any given point of time, or only certain number or types of grid jobs can proceed in parallel, etc.

Ignite comes with the following ready implementations for collision resolution that cover most popular strategies:

FifoQueueCollisionSpi:

This class provides an implementation for Collision SPI based on FIFO queue. Jobs are ordered as they arrived, and only `getParallelJobsNumber()` number of jobs is allowed to execute in parallel. Other jobs will be buffered in the passive queue.

> **Note:**
>
> By setting *parallelJobsNumber* to 1, you can guarantee that all jobs will be executed one-at-a-time, and no two jobs will be executed concurrently.

FifoQueueCollisionSpi can be configured by Spring XML or Java. Let's check a simple FifoQueueCollisionSpi configuretion by Spring XML.

```xml
<bean class="org.apache.ignite.IgniteConfiguration" singleton="true">
  ...
  <property name="collisionSpi">
    <bean class="org.apache.ignite.spi.collision.fifoqueue.FifoQueueCollisionSpi">
      <!-- Execute one job at a time. -->
      <property name="parallelJobsNumber" value="1"/>
    </bean>
  </property>
  ...
</bean>
```

PriorityQueueCollisionSpi:

This class provides an implementation for Collision SPI based on priority queue. Jobs are first ordered by their priority if one is specified, and only first `getParallelJobsNumber()` jobs are allowed to execute in parallel. Other jobs will be queued up. This SPI has the following optional configuration parameters:

1. A Number of jobs that can be executed in parallel (setParallelJobsNumber(int)). This number should usually be set to no greater than the number of threads in the execution thread pool.
2. Priority attribute session key (getPriorityAttributeKey()). Prior to returning from ComputeTask.map(List, Object) method, task implementation should set a value into the task session keyed by this attribute key.
3. Priority attribute job context key (getJobPriorityAttributeKey()). It is used for specifying job priority.
4. Default priority value (getDefaultPriority()). It is used when no priority is set.
5. Default priority increase value (getStarvationIncrement()). It is used for increasing priority when job gets bumped down. This future is used for preventing starvation waiting for jobs execution.

Here is a Spring XML configuration example:

```xml
<property name="collisionSpi">
 <bean class="org.apache.ignite.spi.collision.priorityqueue.PriorityQueueCollisionSpi">
    <property name="priorityAttributeKey" value="myPriorityAttributeKey"/>
    <property name="parallelJobsNumber" value="10"/>
 </bean>
</property>
```

JobStealingCollisionSpi:

Collision SPI that supports job stealing from over-utilized nodes to under-utilized nodes. This SPI is especially useful if you have some jobs within task complete fast, and others sitting in the waiting queue on slower nodes. In such case, the waiting jobs will be stolen from the slower node and moved to the fast under-utilized node. The design and ideas for this SPI are significantly influenced by Java Fork/Join Framework authored by Doug Lea and planned for Java 7. GridJobStealingCollisionSpi took similar concepts and applied them to the grid (as opposed to within VM support planned in Java 7). Quite often grids are deployed across many computers some of which will always be more powerful than others. This SPI helps you avoid jobs being stuck at a slower node, as they will be stolen by a faster node. In the following picture when Node3 becomes free, it steals Job13 and Job23 from Node1 and Node2 respectively.

This is the end of the section compute grid. Next, we are going to explore one of the amazing features of Apache Ignite: Service grid.

Service Grid

You won't find a clear description of what is service grid and how does it differ from a collection of services. In the enterprise application world, a service is *a standards-based way of encapsulating enterprise functionality and exposing it as a reusable component that can be combined with other services to meet new requirements* and provides the following set of ideas:

1. Service described by an interface and provides several methods.
2. The service may have state (stateful service) or can be stateless too.
3. The service has a life cycle.

From the Apache Ignite's point of view, a service grid is a collection of Ignite node (cluster), where you can deploy arbitrary user-defined reusable distributed services. You can imagine services in Apache Ignite as a precompiled execution block deployed in the Ignite cluster. You can use service proxy (client) for accessing remotely deployed distributed services. A classic example of this kind of services would be a service that can return the last 20 transactions for displaying in the client transaction history page of an internet bank or a service that can check the cash withdrawal limit at ATM for a day. Figure 7.23 illustrates a high-level view of the service grid in Ignite cluster.

Chapter seven: Distributed computing 331

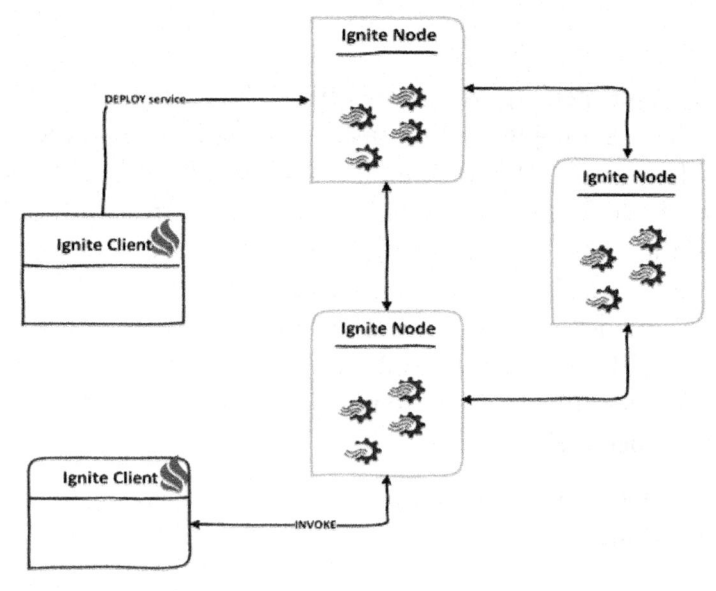

Figure 7.23

Ignite service grid provides the following features:

1. Continuous availability of deployed services regardless of topology changes or crashes.
2. Automatically deploy distributed services on node startup by specifying them in the configuration.
3. Automatically deploy singletons, including cluster-singleton, node-singleton, or key-affinity-singleton.
4. Automatically deploy any number of distributed service instances in the cluster.
5. Undeploy any of the deployed services.
6. Get information about service deployment topology within the cluster.
7. Develop and deploy on-demand microservices in distributed fashion.
8. Create service proxy for accessing remotely deployed distributed services.
9. Create a high-level wrapper (REST/WS) for service proxy for accessing remotely deployed distributed services.

Disadvantages

Just because something is new, doesn't mean it has any drawbacks. Here's a list of some potential drawbacks associated with the Apache Ignite service grid:

1. The developer should spend the time in writing boilerplate infrastructure code to deploy and manage services in Ignite grid.
2. CPU and RAM intensive services could crash the entire Ignite node and should go into separate deployment in the application server. If you are planning to deploy services that consume a lot of RAM (e.g. text analysis, image processing, trained model), you should reconsider using Apache Ignite service grid.

3. Peer class loading is not supported for service grid. It's required to have a Service class in the classpath of all the cluster nodes.

Developing services

Apache Ignite provides two plain Java interfaces to develop and deploy services in Ignite.

Interface **Service**: an instance of grid-managed service. Whenever service is deployed, Apache Ignite will automatically calculate how many instances of this service should be deployed on each node within the cluster. For developing service, you have to implement the interface Service and implements several methods as follows:

- method init(...): Pre-initializes service before execution. This method is guaranteed to be called before service deployment is complete. In this method, we can initialize resources such as connection to any Database or 3rd party services.
- method execute(...): Starts execution of this service. This method is automatically invoked whenever an instance of the service is deployed on a grid node. Note that service is considered deployed even after it exits the execute method and can be canceled (or undeployed) only by calling any of the cancel methods on IgniteServices API. This method is designed for service, whenever it requires a continuously running thread. For instance, polling from a queue. Also, note that service is not required to exit from execute method until cancel (ServiceContext) method was called.
- method cancel(...): Cancels this service. Ignite will automatically call this method whenever any of the cancel methods on IgniteServices API are called.

Interface **IgniteServcies**: Provides functionality necessary to deploy distributed services on the Ignite grid. Java classes that implement interface Service can be deployed from IgniteServices façade. Interface IgniteServices defines a few override method to deploy services in the grid.

- Method deploy(): Deploys multiple instances of the service on the grid according to provided configuration. Ignite will deploy a maximum amount of services equal to cfg.getTotalCount() [defines the maximum number of the instance] parameter making sure that there are no more than cfg.getMaxPerNodeCount()[defines the maximum number of the instance on each node] service instances running on each node. Whenever topology changes, Apache Ignite will automatically rebalance the deployed services within the cluster to make sure that each node will end up with about equal number of deployed instances whenever possible.
- Method deployClusterSingleton(...) : Deploys a cluster-wide singleton service. Ignite will guarantee that there is always one instance of the service in the cluster. In case if grid node on which the service was deployed crashes or stops, Ignite will automatically redeploy it on another node. However, if the node on which the service is deployed remains in topology, then the service will always be deployed on that node only, regardless of topology changes. Method deployNodeSingleton(...): Deploys a per-node singleton service. Ignite will guarantee

Chapter seven: Distributed computing

that there is always one instance of the service running on each node. Whenever new nodes are started within the underlying cluster group, Ignite will automatically deploy one instance of the service on every new node.
- Method deployKeyAffinitySingleton(...): Deploys one instance of this service on the primary node for a given affinity key. Whenever topology changes and primary node assignment changes, Ignite will always make sure that the service is undeployed on the previous primary node and deployed on the new primary node.
- Method deployMultiple(...): Deploys multiple instances of the service on the grid. Ignite will deploy a maximum amount of services equal to cfg.getTotalCount() parameter making sure that there are no more than cfg.getMaxPerNodeCount() service instances running on each node.

So far in this chapter, we created Ignite on-demand compute jobs to validate XML documents. In this section, we are going to reuse our previous two phase validation process as a service and deploy it as service on Ignite grid. Whenever we have a need to validate any XML documents, we will create a proxy and invoke the service in Ignite grid to complete the validation. After deployment of the XML validation service in Ignite grid, it will live till undeployed from the Ignite grid. Full source code of this section is available on GitHub[55]. Let's start with the creation of the interface.

Step 1:

Create the `XsdValidatingService` interface with one method *isOk()*, which has parameter type ValidateMessage and can return the validation result. It's our custom interface for our service for validating XML message.

```
public interface XsdValidatingService {
    boolean isOk(ValidateMessage msg);
}
```

Step 2:

Next, create a new Java class with name XsdValidatingServiceImpl and implements the next two interfaces: `XsdValidatingService, Service`.

---

[55] https://github.com/srecon/ignite-book-code-samples/tree/master/chapters/chapter-dist-computing/src/main/java/com/blu/imdg/example7

```java
public class XsdValidatingServiceImpl implements XsdValidatingService, Service {
    private CloseableHttpClient auditClient;
    @Override
    public boolean isOk(ValidateMessage msg) {
        Boolean validateXsdResult = XsdValidator.validate(msg.getMsg(), msg.getXsd());
        sendResult(msg, validateXsdResult);
        return validateXsdResult;
    }
    private void sendResult(ValidateMessage msg, Boolean validateXsdResult) {
        try {
            HttpAuditClient.sendResult(auditClient, validateXsdResult, msg.getId());
        } catch (Exception err) {
            err.printStackTrace();
        }
    }
    //service methods
    @Override
    public void cancel(ServiceContext serviceContext) {
        System.out.println("cancel service");
        try {
            auditClient.close();
        } catch (IOException e) {
            e.printStackTrace();
        }
    }
    @Override
    public void init(ServiceContext serviceContext) throws Exception {
        System.out.println("init service");
        auditClient = (CloseableHttpClient) HttpAuditClient.createHttpClient();
    }
    @Override
    public void execute(ServiceContext serviceContext) throws Exception {
    }
}
```

Let's go through the above code line by line. First of all, we have implemented the method isOk(), where, we have invoked our XsdValidator.validate method to validated the XML document. Next, we send the result of the validation process for audit and return the result. Later, we override two Ignite service method:

- Init(): in this method, we initialize the auditClient for sending the validation process for audit.
- Cancel(): in this method, we released the auditClient connection and rest of all resources.

Step 3:

Chapter seven: Distributed computing   335

Now that, we have developed our service, let's deploy it and run some test to validate XML documents. Create a new Java class with a main method and add the following contents to it.

```java
public class TestXsdValidatingService {
    private static final String VALIDATING_SERVICE = "validatingService";
    public static void main(String[] args) throws IOException {
        try (Ignite ignite = Ignition.start(CommonConstants.CLIENT_CONFIG)) {
            String sample1 = TestDataGenerator.getSample1();
            String sample2 = TestDataGenerator.getSample2();
            byte[] vaidateSchema = TestDataGenerator.getValidateSchema();
            String validateScript = TestDataGenerator.getValidateScript();
            ignite.services().deployNodeSingleton(VALIDATING_SERVICE, new XsdValidatingSer\
viceImpl());

            XsdValidatingService xsdValidatingService = ignite.services().serviceProxy(VAL\
IDATING_SERVICE, XsdValidatingService.class, /*not-sticky*/false);
            System.out.println("result=" + xsdValidatingService.isOk(new ValidateMessage("\
1", sample1, vaidateSchema, validateScript)));
            System.out.println("result2=" + xsdValidatingService.isOk(new ValidateMessage(\
"2", sample2, vaidateSchema, validateScript)));
            ignite.services().cancel(VALIDATING_SERVICE);
        }
    }
}
```

First, few lines of code are very familiar with us from the previous section. We have generated two XML documents, get the XSD schema and the JS validator script from the TestGenerator class. Next, we **deploy** our service through IgniteService interface. As a parameter of the interface, we declare the service name and the implementation of our service as follows:

- Service name: validatingService
- Service implementation: XsdValidatingServiceImpl

> **Note:**
> We are using **deployNodeSingleton** method to deploy our service, it means, there is always only one instance of the service running on each node.

In the next line, we create a **proxy** of the *XsdValidationService* and invoke the service method isOk() two times. During the invocation, we also pass the XML document for validating over XSD schema and JS validator.

> **Note:**
> `ignite.services().serviceProxy(…)` method returns a remote handle on the service. If service is available locally, then local instance is returned, otherwise, a remote proxy is dynamically created and provided for the specified service.

Also, note that we are using a **non-sticky** version of proxy in our example. If the proxy is sticky, then Ignite will always go back to the same cluster node to contact a remotely deployed service. If the proxy is not sticky, then Ignite will load balance remote service proxy invocations among all cluster nodes on which the service is deployed. There are a few rules that need to be taken into account whenever use a sticky or non-sticky proxy. If you are developing stateful services then, you should consider using a sticky proxy to invoke the remote services, otherwise non-sticky proxy is the best choice for you.

In the last line of the pseudo-code, we cancel the service deployment and release all the resources of the service.

Step 4:

Let's run the application, start an Ignite node with the following command:

```
mvn clean package exec:java -Dexec.mainClass=com.blu.imdg.StartCacheNode
```

Now, start the HTTP server as follows (if it is not already started).

```
mvn exec:java -Dexec.mainClass=com.blu.imdg.common.HttpAuditEmulator
```

Next, run the application by the command as follows:

```
mvn exec:java -Dexec.mainClass=com.blu.imdg.example7.TestXsdValidatingService
```

If everything goes fine, you should have the following message on the console:

```
init service
msg=1 result=true
msg=2 result=true
cancel service
```

Very straightforward way to deploy and execute the services in Ignite grid. Note that, for simplicity, we use the same class to deploy and execute the service by proxy. However, in a real world, you should use a separate class for deploying and invoking the services as well. In the next section, we are going to study the different ways of deploying Ignite services.

Cluster singleton

IgniteServices facade allows deploying any number of service instances on the grid automatically. Although, the most commonly used features is to deploy singleton services on the cluster. Ignite proposed automatically deploy singletons, including:

- Node-singleton
- Cluster-singleton
- Key-Affinity-singleton

Node-singleton:

In the previous section, we used the node-singleton option to deploy our XsdValidation service. In this case, each node contains only one running instance of the service. Whenever new nodes are started within the underlying cluster group, Ignite will automatically deploy one instance of the service on every new node. Deploy node-singleton is accomplished with the following code:

```
ignite.services().deployNodeSingleton(VALIDATING_SERVICE, new XsdValidatingServiceImpl());
```

Where,

- VALIDATING_SERVICE – is the name of the service.
- new XsdValidatingServiceImpl() – is the service instance.

The above method is analogous to calling

```
deployMultiple(VALIDATING_SERVICE, new XsdValidatingServiceImpl(), 0, 1)
```

Let's start two Ignite nodes and deploy the XsdValidation service with option `node-singleton` as follows:

```
mvn clean package exec:java -Dexec.mainClass=com.blu.imdg.StartCacheNode
```

Now, deploy the `XsdValidation` service by executing the Java class *DeployNodeSingleton* (see the example7 on GitHub for more details). After the deployment, you should see the following messages on the console.

Figure 7.24

Above figure confirms that each node on the cluster has one instance of the `XsdValidation` service. If we invoke the remote service via proxy, one of the services will be invoked and returns the validation result. Let's run the Java class `RunXsdValidationService` and see the action as follows:

Chapter seven: Distributed computing   338

```
mvn clean package exec:java -Dexec.mainClass= com.blu.imdg.example7.RunXsdValidationService
```

Figure 7.25

Cluster-singleton:

A cluster singleton service is a service running on a cluster that is available on only one node of a cluster at a time. In case if grid node on which the service was deployed crashes or stops, Ignite will automatically redeploy it on another node. However, if the node on which the service is deployed remains in topology, then the service will always be deployed on that node only, regardless of topology changes.

> **Note:**
> In the case of topology changes, due to network delays, there may be a temporary situation when a singleton service instance will be active on more than one node (e.g. crash detection delay).

Deploy cluster-singleton service can be achieved by the following code:

```
ignite.services().deployClusterSingleton(VALIDATING_SERVICE, new XsdValidatingServiceImpl(\
));
```

Where,

- VALIDATING_SERVICE – is the name of the service, for instance «validatingService-cluster-singleton».
- new XsdValidatingServiceImpl() – is the service instance.

Let's deploy the XsdValidation service by executing the Java class `DeployClusterSingleton` (see the example7 on GitHub for more details).

```
mvn clean package exec:java -Dexec.mainClass= com.blu.imdg.example7.DeployClusterSingleton
```

After the deployment, you should see the following messages on the console.

Figure 7.26

Chapter seven: Distributed computing

In this time, only one instance of the service is deployed in the entire cluster (see the console from the right-hand side). What will happen, if the node with the instance of the service crashed? Let's force quite the Ignite node from the right-hand side of the console.

Figure 7.27

The above figure shows that Apache Ignite automatically redeploy the service on another node.

Key-Affinity-singleton:

In this option, you can deploy one instance of this service on the primary node for a given affinity key. Whenever topology changes and primary node assignment changes, Ignite will always make sure that the service is undeployed on the previous primary node and deployed on the new primary node. The deploy option is very similar to the previous option as we have done before.

```
ignite.services().deployKeyAffinitySingleton(VALIDATING_SERVICE, new XsdValidatingServiceI\
mpl(), "myCache", new MyCacheKey());
```

Where,

- VALIDATING_SERVICE – is the name of the service, for instance, «validatingService-affinity-singleton».
- new XsdValidatingServiceImpl() – is the service instance.
- myCache - Name of the cache on which affinity for key should be calculated, null for default cache.
- new MyCacheKey() – affinity cache key.

The service deployment contains a value for the affinity key as well as a cache name (myCache) to which this key belongs to and Ignite service grid will deploy the service on a node that is primary for the given key. If the primary node changes throughout the time then the service will be re-deployed automatically as well.

Service management and configuration

IgniteService interface provides `serviceDescriptors()` method to get metadata about all deployed services. `serviceDescriptors()` method returns an instance of the Service deployment descriptor, which contains all service deployment configuration, and also deployment topology snapshot as well as origin node ID. Ignite service descriptor provides a collection of methods that can return the following deployment configurations:

Method name	Description
name()	Name of the service
serviceClass()	Name of the service class
totalCount()	Maximum allowed total number of deployed services in the grid
maxPerNodeCount()	Maximum allowed number of deployed services on each node
originNodeId()	ID of the grid node that initiated the service deployment
topologySnapshot()	Service deployment topology snapshot. Service topology snapshot is represented by the number of service instances deployed on a node mapped to a node ID
affinityKey()	Affinity key used for key-to-node affinity calculation. This parameter is,optional and is set only when key-affinity service was deployed.
cacheName()	Cache name used for key-to-node affinity calculation. This parameter is,optional and is set only when key-affinity service was deployed.

Create a Java class ServiceManagements and add the following contents to it:

```java
public class ServiceManagements {
    public static void main(String[] args) throws IOException{
        try (Ignite ignite = Ignition.start(CommonConstants.CLIENT_CONFIG)) {
            for(ServiceDescriptor serviceDescriptor : ignite.services().serviceDescriptors\
()){
                System.out.println("Service Name: " + serviceDescriptor.name());
                System.out.println("MaxPerNode count: " + serviceDescriptor.maxPerNodeCoun\
t());
                System.out.println("Total count: " + serviceDescriptor.totalCount());
                System.out.println("Service class Name: " + serviceDescriptor.serviceClass\
());
                System.out.println("Origin Node ID: " + serviceDescriptor.originNodeId());
            }
        }
    }
}
```

In the above class, we used the Ignite ServiceDescriptor to print all the service metadata into the console. Let's execute an Ignite client to quick view the deployment configuration of our deployed services.

```
mvn clean package exec:java -Dexec.mainClass=com.blu.imdg.example7.ServiceManagements
```

See the example7 on GitHub[56] for the full source code of the Java class. The above command should return the following output on the console:

---

[56] https://github.com/srecon/ignite-book-code-samples/tree/master/chapters/chapter-dist-computing/src/main/java/com/blu/imdg/example7

```
Service Name: validatingService-cluster-singleton
MaxPerNode count: 1
Total count: 1
Service class Name: class com.blu.imdg.example7.XsdValidatingServiceImpl
Origin Node ID: 26090345-63bf-42b3-8206-114b34a17e6b
```

Service configuration:

So far in this chapter, we have deployed service after the Ignite node startup. However, you can automatically deploy service on start up of the Ignite node by setting serviceConfiguration property of IgniteConfiguration. Uncomment the following spring configuration into the file base-config.xml *(chapters/chapter-dist-computing/src/main/resources/META-INF/org/book/examples/base-config.xml)*.

```xml
<bean class="org.apache.ignite.IgniteConfiguration">
    ...
    <!-- Distributed Service configuration. -->
    <property name="serviceConfiguration">
        <list>
            <bean class="org.apache.ignite.services.ServiceConfiguration">
                <property name="name" value="validatingService"/>
                <property name="maxPerNodeCount" value="1"/>
                <property name="totalCount" value="1"/>
                <property name="service">
                    <ref bean="xsdValidatingServiceImpl"/>
                </property>
            </bean>
        </list>
    </property>
</bean>
<bean id="xsdValidatingServiceImpl" class="com.blu.imdg.example7.XsdValidatingServiceImpl"\
/>
```

In the above spring configuration, we have defined all the necessary service configuration to deploy the service on startup. We set service name, total count, and the service class to deploy the service.

> **Note:**
> In this approach to deploy services, service class should be located on Ignite node classpath.

After changing the spring configuration, you have to restart the Ignite node as shown below:

Chapter seven: Distributed computing 342

```
mvn clean package exec:java -Dexec.mainClass=com.blu.imdg.StartCacheNode
```

During node startup you should notice the service startup message (init service) on the console as follows:

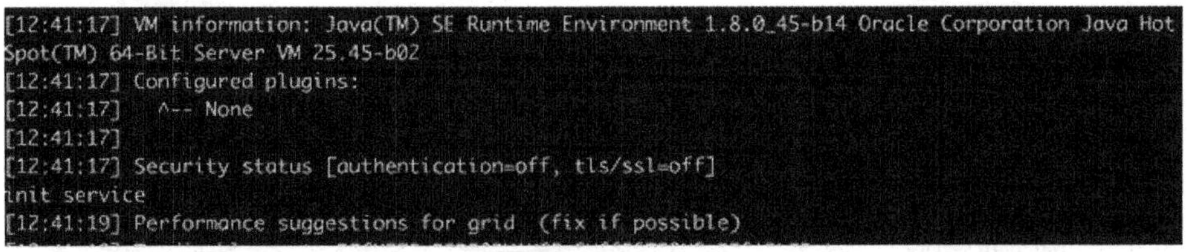

Figure 7.28

After the node bootstrap, you can invoke the remote service through service proxy as described earlier in this chapter.

Developing microservices in Ignite

Microservices is a paradigm of breaking large software (monolith) projects into loosely coupled modules (fine grained), which communicate with each other through simple APIs. Sometimes Microservices are very analogous to Unix Utilities. The concept is the same, just different decade.

Write programs that do one thing and do it well. Write programs to work together. Write programs to handle text streams, because that is a universal interface - Doug McIlory.

Unix executable: Does one thing and do it well	Microservice: Does one thing and do it well
Runs independently from the other commands	Runs independent of other microservice
Produces text-based response	Produces text-based response to clients

From my point of view word microservice misleads itself. In a nutshell, design model under this concept is as follows:

1. Service should be loosely coupled.
2. High cohesion in functionality.
3. Service should be change with minimal effect on other services.
4. Automated in deployments.
5. Scaling out easily.
6. Can use a polyglot programming language and polyglot persistence store.

Chapter seven: Distributed computing

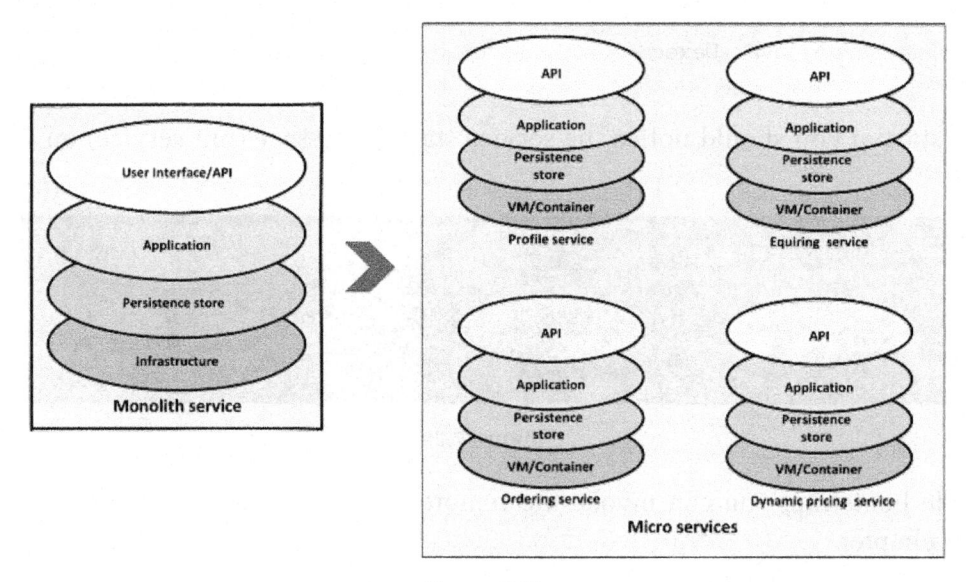

Figure 7.29

Most of these requirements are nothing new at all. Developers or IT Architect who are familiar with SOA already know all the above concepts very well. However, benefits of using microservices over monolith system are very obviously. You can find the best explanation from the Martin Fowler article[57].

As microservice architecture, recommended independently deployable units with minimal shared data, in-memory data fabric is not completely aligned with this architectural approach. However, in-memory data fabrics/grid like Apache Ignite can provide independent cache nodes to corresponding microservices in the same distributed cluster and gives you the following advantages over traditional approaches:

1. Maximum uses of the data fabrics/grid resources (nodes can be added/removed on need basis for scalability in the cluster). Services running on the in-memory cluster is much faster than the disk-based application server.
2. Services can be deployed alongside with the data in the same node, where services compute only the local data (data locality).
3. Automatically deploy any number of distributed services instances in the cluster.
4. Continuous availability of deployed services regardless of topology changes or crashes.

The figure 7.30 shows the main building block of the Apache Ignite microservice solutions. Let's explain all the layers shown below.

---
[57] http://martinfowler.com/articles/microservices.html#MicroservicesAndSoa

Chapter seven: Distributed computing   344

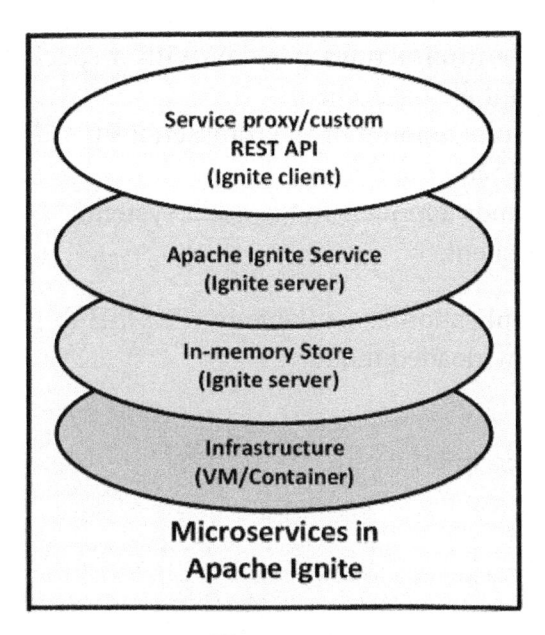

Figure 7.30

Service proxy/custom REST API: this is the client-side proxy for the Ignite microservice. The service proxy enables the application to send and receive messages as a method call. Service proxy can be resided in the Ignite client node (separate node) and can provide high-level interface to interact with the Ignite microservice. Service proxies are created as needed, opened, used to call a service, and closed when no longer needed. Out of the Apache Ignite service proxy is not a REST style proxy, you can create a wrapper REST client around the Ignite service proxy.

Apache Ignite service: each microservice in Ignite implements the Ignite service interface, which makes it inherently fault-tolerant and provides an easy way to call one microservice from another. Apache Ignite service implements the business logics of the microservice. Ignite microservice can also be called from the Ignite compute task as needed. Apache Ignite takes care of continuous availability of this deployed services regardless of topology changes or crashes.

In-memory store: it's an Ignite server node that holds the portion (or a full copy) of the datasets. It also enables the execution of the microservices.

Infrastructure: describes how the Ignite node will be deployed in the cluster. It can be any dedicated server or can be any container to hold the Ignite node in the cluster. Most popular container to deploy and run Ignite node is the docker container.

Now that we have got the basics let's build something useful. We are going to build an application that allows us to validate the cash withdrawal limit of ATM for each user. Business requirements of our microservice are as follows:

- The microservice accept the customer account number and the transaction amount as input parameters.
- Microservices looks for the client by the customer account number.

- Check the amount of the transactions per day with a specified limit for the account. For example, 3000$ is the limit for basic clients.
- Add the amount to the total amount of the transactions per day (reset the number to zero in the case of the first transaction of the day).
- The Microservice also sends a request to the audit system.
- Return the result to the client.

The full source code of the application is available in the GitHub repository[58]. Let's create a new Java projects or modify the downloaded module.

Step 1:

Let's start with the `BankService` interface.

```
public interface BankService {
    String NAME = "BANK_SERVICE";

    boolean validateOperation (String account, BigDecimal sum) throws AccountNotFoundExcep\
tion, LogServiceException;
}
```

The `BankService` interface has one method: *validateOperation*, which accept the client account number and the cash withdrawal amount as input parameters. The above method also throws *AccountNotFoundException*, whenever the account number is not available in the Ignite cache.

Step 2: Create another interface to log the client operation. Create a new Java interface with name LogService and add the following contents to it.

```
public interface LogService {
    String NAME = "logService";

    void logOperation (String operationCode, Boolean result) throws LogServiceException;
}
```

The above interface also contains one method `logOperation`, which accepts the operationCode and the result of the operation for sending to the audit system.

Step 3:

Let's implements the LogService first, add a new Java class with name LogServiceImpl and implements the following interfaces:

- LogService
- Service

Where, Service is the Ignite Service interface. By implementing the Ignite Service interface, Our `LogService` becomes a microservice. Add the following contents into the LogServiceImpl class:

---

[58] https://github.com/srecon/ignite-book-code-samples/tree/master/chapters/chapter-dist-computing/src/main/java/com/blu/imdg/example9

```java
public class LogServiceImpl implements LogService, Service {
    private CloseableHttpClient auditClient;

    @Override
    public void logOperation(String operationCode, Boolean result) throws LogServiceExcept\
ion {
        try {
            HttpAuditClient.sendResult(auditClient, result, operationCode);
        }catch (Exception err) {
            throw new LogServiceException(err);
        }
    }

    @Override
    public void cancel(ServiceContext serviceContext) {
        try {
            auditClient.close();
        } catch (IOException e) {
            e.printStackTrace();
        }
    }

    @Override
    public void init(ServiceContext serviceContext) throws Exception {
        auditClient = (CloseableHttpClient) HttpAuditClient.createHttpClient();
    }

    @Override
    public void execute(ServiceContext serviceContext) throws Exception {

    }
}
```

The above-implemented class is very similar to what we have done in the previous section. First, we implemented the method logOperation, where we are sending the result of the operation to the audit system. Next, we populated the LogServiceImpl as an Ignite service by implementing the methods: init(), execute() and cancel().

Step 4:

Now create a new Java class with name BankServiceImpl and implement the following interface:

- BankService
- Service

Where Service is the Ignite Service interface.

Chapter seven: Distributed computing

```java
public class BankServiceImpl implements BankService, Service {

    @ServiceResource(serviceName = LogService.NAME)
    private LogService logService;

    @IgniteInstanceResource
    private Ignite ignite;

    IgniteCache<AccountCacheKey, AccountCacheData> accountCache;

    @Override
    public boolean validateOperation(String account, BigDecimal sum) throws AccountNotFoun\
dException, LogServiceException {
        AccountKey key = new AccountKey(account);
        Lock lock = accountCache.lock(key);
        try {
            lock.lock();
            AccountData accountData = (AccountData) accountCache.get(key);
            if (accountData == null) {
                throw new AccountNotFoundException(account);
            }

            //clean today operations
            if (!accountData.getToday().equals(LocalDate.now())) {
                accountData.setTodayOperationSum(new BigDecimal(0));
                accountData.setToday(LocalDate.now());
                accountCache.put(key, accountData);
            }

            BigDecimal newOperationSum = accountData.getTodayOperationSum().add(sum);
            if (newOperationSum.compareTo(accountData.getDailyLimit()) > 0) {
                logService.logOperation(account, false);
                return false;
            } else {
                accountData.setTodayOperationSum(newOperationSum);
                accountCache.put(key, accountData);
                logService.logOperation(account, true);
                return true;
            }

        } finally {
            lock.unlock();
        }
    }
// implementation of the method init(), execute() and cancel() are omitted
```

}

First, we inject the Ignite LogService as a resource. If more than one LogService is deployed on a server, then the first available instance will be returned. Next, we injected the current Ignite instance as the resource. Note that, in this example, we are also using AccountCacheKey and AccountCacheData for data co-allocation. Please refer to the previous section for more information about data affinity. Later in this class, we implemented our business logic interface to validate the cash withdrawal operation. In the `validateOperation()` method, we first created the AccountKey instance from the given account number and locked the cache key. In the next few lines of code, we acquired the lock.

> **Note:**
> If the lock is not available then the current thread becomes disabled for thread scheduling purposes and lies dormant until the lock has been acquired. This lock is optimistic lock and guarantees that any other thread or operation on this cache entries will not interrupt our operation and the data.

The rest of the business logic is very straightforward; we clean up the cache entry if the current operation is the first transaction of the day. If the new operation exceeded the limit of the cash withdrawal, we send a message to our microservice LogService. Otherwise, we increased the total amount and registered the operation by sending a message to the LogServcie. Finally, we unlock the entries of the cache.

Step 5:

Let's deploy our above two microservices and run some test. Create a new Java class with name `TestMicroServiceMain` and add the following contents.

```java
public class TestMicroServiceMain {

    public static void main(String[] args) throws AccountNotFoundException, LogServiceExce\
ption {
        try (Ignite ignite = Ignition.start(CommonConstants.CLIENT_CONFIG)) {

            IgniteCache<AccountCacheKey, AccountCacheData> cache = BankDataGenerator.creat\
eBankCache(ignite);

            IgniteServices services = ignite.services().withAsync();

            services.deployNodeSingleton(LogService.NAME, new LogServiceImpl());
            services.future().get();

            services.deployNodeSingleton(BankService.NAME, new BankServiceImpl());
```

Chapter seven: Distributed computing   349

```
            services.future().get();

            BankService bankService = services.serviceProxy(BankService.NAME, BankService.\
class, /*not-sticky*/false);

            System.out.println("result=" + bankService.validateOperation(BankDataGenerator\
.TEST_ACCOUNT, new BigDecimal(50)));
            System.out.println("result1=" + bankService.validateOperation(BankDataGenerato\
r.TEST_ACCOUNT, new BigDecimal(40)));
            System.out.println("result2=" + bankService.validateOperation(BankDataGenerato\
r.TEST_ACCOUNT, new BigDecimal(180)));

            services.cancel(BankService.NAME);
        }
    }
}
```

In the above fragment codes, we deploy our two microservice as a node singleton service. Created a service proxy bankService to invoke the BankService. Next, we generate some data for test and run the test. Next, we will start a few Ignite node and the audit service to test our application.

Step 6:

Start the Ignite node with the following command:

```
mvn clean package exec:java -Dexec.mainClass=com.blu.imdg.StartCacheNode
```

Start the audit http service as follows:

```
mvn exec:java -Dexec.mainClass=com.blu.imdg.common.HttpAuditEmulator
```

Next, run the following mvn command to execute the TestMicroServiceMain application.

```
mvn exec:java -Dexec.mainClass=com.blu.imdg.example9.TestMicroServiceMain
```

If everything goes fine, you should have the following output into the console.

```
[20:42:31] Topology snapshot [ver=4, servers=1, clients=1, CPUs=8, heap=4.0GB]
result=true
result1=true
result2=false
```

Figure 7.31

Note that, the last result is false because our cash withdrawal limit is exceeded, whenever we have asked for 180$ from ATM. Our everyday cash withdrawal limit is only 200$. Let's create a REST client for our microservice.

Step 6:

Create a new Java class ServiceHttpClient; it will be our HTTP client proxy for BankService.

```
@Path("/service")
public class ServiceHttpClient {
    private static BankService bankService;
    @GET
    @Path("/withdrawlimit")
    @Produces(MediaType.TEXT_PLAIN)
    public boolean acceptResponse (
            @QueryParam("accountnum") String accnum,
            @QueryParam("amount") int amount
    ) throws Exception
    {
        System.out.println("account number=" + accnum + " amount=" + amount);

        return bankService.validateOperation(accnum, new BigDecimal(amount));
    }

    public static void main(String[] args) {
        URI baseUri = UriBuilder.fromUri("http://localhost/").port(9988).build();
        // start the Ignite client
        Ignite ignite = Ignition.start(CommonConstants.CLIENT_CONFIG);
        IgniteServices services = ignite.services().withAsync();

        bankService = services.serviceProxy(BankService.NAME, BankService.class, /*not-sti\
cky*/false);

        ResourceConfig config = new ResourceConfig(ServiceHttpClient.class);
        HttpServer server = JdkHttpServerFactory.createHttpServer(baseUri, config);
    }
}
```

We used javax.ws.rs annotation to exposed the Java class as an HTTP service. The service will be available at http://localhost:9988/service/withdraw limit?accountnum=0000*1111&amount=100. You can change the host and the port number in the source code. The service just wraps the Ignite service proxy and expose an HTTP interface to interact with it. Let's run the client with the following command:

mvn exec:java -Dexec.mainClass=com.blu.imdg.example9.ServiceHttpClient

Make sure that, your Ignite node is running and BankService is deployed. If you just want to deploy the BankService in Ignite cluster run the following application.

mvn exec:java -Dexec.mainClass=com.blu.imdg.example9.DeployService

The deployservice application will just deploy the BankService and the LogService in the Ignite cluster. Now, open up your favorite browser and go to the next URL.

Chapter seven: Distributed computing

```
http://localhost:9988/service/withdrawlimit?accountnum=0000*1111&amount=100.
```

First two times you should get the result TRUE in your web browser page, in the third time, it should return the result FALSE because the cash withdrawal limit is 200 dollar.

Limitations:

In Microservices architecture, the number of microservices that you need to deal with is quite high. And also, their locations change dynamically owing to the rapid and agile development/deployment nature of microservices. Therefore, you need to find the location of a microservice during the runtime. The solution to this problem is to use a Service Registry. Unfortunately, Apache Ignite doesn't provide any service registry. However, you can develop your own service registry and service discovery application with a little effort.

Conclusion

In this last chapter of this book, we have covered the following topics by examples:

- Developing and deploy distributed closure
- Developing Map-Reduce and fork join
- How to use Ignite Per-node share state
- Compute task fault-tolerance and checkpointing
- Distributed job scheduling
- Developing and deploy Services in Ignite cluster
- What microservice is and how Ignite service can differ from the traditional microservice
- Developed and deployed microservice in Ignite cluster
- Create high-level REST client to interact with Ignite microservice.

Lightning Source UK Ltd.
Milton Keynes UK
UKOW07f1906071217
314084UK00005B/429/P